For someone who wasn't there, this is enthralling stuff. I want to frame some of the text and hang it in our foyers, the lavish and the ugly. It works as an insight into the nature of the ongoing struggle for the Australian stage, the discovery of, and advocacy for, a national (read 'democratic') imagination.

Ben Ellis

Of all Australia's arts critics, she has been the most influential ... her sort of authority in the theatre, or in journalism for that matter, no longer exists.

Robert Drewe

She is the wise old woman of Australian theatre—the one who has seen everything with cold eyes and a warm heart. As a critic Katharine Brisbane became the force she is because right from the start she saw theatre, not as something happening in the dark behind closed doors, but a necessary part of this country's story.

David Marr

Katharine Brisbane, through her publishing and writing, has made a significant and passionate contribution to the development of an authentic voice and character in our theatre.

John Gaden

When Katharine Brisbane wrote her 'think pieces' in the 1980s, there was, however briefly, the sense that someone was prepared to divine the undercurrents of Australian theatre, locating trends, shifts, innovations that might hint of artistic policy, a body of work or even a world view. Whether you agreed with these analyses or not, they reassured practitioners that their contributions would not be viewed solely as phenomena devoid of context or wider social implications.

Wayne Harrison

There are many critics writing now who envy her that exciting period to write about, but none of us who think it should have been anyone else. ... The breadth of her knowledge about Australian theatre and drama, and the astuteness of her commentary are astonishing.

John McCallum

For Philip

who was there

'It is criticism that by concentration makes culture possible.'
Oscar Wilde

Katharine Brisbane
NOT WRONG—JUST DIFFERENT

Observations on the rise of contemporary Australian theatre

Foreword by Robert Drewe

Currency Press, Sydney

First published in 2005 by
Currency Press Pty Ltd
PO Box 2287
Strawberry Hills NSW 2012 Australia
www.currency.com.au
enquiries@currency.com.au

National Library of Australia Cataloguing-in-Publication Data:

Brisbane, Katharine.

Not Wrong—Just Different: observations on the rise of contemporary Australian theatre.

Includes index.

ISBN 0 86819 777 7 (pbk).

ISBN 0 86819 764 5 (hbk).

1. Brisbane, Katharine. 2. Theatrical producers and directors – Australia – Biography. 3. Performing arts – Australia. 4. Theaters – Australia. I. Title.

792.0994

Book and cover design by Kate Florance, Currency Press
Cover shows article first published in the *Australian*, 20 March 1971.
Produced by The Australian Book Connection.
Printed in Hong Kong.

FOREWORD

I was an eighteen-year-old cadet reporter typing up the vegetable market reports and TV programmes when I first encountered Katharine Brisbane. She appeared suddenly in the newsroom one evening, moved determinedly through the cigarette smoke of the sports' section like a ship's figure-head slicing an ocean fog, and set off south-west towards the pipe smoke of the sub-editors' desk.

Scruffy young reporters looked up in awe. Our territory, a sort of demilitarized zone of unnewsworthy news, lay between sport and subs. We worked on huge, industrial-strength Siemens typewriters, which were chained for security purposes to unwieldy metal trolleys. A panicky rumble and clang of metal broke out. Everyone was trying simultaneously to wheel their cumbersome machines out of her way. Urgently I followed their lead. *Hurry, hurry.* Clear a path. The *West Australian*'s theatre critic was delivering her copy.

Katharine must only have been in her late twenties, but she was a commanding presence. It was hard not to notice her. Not that she was trying to make an entrance. (On the *Australian* in Sydney years later, a vastly more important, national, figure, she seemed somehow shyer: she always hurried, and sometimes *sidled,* into that eccentric newsroom.) But her height and leading-lady bearing, the well-modulated voice, the air of not suffering fools whatsoever, ensured she'd be noticed. And not least with us, for the reason—the rare and enviable fact—that in the Perth of 1961 she was allowed to voice an opinion and her work carried a byline.

As it happened, my acquaintanceship with Katharine Brisbane had indirectly begun a couple of years earlier. Writing of her days directing plays for the University of Western Australia's Dramatic Society, she notes in this book: 'My production of *Waiting for Godot*, in 1959, is still remembered by some in Perth.' Indeed it is. My school English class saw that production, and I recall it vividly today, just as I like to remember the impact of Brisbane's Beckett on those sixteen-year-old footballers and farmers' sons.

Our paths were to cross again, more directly, in the early 1970s. In the sort of wild coincidence that characterises life in this small commonwealth (where one or two degrees of separation, not the six degrees of John Guare's play, seems the norm), I became, briefly, features and arts editor of the *Australian*. Thus it was to me, technically, as overseer of the arts pages, that the paper's distinguished national theatre critic submitted her copy. I never had to worry about changing a word; fortunately I was not to be faced with that quandary. After the famous defamation case brought by the actor Peter O'Shaughnessy over her review of his *Othello*, Katharine's columns went straight to the editor and the lawyers.

That I should, soon after, unknowingly buy a house in the same street as Katharine in Sydney—our paths crossing rather more regularly in the greengrocer's or newsagent's than at the theatre—by now seemed almost to be expected. We left the *Australian* in the same month in 1974, she to concentrate on running Currency Press, the estimable publisher of Australian drama that she had founded with her husband, Philip Parsons; me to attempt to write fiction.

Through all those years and strings of coincidence I have felt a strong admiration for her. Of all Australia's arts critics, she has been the most influential not only in bringing the news of the times and joining the cultural debate, but in very many cases in leading the debate. Sadly, her sort of authority in the theatre, or in journalism for that matter, no longer exists. This book is more than a fascinating record of the striving for a national character in the theatre; it is a cautionary tale of lost opportunities on the bigger stage.

Robert Drewe
July 2005

CONTENTS

Part III: The Tide Turns 1970–71   *131*

Part IV: The New Wave Rolls 1971–72   *169*

LIST OF ILLUSTRATIONS

ACKNOWLEDGEMENTS

I am deeply indebted to many people who have supported me in this long venture. My daughter Harriet, who has taken Philip's place as my favourite editor, read and advised on several drafts. John Senczuk offered further encouragement and sound sense on the book's structure. Ben Ellis' report gave me heart to believe the book has something to offer the present generation of theatre artists. Jean Cooney, who as my assistant shared many of the stirring times depicted, confirmed the detail of the events. Intrepid researcher Margaret Leask generously spent many hours searching for lost dates, articles and photographs; and Victoria Chance many more hours wrestling with intransigent material and creating a way to give smooth passage to my narrative. The ease with which the story now emerges is due to all these friends. And for the look, feel and successful launch of the book I have to thank my skilled and patient Currency staff, editor Claire Grady, designer Kate Florance and marketing director Deborah Franco.

But more than all these people, I extend my gratitude to those actors, directors, designers and composers who took the journey with me and gave me so much joy. One of that company, as I was writing this, was dying in a Sydney hospital. Neil Fitzpatrick was a complete actor, one of the abstracts and brief chronicles of the time, whose contribution to our theatre was less recognised than he deserved. My review of *The Philanthropist* that opens Part IV is my tribute to him. I hope this book might serve to remind all of its participants, as it will the reader, of some of the excitement, the laughter, the frustrations, triumphs and the tragedies we shared; and more importantly the lessons that we learnt. That the best kind of theatre reflects upon the time and its passions is transparent from my writings, as is the fact that theatre, like the times, must go on changing.

LIST OF ABBREVIATIONS

ABC: Australian Broadcasting Commission
ACA: Australian Council for the Arts
AETT: Australian Elizabethan Theatre Trust
AGDC: Australian Gallery Directors' Council
ALP: Australian Labor Party
AMC: Almost Managing Company
ANPC: Australian National Playwrights' Conference
APG: Australian Performing Group
ATYP: Australian Theatre for Young People
CLF: Commonwealth Literary Fund
HVTC: Hunter Valley Theatre Company
IAC: Industries Assistance Commission
JCW: J. C. Williamson's Ltd
MRPG: Murray River Performing Group
MTC: Melbourne Theatre Company
NIDA: National Institute of Dramatic Art
QTC: Queensland Theatre Company
SATC: South Australian Theatre Company
SGIO: State Government Insurance Office
STC: Sydney Theatre Company
TNP: Théâtre National Populaire
UNSW: University of New South Wales
UTRC: Union Theatre Repertory Company

INTRODUCTION

This book began as a collection of recent ruminations, inspired by a growing sense of disillusion with the performing arts, in which I had played a part for over 50 years. Disenchantment with the present led me on a journey into the past. Was it just age that made me feel this way? Or was there really a time of radical action when we could effect change? As I began to delve into my scrapbooks going back to the 1950s, a narrative began to emerge. And so I followed it.

I grew up in Perth, the most isolated capital city in the world. I was introduced to the theatre via my history teacher, Mrs Pinnock, who stretched our imaginations with deeds of derring-do and the aid of a puppet theatre. It was an age long before television and we made our own entertainment, unaffected by the seductions of the greater world. Nevertheless, I cut photographs of stage stars like Laurence Olivier and Paul Scofield out of magazines, joined the dramatic society at University and dreamed of the day I could get to London and see it all for myself.

On completing my cadetship on the *West Australian* I spent 1955–57 in the United Kingdom, working as a typist and seeing as much theatre as time would allow. It was a vintage period for theatre critics: Kenneth Tynan in the *Sunday Times* and Harold Hobson in the *Observer*—and Walter Kerr in the *New York Times*—were my mentors; and a scrap book of their writings was my primer in my early years as a reviewer. It was 1959 before my pleas gained me the job on the *West Australian* as part of my general duties as a reporter.

In 1960 I married Philip Parsons, whom I had known since undergraduate days in the University Dramatic Society, where he was playing glamorous leading roles in the classics and I began life as wardrobe mistress. Those plays, like Webster's *The Duchess of Malfi*, Euripides' *The Trojan Women*, Congreve's *Love for Love*, Shakespeare's *Love's Labour's Lost*—whole sections of which I can still recite—were as much my education as the London theatre. I later furthered that education by becoming a director for undergraduate and graduate productions. My production of *Waiting for Godot*, in 1959, is still remembered by some in Perth.

Philip had spent nine years in the United Kingdom at Kings College, Cambridge, latterly as a research fellow at Christ's College. His studies had been in seventeenth century drama but, as in my case, a return from absence soon alerted him to the undiscovered history of our own theatre. A decade later this would be the genesis of our idiosyncratically founding a publishing house for the Australian playwright. We named it Currency Press, after Edward Geoghegan's *The Currency Lass* (1844), the first extant play known to have been written and performed professionally in Australia. The name seemed appropriate on many grounds—the Currency lads and lasses were the first colonial children born here and known for their rough manners and self-reliance, compared with the supercilious Sterling children born in the United Kingdom. The word also has a sense of current affairs. The reference to money, however, was not the good omen for which we might have hoped. It was quickly noted that the classical figure chosen for our colophon, was scattering the contents of its cornucopia with unseemly prodigality.

But all that was in the future. In 1962 we returned to Cambridge with our 11-month-old son Nick for Philip to complete his PhD dissertation. And in March 1965, by then with our baby daughter Harriet, we moved to Sydney at the invitation of Professor Robert Quentin, who had founded the first Department of Drama in Australia, at the University of New South Wales.

We bought a house by mail order, after we stuck a pin in a map of Sydney between the University and the city and came up with Paddington. Or Woollahra, as the house at 87 Jersey Road proved to be, on the 'safe' side of the boundary. Woollahra was just respectable then, though no bank would give us a mortgage on a terrace house with a sixteen-foot frontage. But we had thirty happy years there and it became a haunt in turn of students, budding theatre directors and promising playwrights.

In 1967, when I applied for the job of national theatre critic of the infant *Australian* newspaper, I had no inkling of where it might lead. To work for our first national daily seemed a unique opportunity for a journalist with two small children looking for a flexible part-time job. And so it proved.

My brief was to write two columns a week reviewing the theatre. It was quickly apparent that if I was to gain a national readership, then my columns must reflect the national interest. Here the *West Australian*'s strict training stood me in good stead. After nearly forty years these columns emerge as reports on the times; and the times were in all senses critical. Part I opens with a piece setting out what I then believed was the role of the reviewer; it gives no hint of what it offered me as a reporter.

My columns were published on the leader page for most of my time at the *Australian*. Very soon I was writing news items and Saturday feature articles. The *Australian* was a larrikin newspaper, only three years old, and preoccupied with the challenge of distribution. And this was formidable. Newspapers were still using metal casting to print. A matrix or papier maché mould of the cast of each page was made at the paper's headquarters in Canberra and flown by light plane to Melbourne for printing and distribution to the southern states. Relief came in the early 1970s with offset printing, which reproduced type photographically.

So in the early days I had no supervision except from my sub-editor. After a few months I asked the then editor, Walter Kommer, if he liked what I was doing, to which he replied: 'I don't know. I've never read you.' Kommer moved on soon after to run the Murdoch mining enterprises and was replaced by the *Australian*'s finest editor Adrian Deamer. Adrian read my columns, especially after News Ltd received a writ for defamation from the actor Peter O'Shaughnessy over my intemperate review of his *Othello* during my first year. After that they employed a lawyer to watch the pages. Adrian was the only editor ever to pull my copy—a column about the Purple Onion, a gay club that presented satirical drag shows with some style. Some of the figures later prominent in the rise of Sydney theatre were guest directors at that time.

The *Othello* case made gossip for a good two years but I was overseas when it was finally settled. My review, headed 'What a Tragedy', was published in the *Australian* on 19 October 1967, and the complaint of malice lay chiefly against my phrase 'the waste and dishonesty of this production'. The writ was issued against Mirror Newspapers Ltd, which won the case in the Supreme Court. It went to appeal and then the High Court, where a new trial was ordered on the ground the judge had misdirected the jury on a technicality over opinion and fact. Mirror Newspapers then settled. O'Shaughnessy left immediately for overseas and worked in Australia only occasionally thereafter.

The early months were spent getting to know the field. I travelled to other capitals once or twice a month, seeing shows, introducing myself, seeking out innovation. And I found it. Within months I was swept up by the winds of change. The Federal Government's decision in 1967 to provide funding to the arts set the many small theatres plotting to be part of the big handout. In the back streets student playwrights and actors were rising, lampooning the outdated censorship laws; and TV workers were marching in the TV: Make-it-Australian campaign. Old theatres were demolished and new palaces of culture rose. At the centre of which was the Sydney Opera House.

The traditional view of a critic of the arts is that he or she should remain remote from the turmoil of creation in order better to judge it. Coming as I did from a small town in which I had moved from participating in the lively amateur theatre to becoming its judge, I had already learnt that if you can't know nobody then it's better to know everybody. And that's what I did.

Living with Philip, of course, dictated that. He loved the theatre and the people in it. And causes. We had been in Sydney only a few months when we were caught up in the row over the resignation of Jørn Utzon, architect of the Opera House. He and Francis Evers, who was then theatre reviewer of the *Australian*, wrote several articles on the affair and Philip remained in the trenches for some years, attempting with others to engineer a reconciliation between Utzon and the new architects. But that's another story. For most of my time as a columnist I was involved in some behind-the scenes activity: as a member of the Friends of *America Hurrah!* protest in 1968, as one of Dr Coombs' interim drama committee charged with planning criteria for subsidy in 1968–69; as a founding committee member of the Australian National Playwrights' Conference in 1972; and in the same year on the selection committee for the first director of the reconstructed South Australian Theatre Company; campaigning to have the writer and recidivist prisoner Jim McNeil released on parole in 1974, giving evidence to the Industries Assistance Commission on the Arts in 1976. All that made me a better commentator, I believe. And it made us a lot of friends.

My few months in 1968–69 as a member of the Interim Drama Committee of the Australian Council for the Arts were probably the most insightful for me as a journalist. As one of the few people familiar with theatre around the country I was not an unexpected choice but I think I was probably invited in to keep me quiet. We took our brief very seriously: to draw up the criteria for theatre subsidy (ie to define the basic needs, set a long-term goal and recommend the best way to begin). But every step at our few meetings was pre-empted. Even my invitation. This came by phone one day in August and my response was that I needed to consider whether it represented a conflict of interest. Next day my name was released to the press. This became the pattern. No time was taken for research. Decisions were consistently announced before reports were released. A minority report drawn up by a group of us was probably filed without reading. Dr Coombs, wisely, was determined to achieve the first funding in the May 1969 budget, and to have his Council survive any change of government. As we know from *Don's Party* there was no change of government in 1969; and the Council got its budget, but the problems foreseen at that time have multiplied exponentially in the years since.

In looking over the selection in this book, three trajectories can be perceived. The highest is the politics of subsidy, the rapid change that money brings. By degrees come complications, corporations, disappointment and conservatism. Below this arc lies the diligent groundwork: the search for new voices telling us we are 'not wrong, just different'. Firstly directors and actors and then playwrights, discarding the English repertoire for American radicalism, challenging censorship and good taste and discovering at last the sound of our own voice. Lastly, supporting the structure, is the story of our theatre architecture. Reviewing in the 1960s and

70s took me first to church halls, factories, cavernous old theatres and by degrees to designer-built arts centres. Buildings came down as others went up. Often it was the work that found out the space; often the buildings became in time the obstacle. Each of these factors has, in its way, contributed to the making of our drama and our theatre-going practice.

The movement of the trajectory also has its own pace. The writing for the *Australian* consists largely of short pieces, aimed at bringing the news, capturing the attention of the distant reader, gathering the energies of the theatre community across the country. Sometimes I proselytise, sometimes I am hasty; many times I am attempting to share with the reader a moment of superlative achievement.

In Part VI the style changes. I left the *Australian* in October 1974. By that time theatre performance had increased to a degree impossible for one person to cover. I was losing ground and Philip and I had started Currency Press to publish the new drama. I wrote occasionally for the *Australian* which by then had an arts page and editor; and from 1976 for *Theatre Australia*, that admirable journal that against the odds lasted until 1983; and during 1980–82 the *National Times*. These were periodicals, and the emphasis was no longer on bringing the news but in joining the debate. Some of my best commentary, I think, was for these journals. They gave me generous space to develop both opinion and reportage, and on reading these I was pleased to see how careful I was to give my views context.

The reader will find some of the content quaint. Forgotten are the extraordinary powers exercised by the Australian Elizabethan Theatre Trust; and the pathetic resources available to most theatres. It may come as a surprise in these days of middle management that the first act of the successful tenderers in 1969 was to contract a company of actors—in some cases over twenty—as well as designers and workshop staff. The quality of performance rose dramatically. The Old Tote Theatre Company, Sydney's first state company, exploded from a tin shed to an Opera House: in little more than a decade it sparked, flared and died. As did the legendary Australian Performing Group.

The reader may also find curious my preoccupation with national character and striving for 'maturity'. And my reversal from nursing the theatre's 'children of nature' in 1967 to, by 1973, demanding their right to self-government. But it was like that. My attitude to Dr H. C. Coombs, architect of both the AETT and the Australian Council for the Arts, was undeservedly suspicious, reflecting the disrepute into which the Trust had fallen by the mid-1960s. I later came to regard him with great affection. Reading my reports of his statements today it is evident the Government gave him little room; and his achievement in getting up arts subsidy at all, in the circumstances, was immense. We owe him a great debt.

My admiration for Dr Jean Battersby, too, has grown over the years. The founding chief executive of the Australian Council for the Arts and its successor the Australia Council, she survived for 16 years the repeated interventions of both the Government and artists, retaining her cool and becoming a powerful advocate with government. Despite the conflicting demands with which she regularly found herself—'I had come to embody that whole focus of antipathy from everybody, about the Australia Council', she told Justin Macdonnell in 1986 (*Arts, Minister?* 1992)—her discretion as a public servant was impeccable. Since that time she has put on record her concern at the direction in which the Council had gone; and how interim measures taken in its infancy had become fixed practice.

Much of my writing for the *Australian* is no more than hasty journalism. Its virtues are the immediacy of an eyewitness and a passion that has gone from most arts journalism today. The reader will see that once I had found my audience I acquired a style of intimate correspondence with them by which I relayed the rapid changes that were taking place. Indeed the extravagance of some writing is less my own style than my interpretation of the feelings privately expressed by those involved in the subject matter. There are occasional vintage pieces but the columns reproduced here have been chosen not for their eloquence but for their information. I have tried to choose pieces that record steps in our progress and give us a glimpse of the early work of those artists and companies that have come to be seen as the makers of the Australian theatre today.

In selecting the pieces, which must represent less than a quarter of the output from this period, I have sought to invite the reader to share in the struggles, the revelations and the occasional victories that marked the path to the performing arts we have today. Because it is the story of the making of a new theatre, the core of popular comedy, drama and musicals that continued to provide entertainment to a loyal following have been given only the occasional glimpse. In the wake of the upheaval little of it remains today. The seven parts into which I have divided the writing seemed to follow of themselves. Part I is largely report and opinion on the erupting political climate. Part II demonstrates the burst of activity that accompanied the expectation of federal subsidy. Part III expands on a growing confidence; and Part IV establishes major figures in this development. Part V plots the groundwork for today's industry. Part VI contains the post-*Australian* commentary and documents the demise of some early hopes, and Part VII reflects from the distance of 2005 the lessons of half a century of observations.

It was a vintage time to be a reviewer, and one, sadly, that will not come again. Newspaper culture has changed too radically. Most journalists have lost the authority they once held on the floor of the reporter's room. Too many publicists, too many vested interests, too little time to gather facts, too many personalities waving opinions, too easy access to half-truths over the internet. With this book I hope I can give the artists of today some insight into what has been lost by this, and why the arts in the public arena are today no longer influential.

As most people know, journalists rarely choose their own headlines. Where necessary for clarity I have reclaimed the privilege and in the case of reviews have added the play's title for easier reference. I have done some trimming of text, mainly to the work for the *Australian,* and repaired the typographical and spelling errors that are inevitable in newspaper writing. The style at that time was more discursive than would be permitted today—in some cases irritatingly so. To assist continuity I have also omitted information that has been too often repeated elsewhere.

The style will cause other problems to the present-day reader. The universal use of the male pronoun hit me between the eyes on first reading. The universal use of Mr and Mrs was a milder irritation. (This lasted to the 1980s.) After thought I rejected the idea of updating and, with occasional exceptions, have left them as they were. More awkward is the word 'indigenous' which I use to describe the work of emerging writers, to distinguish them from British or American work. I have deleted the word where it is unnecessary. I succumbed occasionally to the green lines on my computer program that reprove me for too-long sentences and use of the passive voice but at no point have I altered the opinion expressed in the original.

Finally, among the many I have to thank for their support is the late Francis Evers, founding theatre critic of the *Australian*. Francis, a lean Irishman perpetually wrapped in a navy overcoat, suffered all the early inconveniences of a fledgling national newspaper, travelling interstate with the midnight plane that flew the matrices between states. Francis became a friend and when he decided to return to France, his second home, he bequeathed me his job, for which I shall always be grateful. In deference to my gender I was permitted to travel by commercial airline.

PART I
THE CHALLENGES
1967–68

In 1967 the theatre was truly a cottage industry. J. C. Williamson's Ltd, the near-century old production company familiarly known as the Firm, still controlled the largest theatre chain in the world. But it was in terminal decline following the death in 1965 of Sir Frank Tait, the last of the Tait brothers who had headed the company since 1920. Times were changing, television was a decade old and young Turks like Harry M. Miller were knocking at the door.

The art and community theatres, occupying a totally different world, were mostly amateur or semi-professional; run by salaried management but with stages occupied by actors at best intermittently and inadequately paid. The exceptions were the Union Theatre Repertory Company in Melbourne, founded by John Sumner in 1953 under the umbrella of the University of Melbourne; and the National Theatre Company in Perth, which had developed from the Perth Repertory Club and been fully professional since 1960.

A few companies had their own purpose-built theatre, like the Perth Playhouse, St Martin's Theatre in Melbourne and the art theatres in Brisbane and Adelaide. Most played in church halls; and before long new wave ventures proliferated in converted factories and warehouses. The old, privately-owned gilt theatres were pulled down and new government-funded arts centres replaced them.

The earliest breeze to bring change was the establishment of the National Institute of Dramatic Art (NIDA) on the University of New South Wales campus, which accepted its first students in 1959. This was Australia's first government-sponsored acting school, though private studios had existed since the 1920s. It was part of a ferment of activism that rose from universities in every state during the 1960s which spearheaded the demand for government subsidy for the performing arts. It also led in 1963 to the formation of the Old Tote Theatre Company in NIDA's tiny theatre. From 1968 the new subsidised theatre system changed the

Davis Hughes showing a view of a model of the Concert Hall Platform, the choir seating and sound reflectors, 16 February 1968.

structure of the performing arts irrevocably. The decade that followed saw the meteoric rise of the anointed state theatres and the equally rapid decline of the rest. By 1978 almost all the small theatre managements were gone. Even the Firm was dead.

Overshadowing it all, a monument to these ambitions, was the Sydney Opera House.

In 1956 the Danish architect Jørn Utzon had won an international competition for an opera house in Sydney. The idea had been embraced by the Labor Government of Joe Cahill but from the start it was plagued by warring factions. The death of Cahill in 1959 and a change of State Government in 1965 had brought this to crisis point. In March 1966 the Minister for Public Works, Davis Hughes, blocked supply and forced Utzon to resign. Public meetings and marches were held in protest against the dismissal. Chief among the quarrels was the battle over the major hall, intended as a dual-purpose hall for opera and concerts. The powerful ABC with its subscription concerts and its wily chief, Sir Charles Moses, laid claim to be sole occupier and won the fight. The minor hall, intended as a drama theatre, was converted to opera and the small community theatre became the Drama Theatre we know today. The monumental nature of the building had a powerful attraction for the other states, which set about raising their own edifices; while the artists in New South Wales came to terms with yet another flawed realisation of a prospect that had captured their imagination.

I began work at the *Australian* in May 1967 and in my second column, examined my function there.

The Role of the Critic

Australian, 5 June 1967

What purpose does a critic serve? What makes him or her influential? Let me say at once that although I believe the critic to be a good servant of the theatre, ten years' experience has shown me that where it hurts most—at the box office—he has very little influence. Good reviews cannot save a bad play, nor can bad reviews kill a good one, although there may be a temporary setback. Word of mouth is the only true arbiter and no matter what a critic says, if the reader's friend tells him to go or not to go, the advice will be taken.

What service, then, does a critic provide? First of all he must be read, for he is employed by a commercial enterprise seeking the widest possible audience and if he is too dull, too opinionated or too ill-informed he becomes not only powerless but jobless.

The critical writer's role, whether in sport, foreign affairs or theatre, is mainly historical, not judicial. The job is not to tell people what to do, but to analyse and clarify what they have done. Despite what he or she may know about what happened during those trying rehearsal weeks, the critic may only write about what happens between the stage and the audience. He is the audience's trained eye, an eye the critic has acquired by years of exposure. Like too much of any pleasure, he reaches satiation after a while or learns discrimination. Theatre critics must have learned discrimination. Whatever their tastes, they must remember that the public is being asked to pay money for certain goods and deserves protection. The critic's personal taste is a yardstick in evaluation but beyond that he has only the standard set by the theatres themselves.

One of the most important tasks of a critic is to recognise the thing attempted before labelling it good or bad. The second is to differentiate between the contributions of the writer, the producer and the actor; this is often an impossible task, especially in the case of a new play. The Sydney actress Jacqueline Kott once remarked that she thought reviews were written by racing writers because they told you who won and who ran. This is not entirely true but it is a danger.

Then there is the matter of what is 'good' theatre. Why is it that for so long there has been this dichotomy between 'good' and 'popular' theatre? Many critics have come to despise commercial theatre, others aggressively prefer it. It seems to me that box-office success has less to do with quality than opportune timing. If I may be allowed a wild generalisation, the theatre which has come down to us as 'good' has been successful with the audience that created it. Much good theatre well done has failed because the time was wrongly chosen. Much ephemeral work has succeeded because the time was right.

A current example is the farce *There's a Girl in My Soup* with Ron Randell and the delicious Amanda Reiss now packing the Theatre Royal, Sydney. Any play that draws people to it deserves our serious attention and I say this despite having despaired at the inanity of many long-run productions.

Australia has some bad critics (and you will soon find out if I am one of them) but I do not believe they do lasting damage. Good critics have the power to do much good in helping the theatre to understand itself. Audiences, I think, know pretty clearly what they want and when it comes they recognise it, with or without the critics.

The first task I set myself was to get to know theatres in states other than my own. Melbourne's Union Theatre Repertory Company (URTC) was legendary, the company that had put Australian theatre on the map with *Summer of the Seventeenth Doll*. The UTRC had been founded in 1953 by John Sumner, a former merchant seaman with experience in the British theatre, who had come to Australia to manage the University of Melbourne's student Union Theatre. George Ogilvie joined the company in 1965 and had a profound effect upon the standard of its work. This was my first visit to the Russell Street Theatre, the tight little converted church hall seating 374, which was briefly closed for remodelling later in the year.

Incident at Vichy: A Look at the World Outside
Australian, 12 June 1967

I regret having seen only the last play of the Union Theatre Repertory Company's season. The productions have reportedly been of exceptional quality as they must have been if they compare with the extraordinary performance now on stage at Russell Street, Melbourne.

The play is Arthur Miller's *Incident at Vichy*, a passionate indictment of our apathy towards war crimes and written with better control and economy than anything he has done so far. It is his best since *The Crucible*; it has all his virtues and none of his pomposities, and the extremely moving production by George Ogilvie fills me with respect for both the author and the company.

The play is set in a seedy railway yard in Vichy in 1942, where an ill-assorted group of suspected Jews is herded for examination. Gradually we learn about each of them and gradually the terrible reality of the gas ovens becomes the central common factor. It is a stifling play, especially in this little theatre; and one of its virtues is that there is no interval. There is no easy let out, no easing of tension—only a variation of it. It places the responsibilities not on some safe shoulder on stage but on all of us—Nazi, Jew and Gentile. And it does this in dramatic terms: the play is not a sermon.

Mr Ogilvie has assembled a distinguished number of performances: David Turnbull, for example, as a shabby perplexed artist; Michael Duffield, gravely courageous as a railway worker; Dennis Olsen as a successful actor; John Gregg in a splendid hysterical outburst as a Nazi officer who revolts; and the central characters George Whaley, as a Jewish psychiatrist, and Robin Ramsay as a Catholic intellectual. These two in particular articulate the circular horror of facing death or being left alive. 'It is not your guilt we want', says the doctor. 'It's your responsibility.'

This is that rare essence of dramatic experience—the capacity to make an audience join the actors on a predestined road and through their eyes take another look at the world outside. The opportunity does not come so often in the theatre and those who live in Melbourne should make the most of it.

The following week I returned to Sydney, and two very different theatres. Hayes Gordon had established the Ensemble Theatre and studio in 1958, introducing 'the Method' to Sydney. The news of his return to the musical stage, a world away from such gritty realism, had been greeted with anticipation. In contrast, the Old Tote Theatre Company was beginning to show the paces of the first NIDA graduates in its tiny art theatre. Robin Lovejoy, its director, was also a talented designer.

Triumph for Two Plays and One Man

Australian, 19 June 1967

Sydney has enjoyed the triumph of sentiment in two productions that opened on Friday—the Jewish musical *Fiddler on the Roof* for J. C. Williamson's at Her Majesty's and Sheridan's *The School of Scandal* at the Old Tote. It has also enjoyed the personal triumph of Hayes Gordon, who makes a comeback after eleven years to Her Majesty's as Tevye, the milkman of Anatevka, a Jewish quarter in Russia at the turn of the century.

Tevye is a mixture of Don Camillo and Mother Courage, with a direct line to God and a stoic acceptance of the fate of the poor wandering Jew. Mr Gordon, an American who settled in Sydney after playing the leads in the boom of post-war musicals here, remarked in a television interview that perhaps there was some gesture in the fact that his last role had been an Arab in *Kismet*. And certainly *Fiddler on the Roof* is an open plea for peace and brotherhood, demonstrating the principle that Jews are real people—or at least real musical comedy Americans.

It has become customary to sneer at sentiment but it not always honest to do so and *Fiddler on the Roof* is an honest musical, not overly memorable but refreshingly different, and it gives one an extra aesthetic pleasure in having an integrated style of its own. Based on the homespun tales of Sholem Aleichem, it tells the story of Tevye, his shrewish wife and five comely daughters; and how, once a chink appears in the strong wall of tradition that surrounds him (he agrees to let his eldest marry the man of her choice) his whole house comes tumbling down.

The production, including mounting and choreography, has been reproduced from Jerome Robbins' original in New York. The sets are too comfortingly like a child's storybook for what is a fairly sophisticated downbeat piece of naivety, though some of the scenes have a nice peasant woodcut style about them. The Russian folk-type music by Jerry Bock is, as one might expect, stronger on the choral work than on solos and belongs also to the stamping dances directed by Betty Pounder with her own admirable style of attack and precision. As a folk piece the music and dancing are much better integrated to the action than is usual in a musical and the whole has a simple, steady pattern which is undemandingly satisfying. Added to this we have a first-rate performance from Hayes Gordon, alternately sardonic and sentimental, and with a calculated sense of timing which is a pleasure in itself to watch. *Fiddler on the Roof* is clearly

Hayes Gordon (centre) and the cast of the J. C. Williamson production of *Fiddler on the Roof*, 1967. (Mitchell Library, State Library of New South Wales)

set for a long run in Sydney and the other capitals.

If *Fiddler on the Roof* is sophisticatedly naïve, *The School for Scandal* is exactly the reverse. Robin Lovejoy's café-au-lait production of this 18th century classic, which makes a fine flurry of the scandal-mongers, places the emphasis squarely and with effect on the lustily sentimental second half of the play. Two Saturdays ago I wrote that I thought the play would be accepted less for itself than for the echoes of Restoration comedy in it. But Mr Lovejoy discards the echoes, rightly, because there is not much bite left in them. The school's barbs, after all, are aimed chiefly at those we never meet. Its references to the protagonists are made obliquely or in a manner that proves harmless.

In Sheridan's time the gossips were probably slanderous. Today the only way to give them back their sting would be to convince us their viciousness could triumph, as it does in *The Country Wife* (produced by Mr Lovejoy last year); and that Lady Teazle is a modern thrill-hungry adolescent. Sheridan is making a valid claim that there are moral values worth hanging on to; but he does not persuade us today they are really in danger.

Mr Lovejoy offers us instead the scandal-mongers as a decoration to the play, for the elegance of their balanced dialogue, the pleasure of a neat rivulet of text meandering through a meadow of margin, in Sir Benjamin Backbite's words. What we have left is a genuine 18th century domestic comedy in which the characters succeed in proportion to how 'real' they can be made. The play was written as a satire on false sentiment but it is Sheridan's own brand of sentiment that triumphs.

Accordingly, in Mr Lovejoy's quality team our praise must go first to Peter Collingwood as Sir Peter Teazle and Helen Morse as Lady Teazle; to Richard Meikle and John Norman as Joseph and Charles Surface; Ron Haddrick as Sir Oliver, Ron Graham as Rowley and John Krummel as the amiable toper Sir Harry Bumper. The drinking scene, the action of Charles' ancestors, the famous screen scene—these romantic set pieces could hardly fail and the mood is deliciously captured by Ron Reid's rococo folly setting, monochrome with touches of gilt.

The costumes, which fill to bursting the tiny stage, are a profusion of lace and satin, brilliantly subdued in being solely in shades of milk and coffee (and the bulk made, the theatre is proud to confide, of mattress ticking). The whole has an enchanting rococo unity of painted stucco— extravagant, whimsical and insubstantial—which places the play where it probably belongs today—far removed from our own pressing perplexities.

My description of Teyve as a mixture of Don Camillo and Mother Courage has less resonance today than in 1967. Don Camillo, a small-town Italian priest with a literal faith and a cosy friendship with the Communist mayor, is the central character in a series of then-popular comic novels by Giovanni Guareschi. Brecht's *Mother Courage and Her Children*, familiar from amateur productions at the time is, of course, a much tougher critique of what war and poverty do to human relations.

It is difficult to recapture now how wide the gap stretched between the world of J. C. Williamson's musicals and that of the art theatre. *Fiddler on the Roof* played in an art-deco theatre in Quay Street, Haymarket, seating 2,500, originally the Empire Theatre built in 1927 and refurbished in 1960 as Her Majesty's. Opening nights were extravagant formal dress affairs.

Australia's art theatre, on the other hand, with a mission to bring its audiences 'the world's best plays', performed for the most part to tiny audiences in uncomfortable halls. The University had converted the Old Tote Theatre from the totalisator of the old Randwick racecourse in High Street, Randwick, into a theatre seating 160 for student productions; but it soon became a professional venue for the classics with Robin Lovejoy as principal director.

It was into this makeshift world that the first NIDA graduates emerged; and their audiences found no incongruity in seeking them out on a university campus or a suburban back street, to sit on benches and admire the ingenuity of mattress ticking and improvised settings. The budgets were tiny and conditions hard in these pre–Australia Council days; but the seriousness of the attempt was uncompromising. The very makeshift nature of this theatre architecture provided a freedom to abandon the proscenium arch of the traditional theatre and open it to new forms and naked confrontations. It was not long before the demands of this new performance style began to dictate the architecture of more substantial conversions.

While there were already proposals for a new Performing Arts Council, the national public funding body for the performing arts at this time was the Australian Elizabethan Theatre Trust. It was founded in 1954 by Dr H. C. Coombs, then governor of the Commonwealth Bank, and others, as a non-profit public company limited by guarantee and was supported by government funding and tax-deductible donations. The Trust ran the Australian Ballet, the Elizabethan Trust Opera and the Elizabethan Orchestra, which in 1970 it split into two, to create resident orchestras in Sydney and Melbourne. Between 1959 and 1961, it had a short-lived national touring company, the Trust Players, directed by Robin Lovejoy. In 1967 it inaugurated an interstate theatre season. This was planned as an annual exchange between the major theatre companies, but it was not repeated.

Democracy and the Trust

Australian, 26 June 1967

At 5.30 this afternoon the Australian Elizabethan Theatre Trust (AETT) will hold its yearly forum, the annual general meeting, in Melbourne. If it follows the pattern of preceding years there will be more directors than members present. But the voice of public opinion has been strident on Trust politics during the past twelve months and if Victorians want to air their complaints this is their biennial chance. Next year the meeting will be held in Sydney.

Thirteen of the 25 directors are up for re-election. Some of them, because of the vast distances between the capitals, seldom or never come to directors' meetings. As with most boards, some of the elected members are sincere and conscientious, others have too little time to spare. On the other hand it must be said that the position is a thankless one. It is time-consuming, controversial and expensive, entirely honorary with not even the courtesy of a free theatre ticket.

It is a sore point among critics of the Trust that it is an anomaly—a private, commercial company given charge of an annual $600,000 in public cash. The sooner the Prime Minister is pushed into putting this right the better. The Trust's constitution is the fault of the originators, not the present executives, but there are ways in which it could become more nearly a democratic institution.

The AETT insists that it is open to nominations for directorships. There is provision in the articles of association for proxy forms to be lodged before the annual meeting. Surely, if proxy forms were included with the annual report, as is usual in a shareholding company, members in outlying states might be encouraged to demand the representation they want? Nor, for practical reasons, has the Trust publicised the fact that the articles provide for local boards of directors where required.

Efficient control at the centre, and adequate fact-gathering over distance, have always been opposing problems in the Trust. The past year has been particularly important. The ballet company has further established itself and foundations have been laid for a permanent orchestra with an eye to future year-round activities at the Sydney Opera House and the Melbourne Cultural Centre. It also ventured into national drama with its interstate theatre season, which, if kept up, could be valuable in promoting a national style of theatre.

And of course, there was the furious controversy about the proposed Performing Arts Council at the time of the last annual meeting. This ended in an eleventh-hour rescue from the danger of being rushed into a new organisation without proper public airing. Now Dr H. C. Coombs says in his annual report: 'Submissions to the Australian Government urging action to establish a council for the performing arts continue to receive the sympathetic consideration of the Government, and it is hoped that effective progress will be made before the next report of the board'. Governments being what they are, unless there is another public outcry, Dr Coombs will find himself writing this in his next report and the one after that. We have told the Federal Government our objections and the arts-versus-performing arts council debate is still to be thrashed out. If we don't press for what we do want we are likely to waste five years and put up with the original proposals in the end.

There are, however, subterranean stirrings, and a pilot project in New South Wales—the two-year-old Advisory Committee on Cultural Grants—is being closely watched. From its activities so far it is clear that a subsidising council on a national scale will need to be an Argus if the money is to be used to best advantage.

The AETT report shows a healthy drop too in the number of seasons undertaken in partnership with commercial managements, apart from the Ballet Folklorico of Mexico (a Harry M. Miller venture) which was the Trust's only profit-maker at $16,318. The entrepreneurial losses were: the Marionette Theatre of Australia tour ($3,584); *Private Yuk Objects* ($13,302); and that bumble-headed venture the Athens Drama Company ($37,294). No mention is made of the *Pageant of Asia* losses.

Subsidies included $220,285 to the Australian Ballet, $105,374 to drama and $162,700 to opera. A total of $32,224 in bad debts has been written off. While only a proportion of State Government funding to the AETT returns in grants to the states—$6,791 of $32,000 to South Australia and $1,130 of $32,500 to Queensland, for instance—some trouble seems to have been taken to provide the capitals with tours in proportion. It cannot be claimed, however, that the choice of entertainment is always what resident theatregoers would like. Only money for state offices and audience surveys is likely to improve the situation.

The Melbourne Cultural Centre, for which plans were first drawn in 1967, is now the Victorian Arts Centre. The proposed Performing Arts Council became the Australian Council for the Arts, established in 1968.

By this stage the complaints against the Trust had sunk its reputation to its lowest ebb. It was protected from public scrutiny of its books, and provided a somewhat dubious tax-deduction service by channelling donations to other performing arts organisations. There were criticisms, too, about the poor return received by the outer states for their contributions, the quality of some board members, and the Trust's virtual monopoly of rights to overseas plays. Peter Scriven, the puppeteer who founded the Marionette Theatre of Australia, then under the Trust's umbrella, was disillusioned, like many practitioners, with its internal management. In 1968 he stood for the board and brought matters to a head. With the help of his fellows he collected sufficient proxies but was outmanoeuvred by the chair, Sir Ian Potter, who declared that as a Trust employee Scriven was ineligible.

The Trust's invidious position as both a dispenser of public funds and a commercial investor was not helped by a litany of poor entrepreneurship. Alan

Hopgood's *Private Yuk Objects*, which debates the morality of the Vietnam War, had some success in Melbourne for the UTRC. But the Trust transferred it to the Phillip Theatre in Sydney, a light comedy and revue house whose audiences expected nothing more serious than a mother-in-law joke. The play's failure badly affected audience confidence there for the following twelve months. The Athens Drama Company, claiming to be Greece's major company, proved to be a troupe got up for the tour. They performed in Greek. The *Pageant of Asia* was mounted in the Sydney Showgrounds and featured dancers set at such a distance from the audience that the intricacies of their dance were lost. It was the brainchild of Stefan Haag (1925–86) who had come to Australia as a member of the Vienna Boys' Choir during World War II and remained. He was the third executive director of the Trust (1962–67) and, later, a freelance opera director and theatre producer.

The Wind of Change is Blowing

Australian, 12 July 1967

This week there are more signs of the winds of change blowing a healthy air of permanence over our community theatre companies. Three circulars have come to hand—one from Melbourne, one from Adelaide and one from Sydney.

The first is the Union Theatre Repertory Company's prospectus for a five-month season, which begins next month and will bow out its present title. On 1 January it will become the Melbourne Theatre Company and, with financial help of the Melbourne City Council and the Australian Elizabethan Theatre Trust, will take on its responsibilities as a civic theatre with an eye on the proposed theatre complex of the Melbourne Cultural Centre. The UTRC, now fifteen years old, began life in Melbourne University's Union Theatre. As student activities increased it has gradually moved away from the university and with the change of name will sever the final connection.

In Sydney, a much newer private-enterprise group, Community Theatre Company Ltd, directed by former British actor Alexander Archdale, has been granted a five-year lease of the Killara Soldiers' Memorial Hall and will spend about $1,000 on renovations before opening a nine-month season in March. The group was begun three years ago with the idea of providing a permanent professional theatre for Sydney's North Shore, a wealthy but notoriously stay-at-home area which does not, on the whole, much patronise the smaller city theatres.

Jennifer Hagan as Annette and Anne O'Shaughnessy as Louise in John Tasker's South Australian Theatre Company production of *Night of the Ding Dong*, 1967. (Photo courtesy of the John Tasker archive from the Performing Arts Collection of South Australia)

Mr Archdale has gathered a basic company of eight theatre people from the area and has to date been preoccupied with money-raising (he now has 782 subscribers) and presenting plays at irregular intervals and in unsatisfactory conditions. In May he received $2,000 from the New South Wales Cultural Grants Advisory Committee with promises of more substantial help if he shows results.

In Adelaide there is news, at last, of the South Australian Theatre Company with a two-month season of three plays opening next month at the Adelaide Teachers' College theatre. The word 'company' is still a misnomer and its home is the person of Mr John Tasker, the Elizabethan Theatre Trust director, whose presence in Adelaide is the outward sign of the group's existence. Mr Tasker launched the SATC in 1965 with a season of four plays and a musical and since then has busied himself with the Young Elizabethan Players and productions in various cities of *The Royal Hunt of the Sun*. His stylish *Night of the Ding Dong* was one of the highlights of the interstate theatre season and it is to be hoped that, having employed actors from Melbourne, Sydney and Perth for the new plays, he will be able to make a further step towards giving Adelaide a serviceable company.

The healthiest side of our theatre today, if anything is healthy, is the strong new climate of opinion that, if we are to improve the quality, we must have permanent companies. A team which works together shows in its results enormous advantages over an ad hoc group; and contrary to the belief that audiences tire of the same faces, the evidence shows that a good actor builds up a personal following and a good company becomes a property in which the community takes pride. Ten years ago the now-forgotten director of the Elizabethan Theatre Trust, Hugh Hunt, waged a lone battle to stamp out amateurism in our professional theatres. Now we have thought of the idea for ourselves. Better late than never.

My comment about the advantages of an ensemble company derived from my experience in Perth where the Playhouse, under the direction of Edgar Metcalfe, had a nucleus of mainly English repertory actors who appeared in a new play every month and gained a loyal following. Perth has not been so well served for theatre since his time at the Playhouse (1963–67 and 1970–72).

Alexander Archdale (1905–86) settled in Sydney in 1951 and quickly made a reputation with acclaimed performances at the Mercury Theatre, including the title role in Strindberg's *The Father*. He established the Community Theatre in 1965 but retired due to illness in 1970. The theatre was renamed the Marian Street Theatre in 1974 and closed in 2002.

John Tasker (1933–88) was one of Australia's most brilliant and erratic theatre directors, who had directed the early plays of Patrick White between 1960 and 1964 and a spectacular production of Peter Shaffer's *The Royal Hunt of the Sun* for the 1966 Adelaide Festival. He also worked with the Trust's Young Elizabethan Players which toured schools with abbreviated, small-cast versions of the classics, notably Shakespeare. Many of the early NIDA graduates did time with the Young Elizabethans and remember it with no great fondness.

In the ambience of the Federal Government's promise to replace the Australian Elizabethan Theatre Trust with a properly constructed funding body, it became imperative for the established small theatres to prove themselves capable of making the leap to professional status. The doomed enterprise of the Independent Theatre described below was the most hair-raising of the expansion plans, but I, too, was caught up in the mood of anticipation.

The Independent Repertoire

Australian, 19 August 1967

Almost without exception every actor in Sydney has been on the phone to the Independent Theatre in the past seven weeks in a bid to join in the most forward-looking step any of our small theatres have made in recent memory. With private enterprise, faith and a substantial grant of $8,000 from the State Government, the Independent's crusading director, Miss Doris Fitton, has formed Australia's first permanent repertory company since the Elizabethan Theatre Trust disbanded its Trust Players.

The term 'repertory theatre' is loosely used these days, especially here where we have no such system in practice outside opera and ballet. The proper definition is a theatre with a permanent company that has two or more plays in production at the same time and performs them in rotation. An acting company of eight has been announced and in October the theatre will begin its repertory system with two plays. As long as a play is in demand, it will be kept in production, until the theatre is playing, ideally, six plays each week. Eight is clearly not a big enough company for such a project and the difficulties are formidable but the start deserves encouragement.

The advantages of running plays concurrently are, of course, enormous. A play will run only as often and as long as there is a public for it, the theatre will always be in use and able to channel audience into the poorer nights of the week. And each actor, while he or she will have the satisfaction of playing a variety of roles, will not have to perform them six nights out of seven. The reason such a common practice has not been employed elsewhere in Australia is simply that the initial outlay has been too great. Six plays a week means six sets, backstage manpower and storage space on city property already too expensive to spare even for adequate working conditions. It also means employing a full-time company of actors at a wage comparable with television; and paying (as is not very often done) for their rehearsal time. Once the plunge is taken, however, the rewards which follow are considerable: a full company available for every rehearsal; and time left for actors to work with writers on a new script or perform other services for the improvement of the theatre's program. In fact, the conditions available in all famous government-subsidised theatres overseas. That our actors are attracted by the idea of a more settled and more honest way of practising their craft is clear from the overwhelming response to the Independent's new policy.

The first eight actors have been chosen for their ability, versatility and their capacity for teamwork. They are Jacqueline Kott, Carmen Duncan and Aileen Britton, Alexander Hay, Brian James, Donald MacDonald, James Condon and Ross Thompson. Also associated (they have other commitments) are Diana Perryman and Ron Haddrick.

Six of these have been cast in Strindberg's three-hour *The Dance of Death* which will open on 13 September with time off for dinner. The first repertory play will be T. S. Eliot's *The Cocktail Party*. Other plays will be a new London play for two actors, *Staircase* by Charles Dyer; and standards like *Blithe Spirit*, *The Lady's Not for Burning*, *A Streetcar Named Desire*, *Uncle Vanya*, *Death of a Salesman*, *The Little Foxes* and Schiller's *Maria Stuart*.

Planning for long thin runs instead of short fat runs should put weight into one end of the Independent's program and daring into the other. Several of the plays listed are successes from the Independent's past and most of them have been chosen to please the theatre's large following of people in late middle age. This group is the biggest supporter of the theatre (apart from dragooned schoolchildren); the new multi-season program will help solve the vexing problem of how to hang on to the regulars while introducing more adventurous fare.

Resolving how to expand the repertoire without disturbing the habits of the regulars is one of the most difficult challenges our theatres face. I believe that there is no theatre that would not follow the Independent's example, had it the resources.

A permanent company offered other advantages as well. Traditionally performers were only paid for performances—Doreen Warburton believes that the Q Theatre was the first to introduce rehearsal pay in 1963. If a show closed early due to lack of patronage they could find themselves in debt. Conversely, producers had to release actors from rehearsal for paid radio work, and film and TV roles were already an endemic problem. Melbourne's UTRC was clearly enjoying the benefits of a regular company.

Herman Melville's Tragic Vision

Australian, 23 August 1967

The first of five revivals in which the Union Theatre Repertory Company is having a final fling before adopting its new garb as the Melbourne Theatre Company, is now playing to crowded houses at Russell Street. It is *Moby Dick—Rehearsed* by Orson Welles, from the famous nineteenth century novel by Herman Melville.

The admirable thing about the performance, and I keep saying this about the company, is its togetherness: the rewards of working a familiar team are particularly apparent in this production, which is as much choreographed as directed. John Sumner's production is first rate, as is Frank Thring's performance as Captain Ahab—and together they make an impact which, although not strictly dramatic, is memorable.

Moby Dick—Rehearsed is an individual creation designed by Orson Welles as a vehicle for himself. Welles has attempted to reassess its spirit in theatrical terms and, to a certain extent, he succeeds. The play is a product of the 1950s, when writers were concerned with restoring the grandeur of theatre and finding a form among the older forms which could present our modern dilemma in tragic proportions.

Welles sees Captain Ahab as an Old Testament Lear, a blind autocrat who is driven by divine madness towards his doom and his salvation. Pip, the cabin boy, is his Fool and Starbuck, the mate, his Kent. Welles drives home his message by putting his play on stage with a *King Lear* company of actors. For me, in fact, the best part of the evening was the glimpse of Act I of *Lear* which opens the play. In this Mr Thring relives the grand days of the actor-manager and shows us the splendid dramatic leaps from truth to illusion which make the dramatic experience for actor and audience.

What followed was exciting but not drama. It is the creation in poetry, art and ballet of a myth. The myth demonstrates Melville's conflict of black and white, will and passion, fear and death; but it is not the conflict itself. The difference is exemplified by the narrative figure of Ishmael, the sailor who at the high points of the play holds the action frozen, as it were for contemplation.

John Sumner overcomes the disadvantages of Welles' approach by the theatrical impact of this production and the dazzling (figuratively and literally) and complex effects of his lighting plot. His collection of ropes, barrels and crates is imaginatively assembled as he uses his cast as a living conjuration of the whaler *Pequod*, which is being hounded to its death with those aboard by Ahab's tragic vision of the white whale. The flashing storms, the supernatural first appearance of Ahab, the gentle swaying of the ship in time to a sea shanty and the final dramatic overthrow of the *Pequod*—these rather than the vestiges of the Melville novel are the objects for contemplation that remain in the mind. And it is for these that *Moby Dick—Rehearsed* is worth a visit.

A plentiful and diverse scene for children's theatre, albeit of varying quality, was another feature of the period.

It's a Mini-boom

Australian, 9 September 1967

Business is booming in children's theatre over the September vacation and one new venture, which set off this week, is a tour of 93 Queensland towns by the Australian Theatre for Young People, in association with the Arts Council of Australia (NSW division). The project is another by-product of the state cultural grants policy in New South Wales. The Australian Theatre for Young People, run by Sydney actors Alastair Duncan and his wife Diana Sharp, has been steadily expanding since 1964 and this year received a grant of $3,000. The Arts Council also received a grant of $6,000 to tour this group and the Young Elizabethans.

ATYP provides theatre on a professional scale for children from 5 to 18 and has launched ten productions so far this year. Their package-deal programs, which are mainly performed by young companies, have a life of two years in New South Wales, being taken into schools and public halls and presented as far as possible with an audience limited to 300.

The Queensland tour, which has already been playing for eighteen months in NSW, has a program of three fairy tales for primary schools, designed to introduce children to the conventions of theatre. For the older children will be *The Sword of Pendragon* written for the ATYP by Barbara Vernon. The group will also send two new tours this week to metropolitan and country areas of NSW and begin Saturday drama workshops for 9–14 year olds, and Friday evening workshops for the 15–20s.

In Sydney the ATYP has been running a production of *Hoddel's Remarkable Handcart* at the Killara Memorial Hall. It is simple and direct entertainment with no superfluous words and plenty of easily-understood action; and the children have their own part to play in bringing the story to a conclusion.

There has been a lot of development in children's theatre over the past few years and much of it has come from theatre people themselves, who realise that the theatre-going habit has been broken by other entertainment media. The Old Tote Players in NSW and the Young Elizabethans in Victoria have been going for some years; and there have been many Arts Council tours. In South Australia actress Marie Tomasetti and her husband, television producer Tony Roberts, are successfully running their Children's Theatre of South Australia. They tour SA private schools and at present have a season of *Winnie the Pooh*.

Sydney has the Independent Theatre's children's theatre and the little Pocket Theatre which have performances most Saturdays and are almost always packed. And in Melbourne the actress Bunney Brooke has announced plans to open her own children's theatre. Perth has the Children's Activities' Trust (the CATs) who mushroom each holiday with creative projects for schoolchildren. Then there are individual performers like the Rayner sisters in Victoria and Thea Rowe in Sydney who visit schools. The Tintookies puppet theatre is at present touring the states for the Elizabethan Theatre Trust; and there are schools' Shakespeare seasons like the National Theatre's at the Princess in Melbourne; and the Genesians in Sydney. And so on.

Some of the work is very good, some of it bad, and most of it profitable. The Tintookies, for example, although an excellent production, are not being properly exploited for the children's benefit. The stories still depend too much on words and too little on action. In the big theatres they are altogether too remote for anything like the old attraction of the Punch and Judy Show. As puppets they are already once removed from reality; with recorded voices they become doubly removed.

Shakespeare, of course, is the curliest problem of all; and cost is not the only reason. I saw part of an extremely expensive, well-elocuted and almost totally lifeless production of *The Merchant of Venice* in Melbourne recently, designed as an official teaching medium. The children around me were in agonies of boredom and will certainly return to the theatre only under protest.

Children's theatre may be big business but it still depends on individuals. What good is being done in some directions is being undone in others. [With the coming of subsidy] some overall policy is needed and some more enlightened standard of evaluation from the education departments.

Of the companies mentioned, the Australian Theatre for Young People, founded in 1963, survives and flourishes, as does Melbourne's National Theatre Company (founded 1956), now a performing arts school; and Sydney's amateur Catholic dramatic society, the Genesians, formed in 1944. Joan and Betty Rayner, founders of the Australian Children's Theatre, began their career in the UK and toured Europe and America for many years. They first came to Australia in 1929 and later settled here. They continued to perform until the 1970s. Thea Rowe was a drama teacher in Perth who gave solo performances, telling stories in character.

Hedda as a Young Woman

Australian, 25 September 1967

The production of *Hedda Gabler*, which opened at the Old Tote on Saturday, is the first major public showing of a cast made up entirely of graduates from the 7-year-old National Institute of Dramatic Art. It is hoped that when the Old Tote builds its new premises such young people will form the nucleus of a permanent company.

As a display piece *Hedda Gabler* was not the best play to choose, although it does offer a bright opportunity to two shining new talents, Jennifer Hagan as Hedda and John Krummel as Tesman. Although the main characters are comparatively young, Ibsen at the time of writing had turned 60, and the play is oppressed with the disillusionment and hard experience of old age. It is about the frustration of romantic dreams and the painful settlement for second-best which comes with the loss of youth; and while there was a high level of competence in the cast there was also a limited understanding and attack.

The weakness lies at the centre of the performance in the strong melodramatic triangle of Hedda, Judge Brack and Ejlert Lövborg. Hedda, as I see her, is a kind of frustrated Bronte sister, a dilettante with an emancipated mind but no first-hand experience, who likes to dabble with the black-and-white sides of the *fleurs du mal*—Brack the accomplished roué and Lövborg the young Dionysius.

At the same time she is a punctilious observer of conventions and lacks the courage to commit to either man. Instead, she settles for the one who will make no demands—the gentle Tesman. She is barren and rootless, with so little grasp of commonplaces that she can tempt a man back to alcoholism for the sake of a grand Gothic gesture; and her triumph, her one orgiastic action of committing suicide, is, like all her actions, destructive, sterile and finally bathetic.

Edwin Hodgeman and Charles Little, in the extraordinarily difficult roles of Brack and Lövborg, the fascinating demon lovers, were not able to match in size Miss Hagan's venomous Hedda; and not seeing her among equals in the play did some damage to the total conception. Miss Hagan does, however, make a fine cold, caged woman with a masculine stride and a splendid presence. A little better response from all her companions would give greater variety to Hedda's fanatical nature—shrewd and sophisticated with Brack, romantic with Lövborg, hypnotic with Mrs Elvsted.

John Krummel gives a very fine performance indeed of an eager, short-sighted academic. One delights in the details of his realisation and having a younger-than-usual Tesman is the most interesting contribution the production makes. The minor characters are less rewarding, except for Pat Bishop's timid maid, Berte.

It is good to see the Old Tote making experiments towards a permanent team, and as a young group this cast does remarkably well. But from the public's point of view it is a slightly empty gesture. One or two older actors could have given the rest the support they needed for their admirable and undoubted talents. The gentle and rather restrained production is by Robert Quentin and there is a good, carefully-furnished set by Robin Lovejoy.

Robert Quentin, a former AETT executive, was foundation professor of Drama at the University of New South Wales, and the strategist behind the expanding theatre activity on its campus. He was the founder of NIDA and the Old Tote and had incorporated the University of NSW Drama Foundation to finance activities.

While the production of *Hedda* was standard fare for the Old Tote, by this time the effects of a world-wide cultural revolution were beginning to inform a new generation of practitioners and the long-standing conventions of realism pioneered by Ibsen were being discarded for new forms and rebellious attitudes. Experiments became plentiful and gradually took shape as what we now call the New Wave. The director Jim Sharman, an early graduate of NIDA, had already made his mark by mounting in Sydney a small iconoclastic revue called *Terror Australis* and directing a production of *Don Giovanni* for the Elizabethan Theatre Trust Opera which had caused scandal among the aficionados.

Theatre for the Space Age

Australian, 14 October 1967

When one considers that from raising a few pieces of wood and canvas in the air we have in this century reached the dark side of the moon, the arts, in comparison, have made very modest progress. A group of young people in Melbourne this week were bemoaning the isolation of the arts one from another and how little research is being given to the creative use of our lives, compared to what was spent on keeping us alive. The group is involved in a 90-minute assault on the senses called *The Flower Children* at a Little Bourke Street discothèque and the producer is that *enfant terrible* and despoiler of opera Jim Sharman—whose newest enthusiasm is environmental theatre.

The mechanical sound and image idea had recently aroused interest. A few weeks ago in the Wayside Chapel, Sydney, I attended a performance of 'psychedelic' music by young Sydney composer John Terry, played on the electric organ and a number of smaller odd instruments with improvised visual accompaniment on projector and mirrors by Francis Good. In Adelaide the art collector Derek Jolly and his associates have presented a number of concerts and at present he is preparing his most ambitious feat for later this month—a stereophonic performance of Benjamin Britten's *War Requiem* in the Bonython Hall. The hall will be set with a hundred microphones and Mr Jolly will accompany them on the projector for which he has several hundred slides of the Great War—photographs, official sketches and some paintings commissioned from Adelaide artist Vytas Serelis.

The *Flower Children* happening is an apologia for LSD and the hippie cult of love and peace and extra-sensory self-awareness. The material includes two pop groups, dancers, op-art and art nouveau psychedelic images; and excerpts read by Helmut Bakaitis from Genesis and Exodus, the poets Coleridge and Blake, and from Aldous Huxley's *Doors of Perception* and Antoine de Saint-Exupéry's *The Little Prince*.

The performance assaults the audience with thoughts, sounds and coloured images, thrown on the scrims or in the flickering light of a stroboscope which transforms the moving figure into something from a dream or an old movie. The effect is dizzying and the amplification sometimes up to 120 decibels—an everyday thing for a discothèque but extremely painful to my ears. As art it has no special significance but it does make one or two points.

The first Mr Sharman himself made about the amplification. For young people to whom the cinemascope screen, extreme stereophonic sound, dazzling lights and hysterical screaming are a form of expression, surely the average theatre entertainment is rather tame. He would like to use all these things in his environmental theatre, surrounding the audience with sensual effects.

The idea is not original and many of the new theatre movements have been groping towards something like this. One thing that does perturb me, however, about mechanical devices and about my discothèque experience is the curious passivity of the audience. A lasting stimulation requires an active concentration and commitment from both the stage and the auditorium (the imaginative effort of being both in and out of the action at the same time) which stimulates not just feeling but understanding.

There is something in this psychedelic idea for our artists but it is not art in itself. It is pre-art or pre-theatre, the breaking down of natural responses in order to make room for new stimuli. To be art there must also be a building up and a unifying.

The time is coming for a great release in our audiences. We can now eat in some of our theatres. Soon we shall be able to stand up and walk. We might do worse than take another look at the mediaeval theatre.

Staircase: **Behind the Camp Humour**
Australian, 11 November 1967

Sydney's Independent Theatre has achieved a coup with its second repertory production, a play that will provide the opportunity to demonstrate the potential of the repertory system. It is *Staircase*, a comedy for two actors by Charles Dyer, a recent *succès d'estime* in London with Paul Scofield and Patrick Magee, and performed at the Independent by two of Australia's most gifted actors, Alexander Hay and Brian James. As theatre it is something of a landmark, being about two homosexuals in a middle-aged marriage relationship, but it is more than that.

When *Summer of the Seventeenth Doll* was presented in London the critic Kenneth Tynan remarked (rather quaintly, in our terms) that the play had made a place for itself in history by portraying the working class without condescension. One is tempted to say much the same about *Staircase*, that it represents homosexuals without condescension. By this I do not mean that they are not comic in the conventional way for they are ridiculous, clownish figures and the play is bursting with cockney music-hall wit. The author's point goes deeper than this. It is a search for self-recognition by two people who are trapped in this commonplace, but commonly unmentionable, relationship and denied the right to be human beings.

Charlie, a former small-time actor, and his friend Harry run a broken-down barber's shop in Brixton and rub along on their illusions as best they can. Charlie, the apparently stronger of the two, lives on memories of his theatrical past, hopes of a comeback and the claim to respectability that he was once married. Harry is fat, flabby and defeated. His tragedy is that his blond curls fell out one night, a blow to his vanity and their hair-restorer trade; he now wears his head bandaged because it feels 'safer'. He broods on a lifetime of unkind cuts by ignorant mothers, wishes that human beings had been arranged differently and yearns for the right to stop being a non-person. Their moment of truth is brought about by a summons Charlie receives after being caught parading in female attire. Between them they sort truth from illusion and decide with which they prefer to live.

The question of identity is important in this kind of relationship which in its essence is unreal and has in it something of the desire to assume someone else's identity and something of the need to make someone else oneself. It is a curiosity of this play that the author Charles Dyer has given his own name to one of the characters, and that all the people associated with Charlie are in a symbolic way linked with the same identity.

The crunch comes for Charlie when he realises that even Harry himself may be a figment of his imagination, just as everything in his past has proved to be, and that he is, as he has so much feared, alone. When he and Harry are reunited it is not the truth about themselves they want; and so laboriously they set about rebuilding the rules of their old relationship.

The serious side of this play is not all there yet in Doris Fitton's production but the framework is set. Alexander Hay is still panting from having performed Harcourt-Reilly in last week's *The Cocktail Party*. He gives a witty interpretation of Charlie's viciousness, self-deception and fear; in time the performance will grow to a higher level of subtlety. Brian James' performance as Harry is already something remarkable, from his ridiculous gait to his sad maternal gestures of comfort. And it is because *Staircase* gives the opportunity for these two outstanding performances that one is grateful for the Independent's new repertory system. Time will bring maturity, toss out the conventional campery and in the end give us something we can hold up as a classic.

An interesting feature of its exploration of self-deception is that all the names in the play are anagrams of Charles Dyer, even his partner who is Harry C. Leeds. I focus on this being a gay play because it was one of the earliest to speak out about homosexuality in the mainstream theatre. Arthur Miller's *A View from the Bridge*, for example (in which there is only a malicious accusation of homosexuality), was given a closed club season at its premiere in London in 1956. A note in the 1966 Penguin edition of *Staircase* reads: 'This reading edition is not necessarily identical with the text as licensed for production by the Lord Chamberlain.'

The Independent's repertory experiment proved too demanding for such a tiny company. It offered the kind of formidable repertoire that our state companies today would hesitate to undertake, even in sequence and with a subscription base. No others tried until Jim Sharman's period directing the Lighthouse Company (the State Theatre of South Australia) in 1983–84. The Independent lasted six months, leaving the actors and stage crew exhausted and the theatre bankrupt. It returned to its semi-professional status. Despite attempts to revive the theatre the directives of the new Australian Council for the Arts meant it never recovered. It closed in 1977 when Doris Fitton retired. She had been proprietor and director of the theatre for its life of 40 years. The theatre building survives as the SBW Independent Theatre.

Through 1967, after Utzon's forced resignation in 1966, new work on the Sydney Opera House stalled while a new architect was sought; and vociferous demands for Utzon's return continued. But for all the controversy the building had its effect on other capitals which by now were planning their own cultural edifices.

Confusion and Conflict over Culture

Australian, 7 December 1967

Why is it that the idea of building a cultural centre brings down on our heads such a multiplicity of confusing demands? Melbourne, by keeping its building under tight security regulations and its building committee remote from politics, is managing to give the people of Victoria what is good for them with as little fuss as possible. The Sydney Opera House affair has become a scandal of international fame. And now both Adelaide and Perth are embarking on this slippery dip of political and cultural vested interests.

The Adelaide controversy concerns its Festival Hall. Last week, after four years of discussion, the Adelaide City Council voted that it be a multi-purpose hall available to all the performing arts and popular entertainment as well as for concerts. While a widely-used hall has obvious economic advantages, the building cost of the new plan is estimated now at $4.8 million, which puts it outside the agreed range of city council and State Government and into the hands of the Federal Government.

Which leaves Adelaide citizens with the thought: Will it ever be built?

The seating capacity estimated at between 2,000 and 3,000, also puts it within the danger range acoustically for a dual-purpose hall, according to the evidence presented during the Sydney Opera House controversy. But the most serious decision that must be made concerns who is to use it.

The Adelaide Festival of Arts is at the crossroads. It has no festival centre and many of its venues are scattered, acoustically bad or suffer some other disadvantage. Such a hall will set the festival on its feet as a national event, but it is only a biennial one and the question must be asked: Who, apart from the South Australian Symphony Orchestra, is going to use it? The question was asked when the Sydney Opera House was started and no answers were forthcoming. Had a theatre manager been appointed then to determine the most economic way of running the complex, much of the confusion and waste might have been avoided.

In Melbourne the question of tenants is fairly clear. Adelaide relies largely on imports. The obvious contender for the job of Festival Hall manager will be the new administrator of the Festival of Arts at present being chosen, and on his strong organising hand will depend how costly this lavish new project will be to the city of Adelaide. But before building can go ahead two controversies must be resolved: first the site and second the money.

Perth seems to have solved its problems simply by having no plan at all. Work is to begin next year on a $23 million cultural centre project on nineteen acres on the north side of the city railway station. It is expected to take fifteen to twenty years to finish. The centre will comprise a museum, library and art gallery and an education department building to serve the needs of commerce in the city; a national fitness headquarters and lecture rooms for drama, music and literature societies. Tenders have also been called to sink underground the central railway station, which would allow for a pedestrian way to Forrest Place in the city shopping centre.

This is the most ambitious project of its kind attempted in WA and $2.2 million has been allocated over the next three years to launch the project. No overall plan, however, has been drawn up. And, what is more, the planned concert hall, for which a site has been sought for over a year, is not to be included in this project but placed on the other side of town.

It seems a pity that Perth, which has more available space than Melbourne or Sydney and more money available than Adelaide, should not be able to design a really spectacular leisure time centre for itself. Some time ago such a scheme was put forward by a group of young architects to develop Heirisson Island, a piece of swamp land in East Perth at the poor end of town. The site conflicted with the Metropolitan Regional Plan, however, and the Government has had trouble in the past making foundations in the bed of the Swan River. But with a budget of $23 million the principle at least is worth preserving that the more reasons one can find to lure people to a community centre, the more widely used it will become.

It is a curious idea to build a cultural centre without catering for the live arts or other social needs. Premier Brand's hope seems to be that such recreation facilities would be provided much sooner than would be possible under the long-term plan for the cultural centre. But Perth appears no nearer to getting its concert hall now than in August 1966 when the Capitol Theatre was sold, or in 1964 when the plan for the civic banquet and concert hall beside the Council House was abandoned. The present site favoured by the Government is at the east end of St George's Terrace on less than three acres of land—enough to provide only the minimum of facilities.

It all seems to go back to the tiring fact that while our governments have come round to believing that a selection of the arts is necessary to make a community appear respectable, theirs is still not to reason why.

I review the opening of the Adelaide Festival Centre on page 230.

The Perth Cultural Centre today is on James Street Mall, Northbridge, on the north side of the railway station. Its construction comprised a major development of the existing Perth Museum and Art Gallery, the Battye Library, with addition of the Alexander Library building; and the development of the former Perth Boys High School buildings into the Perth Institute of Contemporary Arts and the Performing Arts Centre, which contains a small performance space, the Blue Room. Music and hybrid arts programs are conducted by both institutions. The State Government has plans for a new dedicated lyric theatre on an adjacent Northbridge site. The surrounding area is a popular centre for restaurants, pub music and film. It has also become a venue for drug trafficking and the State Government recently imposed a curfew for teenagers. The Concert Hall opened in 1973. Heirisson Island in East Perth is now a wildlife sanctuary.

Along with the competition for the best new cultural centre, the proposal for a federal council was hotting up. The following piece is a conflation of two articles, written as one but divided for publication. It is intemperate and unfair to Dr Coombs, without whom federal subsidy would never have been realised. But it does reflect the widespread fears of another Australian Elizabethan Theatre Trust and the suspicion with which the appointment of its founder and former chairman to head the new funding body, was met. At this time the Trust not only provided subsidy for performance groups but selected or approved its staff appointments and board members, thus actively intervening in the day-to-day business of those it supported.

Sergey Diaghilev (1872–1929), a Russian impresario, introduced to Europe the splendours of the Russian Ballet and was known for his empathy with the life of his artists.

Bring Us a Diaghilev

Australian, 9 and 16 December 1967

My recent trip through three capitals has only reinforced the view that there could be no more tactless appointment than Dr H. C. Coombs to head the vague new federal Council for the Arts. This is regardless of the final form of the council and the obvious advantage to the Government of having the omnipotent Dr Coombs in the driving seat.

Dr Coombs and his Australian Elizabethan Theatre Trust are disliked and distrusted by members of the performing arts to an extent only partly understood by those who buy their theatre tickets. The reasons include the monopoly of government monies, the domination of performing rights and employment opportunities and the autocratic decisions made in Sydney about Trust-subsidised programs without sympathetic consideration of local conditions.

Despotism is usually more efficient than democracy but the lack of a driving plan and the idiotic failure to make use of its resources by putting the right person in the right job have resulted in a criminal waste of money and talent. The waste of money is bad enough. To waste lives is more serious. The Trust has often been despotic but seldom enlightened. And seldom has it been ruthless enough to follow through a scheme to the point where it is a 100 per cent success or failure.

This applies equally to opera, ballet and music. Successful groups have got somewhere only through the driving force of leaders who personally see that the standards, efficiency and vision are maintained. To the Elizabethan Theatre Trust has fallen the opportunity to support such people. Some have asserted themselves, others have not. But overall the Trust has failed miserably in that function which originally it saw itself as undertaking—of being a Diaghilev, a patron capable of building an environment in which it was possible for the creative artist to work.

In management there are three kinds of people (basically incompatible): the businessmen with an amateur interest, who sit on the board; the administrator, trained in most branches of the profession, on whose judgement over creative, financial and promotion matters the success of a theatre depends; and those children of nature the artists, who create the excitement that theatre is all about.

For financial reasons the two jobs of business and artistic director of a company have mostly fallen to the same person and he rubs along as best he can. But the qualities required for the first job are shrewdness, practical knowledge, a well-educated understanding of the world in which his audiences live, and artistic sensibility. The second job is one of the heart rather than the head; its currency is emotion. The two imperatives are very rarely present in the same person. A man who can generate theatrical excitement is far from the kind of comfortable committee-man whom most boards would like to head their company.

In this light, the job of administrator is by far the most important if a company is to keep on an even keel. But curiously, in this country the job is without status and in most cases not considered at all. If the Council for the Arts is to start the performing arts off on a new footing, one of its first jobs should be to follow the steps of the Canada Council and send six people a year abroad to learn theatre administration.

There are two current cases which demonstrate the total lack of understanding of theatrical needs and personalities by the Elizabethan Theatre Trust and by the men and women of goodwill who constitute theatre boards.

The first is the case of Allen Harvey at the Playhouse in Perth. Mr Harvey was imported twice from Tasmania by the theatre at the instigation of the Trust, the second time last January with his family; and he understood that he was to inherit the directorship vacated last June by Edgar Metcalfe. The position was, however, advertised after the departure of Metcalfe (this was delayed in the hope that this highly-popular director would indicate an intention to return). While it was clear that Mr Harvey was not the man the committee wanted to step into Metcalfe's shoes, they kept him on a string for nearly twelve months until he finally accepted a job in Sydney.

Allen Harvey has a reputation as a good planner, stage manager and administrator. He might not have been the person the theatre dreamt of but he might have been the administrator it needed to get it out of the present confusion. Meanwhile time and audiences are moving on, the theatre's finances are in a miserable state and the heart has gone out of it all.

The second case is a more complex one and involves two separate issues—the puzzling fact that with two years to prepare the South

Australian Theatre Company could not agree on a play for the Adelaide Festival of Arts; and the fact that the director, John Tasker, was last month summarily sacked.

John Tasker is a far more controversial figure than Allen Harvey and has been so since he first produced three of Patrick White's plays in the early 60s. But he belongs among the two or three directors in Australia in whose work there are elements of greatness. This is a fairly widespread view among those who know him. In Adelaide, even among the members of the board that sacked him, this opinion was greeted with neither surprise nor denial. His board members were emphatic about both his efficiency and his ability as a director of plays. The reason for the dismissal appears to be a purely emotional one. Attached as they personally seem to be to each other, Mr Tasker and his board are totally incompatible and blame for this unholy marriage must be laid at the feet of the Trust.

When Mr Tasker took up his appointment in April 1965 he found himself alone in Adelaide, with a salary but no budget and no administration. Not long after, a board representing various educational institutions and the Trust was appointed from Sydney by Dr Coombs. Like Mr Harvey, John Tasker had no written contract or outline of his duties. The board, on the other hand, is permanent, autonomous and, at the time of its appointment, without a charter. Mr Tasker did not choose the board, nor did they choose him. Nor, probably, would they have chosen him.

Since 1965 the Trust has channelled $34,000 into the South Australian Theatre Company and nothing has been achieved beyond the occasional employment of local actors and a consolidation of Mr Tasker's talents. No theatre-going pattern has been set, no attempt was made by the SATC board to raise funds locally by annual subscription to support a permanent company of actors, although the last season of three plays had 900 subscribers and made a profit.

The position was further complicated by the fact that the company had no permanent home. It was first housed temporarily in Theatre 62 and now for part of the year in the Teachers' College Theatre. Things did not go too badly at first but the interstate theatre season last year (again instituted by the Trust) over-stretched the company's resources and forced them into virtual inactivity for almost a year. During this time a mutual distrust grew up which made decisions almost impossible—all decisions, that is, but the final one. The SATC board, like the Perth board, knows what it does not want, but it is not at all sure what it does want.

John Tasker is a highly erratic, instinctive director whose range from the superlative to the disastrous seems to depend on his state of mind. Strong men are moved when they describe the emotional cord between him and Zoe Caldwell in rehearsal; without life-blood like this the theatre cannot go on existing. But it is foolish to expect this kind of temperament to be also a shrewd promoter or financier. That is another man's job and if you force both on one man he will end up able to do neither.

In 1962 when she was playing St Joan at the Adelaide Festival Zoe Caldwell was asked at a dignified reception at the South Australian Hotel to reply on behalf of the Elizabethan Theatre Trust. Her speech was brief and to the point, confining itself to one four-letter word with reference to that august institution. It is this terrible public honesty and disregard for the consequences that make her an embarrassment to officials, adored by the public and able to play Cleopatra better than anyone. But no one in their right mind expects her to be responsible. And that is why I pray that the new Arts Council will learn to nurture both its exotic and its household plants where they are and not transplant them to some climate against their nature.

Take back Dr Coombs, Mr Gorton, and give us a Diaghilev.

This view that practitioners should not be required to be administrators is a theme to which I returned in the early years of subsidy. Now directors have gained management skills and have generally assumed the dominant role, supported by a general manager. But at that time there were almost no skilled arts administrators beyond the national institutions—a problem that emerged starkly with the first applications for government funding. The question of what skills and attitudes board members should bring to the table, however, is still contentious.

Theatre 62 (1962–75) was a semi-professional theatre founded by John Edmund in a converted building on the Hilton Road, Adelaide. It was leased to the SATC for its first season. Zoe Caldwell, now an internationally-acclaimed actor based in New York, created the role of Nola Boyle in *The Season at Sarsaparilla* (1962).

In February 1968, I returned to Perth for the first time as critic of the *Australian*, for the Festival of Perth. The Festival was a leisurely affair then, based at the University of Western Australia, made up of film, concerts and plays brought from interstate. So for me it was a family holiday. One of the Festival features was a production by my husband Philip of *Richard III*, at the New Fortune Theatre, the university's replica of the dimensions of the Fortune Theatre of Shakespeare's time. Dorothy Hewett reviewed it in the *Australian* on 12 February 1968.

Perth's principal art theatres were the National Theatre at the Playhouse and the Hole-in-the-Wall Theatre, both of which regularly produced up-to-date work from the British, American and Australian repertoires.

Perth Festival: Blasts of Stage Discord

Australian, 24 February 1968

My last column from the brass bands and the sun-music of the Festival of Perth ends on a strident note with two discordant trumpet-blasts from the repertoire of the 60s—one from the American cartoonist Jules Feiffer and the other from the grim German, Peter Weiss.

Feiffer's work is a play called *Little Murders*, which proved understandably unpopular in America and hysterically successful in London. It is a broadside at the all-American family of the Great Society and is being presented on the festival fringe by the Hole-in-the-Wall theatre. The venue is the Guild Theatre—the company's Hole-in-the Roof open-air theatre, about which I wrote recently, under the heading 'The Wall Is Always Open', having been closed by the Health Department.

The Weiss work is the film of the *Marat-Sade* directed by Peter Brook, which begins a season in Perth on Thursday. It will, I understand, not be released commercially in Australia for no doubt the same reasons that gave the censors queasiness about *The War Game*. It is certainly the most shattering two hours I can remember spending in the cinema.

Little Murders is not very easy to write about. It is a collection of cartoon ideas, each of them satanically funny and adding up, if there is cohesion at all, to the widely-held belief promulgated by Feiffer that America is sick, sick, sick. The style is half satire and half N. F. Simpson absurdism; for the former one is tempted to yearn for a setting by Feiffer himself and for the latter a style of earnest and elaborate naturalism.

Producer John Gill is probably right in plumping for something like the latter but the production did not achieve on the opening night quite the degree of humourlessness appropriate to the outrageousness of the author's nonsense. *Little Murders* is set in the New York apartment of the Newquists, a normal Feiffer family with a cheerful mother who has a wise word for every situation and makes the best of things; a father whose personality problem is that his Christian name is Carol; a transvestite son who lives in his sister's wardrobe; and a daughter who is both the brains and the brawn of the family.

They are entertaining the inanimate Alfred, whom daughter Patsy plans to marry and mould to her own pattern of a husband—a desire made manifest by her habit of punching him about the stomach and head in a playful manner. He affects people this way, he explains. Strangers keep beating him up and he has learned to live with it by humming and day-dreaming of something else during the punch-up.

Alfred and Patsy get married in a blasphemous and allegedly anti-hypocritical marriage ceremony delivered by an 'existentialist priest' whose message is that since Christ died for our sins we should prove ourselves worthy of the sacrifice by committing them. The moulding process begins and Alfred is soon able to assume the master role when Patsy is shot by a passing sniper.

The play has many memorable moments, like the opening of Act Two which reveals the exhausted figure of Carol feebly punching the rock-like stomach of Alfred: 'Stop it, Daddy, you've been at it for hours.' And the wedding reception, at which six desultory guests circle in and out of the living room perpetually shaking hands with the bridal party.

Mr Gill has a competent quartet in Margaret Ford and Evan Taplin as the parents and Kim Mills and John Turner as Patsy and Alfred; but as a team they could not reproduce the ghastly Feiffer style of intense Americanness which could add a third dimension to what he has drawn so many times in two dimensions. A good satirist is one who loves his victim passionately enough to want to shake him for his own good; and it is interesting that Feiffer is so eager to make more immediate contact with his public that he has chosen to try the theatre. But the play itself does not generate the feeling that it is administered for medical purposes, but rather it is an outburst of despair against a nation which he makes us feel is beyond recall.

Peter Weiss' outburst of despair has a source in common with Feiffer but his is not a wild broadside at one nation but a global holocaust of atomic proportions. The film is a reconstruction of the stage production by the Royal Shakespeare Company and is remarkable not only for the extraordinary beauty and sympathy of the photography but for an overwhelming immediacy of impact which is rare to the medium.

The play—*The Persecution and Assassination of Jean-Paul Marat as Performed by the Inmates of the Asylum of Charenton under the Direction of the Marquis de Sade*—is probably the major theatrical document of despair which has yet emerged from the decadent 1960s. It is a celebration of the repeated pattern of high ideals and venal execution which has been the shape of history, and of the belief that nothing is so bad that we are not capable of it.

It is set in the bathhouse of Charenton where the director and his wife and daughter, and by implication the public, are invited to see a therapeutic performance arranged by de Sade himself as a voluntary inmate and refugee from the enormities of the French Revolution. The impact of the play has three levels. First the story of Marat, the idealist for whom the Reign of Terror is a sacrifice by France to the new age. Then come the implications of its performance by madmen and the dialectic argument between the Marat actor and de Sade; and finally the application of the action to the atrocities of this century.

De Sade is the realist and the intellectual who sees man as a mad animal and despairs of the meaninglessness to which the act of death has fallen. We have lost the art of killing with emotion, he says. There is no personal death left, only statistics. And so the argument is played out in song and action between de Sade and Marat against the background of the horde which demands revolution with no further understanding than the satisfaction of immediate needs.

Marat is murdered and de Sade leaves the end of the argument open to hope for those who offer it, while at the same time, in Mr Brook's brilliant production, lashing into life one of the most terrible exhibitions of anarchy the cinema has ever presented. Physically the film is dominated by the painful and beautiful faces and voices of Patrick Magee as de Sade, wise and intellectual; and Ian Richardson, lean, liquid-eyed and ascetic as Marat; and by a blue-white cement colour which covers both the bathhouse and the people. The almost total absence of colour is relieved by the occasional tricolor and slash of scarlet which, together with the abstract shapes, the preoccupation with madness and yawning mouths, gives the film the appalling beauty of a Francis Bacon painting.

In short, the censor is right in implying it is not the kind of film to take one's best friend to; but I cannot remember being in an audience so united and shaking with dry-eyed emotion as this one was, as it blundered out into the beach weather and the traffic.

The War Game (1965) was a controversial BBC documentary drama by Peter Watkins which used World War II footage to depict the impact of an atomic bomb landing on Britain. The BBC refused to broadcast it until twenty years later but in 1967 it won an Oscar for best documentary.

The aggression in these works is typical of the period. Conflicting emotions aroused by Australian involvement in the Vietnam War had begun to focus on violence, political protest and censorship. The phrase 'alternative theatre' was imported to express this wave of outrage, mainly from North America. Within twelve months writers like John Romeril, Alex Buzo and David Williamson were creating their own kind of alternative theatre. The *Marat Sade* project had visible impact upon the thinking of the New Wave, though it received only student productions in Australia. Peter Brook's manifesto, *The Empty Space* (1968), along with Jerzy Grotowski's *Towards a Poor Theatre* (1968) became its bibles.

The production of *Fortune and Men's Eyes* by the little Ensemble Theatre became a milestone on the route towards a new form of theatre and a triumph for its director, Brian Syron. A former Ensemble student, Syron had recently returned from nine years in the United States and he brought with him an aggressive style of performance that embodied the public emotion surrounding the Vietnam War. The impact was the greater because the Ensemble was then a theatre in-the-round and the audience was presented with the actors in their centre, inside a cage. (The theatre was renovated in 1980 and converted into three-quarters in the round to provide more seating.)

Coming Out Fighting: The Case of *Fortune and Men's Eyes*

Australian, 29 February 1968

Sydney's Ensemble Theatre has for some time been falling between stools in a rather aimless search for direction. A theatre-in-the-round with a school based on the New York Actors' Studio principles and pioneering ambitions, it has been looking for something to reform. But somehow only occasionally has it found the right theme at the right time. At others there has been much that is soft-centred, even sentimental, about its attitude to social realism.

But now, unexpectedly, it has hit us between the eyes with a play by a Canadian ex-convict, John Herbert: *Fortune and Men's Eyes*, which comes with a recommendation from Darcy Dugan. It is a fighting documentary drama aimed at exposing the viciousness of society's belief that prison can in any way be remedial, can in fact be anything more than Old Testament justice of an eye for an eye.

It has all the toughness that belongs to the confined quarters and the young and muscular quality of this company; and it has been given a strong and violent, dedicatedly naturalistic production by Brian Syron. It is also a play which makes me feel rather hoist with my own petard, for it is the kind of committed drama I keep demanding to put some virility back into the theatre—yet I can't say I liked it.

Well, not all of it. It may be I have had enough lately of suffering homosexuals but I think it is the irritation of it being almost a very good play indeed, just spoiled by the American vice of humourlessness and didacticism.

The play is set in a prison cell into which a youthful first-offender, Smitty, is thrown with three homosexuals—Queenie, a raving bleach-blond whore; Rocky, a neurotic yellow-bellied sadist; and Mona Lisa, an over-sensitive aesthetic youth whose presence and ill-treatment in gaol is the natural consequence of a lifetime of victimisation. They each teach Smitty their own recipes for survival and from being the victim he learns gradually to become the leader.

The process is the hardening one of learning to treat other people not as human beings but as objects for use or misuse. It is only Mona who manages to preserve some kind of inner life and self-esteem by submitting passively to his bodily insults and keeping them separate from his personal relations. This, in the circumstances, is the only answer, but it did remind me rather too much of Jules Feiffer's Alfred for my comfort.

But before I elaborate on the weaknesses I must say that this is a first-rate production by Syron, who brought the play from America, where it is running off-Broadway. He has a high-quality cast dominated by a superb performance from Max Phipps as Queenie. Max Cullen's Rocky is also distinguished, developing from an orthodox bully to a nervous psychotic with a facial tic and a compulsive laugh. Sandy Harbutt as Smitty and Fred Sims as Mona were only slightly less successful, partly due to a weakness in the writing.

The play suffers the pitfall of all thesis drama: that when one takes a slice of life one has to twist it first into the shape of a play and then into the shape of the thesis. Smitty is the one who is twisted, but although we see the changes we do not really know any more about him at the end of the play than we do at the beginning. Whenever a naturalistic writer gets stuck for emotion you will find him quoting poetry. Poor Mona gets stuck with 'The quality of mercy' and 'When in disgrace with fortune and men's eyes'. It is a cheat and an aesthetic error that deals a body blow to the character. Another occurs in his final dialogue with Smitty, in which he is asked to vocalise what should have been made clear to us in the action.

These points, plus the moral finger shaken at the audience at the final curtain, are vulgarisations which undo some of the good of the powerful first two acts and send us away feeling irritatedly that this is one more earnest, socially-responsible American play. But it is an honest drama, which does not seek to shock for its own sake. It is also considerably more alive than many available and for this reason should be seen. As an instrument of prison reform it is, I do not doubt, a factual document, and it is a pity it has been issued in isolation and not as part of an organised campaign.

The campaign was not long in coming. On 30 March 1968 I resumed the case:

On my return from the Adelaide Festival I found Sydney the centre of an outspoken press campaign involving most of the current affairs columnists, TV documentary programs, Hazel Phillips, the Minister of Justice and, in the role of wise old father-figure to them all, New South Wales' most lionised ex-convict, Darcy Dugan.

First into the field a fortnight before it opened was *Daily Mirror* columnist Ron Saw, who summed up most of what need be said about the play.

Last night at the Ensemble Theatre I saw a preview of a play called *Fortune and Men's Eyes*, a play that forced me to think about both sides of the problem. At least that is a start. It's more than I've ever bothered to do before. It is a brutal, dirty play, a play of the kind, which, only a few years ago, would have brought Vice Squad men at the full gallop. [12 February 1968]

Mr Saw goes on to outline some of the arguments raised by government, Church and medical representatives who attended the preview and sums up baldly with two written quotes from Darcy Dugan and the Comptroller-General of Prisons, Mr J. Morony, both of whom declined to attend.

DUGAN: *Fortune and Men's Eyes* is a factual account of a recurring aspect of prison life.

MORONY: Repugnant. I doubt its essential truth. I want no further part of it.

Take your pick.

Reviews of the opening night were not on the whole encouraging and I suspect some of my colleagues of covering up shocked feelings with expressions of boredom. The public, however, has chosen to disregard us and has assured the play of at least another six weeks' run. On Tuesday I

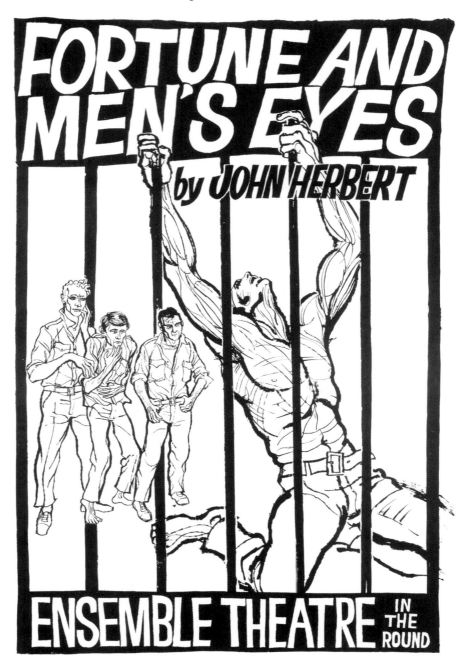

Theatre poster for the Ensemble Theatre's production of *Fortune and Men's Eyes*, 1968. (Mitchell Library, State Library of New South Wales)

attended the play again for the weekly after-show discussion and found the audience overflowing onto the stairs. Several hundred replies to a questionnaire enclosed in the program have been received by the theatre, along with a pile of letters, some from ex-convicts, adding ammunition to the play's argument.

On television Darcy Dugan was reported as saying that prison warders were homosexuals. It turned out he had merely said: 'A turnkey is a man too lazy to work and who hasn't the courage to steal. He bludges on men better than himself.' Whatever he said, the Minister of Justice, Mr J. Maddison, and Mr Morony, were 'appalled' by some of his remarks and demanded an apology. A TV program followed, devoted to the life of a prison warder. The majority verdict on this effort was that it begged the question.

Channel Seven, however, proved to be the hero of the hour with its *Seven Days* documentary, 'A Queer Kind of Hell'. This was hailed as 'a giant step forward' and 'one of the most powerful public affairs programs we have seen for months'. It showed part of the play in action, followed by a heated argument among Mr Maddison, Mr Dugan and another ex-convict, warders, a criminologist and a gaol chaplain. The program is to be screened again.

Except in isolated cases there has been no attempt to deny that conditions are both atrocious and wholly corrupting in our prisons. The Minister of Justice has said that he knows young prisoners are gaoled with homosexuals and standover men. He has also announced that a Bureau of Crime Statistics and Research will be set up to inquire into prison conditions.

Theatre-wise the point about this controversy is that the reason theatre is dying in this country is that the theatres themselves are failing in their duty to the public. Just as some churchmen drive away their parishioners by assuming a solemnity that isolates them from the very people with whom they wish to communicate, so, too many theatres make solemn claims to art as a way of disguising the fact that they have nothing to say. When a play speaks urgently the public will seek it out. One phenomenon of this production is that people find it demanding enough to go two or three times. One person admitted to having been seven times.

The theatre's role in a public matter like this is a simple one—to raise it and to find a way of involving people. Its job is not to find solutions. The argument on prison reform is going on and the arguers are beginning to forget the play which started it all in favour of more important and more damning facts gathered closer to home.

Darcy Dugan, a legendary prison escapee and, at the time, a 'retired' convict, became after this affair a social worker at the Wayside Chapel, Kings Cross. The following year he made his stage debut as the warder in another production of *Fortune and Men's Eyes* at the Anzac Auditorium, Sydney. During the season he was arrested in connection with a $40,000 armed robbery and later sentenced to 14 years' gaol. My remark that 'I have had enough lately of suffering homosexuals' is a comment on the fact that following *Staircase* a number of overseas plays about gays had been performed, breaking an historical tabu. Hazel Phillips was a popular actress and television personality of the day.

When John Grey Gorton became Prime Minister in January 1968, work began in earnest on setting up the Australian Council for the Arts. A growing arts lobby, particularly from the embryonic film industry and a 'TV Make-it-Australian' campaign, persuaded Gorton to take up the plans approved by his predecessor, Harold Holt. Things moved quickly. Dr Coombs was determined to have a Council appointed, and seeding funding allocated, in the 1968 budget, ahead of the federal election looming in late 1969. The frank speech quoted below reveals the compromises he was forced to accept, some of which have had a lasting effect upon how the Australia Council developed.

Mobilising for the Big Arts Battle
Australian, 6 April 1968

Any day now it is expected that the Prime Minister will announce his nine-man committee for the new federal Council for the Arts. The announcement is long overdue and was delayed by the sudden death of the late Prime Minister, Harold Holt. The air is full of rumours about who these faceless men might be. But I must say that one or two of the rumours do not sound too bad.

All we know for certain is that the Governor of the Reserve Bank, Dr H. C. Coombs, is to head the Council; and recently at the Writers' Week conference in Adelaide, he gave an unofficial account of his intentions. Dr Coombs' career in the arts has been paved with good intentions and bad advice and he has reaped the reward of becoming an ogre of a size more in proportion to his remote and aweful position at the head of the Reserve Bank than to his diminutive personal stature.

We have all had our say about the Australian Elizabethan Theatre Trust and it is now blessedly shrinking back into the pigeonhole it deserves. It is time to stop giving all our attention to this rancid old bone and start thinking about the best way of carving up the new joint. Dr Coombs has again expressed his good intentions. He has expressed himself eager for advice from practitioners of the arts with equal good intentions. My guess is that he is heartily tired of the AETT and hopes this time to set up a genuinely philanthropic body with a more easily controllable structure. But the obstacles are as formidable as ever and when bureaucracy takes over good intentions are inclined to get lost in the out-basket.

So what Dr Coombs said in Adelaide I have taken down so that it may, later, be used in evidence.

It has been argued that the establishment of this Council should have been preceded by an inquiry reviewing the state and needs of the arts and developing a broad plan. I myself believe strongly that such an inquiry has been necessary for a long time and the original recommendation from the AETT for the establishment of a council for the arts included [it]...However, the Government did not accept this particular piece of advice and has proceeded to establish the Council, which has a widely-spread but ill-defined charter so that it is difficult to see where the responsibility of the Council begins and ends. ... Frankly I do not find the compromise wholly unsatisfactory. It ensures that, unlike Canada, we will not have to wait eight years before anything happens, but can move step by step as investigation justifies.

I personally advocated that the Council should be concerned mainly with the performing arts. This has been taken to mean that this is where my heart lies. I do not think this is the truth. The recommendation reflects a conviction that there is a danger in a too-concentrated bureaucracy of the arts. Once government supports the arts, bureaucratic elements are inevitably introduced. I felt that there was a need for other bodies similar and equal in status to the Council, which, while they could collaborate, were in claims for public support competitive. I saw these separate councils as means of persuasion that the arts they represented warranted greater public support, and as channels through which such support should flow. I may have been mistaken in this conception but it was genuinely held. In the light of the decision the Government has made I will now approach the question with a completely open mind. The Council will carry out, or see carried out, studies to guide further developments.

My own views about membership of the Council would, it seems, not find favour. I have suggested to the Government that the Council itself should not pretend to be representative of practitioners in the arts.

A council of nine cannot hope to be representative. It seems preferable that the Council should be formed from persons of known wide-ranging interest in the arts. This does not preclude practitioners, but the essential requirements are: firstly, a wide and discriminating interest in the arts, secondly an understanding of the problems associated with the support of the arts, and thirdly a capacity to persuade the Government.

I take this to be one of the main functions of the Council: to act as an advocate for the arts and an influence on government ways of thinking. I do not think that a practitioner is necessarily the best advocate. However, an advocate must be in touch with, and advised by, practitioners and the Council should have a panel of advisers drawn from practitioners. I can see great advantage in these advisers being chosen by their fellow artists if this can be done. You will forgive a certain scepticism about the probability of artists choosing and continuing to support such representatives. Whether artists accepting the task of representing their fellows would find themselves handicapped in relations with their fellows is a risk, but one that should be taken.

In any field there is a tendency for an establishment to develop and this is the stronger when judgements are of a corporate and compromise character. My own answer to this problem lies in the maintenance of a multiplicity of channels of possible support. I have been personally concerned in trying to interest private corporations, universities and other bodies in independent action for support of the arts. The Australian National University has established several fellowships … Already these fellowships have led to the creation of new works of art, but also have enriched the life of the campus … I hope the Council will be able to stimulate in different sections of our society alternative channels through which artists can seek support in the periods of creation, or access to a wider and richer audience for their work.

My colleagues' ideas may differ from my own, but I would say that the first task of the Council would be to carry on and develop support for the arts now accepted. In this development regional or state support for the arts is as important as support from the Commonwealth. I believe that an early priority is for the Council to establish direct working relationships with such state bodies and to encourage their establishment where they do not exist. The existence of such bodies along with parallel developments in universities and other places will help prevent the Council becoming a monopoly.

Space defeats me today but I shall return to discussion of the Council from time to time and refer to some of the constructive suggestions which have been put to me, and others which readers may care to offer. If the Council can genuinely stimulate a climate in which the arts are accepted as necessary; if it can persuade local groups and private enterprise to subsidise it for their own purposes; if it can help make the arts a familiar part of community life, there is nothing better it could do.

One problem for a government instrumentality is that in the personality of the working artist lies its chief asset and this cannot be quantified in an annual report. But without that driving force no artistic production unit can succeed, however efficient it may be.

Another problem to which some answer must be found before subsidy to the arts will be of any benefit is how to define the needs of such a disparate society. Many of our bravest experiments are failing because there is no efficient way of gathering together those to whom this giving and receiving process would be most beneficial. The AETT opera and ballet have succeeded not just because they receive so much money but because the audience for these traditional forms is well-defined. But how do you persuade potential consumers that they will like something totally outside their experience? And which consumers do we choose to persuade? The closer one looks the more formidable the problems become. Dr Coombs has chosen to run the government [ie the arts bureaucracy] and one wishes him luck. But from where I sit the view from the opposition benches looks more attractive.

In the event, Dr Coombs played no part in the choice of the new Council and told me in an interview published on 13 June that he knew nothing of some of the members. Of the administration he said he hoped to find someone of high qualifications and experience but this would require a higher salary than had been budgeted. Staff facilities would at first have to be borrowed from another government department. Later that year Dr Jean Battersby, a broadcaster and research scholar, was appointed the Council's first executive officer. She became chief executive officer in 1973 and resigned in 1981. The Council's budget in 1969 was $1.7 million.

As subsidy encouraged the theatre to expand, the idea that we might have our own playwrights had begun to take hold. In 1966 the University of New South Wales Drama Foundation mounted an experimental season of Australian work in the 100-seat converted church hall renamed the Jane Street Theatre. After two seasons the decision to repeat the experiment in a larger space—even one with only 60 more seats—proved such a financial disaster that it threatened the Tote with closure. The pressures on the Old Tote were already telling. It was heavily subsidised by the AETT, a cause of envious criticism by its rivals, and it was countdown time for subsidy.

The 1968 season consisted of a revision of Rodney Milgate's *A Refined Look at Existence* which had received its premiere in the first Jane Street season; and his second play, *At Least You'll Get Something Out of That*; Dorothy Hewett's *This Old Man Comes Rolling Home*, which had had a season at the New Fortune Theatre in Perth; a double bill of Douglas Stewart's *The Fire on the Snow*, a classic radio play in blank verse adapted for the stage, and Alex Buzo's *Norm and Ahmed*, his first play to gain national attention.

The Old Tote: A Duty to Lose Money

Australian, 25 May 1968

Tonight is the last night of the much-fussed-over Australian play season at the Old Tote and the critics, the public and the management are resignedly agreed that the effort was pretty much a disaster all-round. I myself have been prominent in the game of critical target practice; my remark about the Tote being a hotbed of conservative thought seems to have caused some reverberations. But all this is the daily stuff of the battle of the box office.

What we should consider is whether the season was worth doing at all—and the answer is that only serious theatre projects of this kind can possibly justify the existence of this non-commercial out-of-town, most subsidised Australian theatre. Success or failure at the box office has nothing to do with the value of the experiment. The value lies in the unique and unheard-of fact that a major professional theatre was willing to gamble more than half its year's program to promote local scripts of mostly untried and only embryonic shape.

Nor were the scripts as raw material all that bad; and the mounting and performance were well up to the standard of the Old Tote. It was not the plays that were prime cause of the disaster. It was the move from the anything-can-happen atmosphere of that former ladies' auxiliary hall to the formal surroundings of a theatre promoting the idea that it gives us the best new and old plays from the international repertoire at the best standard Australia can produce.

Audiences are a conservative lot and they do not like their habits disturbed or their expectations disappointed. The anger of some of the Old Tote's patrons during this season at being asked to put up with something less than a well-finished, well-seasoned product, was quite out of proportion to the quality of the entertainment offered. Most of the evenings had something to recommend them, and much more allowance would have been made in the workshop atmosphere of the Jane Street Theatre.

The Old Tote building's days are numbered, however, and much more disturbing things are going to happen to its audiences before order is resumed. The next production is *King Lear*, to be produced by Robin Lovejoy with Ron Graham as Lear. It will open at the University of NSW Science Theatre on 28 June and at the end of the season will fly to Brisbane and tour also to Lismore, Armidale, Dubbo and Wagga. The tour has been arranged in association with the Arts Council (NSW Division). After that there will probably be two more seasons at the Old Tote before it closes for demolition in November. Next year the company will play in a temporary theatre seating 350 on the other side of Anzac Parade, Kensington, until the new Old Tote Theatre is built.

Where, among all these temporary arrangements, the two plays already commissioned by the undaunted University of NSW Drama Foundation are staged is the Old Tote's next problem. (One is from Jack Hibberd in Melbourne and the other from Alexander Buzo, the author of the one-act play *Norm and Ahmed* shown in the recent season.) A workshop centre is obviously necessary where producers and authors can work together without involving the public until a much later stage of refinement than a three-week rehearsal period can offer.

What those involved in the Australian play season gained from it had no bearing on the public, except in providing responses that could be gained from an invited audience. As productions, Robin Lovejoy's two Milgates probably made the best use of the material. The experience has not made a playwright of Mr Milgate; maybe one day he will become one. Mr Lovejoy has no doubt learned a lot about how to deal with authors. The other two major new plays were better scripts, but the gestation process for producer, cast and playwright was too short to make more than a superficial binding together of words and action.

Calling the Old Tote conservative in thinking is a paradox when one considers the wild bravery of this venture. The theatre obviously feels a duty to Australian theatre because of the subsidy it receives, and we are grateful for this. But its approach to such wildness is enforcedly conservative because of the extreme insecurity of its finance and reputation—and because it has so little and the little means so much. Experiment without freedom of thought is bound for failure.

When we shall grow out of calling for Australian plays and not simply plays, I do not know, but the sooner a play can stand or fall on its own merits, the better.

The following year the experimental season retreated to Jane Street and the playwrights themselves soon burst out of it. The original Old Tote survives as the Figtree Theatre, now used by students. A new theatre was never built. The temporary Parade Theatre was used by NIDA until it was demolished in 2000 to make way for the new NIDA complex. Jack Hibberd's *The Last Days of Epic J. Remorse* was never staged by the Tote but Buzo's *Rooted* was presented at the Jane Street Theatre in the 1969 Australian play season. Buzo disliked the style of the production enough to desert on opening night and attend a performance of the play by an amateur theatre in Canberra.

We were now at the height of the Vietnam War and the protest movement. The state visit of United States President Lyndon Baines Johnson in October 1966 had produced violent public demonstrations in Australia; and elsewhere marches and demonstrations against prevailing governments were gaining in violence, notably the 'events of May 1968' in Paris and the 1968 Chicago Democratic Convention. President John F. Kennedy had been assassinated in 1963, Malcolm X in 1965. Australian Opposition leader Arthur Calwell, an opponent of the War, had been wounded by a gunshot during the 1966 election campaign. Martin Luther King was assassinated in April 1968 and Robert F. Kennedy on 5 June.

In the theatre, there was a break with realism, when traditional narrative structure and the newer Method School of internalising emotion were overrun by new overseas influences. The culmination by 1970 was outgoing, big-gesture larrikin theatre. *America Hurrah!* was a turning point. George Ogilvie, Brian Syron and John Tasker, together with NIDA students Jim Sharman and Rex Cramphorn, became the leaders of a new kind of directors' theatre.

Actors of a New Breed

Australian, 15 June 1968

We live in an age of assassination, say the headlines. One third of America is afraid to walk in the dark. Here at home our nightmares are of the child-murderer at large, the rape packs, the call-up ballot. In our wars some six civilians are killed for every armed man; and they are not deaths any more but body counts.

'Today we are all mad, and we are all perpetrating madness', writes Jean-Claude Van Itallie. 'Normal men have killed perhaps a hundred and fifty million of their fellow men in the past fifty years.' 'There's no singular personal death to be had—only an anonymous cheapened death', says Peter Weiss's Marquis de Sade, describing with awe the festive tearing to pieces of Louis XV's assassin. Who are Weiss and Van Itallie? They are playwrights, dream-makers, who act out our worst nightmares so that we may see for ourselves what it is we really fear. They are the new poets of destruction who recreate the old rituals of carnage and vandalism.

Australian theatre has so far remained almost untouched by the new wave of theatre abroad, which is feverishly embroiled in the chaos. The few productions here have been only partly successful because their secret truth lies not in the script but in a completely reverse process: the communal work of firstly the actors, then the director and finally the writer.

I want therefore to describe the process of three of our directors, men in their thirties who have received their training abroad, who have become aware of the need for a new kind of actor if the theatre is to become a public voice again. They are George Ogilvie, assistant director of the Melbourne Theatre Company; Brian Syron, a Sydney actor, director and teacher who returned to Australia last September after nine years in America; and John Tasker, until December resident producer of the South Australian Theatre Company. His production of Van Itallie's *America Hurrah!* opens at the New Theatre in Sydney next Saturday.

Of the three, Brian Syron's work is the least known for since his return he has done only one production. Because of the social issues it raised, however, it received more press space and invited more public discussion than any play for a long time. The Ensemble Theatre's *Fortune and Men's Eyes.*

Originally a member of the Ensemble's drama school, Mr Syron chose to go to the United States in search of an 'organic sense of truth' in acting style which he felt was lacking here. In Sydney the bulk of his work is done in a hired studio at the Elizabethan Theatre Trust premises where, with his students, he attempts to define the nature of reality in an actor's terms. There any day you may find a group of actors miming a ball game which is suddenly a traffic disaster or a beach scene. Mr Syron sees the theatre as an organic part of the world and the world as an organic part of people. Machines are part of his world and in his world people are either machines or their victims.

Marie Armstrong as the Motel Keeper, Barry Sterling as the Man and John Hargreaves as the Woman in the New Theatre production of 'Motel', 1968.

What he is after is not interior searching but outward physicalisation. His group transformation exercise, as he calls it, creates itself from actors picking up gestures from each other and adding to them. This forces each actor to be constantly aware of the others, to remain part of a group and yet retain the power to influence the total action. A simple example of this is an exercise devised by Charles Marowitz and Peter Brook for their theatre of cruelty experiment in London, out of which came Mr Brook's production of *The Marat-Sade*. It begins with two actors touching each other and as the others join, one by one, soon no single actor can move without affecting the others. The lesson is obvious. Several of his pupils have, not surprisingly, been cast in *America Hurrah!*

These principles are being adopted by Tasker in his rehearsals of this play, which is really three short plays, based on transformation exercises from Manhattan's Open Theatre and the three sections were originally performed separately at the Café La Mama. In 1966 it opened at the Pocket Theatre, off-off-Broadway, and last October the La Mama Troupe performed it at the Royal Court, London.

The first, 'Interview', is an almost literal acting out of some of the nightmares of American life—fears of inadequacy and anonymity, of life running us down like a steamroller. The second play, 'TV', is a satire on the total irrelevance of its platitudes of real life and the danger of putting trust in them—in soft-soap commercials, self-satisfying adventure programs, or reassuring politicians. What Van Itallie is saying is that there is nothing either inside or outside ourselves we need not fear, and that is the kind of dream we dare not admit. The last play, 'Motel', is like nothing Australia has seen before. It has forced audiences to leave the theatre or get under their seats. It is not a nice play but it belongs to our time. What Sydney will do remains to be seen. This is a new kind of theatre that tosses out the window the preconceptions of the orthodox pattern of production.

George Ogilvie takes quite a different approach; but his application of physical and mental control and his organic ensemble is similar in outcome. Originally from Canberra, he studied in Paris with the famous mime Jacques Le Coq and for two years travelled round European towns and holiday camps with a mime troupe in the manner of Molière. He also received more orthodox acting experience and has been a teacher at London's Central School of Speech and Drama and at the Royal Shakespeare Company.

Although the Melbourne Theatre Company's play requirements are of a more conventional kind than I have been discussing, Mr Ogilvie still feels the pressing need for a more intelligent and inquiring kind of actor than we have been breeding. Every morning he takes a 45-minute class for the company at the Russell Street Theatre. With his strong classical background he works not on associative images like Mr Syron but on actors—drawing from a background of traditional comic and dramatic principles to get a predictable result. At one class I visited, he was showing how the rhythm of movement could affect the comedy of two actors trying to sit on the same chair; and how Chaplin based his comedy on building up an expectation and then confounding it.

Dramatic acting should be similarly based on technique, he says. One of the drawbacks of the Australian actor was that he believed it dishonest not to feel the emotions he created on stage. Actors must first know form, but within that form there is a freedom, says Mr Ogilvie. What the actor does with that freedom is where art displaces craft. Give an actor total freedom and the result is anarchy, he says, and this applies equally in real life.

We need more such directors and actors who are prepared to uncover our dreams and show us, not the thing itself but its distillation within the strict form of the theatre—and then we shall find our theatre has something to say.

America Hurrah! Landmark in Instant Imagery
Australian, 27 June 1968

Because I have an out-of-the-ordinary production to discuss, I need to say at the outset that the total is by no means a rounded success. Uneven as it is, its best is an advance on anything Australia has seen before and at its least is a genuine new form of dramatic communication.

The play is *America Hurrah!* by Jean-Claude Van Itallie, which opened at the New Theatre, Sydney, on Saturday. To have achieved so much is a wonder for a small amateur theatre on the breadline. It did, however, receive charity on this occasion from the Australian Elizabethan Theatre Trust who brought the producer John Tasker from Adelaide for the production.

America Hurrah! is not one but three plays, each on a theme about the emotional pressures in modern life. The first, 'Interview', with a cast of eight, is a compelling series of comic-tragic improvisations on our nightmare anxieties—being interviewed for a job, losing one's way, being ignored, used, operated on, trampled over. And, running through them all, the terrible refrain: 'Excuse me, I'm sorry. Thank you. Pardon me for living'. The second play, 'TV', is a satirical revue-style sketch of commercial television values. Three television control operators, two men and a woman who have a private triangular relationship, squabble and celebrate and take tranquillisers and confess their problems while a television screen and live actors provide synthetic panaceas as politicians, Western heroes, Wonderboy, TV personalities and Billy Graham.

The third, a ten-minute masque for three dolls, is a vandalism ritual called 'Motel'. Centre-stage the giant, granite figure of the motel-keeper intones in a rising stereophonic crescendo the mass-produced happiness features of the motel room, while eight-foot tall boy and girl dolls bulldoze through the apartment, tearing it apart, dancing and copulating on the destruction and scrawling graffiti on the walls.

What is so new about these plays is not just their method of presentation. It is not even the novelty of the subject matter, but on the contrary the extreme familiarity of it all. Van Itallie has put his finger so accurately on our hidden fears—our job, family, social inadequacy, sex, death, God, destruction—that the audience grasps almost without surprise the anonymous group of grey figures who transform themselves on a bare stage from one anxiety image to the next. The message is clear enough but it is written in emotional, not logical terms. Van Itallie is an absurdist in a new guise. He does with action what Ionesco does with words.

The standard of performance is so much higher than one is accustomed to at the New that one cannot make the ordinary judgements. But it is also fair to say that only in a lively amateur theatre of this kind could one find the conditions to rethink the methods of acting and submerge so large a group of actors into an organic whole. In stressing the ensemble work of the group I do not mean that the actors suffer a loss of identity, rather that they assume a chameleon quality of light and shadow. This was brilliantly evident in the first piece in which a series of heartrending figures disengage themselves from the group. Petitioners to an unhearing politician; a girl who thinks being killed in a street accident too poor an excuse for being late to a party; a housepainter at the confessional whose answer is only silence; a switchboard operator who collapses under the pressure of her machine. This was one of the most memorable and uniquely satisfying things I have seen in the theatre.

This was the best of the evening. 'TV' is very funny but less well defined and a bit overcrowded on the confined stage area. Its truth is satirical, not painful and therefore more quickly forgotten. The third, expected to be the tour de force of the three, was the biggest disappointment. This appeared to be partly because Mr Tasker's courage failed him and partly because the economics of the theatre were unable to cope with the play's demands. There was no ritualistic rhythm or orgiastic pleasure in the motions of the dolls, nor was the sound equipment strong enough to approach even nearly the threshold of pain. And the totality was not frightening enough to justify the obscenity. The weaknesses are obvious enough and some of them will be ameliorated before the next performance.

America Hurrah! is not a work of dramatic literature. It is a landmark not because its life is likely to be more than a year or two but because it is a notable example of the new therapeutic theatre of instant, throw-away images that can help us clutch at our own identity in the universal chaos. Out of itself it has created a new style of acting which is so much more recognisably right for this generation than the concrete assurance of the naturalistic actor, that, for the young people who see this production, I doubt if the theatre will ever be the same.

The cast includes Robert Bruning, Barry Sterling, Marie Armstrong, Maggie Kirkpatrick, Roger Millis, John Hargreaves and the motel-keeper's voice by Betty Lucas.

Five weeks later the NSW Chief Secretary, Mr Eric Willis, in response to a complaint from a member of the public, ordered a ban on the performance of 'Motel' anywhere in New South Wales (see p. 70). It's interesting to note here that 'producer' was still the standard term at this time. The word 'director' was regarded as an introduced American term but was adopted into the language during the 1970s.

Away from the Chaos: Council Begins Work
Australian, 8 July 1968

The first meeting of the Australian Council for the Arts is to be held today and formal work will begin on setting up a long-term policy for the arts. So far members of the Council seem to be doing no more than hanging onto an amorphous view that the arts are a good thing. Now is the time to lobby.

Their first job will be to make a widespread inquiry into the arts and this will involve many more people. The second task will be the more delicate one of setting up specialist advisory committees. Here the Council will have to take the bull by the horns and appoint known figures to batter out a policy and set their own work in a context. For, let's face it, the best people are the most involved; there is no point in appointing men and women of lesser stature just because their approach is more arm's length. The fairest thing is to make it a battle of equals with the chances of the finish being a draw.

Since the theatre is expected to be the first consideration, I should like to tender four thoughts for consideration:

1. *The Australian Elizabethan Theatre Trust's abandoned plan to set up a permanent civic theatre in each capital should be pursued as a primary goal.*
   In Melbourne, Adelaide, Perth and Hobart the pattern is reasonably clear. Brisbane has a theatre being built that may be developed to house a professional company. Only Sydney has no suitable theatre within the city limits—except the depressing hope of the Opera House. Once these centres are established it should be possible, and it will certainly be necessary, to circulate personnel. This would have the double advantage of ensuring security of employment while providing the stimulation of differing demands.

2. *Consider establishing a national classical company.*
   Properly organised into an annual subscription series, such a company could well cure, directly or indirectly, most of our problems. It is glamorous and would attract exactly the kind of audiences that now go to ballet and opera. It is prestigious and would encourage both government and private enterprise to see there could be value in subsidising the arts. It is educational and would relieve school students of the necessity to endure so many bastardised renditions of the classics. It could be cast from season to season from the state companies which would help them towards developing a national entity and give them regular classical training. It would provide the kind of company that would attract overseas and expatriate stars to join it for a season. But such a plan would require the kind of investment that has gone into our national opera and ballet—nothing less will do.

3. *The Council should seriously consider backing people before theatres.*
   Much of our theatre subsidy to date has been in terms of bricks and mortar; and grants have been given on the strength of past achievement. But theatre depends on excitement for its life and excitement depends on people, the right people working together on the right ideas. If the people are not there, no amount of money is going to make that theatre better. If subsidy is to be economical some way must be found of capturing and developing original work, rather than prolonging the life of the derivative and the old-fashioned. Audiences may not know what they want but they know enough about the latter to stay away from it. It is time the profession took itself seriously enough to make a proper study of what the theatre is about.

One of the answers is to send practitioners abroad, but just as important is to provide the opportunities for them to stay here. Most of the practitioners in the upper reaches of the profession have worked abroad. They are not short of ideas, only of the freedom to put them to work. If half-a-dozen fellowships were appointed annually they would have no trouble putting the time to good purpose.

4. *A concerted attempt to boost private enterprise backing for the arts must be made.*
Government and civic respectability and permanence are not things that encourage creativity, and the theatre would be better off without them were there some other source of subsidy. The place for government subsidy on a large scale is a museum for the classics like any national company. The job of the other kind of theatre is to disturb the status quo, not to be part of it. Private enterprise money would be more quickly available and a more personal arrangement. Most of the American theatres are run on money from private business. What the Council must do is make the arts a prestigious, glamorous and tax-deductible inducement.

Soon after this Dr Coombs invited me to be one of a nine-person interim Drama Committee of the Council. The members included John Sumner and Jim Sharman. Dr Coombs asked for written submissions from directors and opinion-makers but too little time was allowed and the most considered proposals arrived at our table too late to influence decisions. Most revealed the paucity of strategic planning in our theatres' administration.

My four points had different outcomes. A flagship theatre in each state became a primary goal, with Melbourne and Sydney to lead the way, but a national company, a case that goes back to Federation, was impractical in 1968. Support for individual artists was adopted with the special projects grant scheme established at the outset on our committee's recommendation. The Council has never funded capital works. Lastly, sponsorship was considered inappropriate and did not become Council policy until 1981 under the chairmanship of arts management consultant Dr Timothy Pascoe. Given the preoccupation with censorship at that time my view is understandable although my visit to the United States the following year awakened me to the pitfalls of private subsidy. Today the received opinion is that large-scale and museum theatre attracts sponsorship and that it is the responsibility of government to encourage research and development.

Our committee met three times and then disbanded. As is the way with such advisory boards, our advice was pre-empted by other imperatives.

While the politics of subsidy continued to bubble across the headlines, the reviews in the remainder of Part I show the demolition and reconstruction then occurring across Australia. The review below describes a typical style of protest theatre that sprang up in response to the conscription ballot for the Vietnam War.

Guerrillas in Brisbane

Australian, 17 July 1968

'To the Trades Hall', I said. The taxi-driver looked at me over his glasses. 'Are you going to stop the strike?'

Alas, I pointed out, not only was I powerless to affect the airline strike in any way, I was a miserable victim of it. My pathetic stories of an invalid husband and children turned out on the streets had failed to move the stony-faced men in charge of the last plane out of Brisbane. Nor had my glowers at the fat first-class passengers from the Doomben Cup, patting each other on the back and swearing to stand by Reg Ansett, registered the faintest quiver. Reconciled to a weekend in Brisbane I determined to pursue what excitement offered. 'On Sunday night', I was told, 'you must go to the Trades Hall, to see FOCO'. Foco, it emerged, was Spanish for guerrilla encampment and was a Sunday-night fun house for the under-25s set up by Brian Laver, described as the local revolutionary leader. It sounded promising.

A blood-red light was flashing FOCO and a trail of expressionless youth was spilling over the steps. 'Are you sure this is where you want to go?' said the driver and sniffed. 'You'll get done there.'

Inside my friends and I were escorted to the top of the building in a lift crammed with teenagers in slacks and a girl with a dead-white face and an ancient hat adorned with a pink flower. When the lift door opened we were thrust into a corridor with a hundred or more people all thumbing over copies of *How Not to Join the Army*, *Australian Atrocities in Vietnam*, the weekly review of the Cuba Communist Party and *Peace on Earth* by Pope John XXIII. On the walls were posters for the Ninth World Festival in Sofia this month—*Solidarité*, *Pax*, *Amitié*—and others celebrating Che Guevara and demanding the arrest of Jesus Christ as a political agitator.

We were approached by Doug Anders in a vast navy blue sweater. One usually notices Doug when he approaches because he is about 6ft 4in. tall, dark and given to wearing dark glasses. He is an arts graduate of the University of Queensland and a graduate of the National Institute of Dramatic Art, and is teacher and organiser of FOCO's drama group, the

Tribe. The drama performance of the evening would be on in ten minutes in the Folk Room if we cared to go in, he said. It would be a two-minute piece written by himself and based on one of Paul Ableman's *Tests*. The hat with the pink flower drifted by. There was a boy under it this time.

There were another hundred or so people in the Folk Room listening to a classical guitar. This was in due course interrupted by Anders wearing a drum and three masks, a lean youth and a slip of a person in granny glasses and bird's nest hair I thought at first to be Bob Dylan. But she proved to be Mrs Babs Wheelton, mother of five, whom I had seen earlier in the week seducing the customers at the Mark Twain as Lady Fidget in a musical version of *The Country Wife*.

The play consisted of some crosstalk concerning Aspro, Zanzibar and a spider in the armpit, while Mr Anders did expressive movement in the background. It was intended to mean nothing, he explained later. They had planned a happening that night but they hadn't been able to find any white feathers. I tried to look sympathetic. Nothing will come of nothing. Think again.

An academic friend who had joined us said: 'I know it dates me but the play reminds me of the dadaist Tristan Tzara's play *The Gas Heart*. When was that? 1916?' Then another guitarist began to sing soulfully: 'No one understands. As the sky is blue my love is true.' A couple of boys in the corner were holding hands.

Then came a sitar player and after that we moved to the disco where five or six hundred were having their ears pierced in almost total darkness by a pop group called the Coloured Balls. I retreated to the Folk Room. The couple in the corner was still there but I noticed this time one was a girl. And finally, a visit to the film room where an anti-war documentary from American Documentary Films was in progress. Cracked, blurred at the edges and with the sound track gone, it was still a compulsive piece of film—peace marches in the USA, police action, army combat training and an army funeral in Vietnam.

FOCO is a club which was opened in March by a group of students and young socialists under the guidance of Mr Laver, a research officer for the Trades and Labour Council. It now has 2,500 members and the membership is temporarily closed. Doug Anders' drama group is engrossed in absurdism, improvised texts and the theatre of protest. It has classes at the weekends and performs something each Sunday, though most are longer than their two-minute play. He said he had been delighted by the response from the

FOCO members, most of whom had never been to a theatre. He hoped to make some experiments similar to the New York street performers, the Bread and Puppet Theatre; and next month would begin taking lunchtime theatre to the local factories. So it looks as though before long Brisbane will have its own teenage Centre 42. And there is nothing quite like it anywhere else in Australia.

Centre 42 (1963–71) was an idealistic experimental venue in London founded by the playwright Arnold Wesker and supported by the trade union movement. Doug Anders moved to Melbourne in 1969 and the Tribe briefly joined the Australian Performing Group, the rebellious cooperative then assembling at La Mama in Melbourne.

Below is a different view of Brisbane that confirmed its reputation for prudery. Joh Bjelke-Petersen was just beginning his long incumbency as Country Party (later National Party) Premier, legislating against free expression and running rampant over the separation of powers. Nevertheless his government was swift to see the attraction of sophisticated entertainment offered by Dr Coombs. In 1970 the State Government established the Queensland Theatre Company by statute and housed it in the State Government Insurance Office Theatre.

Brisbane: A Difficult City

Australian, 20 July 1968

Brisbane audiences are so difficult, people kept telling me. They are so sensitive, so easily shocked. *Who's Afraid of Virginia Woolf?* might be all right for southerners but one has to be much more careful here.

Take the Arts Theatre, for instance, a traditional amateur group, well organised and most attractively housed. Its recent season of *Generation* which elsewhere has proved the number one box office hit for small theatres, did not measure up to such plays as *Justice is a Woman* and *When We Are Married*. It is alleged that the heroine's obvious pregnancy had something to do with this. The next play is to be *The Man Who Came to Dinner*, by now sufficiently remote to be respectable. At Twelfth Night, a slightly more advanced group, *Little Malcolm* has been struggling undisturbed against the eunuchs. There the main curiosity seemed to be the number of people who inquired at the booking office whether a eunuch was a horse with one horn. (It's true. I'm not pulling your leg.) The Brisbane Repertory Company, which runs the attractive theatre-in-the-round La Boite, joins the Arts on the side of caution; but at the Mark Twain Theatre Restaurant, where a musical version of *The Country Wife*, *The Sad Case of Master Horner*, has settled down to a long run, the audience knows well what a eunuch is and is prepared to pay to see one.

There is a lot of theatrical activity in Brisbane, almost all of it amateur and most of an exceptionally high order. But it is tending to grow apart rather than together and if the groups are to continue to encourage their audiences some strategy is necessary. This will be one of the jobs of the cultural adviser to the Queensland Government, Mr Arthur Justin Creedy, who is expected to arrive from Britain next month to take up this newly-created position. Mr Creedy (51) is a London and Cambridge graduate, has held appointments in British, New Zealand, Nigerian and Kuwait universities; studied the piano at the Royal Academy and Royal College of Music and is also described as an actor, producer, dramatist and critic.

The centre of the new cultural pattern in Brisbane will be the State Government Insurance Office's civic theatre in Turbot Street, at present half built and due to start operating mid-1969. The theatre is part of a deal with the Methodist Church which sold the Albert Hall to the SGIO on condition that a new hall be supplied in the complex. It has foyer circulation areas on three floors equal to the auditorium space, a movable, adaptable stage and hoists, orchestra pit and fly tower, enough dressing rooms for 40 or more on three floors with lifts between, a rehearsal room of the same dimensions as the stage; luxuries labelled producer's room and musicians' room; a foyer bar. And so on. It will seat 620.

The Elizabethan Theatre Trust has been consultant to the architects, and has been attempting to devise a plan for a professional company in Brisbane. The idea in principle is that the Trust should sponsor a company for six months and for the rest of the year the theatre should be available to the city. The catch is, and I suspect the AETT of taking a shrewd line over this, that the stage mechanics will demand a fulltime crew which, unless they were provided at the expense of the state, will put the theatre beyond the pocket of the established amateur groups. This is why the Twelfth Night Theatre is going ahead with the plan to build a 400-seat open-stage theatre in the city area. A university theatre at St Lucia is also expected to be started within 18 months.

At present the only person providing regular professional work in Brisbane is Russell Jarrett in his theatre restaurants; and the work is of a limited, though useful, kind. Before the present pattern, such as it is, is broken into by the new theatres, some long-term policy for live entertainment should be considered to ensure regular year-round work. Otherwise many happy amateurs will find themselves unemployed professionals. Further, it will be the job of the amateur theatres to find their place in the new pattern, to ensure by co-ordination that at all times at least one theatre is open and to follow an easily-recognisable program policy.

Among the plays I saw in Brisbane was *Little Malcolm and His Struggle against the Eunuchs* at Twelfth Night, produced by a most talented young man, Bill Pepper. The performance was as good as, and in some ways better than, the highly-praised Sydney production and certainly better than others I have seen. Malcolm Scrawdyke (Mervyn Drake) and his trio of revolutionary art-school drop-outs (Graham Howard, Barry Otto and Rodney Neucom) laid more emphasis on the weaknesses of their fascist movement than its strengths, and this did damage to the dangerous elements in the play. But this was compensated by the creation of four very individual human beings who gave the inside view of such excellent frightening comic scenes as the treason trial of Dennis Nipple and the visit of Ann, the girl who tries to make Malcolm see reality.

I also saw *Brief Suspicion*, an orthodox thriller with an all-women cast and had the novel experience of lurking behind the living-room couch at close enough range to pull the murderess's hair. La Boite is a tiny bungalow in Hale Street. Its dramas are acted out in its main room. The members of the audience (about 60 of them) are hung about the walls and enjoy a peep-show view of the domestic tragedies they are witnessing. The seven women sustained with remarkable control the rather contrived world of a barrister called to defend a woman accused of a murder she suspects her sister may have committed.

And I dropped in on the Arts children's theatre to see Bunney Brooke in a new tale of her clown Trumbo, *Trumbo's House*. This is theatre in the simplest elements of the dramatic imagination, and is excellent for the littlest children.

The gibe about Edward Albee's *Who's Afraid of Virginia Woolf?* (1964), refers to the fact that the Old Tote's much-praised production which had toured nationally for two years, produced a public outcry in Brisbane. Wycherley's classic comedy, *The Country Wife* (1674) in which the hero spreads the rumour he is impotent in order to gain access to other men's wives, escaped calumny in its burlesque form at the Mark Twain Theatre Restaurant.

The SGIO new theatre, of course, proved quite impracticable for use by community groups. The Albert Hall (then the home of Twelfth Night Theatre) had been a popular and inexpensive venue and its demolition severely disrupted the status quo and aggravated the rivalries among the established groups. A few years earlier Stefan Haag of the AETT had unsuccessfully attempted to persuade one of these groups to turn professional under the tutelage of the Trust. Now they were all under threat.

La Boite Theatre described here was replaced in 1972 by a more substantial brick building, vacated in 2003 after the redevelopment of the Lang Park Stadium opposite. Its resident company (re-named La Boite in 1976) re-located to the Roundhouse Theatre in Kelvin Grove in 2004. Bill Pepper is now Head of Voice Studies at NIDA.

While the Opera House was pushing forward, this was a bad time for the old theatres in Sydney. The city was in the hands of developers. The Palace was the first to go, followed by the Theatre Royal and the Tivoli. My account of the fight to save the Theatre Royal (see p. 201) outlines the financial imperatives that brought about the change and led to our new theatres being government initiatives. The Palace was situated in Pitt Street, now the site of the Hilton Hotel.

Death of the Palace Theatre

Australian, 17 August 1968

I suppose it is to be expected that Sydney developers, while taking great pains to preserve the bar of the Adams' Hotel, have not expressed a word of regret over the death of the old Palace Theatre next door. The famous colonnaded bar is to be taken apart and rebuilt into the first floor of Stocks and Holdings Ltd's proposed forty-storey office block. There are, of course, overwhelming practical reasons why the Palace site should be put to more profitable use. For fifteen years it has been leased by Hoyts as a not-very-satisfactory cinema, with occasional ventures into live theatre such as the Elizabethan Theatre Trust's sub-lease with Garnet Carroll 1960–61, the Patrick White seasons and the 1964 season of Edward Albee's *Who's Afraid of Virginia Woolf?*

The double-rent requirement, together with the absence of air-conditioning, has made the theatre a luxury of doubtful value. In the words of the managing director of Stocks and Holdings, Mr Erwin Graf: 'We did not consider it at all, quite frankly. In Victoria it might have been possible but not in New South Wales. The Chief Secretary's fire regulations are the strictest in the world. They make building theatres impossible on such valuable land.'

But one cannot let this theatre go without a protest because, with the possible exception of the Theatre Royal, Hobart, it is the best nineteenth-century theatre for straight playing that we have. Any actor will tell you the virtues of its actor-audience relationship. Sydney is badly in need of a theatre of reasonable size in the city centre. As it is, few straight plays are attempted by commercial managements because of this lack. Her Majesty's is out of the question for legitimate theatre, the Theatre Royal is too large for all but the broadest plays. The compact Palace, with its 784 seats and an overhanging circle and gallery, is an ideal size.

Among the big theatres, the Melbourne Tivoli is dead and the Sydney one doomed; in Adelaide the old Majestic and the Theatre Royal have gone. And now the Palace. Soon, if one wants to enjoy the luxury of 'real theatre', as my mother's generation like to call it, we shall have to take ourselves to Hobart. Perhaps we could turn the Theatre Royal into a kind of theatrical Glyndebourne and make an annual pilgrimage there *à la recherche du temps perdu.*

Briefly, the history of the Palace: it was built by the Adams family in the 1890s as a Palace of Varieties, and its original decoration was Byzantine. The proscenium arch was ogee-shaped and the boxes had onion domes. Its present elaborate style of gilt-and-plaster rococo was created in 1923 and the building was regilded recently by Hoyts.

What will probably be the last opening night, as Stuart Wagstaff pointed out in his curtain speech, was held on Wednesday when *Private Lives*, the second of a Noel Coward pair presented by Phillip Productions and Harry M. Miller, opened. *Private Lives* proved to be better than the opening production, *Present Laughter*: it was pleasantly enjoyable. This was mainly due to the author's personal gift to Australian audiences of the delightful Rosemary Martin. Miss Martin, with her exquisitely self-indulgent Amanda, was able to show us some of the possibilities in the hints of the Coward script but there was shallowness in the direction and the Australian cast which kept the play on dangerous ground.

Elyot Chase's two characteristics are intelligence and indulgence. Stuart Wagstaff's weakness is that while he does convey the second he does not help to make Elyot and Amanda notably brighter than their ex-spouses, Sybil and Victor. Helen Morse and John Unicomb give passable support to the main pair to help pass the evening enjoyably enough but the whole production by Anthony Sharp lacked the esprit that should make Coward worth the resurrection.

It was a sad end to an exquisite piece of fantasy architecture; but, as this review suggests, the theatre it represented was already being demolished along with the building it housed.

The theatre attracting most attention was that which tested existing laws. To protest the banning of *America Hurrah!* a select group of eminent citizens and opinion-makers were invited to view the play at the Teachers' Federation Theatre in Sydney. Since any breach of regulations could have given the police cause to close the performance, much care was taken to ensure no more people entered the auditorium than could be seated. However, an unexpectedly large crowd of well-wishers gathered in Sussex Street. Their numbers threatened to bring down the glass entrance doors and finally these were opened to release the pressure. Many of those with tickets were turned away. At the New Theatre the segment 'Motel' was replaced by a parody called 'Hotel' and the season continued.

Friends of *America Hurrah!* Protest

Australian, 24 August 1968

The life of a critic, like everything else, has its ups and downs. Take last Tuesday, for instance. There I was hanging from scaffolding with the sound mechanist up in the flies, trying to review *America Hurrah!* and telling myself I had seen it all before. Outside two thousand citizens were getting restless and trying to push the doors down. 'Am I out of my mind?' I kept saying to myself. 'I should be down in Melbourne at those quiet student riots at Monash University.'

But here I was at the Teachers' Federation Theatre, Sussex Street, Sydney, having been partly responsible for inciting to riot 2,500 Sydney citizens over a play that, but for a grandmother's interest in a few common graffiti, would have passed unnoticed.

I had begun the evening on the steps of the 500-seat theatre along with a group of judges, lawyers, artists, press and theatre people—all armed with tickets—having the coats torn off us. As one of them remarked with feeling: 'What's the use of being a bloody sponsor if we can't see the show?'

However, it was all part of the protest. After a while a lawyer friend grabbed me by the arm and dragged me to a fire escape, up which we climbed eight flights till we found a friendly cleaner who escorted us to the lift, from where we descended in comfort into the foyer. We were no nearer to the inside of the locked auditorium doors, however. The actor Peter O'Shaughnessy resignedly reading a newspaper was one sponsor who had failed to get in. Harry Kippax, holding up a note reading '*Sydney Morning Herald*, Must Review', was still outside, and John Olsen the painter. I managed to smuggle myself backstage until after the first interval when a few of us made it into the auditorium.

The occasion for all this was, of course, the free public performance of Jean-Claude Van Itallie's satirical commentary on the affluent society, *America Hurrah!*, organised by a group of citizens, including myself, calling ourselves Friends of *America Hurrah!*

The play was banned by the Chief Secretary, under the Theatres and Public Halls Act, 1908, for actions prejudicial to good manners and public decorum. It was banned without consideration being given to the context of the play, the nature of the theatre and its audience or the purpose of the author in writing his stage directions. And the law as it stands leaves no opening for appeal, defence or public discussion of the allegation.

A free performance falls outside the jurisdiction of the Public Halls Act and it provided a means of allowing a certain number of citizens to judge for themselves the action taken by the Chief Secretary and to gain support for the claim that the law needs reconsideration. As a result the small play, 'Motel', has received attention harmful to its purpose and quite out of proportion to its quality. Meanwhile what remains of *America Hurrah!* is assuring the New Theatre of a longer run and the moral support of wider audiences than it has known in its little back-street theatre than anything since its anti-Nazi play *Till the Day I Die* was banned in 1935.

At this point I must say that it was theatrically a most exciting evening. It left the audience in no doubt that 'Motel' was an essential but nevertheless only a small part of a serious dramatic document presented in an honest and compelling way. It is also important to note that while the Friends of *America Hurrah!* reproduced as nearly as possible the New Theatre's production and that certain members of the New Theatre offered their assistance, the unnamed cast on Tuesday was not the same as appeared at the New at the time of the banning. Which actors played the offending dolls in 'Motel' remains a well-kept secret though there are rumours that one was played by Sir Robert Helpmann. The police report that they are still searching for them.

The best piece of production for the evening was, in fact, the escape of the dolls from the auditorium. Pursued by two detectives they were led to a kiosk in the foyer and locked in while audience and ushers blocked passage to the police. A sixteen-stoner, smiling benignly, placed his arm gently about the shoulders of the detective sergeant and leant on him. 'No violence', pleaded the sergeant. 'No violence.' And the gentleman smiled again and relaxed more heavily. When at last the door of the kiosk opened not two but six men in their underwear slid surreptitiously into the crowd. What happened after that, the police were told, was a question for their legal advisers.

In the auditorium the Rev. William Pollak, to be known from now on as the fighting parson, was announcing in his soft Viennese accent that 'after a rather wild and dramatic chase the dolls had magically disappeared into thin air'. The backstage crew sweeping the debris from the stage received the wildest round of applause for the evening.

When all that remained were the four-letter words on the white vinyl backdrop, and police and press photographers were photographing them, a spearhead rushed from the audience and tore the offending scrawls to pieces. The police departed disgruntled and the audience happy. Maybe we Friends shall go to gaol in the end but it will probably be worth it. It all seems a long way from a very ordinary, orderly opening night in a 113-seat theatre back in June.

My comment about Sir Robert Helpmann was a bad joke and caused some distress to the newly-knighted dancer who had been named as one of the Friends but was feeling the responsibilities of good manners and decorum that come with a title. The actors were, in fact, John Hargreaves and Rod Williams; and the sixteen-stoner was a volunteer from the Waterside Workers' Federation. Hargreaves (1946–1996) had played the female doll, the one who drew the offending graffiti, in the New Theatre season. In a later reminiscence he said that at the time he was a teacher at Crows Nest High School and had found himself tailed by police. It was these events that determined him to become a professional actor—more exciting than teaching. He became a film actor of international reputation and died at the height of his popularity, aged 50.

The controversy became the subject of an hour-long documentary about censorship on Channel 7. The New Theatre, however, being a small theatre and accustomed to the role of the underprivileged, was unable to gather its resources to exploit the very real sympathy of the public to expand their work. In 1973, though, they did achieve a move from the shabby premises in St Peter's Lane, East Sydney, to their own theatre in King Street, Newtown.

PART II
SEEING PROGRESS
1968–70

The serious work of development now began: the first annual budget of federal subsidy for the performing arts, the selection and establishment of major theatre companies, the first coherent attempts to create and define an Australian style; and the raising of banners proclaiming all-Australian theatre, film and television.

Between June 1969 and January 1970 Philip and I travelled to Italy, Britain, France, Germany, Poland and Scandinavia; then to Canada and the United States. It was a time of extraordinary political turmoil that translated to the stage in assaults on the audience, in the fragmentation of narrative, in the use of obscenity, racial issues and nudity. For both of us it was a transforming experience. It enabled us to better interpret the new forms at home and to recognise what was intrinsic to ourselves. It made me impatient with outdated patterns and indulgent of ill-executed attempts to find new modes of expression. I began to set the New Wave in a wider context.

The experience also produced the spark that became the following year Currency Press.

The progress we found on our return was visible on all fronts. The 'TV make-it-Australian' campaign had achieved an Australian screening quota. There were plans for an Australian Film and Television School. The selected state companies had completed their first year of subsidy and were expanding their ambitions and their workshops. The climate of political activism had bred a vogue for challenging subject matter, which in turn had heightened police enthusiasm for theatre-going. There had been several notable and risible court cases. But *Hair* had opened in spectacular fashion and without police intervention.

Barry Humphries, for the first time, performed a solo show in a lyric theatre. It was the first show he took to London and the beginnings of his move towards an international style and stardom. In Sydney his venue was the creaking and

Barry Humphries as Edna Everage,1968. (Photo: Paul Crowley)

cavernous old Tivoli, a 2,400 seat theatre which had already closed and was awaiting demolition when reopened for this season.

Barry Humphries' Flower for the Dead Heart
Australian, 3 September 1968

I've been this week to Barry Humphries' *Just a Show*, which is now playing on the grand scale at the Tivoli, Sydney. The performance has grown since the relatively modest opening in Adelaide on 1 July. There is much more passion in it and more vulgarity; and it has become less, rather than more, Australian.

Humphries' prime interest is now with people, not with national characteristics. A second viewing makes us more aware than ever that at his best he is a major talent whose work holds its own under analysis. The rest is quality revue; and Edna Everage has become irrelevant to the new Barry Humphries in a way that Sandy Stone has not. Except for Edna's flower power, that is. But more of that later.

Humphries' central thesis is our insensitivity to each other. He plays on this and lays traps for us. Three sketches bear this out and these we remember long after the other are forgotten: Rex Lear, the Toorak father who is marrying off the last of his tiger daughters; Sandy Stone in the repat. after a 'little op'; and the multiple roles of Brian Graham, the fertiliser heir.

The first is set at a wedding reception where Rex, in his morning suit, toasts the bride and belches in a rising crescendo of drunkenness the pain and the frustration of being a self-made man. He has spoilt and educated his daughters out of any communication with him; nor can he communicate in any language but money. Rex has developed into a much more arrogant, fierce, disgusting and pitiable person than he was in Adelaide; his tragedy is that he is a victim of the same kind of prejudice that he uses against others. This is the satirical twist that drives the knife home. The facile ending is a weakness, but even so this sketch is something to make the last days of the doomed Tivoli Theatre memorable.

Sandy Stone's world is a different one: he belongs to the lower reaches of the white collar worker and his life has been innocent and tempered by only the most modest ambitions and imagination. But he too is filled with a sense of loss and waste, a blunted sensitivity that uses words carelessly, that cannot differentiate between a woman's hand and a Thermos flask on an afternoon that lingers in his memory. He has not had the courage to pursue his true path and now can no longer remember the kind of animal distress from which he must at one time, like Rex Lear, have suffered.

The Sandy Stone is a complex piece and it has a peculiar double-edged purpose. For along with the pain and the pathos Humphries urges the audience to laugh at his name-dropping jokes—milk arrowroot biscuits, sequined evening bags, Kia-ora, Gallipoli Crescent, Marmite and walnut sandwiches, Blamey Ward; and so on. As if he were malevolently determined to catch his audience in an act of callousness. He succeeds and the result is uncomfortable.

The third piece is the fertiliser executive Brian Graham and I cannot say much without spoiling the surprise element on which it depends. But again he is showing comically a tortured soul on guard in the business world, his parents' world and his friends' worlds, playing a part in each but belonging to none.

Humphries follows the theme in his other displaced persons—the dissatisfied migrant, for example; the hippie who worries about his parents' moral welfare; the jargon-ridden underground movie director. But these are lesser beings. The major three strike not at our overt prejudice but at our unadmitted ones. The effect is devastating.

Not all Humphries' program is fully assured. It is time he stopped concerning himself with being Australian because this is peripheral. And a lot of the references in his jokes are miscalculated. It is probably time he got himself a sympathetic director. But there is nothing miscalculated about Mrs Everage's finest hour as a gladdie waver. Her carefully contrived character is thrown to the winds as she bowls gladioli into the dress circle and converts the stalls into a garden of sheepishly-waving stalks as she sings: 'When you're feeling melancholy, Take a grip of your gladioli'. There is a familiar meaningless cameraderie about the way she makes the men hold their stems high and shake them until the blooms fall off and are crushed underfoot. Something about this contrast of satirical suburbia and music-hall vulgarity is both companionable and vicious in a way which is much more characteristically Australian than any number of references to the beaches and the RSL. Name-calling is everyday fun. It is revealing the dead heart inside which makes Barry Humphries a clown quite out of the ordinary.

Of course I was wrong about Edna, who did not become irrelevant, but transformed herself by degrees from a small time housewife into a megastar. The surprise element in Brian Graham was that he was gay.

Three Sisters: Chekhov in a Thousand
Australian, 12 September 1968

Two things assured me on Monday night of the Melbourne Theatre Company's ever-increasing stature. One was the minor relief that I did not have to explain to the taxi driver that the Russell Street Theatre was next to the Rapallo cinema. The other was the excitement of seeing one of the wonders of dramatic literature given an interpretation not just excellent but great.

The play, which opens the MTC's second season for 1968 is Chekhov's *Three Sisters*. The producer is George Ogilvie. I can place it easily beside Michel Saint-Denis' production of *The Cherry Orchard* at the Aldwych Theatre with such notables of the British stage as Peggy Ashcroft, John Gielgud and Dorothy Tutin, of which after seven years I retain vivid memories. And I hope that the Australian theatre, in its approach to the classics, will not turn its back upon this moment.

Russell Street was like a cave on Monday night, a cave in which the silence was so clear that the snap of a watch-case and the wind in a chimney sounded unnaturally loud. The provincial world created by Mr Ogilvie and his designer, Kristian Fredrikson, is all grey, peopled by characters who (as the old doctor keeps intoning) do not live, only seem to. There is not a single unnecessary movement on stage, nor a thoughtless phrase, and only two outbursts of violent feeling in three hours; but because of the clarity of every note we listen to it with a pleasure closer to music than to drama.

Three Sisters is about four years in the life of three young women and their brother, who dream of going to Moscow but somehow never get there. It is about fading hopes and unconsummated relationships, and a will to live that survives the loss of a dream to live by.

What comes across so brilliantly in the orchestration of this production is how internal are the ties that bind the characters. The youngest sister, Irina, celebrates her birthday in the first act with a romantic Marxist outburst on the joys of work for its own sake and the common good. And she ends the play with a similar resolve to dedicate herself to teaching. But neither speech, though she convinces herself of their truth, bears any relation to her experience as a worker or that of anyone else in the household.

The sisters and their friends drift in and out purposelessly, tenuously linked and yet each living their own internal life, clinging to the familiar and yet finding no anchor there. There is Olga (Jennifer Claire), the eldest sister, a responsible and efficient chatelaine, a teacher who imperceptibly becomes a headmistress in spite of herself. Second is the restless Masha, who escapes from the boredom of marriage with a fatuous schoolmaster into a brief romance with Colonel Vershinin. It is the distillation of a romance rather than the thing itself, and Maggie Millar's stillness, broken only by the occasional sudden movement, is a distillation more of the spirit than the flesh.

Irina (Lyndel Rowe) is the youngest, the spring life of the house with which most of the occupants are in love, one way or another. For her growing up is to put aside childish dreams of happiness and will herself into another dream of duty done. She engages herself to the Baron Tusenbach, her honest, rather foolish but faithful lover, who finds a reason for dying as good as his reason for living. He is beautifully played by Dennis Olsen.

Helmut Bakaitis gives his most mature performance to date as the gentle brother Andrey. And Elaine Cusick, as his wife, shuttles shallowly between the sickly sentimentality and the tactless brutality of the unimaginative. There is George Whaley as Vershinin, futilely using words to fill the vacuum between himself and other people, and Alan Hopgood as a brilliant Captain Solyony, paranoically self-controlled with a kind of Nazi precision.

A few moments were less than perfect, I suppose—a lack of lightness and humour here and there—an innocence and gentleness about Olga and an entirely hopeful note in her final speech with which I would quarrel. But who cares? It is the so-rare occasions like this in the theatre that make sitting though all those others somehow worthwhile. A Chekhov in a thousand.

George Ogilvie told me recently that this was his first encounter on stage with Chekhov. A month later (9 October) I visited the play again, commenting that the production had drawn visitors from Sydney and other states.

Three Sisters was a less compelling performance than on opening night. The cast, I suspect, were beginning to feel the strain of entering the last stretch of day-long rehearsals for the new Albee play, *Everything in the Garden,* and there was less assurance to the long blissful pauses which were a special delight of the production. But the test of a good producer is how strong a frame he can build to support the play and his actors, and the test of a good actor how strongly he can build his own drama to support him through the vicissitudes of his everyday life.

George Ogilvie's production remains rock solid, revealing all the time new elements which had escaped me in the excitement of first discovery. The performances in *Three Sisters* were interesting in their variations. Those from the least experienced actors had blurred as though they had begun to forget details they had never fully understood, while the stronger performances had expanded and solidified.

Stirring Up and Stripping Down

Australian, 5 December 1968

Down in the theatrical undergrowth things are beginning to stir. Every now and then a little burst of frenzy up there on stage gives a hint on the surface of subterranean activity. Take what I saw at Sydney's Music Hall the other night—Ron Haddrick in his prime, forsaking the boards of the Old Tote for a death-mask face and an opera cloak to do a straw-hat routine with 'The Man Who Broke the Bank at Monte Carlo'.

Or Sunday night at PACT, in Sydney's dockland, where an altruistic group of theatre people meet to give ambitious would-be playwrights some theatre mechanics. Gone were the friends of the author in their cardigans debating the Australian character. In their place was a psychedelic love-in, or rather a brotherhood body-fest, which began with a share-around of loaves and fishes and ended with a core of men—a mixture of performers and audience—dancing naked by the light of a Stroboscope.

I should perhaps mention at this point that in legal terms the performance was not a public one as no admission was charged. However, my invitation states that after this performance 'it is intended to run the production for a short season at PACT Theatre. Later, it is intended to tour it throughout Australia, playing in parks, hotels, underground theatres or private homes.' Which should prove interesting.

The program, called *Ceremonies*, was arranged by a group calling itself the Human Body, 'attempting to make direct communication with people' without calling the result 'theatre'. 'We are attempting nothing less than the total transformation of a vital part of our experience into terms of ecstasy, where there are no terms' is their maxim. Not being accustomed to much ecstasy in my daily round I went along in some state of expectation. And I was not altogether disappointed.

PACT is an old Victorian warehouse with a hammer-beam roof held up at intervals by archways and pillars. In the centre of one ill-defined space a stage has been made between two pillars and when we arrived the half-gloom was filled with squatting figures earnestly passing food and drink. Wine and cheese were pressed upon me and within five minutes of the show's commencement I found myself happily sitting cross-legged sharing a krakerwurst with a young man in a batik shirt.

The performance began with movie clippings of war film thrown onto the wall and overlaid with the silhouettes of the participants moving slowly in a circle holding hands; and this peaceable love-your-neighbour theme ran through most of the improvised group movement. It was based on everyday actions—'Auld Lang Syne' at a New Year's Eve party, eating, fighting, getting married, actions of self-sacrifice and aggression, created with the mood music of drums and clarinet. A group of moving figures—some of them members of the audience—and a couple of lights held in the hand, one a mirror spot with revolving media.

The pace quickened when one young man stripped down to his jockette and danced in a quivering white light to a drum accompaniment in a tribal rhythm of accelerating speed which had the audience panting in unison. It ended with his body being ceremoniously carried through the auditorium. He later appeared in a well-organised and quite riveting piece of improvisation which began with his acting the sulky outsider, led to a fairly dangerous pack hunt through the audience followed by a beating up. An elaborate demonstration of his attempts to rise again took on a religious symbolism and ended with a confused expression of united brotherhood.

This was the only point at which the evening could be called theatre, in that the audience was held by the involvement of the boy in an enacted situation. The rest was a more passive enjoyment of moving coloured impressions in total anonymity.

The evening culminated in the amorphous group stripping and covering each other with coloured paints and dancing in an increasing frenzy in the flashing light of the Stroboscope until the men made the last break for freedom, tossing aside their briefs. It all seemed quaintly vernal and sexless—due, I suppose to a combination of group unity, the psychedelic impression of people as abstracts—and the fact that it did not seem to occur to the women to strip too.

It was an eccentric evening and not well-defined enough to stay in the memory outside in the real world. But theatregoers should not dismiss too lightly experiments like this. The stage lighting made too clear a division between the stage and the spectators to include them wholly in the ceremonial proceedings and there was something a bit precious in creating a totally artificial environment for the purpose of reawakening us to our five senses. But my lasting impression was not of the stage activities but the sense of freedom and community in the audience and its anything-can-happen excitement bereft in a curious way of any sense of genuine physical danger. It will make the cold foyers of our city theatres even more stone cold to this new generation making their own realities.

Which brings me to the ceremonies of the tourist industry to which the music hall restaurants are catering so successfully. I have said this before in these columns that the bear-pit of the Music Hall in Neutral Bay, where the audience eat, drink and pay attention only when the actor is good enough, is probably the best training an actor can get in Sydney.

The Music Hall's new show is *The Face at the Window*, a revival of one of its biggest successes of five years ago. It has been adapted from the Victorian melodrama by John Faassen and Bernadette Alam, and there is an assurance of style about the adaptation which shows how the company has developed

The Human Body production of *Ceremonies*, 1968. (Photo courtesy of Clem Gorman)

in the interim. The theatre's master clown, Barry Lovett, who left last February, is back to play his original role of Detective Paul Gouffet. Other long-standing performers who have come to terms with this very hardworking medium, include Lucia Duchenska as the heroine, Stanley Walsh as her hero and Kenneth Laird as Karl Gottlieb Richter the Mad Doctor, whom he has turned into another charming version of his Wagnerian character Alberich.

Miss Duchenska, whom I still remember with joy saving her caged bird through devastating adventures in *The Worst Woman in London*, is this time accompanied at all times by her violin. Ron Haddrick, as the villainous mad murderer, thwarted in his lust for the heroine, gives an efficient performance and he is obviously taking great pleasure in fraternising with the audience. But he has as yet nowhere near the sophistication of those who have been longer at that theatre and have found out how to play a black-and-white comic character from the inside.

The show will run till February when Mr Haddrick goes to the Community Theatre, Killara, and Mr Lovett to the Old Tote Theatre, for which he recently played the Fool in *King Lear*. Which is the kind of stir-up which will be good for everyone.

Happenings like *Ceremonies* were another casualty of the censorship brouhaha, which temporarily revived the Theatres and Public Halls Act. More stringent health and safety regulations, which had already caused the death of the Palace Theatre, also closed for public use the crumbling buildings being hired by groups like the Human Body.

Help for the Top Dogs

Australian, 14 December 1968

The Australian Council for the Arts has made a promising start in its first annual budget of grants announced by the Prime Minister on Wednesday night. It has wasted no time in discarding the policy of spreading money widely and thinly in favour of strong measures to establish two companies of national importance. And it has preserved a firm national point of view in the ill-defined areas of state and commonwealth responsibility.

The report recommends the setting up of two major companies, the Melbourne Theatre Company and the Old Tote Theatre Company. Last year the MTC received the biggest Elizabethan Theatre Trust grant for theatre of $44,000. This time it received $70,000.

The choice of the Old Tote as the nucleus for the Sydney national company was not as obvious as was the choice in Melbourne. It was governed by the fact that the state authorities had already agreed that the Old Tote should administer the company that will play at the Opera House. The Tote has been granted $49,000 to enable it to put actors on annual contracts for the first time and to increase its activities. It also received $19,000 from the Queensland Government to provide touring theatre there and $15,000 from the Canberra Theatre Trust for a tour there. The MTC also receives two indirect subsidies for tours—$15,000 through the Festival of Perth which includes the MTC's production of *Henry IV (Part 1)* and $6,000 through the Moomba Festival to mount the same production in the Melbourne Arts Centre. With the increased grants will come responsibilities to other theatres in their own cities and other States to provide tours, training opportunities and assistance with personnel and advice.

The other significant sum in the Council allocations (apart from grants to one company in each state and substantial grants to the national touring companies, the Australian Ballet and Opera, the Elizabethan Trust Orchestra and the Marionette Theatre of Australia) is $160,000 for assistance for special projects. This is a fund intended to provide swift and timely assistance in the commissioning and performance of new work, youth activities, and to assemble a pool of professional directors and other practitioners to provide a service. The idea behind the pool is to encourage the dissemination of ideas among workers, the provision of visiting directors and teachers for country areas and to help artists seize an opportunity for experiment when it arises. $5,000 is also allocated to examine the setting up of a training scheme for theatre administrators.

It is naturally a disappointment to many theatres struggling against poverty that certain others have been selected for comparative riches. But it is only by raising the standard at the top and breaking down the barriers between the theatres that we can give artistic talents room to express themselves. And by setting a new standard we will directly raise the prestige and influence of the whole profession.

Loyalty to local theatre companies is an important factor in encouraging the theatre-going habit; and care must be taken to see that while the Old Tote, for example, is being turned into a proper, professional company, it does not starve the rest of the industry. But this is the job of state and civic authorities, not the Commonwealth. As an interim measure the Council has made a good start. A better test will be made next year when the report of the drama committee on future policy is known and more has been done on how to make the good intentions work.

The Ensemble Theatre, Sydney, has opened an interesting adaptation by Arthur Miller of Ibsen's *An Enemy of the People*. It is produced by Hayes Gordon, now back as governing director of the theatre after over a year away on tour in *Fiddler on the Roof*. The production has at its centre a brilliant piece of fervent naturalism by Don Reid as Dr Stockmann, the innocent idealist who finds that to believe in the common good is not a natural instinct in man.

Those who know this, one of Ibsen's most popular plays, will find the alterations by Miller revealing both of the change in theatrical methods in 86 years and unchanging nature of people. It is the story of a doctor whose experiments reveal that the health springs on which the economy of his town depends are being poisoned by a tannery upstream, the property of his father-in-law. His brother is the mayor, and the alterations required would deprive the town of two years' income. Miller's play, while altering the dialogue and incidents to no great extent, simplifies the characters and drives home the polemic, making it a kind of Brechtian melodrama of repeated incidents, each repeating in a different way the townspeople's peccancy.

There were certain difficulties about the production. Not all the large cast were up to the close scrutiny the Ensemble's in-the-round stage inflicts and there was an obtrusive number of awkwardnesses about properties in the formal nineteenth-century setting. But Don Reid, and Rosemary Jones as his wife, whom we last saw together giving two good performances in *The Porcelain Year*, again face each other as partners in a catastrophic domestic crisis. They hold the play together, supported by Lorraine Bayly as their daughter.

Despite a supposedly overt competition, in the battle to become the state theatre company in NSW the Old Tote had the numbers. Dr Coombs had been one of its founders and Professor Robert Quentin, the Tote's founding director, vice-president and master mind, had been one of the principals of the AETT. He was also founding director of NIDA, was on the advisory board of the Opera House, and was an all-round better politician than his rivals. He remained the driving force behind the Tote's ambitious rise until his retirement in 1977. The average wage for an actor at this time was between $70 and $90 a week with half-pay for rehearsals.

The first evidence of the lack of cosy cooperation between the Commonwealth and the states now began to appear; and the first steps towards demolishing the professional/amateur culture that had sustained the theatre. Little thought had been so far given by the states to a coherent arts policy. In August I had inveighed against the Victorian Government's refusal to give urgently-needed assistance to St Martin's Theatre, the reason being, in Premier Sir Henry Bolte's words: 'The Government has no policy for supporting professional theatre.' ('"No Theatre Policy", for Bolte', *Australian* 3 August 1968.) The Victorian Government did, in fact, make a cultural development allocation and in that year's budget had spent $137,468 in small sums to amateur arts groups in such places as Wendouree, Quambatook, Ballarat and Bendigo. The Melbourne Arts Centre, where MTC's production of *Henry IV (Part 1)* was mounted, refers to a space within the recently-opened National Gallery of Victoria.

Sense on Subsidies

Australian, 26 December 1968

Domestically I am having a very happy Christmas. Professionally I am having a perfectly lousy one. I am fed up with managements. I am fed up with actors. I am fed up with government subsidies and I am fed up with Dr Coombs.

The NSW State Government has seen to it that it is a cold Christmas for most of the theatres in Sydney. Without offering enough money to do more than keep the bailiff from the door it has encouraged the small professional theatres to begin projects that have put them into debt beyond their capacity. Now, suddenly, the subsidies have been withdrawn and the total sum reduced. The new policy, it seems, is death. This leaves Sydney's theatre with the inevitable ex-Broadway musical, a handful of vacuous commercial productions, the laugh sensation of the year for queers and one understaffed gold-plated tin shed.

Last time I exclaimed over wasted talent a libel suit for $500,000 was filed against the *Australian*. But since our editor in his Christmas expansiveness says my New Year resolution must be to be less careful and enjoy myself, I would like to tell you all I am fed up with you.

This was meant to be a cheerful holiday piece on children's theatre but the publication of the annual NSW Government grants has intervened. Of the total allocation of $210,250, $68,500 goes to drama—$18,000 less than last year. And of this $30,000 is set aside for professional companies, of which the Old Tote Theatre Company received $20,000. This company is already the recipient of the sole direct Commonwealth grant in NSW ($78,000). The other $10,000 is to set up a pool of directors, actors and technical staff whose services would be shared by the professional theatres companies in NSW.

Amongst the rest of the money, $10,000 goes to the Elizabethan Theatre Trust for rent, pending their removal to the Sydney Opera House. This comes in the teeth of the Minister for Education, Mr [Charles] Cutler's comment that the grants were based on recommendations to widen and improve cultural activities, not to assist financing the administration of such activities. The last big sum is $10,000 for assistance to the National Institute of Dramatic Art for its new third-year course.

I was delighted and reassured by the announcement a fortnight ago of the Commonwealth's first cultural budget because it laid the basis for a national policy: to raise the whole dignity of the theatre as a profession and to expand its skills and ideas. No theatre professional is extended to his or her limits in this country because the conditions are not there and the second-rate is so commonly condoned. Every young man or woman entering the profession in whatever capacity should, if they have the talent, look forward to earning $10,000 a year, to choose their work and give it the honest labour it deserves. But at present there are no riches and no accolades at the top and very little dignity.

That is why I am fed up with Hayes Gordon, who has been expressing his dissatisfaction in the national press. Mr Gordon wrote an extremely good submission on long-term policy to the Council, which as a member of the Council's drama advisory committee I have read, and so far the Council's thinking runs in his direction. And yet Mr Gordon, who for eighteen months has been enjoying the fruits of the top job on the Australian stage, denies the Council the right to make such a position the reward of every capable actor. I sympathise with his chagrin as governing director of the Ensemble oppressed with the immediate problems of keeping open a theatre seating 162. But *Fiddler on the Roof* and the Ensemble are equally necessary and one cannot survive without the other.

I am also, on the side, fed up with the bright young things of the theatre whose ideas I respect and whose future I have fought for more times than I can count. They know what they don't want; but have they thought of how to get what they do want? Among all the reports and suggestions the Council has received, none, as far as I know, has come from the young minds who so much want to be part of a brave new theatre. I think they will get the theatre they deserve.

I am also chagrined that, for all this talk of State–Commonwealth close cooperation, no one has outlined the separate territories. While NSW had little hope of establishing a high standard company there was some sense in making sacrifices for this purpose. Now the Commonwealth has taken the responsibility the State has other priorities. The Commonwealth Council with its limited money has plumped for earning riches at the top with highly subsidised companies in Sydney and Melbourne, and a holding operation in the other states for the present. In the present inefficient condition of the industry, had the Commonwealth found the money to fund a company in each state, I doubt qualified people could have been found to staff them.

But just as we need long-term goals, so we need short-term practical assistance. The little theatres have been living from hand to mouth too long. Sydney's Independent, Community and Ensemble, for instance, have been living on false hopes for months over the present grant and are further in debt than they can endure. It is the small theatres, like these and the amateur and students' theatres too, that are the backbone of the profession. Here theatre people get their first experience. In the upper echelons they no longer retain the right to fail.

And if the Commonwealth is going to subsidise for quality the state and local authorities must subsidise the quantity. NSW had better do something quickly or it will find its theatrical fare limited to relentless reproductions of the Old Tote's standard performances—and heaven preserve us from that. As for this pool of theatre people—this will prove an excellent plan if the Commonwealth can find anyone but the Elizabethan Theatre Trust to administer it. But what is a state annual grants plan doing meddling with it? The Commonwealth has offered $160,000 as a start to provide salaries for innovators and give them the chance to do properly-researched work. What on earth can the Minister for Education do with a puny $10,000?

Dr Coombs, as chairman of the Australian Council for the Arts, has also been adviser to the State Government and his influence is apparent. But the state has no long-term plan and totally inappropriate funds. It would do better to spend its $30,000 for the professional theatre in paying off overdrafts.

The Commonwealth plan came as a shock to the smaller theatres, though not, I think, as a surprise. And they need time to get over this. A gracious and useful thing at this point for the Council to do would be to divide up $100,000 of the [160,000] special projects grant for this interim twelve months; among such companies as St Martin's in Melbourne, the Perth Playhouse, Adelaide's Theatre 62 and the three Sydney theatres I mentioned. With that they could wipe out the past and begin planning to become part of the new wave of which the Council for the Arts has a vision.

The relationship between the state and federal funding bodies was at this stage tenuous. The NSW Advisory Committee on Cultural Grants had been set up in 1966 and had participated in the rush to professionalism in the glow of promised federal money. But these ambitions had, as the *Australian* of 24 December reported, put the theatres 'in impossible situations—they would not continue professional operations without large grants'. The response was to take fright and recommend a reduction of the drama allocation from $86,750 to $68,500—$30,000 for professional companies and less for little theatres.

Hayes Gordon, however, was already steaming at what he called the 'iniquitous' federal decision to decently fund the Old Tote and the Melbourne Theatre Company at the expense of his own, more adventurous, company. And indeed, what had seemed to me an enlightened policy of allocating the bulk of the tiny Australian Council for the Arts funds to first raise the standard in defined areas, was received as pork-barrelling and politicking by those who missed out. Hayes Gordon's paper to the Australian Council drama committee had eloquently put the case for a holistic policy encompassing all aspects of the profession, and aimed at raising work to a level above popular entertainment, in the knowledge that a company like the Ensemble would never survive without subsidy. But the Government's plan was too nebulous and politics-wracked for such forward-thinking. Following the announcement of the federal grants (two weeks earlier than NSW) Dr Coombs had called a meeting of disaffected theatre directors to discuss the disbursement of the $160,000 special projects grant. Gordon, in an account of the meeting (*Sydney Morning Herald*, 6 January 1969) wrote that he had the 'distinct impression that we had been called together … to have us acquiesce to the intention of the Australian Council for the Arts and therefore help to prove that such a policy could be made to work'. Coombs' dilemma was that the ACA at this stage had no administrative resources with which to answer individual needs. In the end he aggravated the unrest by giving the money to the domineering AETT and the unpopular Melbourne Theatre Company to dispense.

Meanwhile, on 18 January 1969 I reported a press conference by Robin Lovejoy, held to account for his windfall of $103,000. 'Mr Lovejoy has formed a company of 26 actors for a 32-week season from February to September to present seven plays… Mr Lovejoy said that despite the publicity over the new grants the Tote had received only $7,750 more for Sydney than last year.'

The establishment of the ACA was a turning point for the Trust, which rapidly lost its reason for existence. It never moved to the Opera House as intended. It remained in its cavernous warehouse in Dowling Street, Woolloomooloo, until losses in the collapse of Harry M. Miller's ticket-sales business forced it to sell the property. The $10,000 allocated to NIDA was well invested. From 1970, through an actors' refresher course, it seeded Rex Cramphorn's Performance Syndicate and the Nimrod Street Theatre.

The 'laugh sensation of the year for queers and one understaffed gold-plated tin shed' are references to *The Boys in the Band* and the Old Tote respectively. The $500,000 libel suit against the Australian was brought by the actor Peter O'Shaughnessy over my review of his production of *Othello* for the Arts Council of Australia (NSW). The newspaper won the case and the appeal but was ordered to a retrial by the High Court. The case was finally settled out of court.

A continuing current of protest theatre, including protest against censorship, led to a series of arrests and public controversies in the period 1968–70. The producer Harry M. Miller had watched with interest *America Hurrah!*'s brush with the law before having printed on the back of his tickets for *The Boys in the Band* and *Hair* a disclaimer stating that the purchaser understood the nature of the product being purchased. *The Boys in the Band,* by American writer Mart Crowley, is a popular comedy about a homosexual's birthday party. Directed by John Tasker, the play had considerable commercial success on national tour. However, the disclaimer did not wholly protect the company. In July 1969, during the Melbourne season, three actors were charged with using obscene language in public, convicted and fined. The season, however, continued uninterrupted.

Keeping Theatre Clean
Australian, 22 January 1969

Theatres are controlled by the different states' legislation giving chief secretaries the power to prohibit or regulate public entertainment when they believe that (in the words of the NSW Act) it is fitting for the preservation of good manners and decorum to do so. All states have broadly the same legislation, although the wording may vary. There is no provision for their chief secretary to explain his reasons for a ban. Nor, unless he chooses to be cooperative, is there any opportunity for a theatre to explore his likely reactions before a play is put on. There is no apparatus for appeal.

Another complication is that chief secretaries have power under the same legislation to revoke a theatre's licence for breaches of a wide variety of health and safety regulations on storage, the number of seats, width of passages, ticket sales and other matters. A chief secretary can, if he chooses, close a theatre without reference to a particular production. The chief secretary relies upon the advice of the police, and police officers regularly visit theatres to assess the attitude of patrons to an entertainment.

Two other types of legislation might also be invoked: the various states' statutes on obscene publications and their legislation on vagrancy. The drawing of indecent words on a stage set comes within the meaning of publication, and so do the scripts used by actors. Under the vagrancy legislation in NSW, for example, someone is liable to a fine of not more than $10 if he 'in any public street, thoroughfare or place, or within the view or hearing of a person passing therein, sings any obscene song or ballad; writes or draws any indecent or obscene word, figure or representation; or uses any profane, indecent or obscene language'. Or, under another section, 'behaves in a riotous, indecent, offensive, threatening or insulting manner; or uses any threatening, abusive or insulting words'.

With the question of male nudity being raised for the first time by a dance improvisation at Monash University in August, the performance of

Ceremonies at PACT, Sydney, in December, and Harry M. Miller's scheduled national tour of the musical *Hair* this year, the sub-section concerning wilfully and obscenely exposing one's person in, or in view of, any street, road or public highway, or in any place of public resort, may also come under consideration.

In one way, it is a problem of Australian theatres that they are subject to a chief secretary's censorship without having the protection from police action which the Lord Chamberlain's certificate used to provide. British theatres are now in the same position as ourselves, since the Lord Chamberlain's censorship powers were revoked on 26 September. But the British development was part of a move to reduce censorship. Instead of being, like Australian managements, cautious about laying themselves open to charges of obscenity or libel, the English theatre has gone to the other extreme.

In Australia the year 1968 saw what was probably the greatest challenge to state censorship laws since colonial days, when righteous citizens denounced theatres as disorderly houses. Previously this century there had been few incidents. Australia's most famous music hall comedian, Roy (Mo) Rene, had many brushes with the law because of his blue jokes; but his chief censors were his managements. In 1935 the Sydney New Theatre's production of an anti-Nazi play was banned after a complaint from the German consul. After the war, the comedy *Rusty Bugles,* by the Australian Sumner Locke Elliott, had to have its 30 expletives reduced to seven before it could continue performance.

There have been occasional complaints of breaches of taste, such as a play by the Western Australian novelist Gerry Glaskin, about Marilyn Monroe, which was closed in Perth in 1957; or the complaint last year against *When Did You Last See My Mother?* in Melbourne. But mostly the worries have been confined to keeping showgirl nudes posed properly, worrying whether God could be represented in a morality play and being coy about titles like *'Tis Pity She's a Whore* and *The Respectable Prostitute*. But in June 1968, controversy about theatre censorship exploded after a woman visited Sydney's Darlinghurst police station to complain about *America Hurrah!*.

The Chief Secretary's action clamped an arbitrary ban on any public presentation of 'Motel' in NSW. This prevented a quite separate production in Newcastle from going ahead—and it made no mention of the parts found objectionable. The law allows for no appeal and the Chief Secretary,

Mr Eric Willis, refused to see three different deputations from the theatre, both before and after the ban was imposed, to discuss a compromise in the performance. He did, however, see a deputation consisting of the editor of the *Sydney Morning Herald,* Mr John Douglas Pringle; Professor Robert Quentin of the University of NSW drama school; and the Elizabethan Theatre Trust executive officer, Mr Stefan Haag, to discuss the principles of censorship.

In Brisbane, *America Hurrah!* was performed briefly without interference; in Perth the play had a closed club season. Finally, in December, a full three-night public season was achieved in Hobart at the Theatre Royal under the supervision of the police.

The protest about the NSW ban culminated in a free performance at the Teachers' Federation Theatre, in Sydney, at which 2,500 people tried to take the 500 free seats available. The final gesture was a solicitor's letter to the Chief Secretary offering to supply the names and addresses of the organisers if the Crown Law Department would prosecute them as a test case. This, however, was refused. The case had repercussions in Victoria where a private-home performance of 'Motel' was attended by the Leader of the State Opposition, Mr Clyde Holding, who caused a press furore by coming out in defence of the play and complaining of his treatment by the police.

Other side effects in Melbourne have been that the amateur Viaduct Theatre's president, Peter Spurrier, was brought to court over *When Did You Last See My Mother?* The action miscarried because the charge had been incorrectly laid. Since then the police have been regular attendants at Melbourne theatres and a great deal of scrutiny has gone into theatre licences. Since very few buildings comply with the stringent health regulations for public halls, many such rely on the goodwill of the Chief Secretary for their continued activity.

One other incident occurred in Melbourne in August—police raided the property of Contact Theatre and confiscated a typed copy of a one-act play, *The Beard*, which is at present receiving a late-night showing at the Royal Court Theatre in London. The play is a dialogue between two American folk heroes, Jean Harlow and Billy the Kid. It employs the repeated use of obscene words and is a banned import. Last month Stefan Frederick Mager appeared before St Kilda Court charged with making an obscene article. Mr Mager said the purpose of the play was to attack the ease with which people accept socially unacceptable images. The magistrate ruled that the play was clearly obscene and corrupting and fined him $100.

As long as it continues to exist, stage censorship will continue to be a hit-and-miss affair. At least two plays presented in the past year, *The Boys in the Band* and *Fortune and Men's Eyes,* might well have been banned in script had the Customs Department got its hands on them in private luggage. But the former has become the *succès d'estime* of the commercial theatre for 1968 and the latter succeeded in engaging the NSW Minister for Justice in a public controversy over conditions in state prisons. Provided audiences keep quiet about what they see, the police are prepared to condone almost anything. At a Sydney coffee-house, as part of a transvestite show, a mock rape has been part of the entertainment for months. The investigating detective's comment to the proprietor was: 'That's all right. It's only two blokes. It is two blokes, isn't it?'

When Did You Last See My Mother? was the first play by the British playwright Christopher Hampton, about a boy who has an affair with his best friend's mother. I had reported on the action against Peter Spurrier on 12 September. The charge was struck off the list because it should have been laid against the theatre, not its president, and within three months of the performance. Therefore the complaint against the content was not raised.

Further charges and closures followed. Actors playing Norm in Alex Buzo's *Norm and Ahmed* in Brisbane and Melbourne were arrested and charged with obscenity over the play's final line: 'Fucking boong'; and two attempts to mount the British critic Kenneth Tynan's nude revue, *Oh! Calcutta!* were foiled. The vogue for nakedness soon faded, the police lost interest, and no stage work has been the victim of censorship since. A side effect of this vigilance was that most of the activist fringe-theatre had died by 1970. In NSW the Theatres and Public Halls Act was superseded by the Summary Offences Act in 1970.

The Sydney coffee house mentioned was the Purple Onion, in Kensington, which had a vogue for its satirical shows, several directed by such subsequently well-known theatre directors as Rex Cramphorn and Richard Wherrett.

Henry IV: Top Shakespeare
Australian, 6 February 1969

Happenings tend to occur apparently unpremeditated in Perth. Without prompting on Saturday Perth theatre lovers packed the 700-seat auditorium of the new Octagon Theatre, which the University of Western Australia had unaccountably discovered on its campus. In place of the lecture theatre it had expected, the Octagon turns out to be the most exciting new theatre building in Australia.

In harmony with the occasion, the Octagon was opened with a speech from Dr Coombs and a spectacular pageant-style production of *Henry IV (Part I)* by the Melbourne Theatre Company. Designed by a Western Australian architect, Mr Peter Parkinson, in consultation with Sir Tyrone Guthrie, it is the third theatre with the famous Guthrie thrust stage and bowl-shaped auditorium to be supervised by him. Unlike any stage but the New Fortune (also on the University of W.A. campus) and the small theatres in the round, it is the only theatre in Australia that discards altogether the picture frame in favour of the three-dimensional sculptural form.

The steeply-raked seating focuses attention sharply on the tongue-shaped stage and in *Henry IV* the focus is boldly concentrated by Richard Prins' weighty wooden set of balcony stage and symmetrical staircases. The functional simplicity of the theatre formed an excellent background for Kristian Fredrikson's extravagant heraldic costumes which, in Perth's memories of legitimate theatre, could hardly have been exceeded in lavishness.

John Sumner's production was a stately one, more decorative than deep. I confess myself disappointed on several counts. I expected a reading more advanced than other Australian theatres could presently produce but found the attention to detail which demanded our admiration was directed at the externals, not the heart of the play.

I also found the stage movement took little advantage of the new stage shape. And that the increase in numbers necessary for this large production destroyed at key points the ensemble, which is the great quality of this company. If I call it a failure, however, it does fail at a very high level because in it we had the delights of seeing and hearing work by the best group of designers and actors we have. The weakness was that, so far as the production had a point of view at all, it was that of an adventure story with an abundance of derring-do, but no feeling in common with us today.

The two contrasting actors—Robin Ramsay as Prince Hal and George Whaley as Henry Percy—appeared to be a pair of driving young men rebelling against the older generation: Hotspur is a Churchillian figure, impatient of committee work and disguising his contempt for ceremony behind rough language. Hal escapes the boredom of being born into a public role, redundant in peacetime, by drinking and adventuring at the Boar's Head Inn.

But the lust for life shown in Hotspur's relations with his wife, and his high heroic standing and salty wit, were subdued on Saturday and Mr Ramsay's Hal, while amusing, was a responsible aristocrat right from the start. I missed the strong kinship of this pair all the way through and at the death of Hotspur, after a spectacularly contrived fight scene, I wished for them to forget their chivalric rules and face his death together. But we had to wait a long time for Hal to put his hand out to his enemy.

There were other examples of a gap in human contact—the mock deposition scene where Hal rejects Falstaff while playing the king, was played with unsubtle pathos, and the real interview with King Henry IV was very little more than a demonstration of a father–son convention.

Raymond Westwell as Henry was hampered by playing too loudly for the generous acoustics, and what personal qualities he might have offered were lost. Frank Thring's Falstaff, though he suffers the same deficiencies of subtlety, makes an engaging, slow, broken down old knight, who pressed each well-known aphorism at the audience in a clear and leisurely fashion. For me the one great moment of the evening was when he drew his dagger upon the dead but still-heaving body of Hotspur. A section of the audience drew in its breath, and one cried out involuntarily, 'Oh no, don't do that'. Mr Thring acknowledged the shouts of laughter with a gesture of gratitude and for a moment there was a friendly understanding of what the business of playing Shakespeare was all about.

The other Guthrie thrust stages are the Festival Theatre, Stratford, Ontario; and the Guthrie Theatre in Minneapolis, Minnesota.

The Parade Opens: Old Tote Comes Alive
Australian, 10 May 1969

This is my penultimate column and my last review for some time because I go abroad next week for eight months. It is good to be able to end with the opening of a new venue and a positive forward step in our taxpayers' theatre. On Wednesday night Sydney's Old Tote Theatre Company—and now for the first time the name is beginning to mean something more than just a registered title—opened its new Parade Theatre in Anzac Parade, Kensington.

The temporary theatre is grander than the pioneering tin shed, seats 400 and has excellent acoustics and a welcoming auditorium which embraces the stage and the audience into the one, rounded space. If disadvantages are going to manifest themselves they will not be in the theatre but in the administration and audience facilities.

The opening play is Tom Stoppard's literary joke, *Rosencrantz and Guildenstern Are Dead*, which receives an elegant and sensitive production. This enormously successful comedy is a curiosity of English verbal acrobatics in a French metaphysical setting. It opens with two figures in Elizabethan dress flipping coins to each other and bickering about the odds of probability and their reasons for being in this unknown anonymous place. They are the flotsam and jetsam of a Shakespeare play: two characters who have no existence beyond the score of lines they have as instruments of the Danish court at Elsinore. And yet they have the right to a game of scholarly speculation upon their life as much as upon the age of Hamlet or the incidents that led to his tragic predicament.

In this situation of suspended existence Stoppard makes of Rosencrantz and Guildenstern an Estragon and Vladimir, waiting for some larger existence over which they have no control but in which they must have faith. They are bit-players in a play which they have never seen right through, whose issues and outcome have never been explained to them. Death, as Guildenstern explains, is not gasps and blood and falling about. 'It is just a man failing to reappear.'

It is as valid and funny an image of the way in which the world is slipping out of our hands as you might find in Beckett, Ionesco, Weiss, Van Itallie, Grass or any of the modern artists of our moral confusion. At the same time it is based very surely on a rock of English mythology, Hamlet the melancholy prince; and on the university wits that go back to Jonson. Stoppard has made English wit out of the French talent for *bouleversement*; he turns time and place inside out and reverses the dual realities of the stage. 'We're actors', says the Player King. 'We're the opposite of people.'

The Player King is the only concrete character in a play populated by shadows. He is the physical manifestation of R and G's philosophical problem, another abandoned relic with his tatterdemalion troupe, reduced to smelling out secrets and giving pornographic exhibitions to keep body and soul together. 'You should have caught us in better times', he says. 'We were purists then.'

Robin Lovejoy's production is beautifully orchestrated and has three fine performances in Neil Fitzpatrick as Rosencrantz, Tim Elliott as Guildenstern and Barry Lovett as the Player King. If one has a criticism it is that too much emphasis has been placed on the harmonies and the aesthetics of the play and not enough on the wit and the incongruities. Sandra McKenzie's soulful music and Yoshi Tosa's designs tend to emphasise this. The picture, for example, of Hamlet in a deck chair under a beach umbrella on his way to England, like an English tourist on the Calais–Dover ferry, seemed, in Mr Tosa's autumnal tones, to have acquired an air of graciousness which rather spoiled the Englishness of the joke.

The play is, to read, a good deal funnier than came across on the opening night. Maybe it was the academic solemnity of the occasion. And something happened to the end of the play that I think neither the author intended nor R and G expected.

The play *Hamlet* is also on the Tote's list for the current season and it would have doubled the joke to see it first. But what I most enjoyed about the production was the quality of ensemble that is at last beginning to take hold of the company. Much should come of this in the next year.

As the state theatre companies were developing, the commercial theatre was failing and reconstituting itself. Sir Frank Tait, the last of the Tait brothers who had run J. C. Williamson's since 1920, had died in 1965 and the company was breaking up. Sir Frank had been chair of both the real-estate parent company and of the production company, then run by the actor John McCallum. Dissension now arose between the two and it had a deleterious effect on the hitherto amicable arrangements with rival producers for buying rights and hiring the theatre chain. The up-and-coming Harry M. Miller solved the problem by renovating the old MGM cinemas in Sydney and Melbourne for *Hair*. In this transition period the music-halls' rumbustious style filled a vacuum for the party bookings and, in Sydney at least, contributed to the search for a characteristic Australian performance style. The following held-over piece was published after I had left for Europe.

Thar's Gold in Them Thar Halls
Australian, 28 June 1969

An Australian theatre? It is a handful of talents in a wilderness, seeking the promised land by government pressure, blown by the winds of public demand and private promotion. A mixture of vulnerable artists and tough-hided businessmen, all seeking the milk and honey; a few only finding rich oases. But one corner of the industry stands inviolate from the quarrels of art and cultural responsibility and has a truly indigenous gilt-edged formula for popular theatrical success, and that is the music-hall restaurants. They exist in all capitals except Hobart, have proved unfailingly successful everywhere but in Melbourne where the licensing laws are inimical to late entertainment, and are now beginning to expand with tours into country areas. The people behind them are theatrical dropouts who have found making money and making people enjoy themselves more attractive than art.

'If you want to succeed you've got to be first in the field', says Frank Baden-Powell, of Perth. 'It's no good being second with an idea.'

'I have no faith in the cultural needs of Australian audiences', says Barry Eggington, of Adelaide. 'None at all.'

'After four years we still provide the only avenue for local people to work continuously in the professional theatre', says Russell Jarrett in Brisbane.

'But we were first', says George F. Miller in Sydney.

The vogue began in the late 1950s when Mr Miller, plying his violin among the tables of a Melbourne restaurant, became aware of the mutual indigestion that curtain-up time in theatres round the corner caused both the chef and the patron. Encouraged by an experimental production of *East Lynne* at another restaurant, he moved to Sydney and in 1960 opened the Music Hall Restaurant, Neutral Bay. A barn-like former cinema, by far the largest and most sophisticated of the halls in Australia, it seats 500 at red-check-covered tables and is heavily hung with high-Victorian clutter. An important part of its attraction is that it indulges to the greatest degree the patrons delight in dressing-up. The menu is fairly large, the food has improved over the years and the entrance ticket is $2.10. With food and wine it is easy to spend $12.00 a head.

Seasons, as with the other music halls, run from six months to a year. Neutral Bay has developed from Victorian burlesque to Regency farce, parodies of Verdi's *Il Trovatore* and Shakespeare's *Macbeth* and a successful colonial divertissement called *The Beaut Country*. Scripts are usually by the hall's director, John Faassen, a former actor and opera singer, and music by Bernadette Alam, a Sydney piano teacher.

In Adelaide, Barry Eggington, a slight, fair man in his early 30s and one of the first graduates of the National Institute of Dramatic Art, has for three years been running the Olde King's Music Hall Restaurant with his sisters Gwen and Dawn, in a turn-of-the-century dance hall.

'Don't be misled by the culture myth', he says. 'Adelaide audiences only like musical comedy.'

The hall has a prosperous costume hire department and in September goes on a 16-week country tour for the Arts Council, SA Division.

His auditorium is decorated with the deep-red and gold bric-à-brac of its Sydney counterpart and hung with canopies and a painted front curtain. His scripts are burlesques based roughly on Victorian plots and put together with no great attention to style. His sets and costumes tend to the tulle, tinsel and feathers of the old variety shows and the songs are mostly from 1940s and 1950s musicals. The hall is small and crowded, with long tables which make the evening seem a permanent wedding party (Andrew Jones' wedding reception was held here) and he seems to have struck the right note of middle-class middle-aged, anti-cultural revolt, making the hall disproportionately popular.

Spartan in contrast are Frank Baden-Powell's two music halls, the Olde Time Music Hole in Perth and the Old Trades Hall Music Hall in Fremantle. A former stage director, bowling-alley manager and second-hand car salesman, Mr Baden-Powell is now a wine promoter with a controlling hand in a theatre and a wine saloon restaurant and has been employing Barry Creyton to star in a local cabaret at $1,000 a week plus expenses.

The Music Hole was a conversion three years ago from a theatre-in-the-round and adjoining club. Since then he and his business partner, John Gill, have opened a more affluent Hole-in-the-Wall Theatre in nearby Leederville. In 1968 Mr Baden-Powell acquired the lease of the Fremantle Trades Hall, a solid Edwardian structure built in 1904. It now offers the best value for money, an all-in evening for $3.80 a head. Overheads are small—a cast of seven, paid not more than $50 for a four-night week, no sets and a restricted but reasonable menu. The turnover for both halls in the Trade's Hall's first year was $280,000.

Quite different is Russell Jarrett's little empire in Brisbane—two halls, the Mark Twain and the Living Room, with all the appointments of elegant middle-class living and more emphasis on the menu. Mr Jarrett, who gave up acting in Sydney twelve years ago, is now the only music-hall proprietor outside Sydney who offers a full-length written, mounted and dressed burlesque play. The Living Room, the larger hall, opened in 1967, has retained solid Victorian melodrama, with long runs of *East Lynne*, *Lady Audley's Secret* and *The Drunkard*.

At the Mark Twain Mr Jarrett indulges his personal taste for comedy. He has produced and played the lead in a 1920s setting of *Charley's Aunt*, and presented musical adaptations by local writers of the Restoration comedies *The Country Wife* and *The Relapse*. For years the only source of regular employment in Brisbane theatre, his restaurants have become staging-houses for artists moving from amateur work to the profession down south.

In Melbourne the liquor laws have militated against the music hall. The comedian Noel Ferrier ran an Edwardian song-and-dance show at Triaca's Hotel for a year but came to a sudden halt at the George's Hotel, St Kilda with a show that had nothing to recommend it. Cautiously prospering, however, is Tikki and John's in Exhibition Street, a tiny coffee shop which Tikki Taylor and John Newman opened during a run of *Funny Girl* at nearby Her Majesty's because they could find nowhere to have supper.

In Sydney since the Millers' hall opened a handful of other theatre restaurants have started up. The best known is Frank Strain's Bull 'n' Bush, which provides a benign host and costumed songsters. At the Comedy Theatre Restaurant Willie Fennell and John Ewart are reviving old radio comedy scripts. The Menzies Theatre Restaurant closed recently after going the gamut of mini-musicals; the Sesame (also owned by Frank Strain) does musical and burlesque; and the Doncaster Theatre Restaurant offers excellent food and lavish cabaret and revue.

What distinguishes these halls and restaurants from the nightclubs is their phenomenal success in attracting crowds to a form of entertainment that depends in no way on importations or mass media entertainers (except for the odd TV personality). But as our repertoire in the mainstream theatre widens the hall is beginning to change the face of Australian acting by setting a challenge for the actor like that of a matador in a bull-ring. The whispered comment on a performance, 'I saw him at the music-hall', is no longer a term of derision, but of respect for a larger-than-life command of the stage.

Andrew Jones was a South Australian parliamentarian noted for being the youngest person elected to Parliament to that date.

The following seven articles have been selected from writings over eight-months' travelling through Europe, Canada and the United States. The political and social ferment of the 1960s had invaded the theatre in agit prop and audience participation, contemporary re-interpretations of the classics and experiments in stage nudity. The extravagance of some of the articles reflects the highly-charged nature of the performances. Most of the articles were also published by the London *Guardian* newspaper. In London I wrote about the Bread and Puppet Theatre a month after I reviewed the anarchist New York troupe, the Living Theatre, who were playing concurrently at London's Roundhouse.

London: Life Among the Puppet People

Australian, 9 August 1969

London's Royal Court Theatre. People in sweatshirts and stray tatters of tulle were scurrying round wiping blood off their hands and faces and gathering up empty packets of chips and salami.

'Has anyone got a Biafran flag?' 'Who knows what an Italian flag looks like?' Peter Schumann, leader, founder and mentor of the itinerant New York Bread and Puppet Theatre was in anxious conversation with two pale-faced women who earlier had been handing out yellow pamphlets about the stopping of relief flights to Biafra. Mr Schumann's ragamuffin troupe of gentle young people who have just ended a season at the Court, had that night enacted the arrival of the Pilgrim Fathers in America and their first Thanksgiving Dinner (which accounted for the blood). He was agreeing that next time the North Vietnamese flag, which had draped the table, would be replaced by a Biafran.

'Forgive me for not shaking hands with you', he greeted me, holding up a bloody cloth.

We were up on stage, the curtains still open to the auditorium, with actors and audience going about the mutual business of cleaning up and going home, as after a family dinner.

The Thanksgiving Dinner is not among the most successful pieces of this famous group of new primitives, but contains most of the elements that divided both critics and audiences so violently. An actor portraying a hostile Indian, with a shark's head and two torches hanging from his chest, stalks the oncoming Christians along an extension ladder placed across the tops of seats from the stage to the foyer. From the foyer then enter the eighteen other members of the troupe with drums and trumpets, wearing oversize tailcoats, ragbag evening dresses and battered cardboard top hats. They recite an account of their landing and how the feared Indians were warded off by their Christian welcome.

The Thanksgiving dinner, for which they give thanks to God with a revivalist fervour and a childlike astonishment, is dispensed from carry-bags from the supermarket a hundred yards down Kings Road, Chelsea, and consists of packaged meats, potato chips, puffed wheat and ready-made apple pies. As their grace dies away they spatter their mouths and hands with stage blood and a black-shrouded figure enters bearing a North Vietnamese flag, with which she drapes the table.

This play, Mr Schumann explained, had been commissioned by a local church for Thanksgiving Sunday, and at the first performance they had used the harvest table. And herein lay the conflict of their qualities and intentions. For none of it had been designed for Bernard Shaw's own theatre—or any theatre, for that matter—and no readjustment had been made to enable these primitive modern mysteries to be properly displayed, understood and accepted by a theatre audience.

The Bread and Puppet Theatre has been working for seven years in its East Side workshop and the streets of New York, performing at demonstrations, fairs and churches, preaching a pacifist message through animated pictures. Its members have nothing of the violence of the Living Theatre. Theirs is a gentle trade, and they have created among them a unique new–old form that rejects art and is not theatrical, and yet which is both art and theatre.

Their chief weapons are their giant puppets, objects of extraordinary beauty which in action take on a life of their own quite unrelated to the manipulators at their feet. Designed by Schumann, they are sometimes twenty feet high with hands as big as a man's torso, manipulated from below by iron rods.

The troupe's major work is *Cry of the People for Meat*, a mystery cycle that traces the predicament of man from the beginnings of the world, with the marriage of Uranus and Mother Earth and the birth of Kronos, to the Crucifixion. Kronos rises armed from a mountain of paper streamers and from this foam of time come Adam and Eve, rolling from under the curtain of heaven in a placenta of plastic wrap, biting their way free. The foam continues with a procession of Joseph's ancestors, the Nativity, the massacre of the innocents (shown as the child coming to Mary in the jaws of a dragon) the flight into Egypt and the Last Supper. Through the course of the play the main figures are pursued by a horde of monstrous, grey, pig-faced beasts.

This bald juxtaposition of the beautiful and the ugly, the impressive and the incongruous, are what give this company's work its unique stature and makes it a paradox of extremely sophisticated naïvety and obdurate ignorance of theatrical presentation. Most moving is the last sequence of *Cry of the People for Meat*. Madonna and Child are received into the house of the grey ladies of Bethlehem—mop-haired totems ten feet high swaying in infantile pity—while the words of a Vietnamese widow describe how her husband had died when he stood up in a field. He had not known what an aircraft was.

Program page from Bread and Puppet Theater's production of *Cry of the People for Meat*, 1969.

We had earlier seen Uncle Fatso, the company's cigar-smoking power figure with a face quite recognisably President Nixon's, failing to enter the door of heaven. Now his demands batter down the defenders of Bethlehem and the grey ladies and their child are swallowed up by a shark-nosed aeroplane.

Next scene is the ritual dressing of the Christ figure with the blessings of the Sermon on the Mount. The shrouded actor receives commonplace objects, weapons of meekness and mercy, life and death. Over the dead-white mask of pity is placed a cavernous red El Greco face of Christ, hung with an ochre gown, and the actor climbs a stepladder until the figure is fifteen feet high. A little lower, under the skirts, sits a second figure, manipulating the long-fingered hands raised in sadness over the scene that becomes the Last Supper.

Sour bread, cooked by the actors, has been distributed to the audience. The apostles—all the races are there—intone as the bread and wine are distributed among them. The end, when it comes, is borne by the same crucifix aircraft with the sharks' teeth, under which the twelve men flee screaming and the sad face on his ladder is toppled into the dust.

What audience is the Bread and Puppet Theatre actually aiming for? The children of Harlem reputedly love them and yet some of their imagery is complex and baffling. The middle-class press in both France and Britain has tended to be irritated by what appears to be a talking down, and there is something academic about their approach to simplicity. What is certain is that they do not belong in an orthodox theatre but in a place of their own making.

The Republic of Biafra was declared in 1967 by the Ibo people of eastern Nigeria in opposition to the Nigerian majority of Hausa people. A bitter civil war broke out within months and the Ibo were suppressed. By 1970 Biafra ceased to exist.

Avignon: The New French Revolution
Australian, 6 September 1969

> Father Legrand said to his son,
> 'What is bloody well going on?
> What are you doing in the street, old son?'
> 'I'm going to make revolution'
>
> 'But finally explain to me, mon p'tit,
> What is he telling you, this Cohn-Bendit?'
> 'He's making me see that you are a—
> And I want to make revolution.'

These, roughly, are the first and last verses of the ballad 'The Revolution' which is now on sale in France recorded by the 'choirs' of the Free Sorbonne and Gavroche revolutionary committees who took part in the student revolution of May 1968. It is sung nightly at the Théâtre Gramont, near Montmartre, where a student revue created by the revolution's cartoonist, Wolinski, is playing under the title of *I Don't Want to Die an Idiot*.

This work first played last year to free houses at Aubervilliers, a Parisian suburb. Now it has committed itself to the backbreaking costs of a city boulevard theatre, which puts most shows beyond the budget of the average Frenchman. There it is a quaint exception among advertised boulevard comedies (*Boeing Boeing* in its ninth laugh-filled year) and stuffy classical productions. The French theatre, the leader in the post-war boom of fresh thought, is now patently in a bad way.

Nor is it unfair to state that the path of good intentions paved for ten years by the Gaullist Minister for Cultural Affairs, André Malraux, has had a deal to do with this. Ask a Frenchman what effect Malraux's ministry has had and he will tell you: 'He cleaned historical buildings and raised the entrance price to museums.'

Decentralisation was the keystone of the Malraux policy for the arts, and his retirement this year upon the reconstitution of the Government has left many more organisations dependent upon him than were at the start of his period in office. The theatres, reliant upon annual grants as they are in Australia, are facing debts of millions of francs while waiting for the new minister, Edmond Michelet, and his bureau to decide a new policy.

Slowly, however, the anti-Gaullist vultures are moving in for the kill and, down in the south during the months of July and August, something stirred which European cultural interests may find it difficult to ignore. One hundred and fifty thousand people of the average age of 28 converged on the small Provençal agricultural town of Avignon (population 100,000) to watch what might be described as a theatrical re-enactment of the events of May.

Avignon is a small town in an area known for its Roman ruins, antique arenas and Mediterranean summer nights. In the twelfth and thirteenth centuries it was the home sought by the popes away from Roman political troubles, and the old town is still dominated by the papal palace and its cathedral. Jean Vilar, now a revered elder of the French theatre and nicknamed *Pape Jean*, but then a young director with breakaway ideas in search of a home for experiment in open staging, found what he wanted in Avignon. It was the vast *cour d'honneur* inside the Palace of the Pope—an enormous quadrangle with stone walls rising 120 feet above huge Gothic entrance arches. In 1947 he launched his first Avignon Theatre Festival.

In 1952, on the strength of his work at Avignon, Vilar became director of the Théâtre National Populaire (TNP) and since then has devoted his talents to the triple purpose of presenting French classics and socialist theatre in a fresh and simple way, keeping ticket prices down to bedrock and capturing a working-class audience. For the bulk of its life, the Avignon Festival has been the summer home of the TNP for a two-week season, and its hero was the actor Gérard Philippe. Philippe died of cancer seven years ago and with him went the era of elegance at Avignon. In 1965 Vilar left the TNP to begin a new career popularising music and to evolve a new policy for the festival.

He began to introduce ballet and music, to extend the venues about the town, and to ensure in other ways that the visitors to the city paid back in kind for the festival costs. But no one predicted the events that followed. In July 1968, immediately after the May revolution, hundreds of young people poured into the city during the festival and held demonstrations, incited by the Living Theatre who saw themselves as leaders in the cultural revolt. Seats had been sold out before the start of the festival and they demanded that the doors of the theatre be flung open to all. Fearing a riot, the town organisers refused. The resulting dispute ended with the Living Theatre disappearing after only three performances with their $80,000 francs, leaving the festival in chaos.

Vilar's solution this year was to hand the star billing over to his old friend Maurice Béjart, one of France's premier dancers and choreographers, who for ten years had chosen to work in Belgium because he got better treatment there. Béjart has brought his company from the National Opera of Brussels, the Ballet of the Twentieth Century, to the *cour d'honneur* with three programs, *The Four Sons of Aymon, La nuit obscure* and *Romeo and Juliet*.

Though middle-aged himself, Béjart's company of 70 is young, virile, and determined to have its own way. He has responded to this by turning the ballets into total theatre and taking as partner for his own performance in *La nuit obscure* the French actress Maria Casares, a familiar figure at former festivals in more orthodox roles. The ballet is based on a poem on the dark night of the soul by St John of the Cross, enacted with considerable violence in Spanish by Miss Casares as an accompaniment in place of music.

This personal and poetic ballet is still, however, more familiar than the other two, which are largely the work of his company. These drew screaming, stamping applause from the youthful audience and filled the nearby town square with giant blow-ups of the long-haired *premiers danseurs* with revolution and love in their eyes—a cult usually reserved for the pop world. *The Four Sons of Aymon* is basically a simple dance drama about four brothers who seek their fortune at the court of Charlemagne and prove their physical and mental strength with weapons and a life-size chess game. The last third of the program is spent reworking the ballet, pulling down the Gaullist figure of Charlemagne to the laughter of children, and showing that today's youth has its own heroes, its own battles, and peace her victories no less renowned than war. By the end of this work, astonishing and at the same time admirable in its innocence, the audience is ready to take on the world.

Béjart's Avignon Festival production of *Romeo and Juliet*, 1969. (Photo: Claire Falcy)

Romeo and Juliet is a mass demonstration of even greater proportions. It plays around freely with the Shakespeare script and the opera. At the centre it has a dazzling pair in Paulo Bortoluzzi and Laura Proença. But again in the last third the style is pulled to pieces by the corps de ballet in their working clothes, while the dead lovers rise and join in a cry of 'Make love, not war'. The slogan is repeated in a dozen languages along with amplified repetitions of body counts, and, in a kind of *Götterdämmerung,* copulating couples are bundled together with those of the picturesquely dying, while the fortissimo orchestra of Berlioz is drowned by the sound of bursting bombs and machine-gun fire.

Not all the programs were so disciplined or so successful but they all showed a real desire to reintegrate the arts into a total greater than before, and were remarkable in the present French climate.

Daniel Cohn-Bendit was the fiery red-headed leader of the student protests in France in May 1968. Today he represents the German Green Party in the European Parliament.

Berlin: Brecht Rediscovered

Australian, 29 November 1969

One of the neatest indications of how theatre companies differ in Europe is their approach to Brecht. Bertolt Brecht is, of course, a classic master of the theatre and is also an exception in being a committed political animal who used his theatre and his pen all his life for a political purpose. He has survived, of course, for quite impolitic reasons—because of the almost Shakespearean depth, breadth and variety of his writing, which Australian audiences have had only small opportunity to gather; and it is his dialectic which finally is his limitation.

In the past few months I have seen an extraordinary variety of Brecht productions. A glossy musical-comedy performance of *The Caucasian Chalk Circle* at the fat Chichester Festival; an uncharacteristically serious production on Shaftesbury Avenue of *The Resistible Rise of Arturo Ui* and a swinging version of *Jungle of Cities* in the Basel Stadttheater which I chiefly remember for its dazzling scenic effects. At the Royal Dramatic Theatre, Stockholm, was a wide-screen version by Alf Sjöberg of *The Threepenny Opera* that lasted four and a half hours, and in which the script played only a minor part. And in the vast baroque theatres of West Germany a variety of jolly productions, where the rich subscription audiences applaud Brecht's verbal qualities with the same respect they give to Goethe and Schiller.

But it was on my last night in Europe that I went for the first time to the place where the cult began—the Berliner Ensemble in Bertolt Brecht Platz, East Berlin. There I saw a production of *Arturo Ui,* a play that had its opening night in 1959 and which has since acquired the status of a classic. The thing that came as the greatest surprise to me was the theatre building itself. Pictures of the company are commonplace—black and white photos of hard-working actors in well-worn 1920s suits, ill-matched military uniforms and old cotton dresses, hard white light and almost no setting, sweating out an epic on the problems of the proletariat. But it had never occurred to me that the auditorium would be that of one of the most charming gilt rococo theatres in Europe; or that we should be out of place in the front stalls for having dressed informally to make the grim underground journey from West to East.

The *Arturo Ui*, as expected, was brilliant, and surprisingly spontaneous and undated for a production that had been in the repertoire ten years. The play is a parody of the rise of Hitler in the 1930s, tracing it in terms of a Chicago protection racket in which Ui's gangsters gain control of the cauliflower market in a campaign of fear, arson, bribery and murder.

The mood is comic; the gang characters are presented by a busker as fairground puppets to be knocked down for a prize. The actors wear painted faces—caricatures of Göring, Goebbels and von Hindenburg in green, yellow and black crayon—to ensure that we keep the issues in our mind's eye. No effort is spared to make it clear how totally untalented and insignificant the little Arturo is and, by implication, Hitler was. Yet, somehow, in his appalling fashion, he worms his way into the confidence of the Cauliflower Trust and the audience until there is a full-scale reign of terror sweeping the stage, a man on a rostrum shouting anarchy, and the terrified market workers marshalled into Nazi salutes.

Michael Blakemore's *Arturo Ui* in London was one of the finest I have seen and drew the admiration of those who saw it. But when Ui comes down to the footlights at the end and says in a voice of warning: 'It has happened before and it can happen again', it was not possible, in the comfortable chaos of Labour London, really to believe him. Nor was it possible to see the power game behind *The Caucasian Chalk Circle* in a theatre where the governing classes fill the seats and Topol, London's favourite musical comedy star, direct from *Fiddler on the Roof* was playing Azdak, the rogue representative of natural justice.

But in this little pocket in East Berlin one can never avoid reminders of Hitler's Germany; where streets still share the same name on either side of the Berlin Wall and there is no way of shaking off a comparison between East and West. There is desolation on both sides because Berlin no longer makes sense as a city; and in the Eastern Zone the grey isolation and physical discomfort look very much like what the Berliner Ensemble represents as Chicago 1933. The threat of Arturo Ui, stunningly performed by Ekkehard Schall, is still frighteningly real.

There is much talk in the West of how the Berliner Ensemble is failing; and, with productions that last until the actors outlive their roles, it is difficult to see how anything else could happen. But the question is less that the Ensemble has deteriorated than that the other theatres have expanded in a way that is rapidly leaving no room for the Ensemble. East Berlin was far more fortunate than West Berlin in retaining most of the city's surviving theatres; and these, both because of their inaccessibility and the personalities which they have gathered into them, have acquired a mystique which attracts a thriving trade of tourists from all over the world.

Zürich: A Child's Brutal View of Historical Horrors

Australian, 13 December 1969

'Stop it! We want no kindergarten here!' shouted a spectator as Gladstone was demonstrating how to kick a handcuffed victim into insensibility. 'Ask the director when we are going to get good theatre again.'

A woman in the front stalls had risen from her seat at the sight of the Lady with the Lamp, in a bikini and transparent plastic mac, ministering to the soldiers of the Crimea.

There had been rumours that the premiere of Edward Bond's *Early Morning* would not pass without incident, and the Zürich Schauspielhaus was crammed. There had even been rumours that some of the actors had considered making a speech before the curtain dissociating themselves from their roles. The productions of the German director, Peter Stein, a left-wing rebel still in his 20s, have a history of bringing out the aggressive in people. But no one quite expected the violence with which his first production of *Early Morning* in German would be received. The man who called the play a kindergarten was right, in a way, because this piece, which caused a similar public outcry when it was performed at the Royal Court Theatre in London, is very much a child's eye view of historical characters.

'They are contained in the nightmare of elementary schoolboys who have class work in history next morning', wrote the eminent critic Ivan Nagel in the *Suddeutsche Zeitung*.

> The bloody episodes of *Early Morning* unroll as before the staring eyes of a child who, for the first time, hears of the incomprehensible but actual horrors which are honoured as national history. Edward Bond asserts this is history for it happens to men. At the beginning he places this sentence: 'The events of this play are true.'

The outrage in Zürich, however, was different from the kind expressed in Britain, which naturally centred on the violence done to the person of good Queen Vic. Bond's characters, in fact, bear no nearer resemblance to reality than Daisy Ashford's Prince of Wales. The outrage was directed elsewhere—to the monstrous, bloody capacity of the characters to swallow each other up. Killing and eating are Bond's physical images for his diagnosis of our moral disorder. German-speaking audiences over forty, on the whole, do not wish to know about violence; and the revolutionary post-war generation, they feel, does not know that of which it speaks.

Two attempts were made to stop the play and scene eight, in which

Gladstone is represented as a Fascist, brought the steady undertone in the auditorium to a pitch that forced the actors to leave the stage. Prince Albert's ghost was hastily wheeled on as a diversion and the rest of the scene inserted later. Feelings rose as the play progressed but sides were quickly taken by youth against age. At interval, the audience held a peace conference and agreed on a truce, that the actors be allowed to continue the performance as planned on condition the directors hold a civilised discussion at the end. By then, however, the older members had departed and the harrowed actors, looking shaken and blue under the cement-colour they had worn for the final act in heaven, took twenty curtain calls to a half-house of frenzied partisans.

Peter Ehrich, a giant of an actor who, as Gladstone, had taken the decision to retreat in scene eight, said afterwards: 'I don't know if I did the right thing. But I thought: "I'm an actor. I'm there to serve the audience. If they don't want me I go".'

Asked if the cast had expected such a reaction, he said: 'We had hoped for it, but we did not expect it. I do not like the play and I do not think such a production is necessary. But there is too much blood in the German theatre today. Whenever they do Shakespeare they have blood all over the place. It's not necessary.'

Peter Stein's previous productions in Munich, Berlin and Bremen are few, and include Bond's *Saved* and Peter Weiss's *Vietnam Discourse*. But each had been noted for its shock value as well as its dramatic merit, and he is now a director in great demand. Whether or not this new production remains in the repertoire at Zürich there is no doubt of the quality and originality of this young director.

Though the main characters are called Queen Victoria and her family, in its new setting *Early Morning* reveals a face which has nothing to do with British tradition. Gone are the Union Jacks and references to Windsor Castle and Beachy Head. The only stage furniture is an iron juggernaut on wheels atop which the graven image of monarchy, enveloped in an enormous mantle of animal hair, delivers her first address to her subjects; and a giant deckchair in and out of which the instruments of revolution and counter-revolution climb and shelter.

The play is about power amounting to terror. The unrelenting brutality of the last act which ranges through beatings, shootings, open wounds, hanged puppets and vomiting blood, culminates in the buckets of dismembered joints and limbs being torn apart and eaten by the company of heaven. These then grow again as mutated deformities on the bodies of the consumers.

What was missing altogether at the end, and was present only by chance at the beginning, was a kind of Belloc humour, which asks us to enjoy the predicament of Little Jim as he is eaten by the lion. In an interview before the performance, Dr Peter Loeffler—who, in his first season as artistic director of the Schauspielhaus, has already instituted some radical reforms—said he had chosen the play because he believed it opened a new era in the history of modern theatre.

'The neo-naturalism is just not interesting any more. We must find new images and Bond is showing us how', he said. 'The theatre must change. Crisis means action. Audiences are conservative because they know only the old things because they do not know the new ones. A theatre has to lead its audience.'

Early Morning is not a nice play, and the fact that its instruments are emotional, not logical, makes it hard to justify. But it demands that we recognise our fascination with violence; it accuses us of unnamed crimes and forces us to admit to the truth of some of them. Whether Bond is leading or dragging his audiences it is difficult to say; but they will certainly not remain indifferent.

The Swiss reaction was very different from the German one. Edward Bond was one of the most popular playwrights in Germany at this time, with his merciless assault on social injustice and British imperialism. The leaders of the new wave of German theatre directors, Peter Zadek and Peter Stein, both had a taste for anarchism and the grotesque. The very English humour had probably escaped the Swiss audience, too shocked by the violence, but the text offered plenty of opportunity for shock, presenting Queen Victoria and Florence Nightingale as lesbian lovers, Prime Minister Gladstone as a racist thug and Princes George and Arthur as Siamese twins. Daisy Ashford wrote *The Young Visiters* (1919) at the age of nine. It is a classic child's view of the domestic life of the British upper classes.

Hellebaek, Denmark: Sydney's Unfinished Symphony

Australian, 27 December 1969

I had the best job anyone could get. I had the possibility to concentrate upon an extraordinarily great structure for a purpose not for profit but for the stimulus of the mind. You could not dream of a better entrance to this new world. When it became clear that our function was to stimulate the audience before the drama, to take them away from their daily lives, the architecture came by itself.

Paying a call on Jørn Utzon, the exiled architect of the Sydney Opera House, is not a simple pilgrimage. He lives outside the small town of Hellebaek, an hour's train journey from Copenhagen, in a kind of non-house of his own design, with no address, in the depths of a beech forest, buried in turn by green foliage, falling autumn leaves and heavy snows. It is a low-slung house of gracious but spartan simplicity with the purpose, characteristic of the man, of making more vivid to the inhabitants the remarkable natural beauty of its surroundings.

Exclusiveness has always been an accusation made by the people of Sydney against this tall, athletic, ascetic figure who came apparently from outer space to thrust an unwanted greatness upon their inner harbour. The idea of a great building was to the government of the day a flattering one and to the Public Works Department strong grounds for resentment. But the difficulties of communication between the government administration and this solitary outsider were intense: he had new building methods, a new approach to working drawings and new production methods, together with an impetuous, thickly-accented English which conveys itself by excitement more than by vocabulary.

Since he summarily abandoned the project four years ago he has become a kind of Grotowski of architecture both in Australia and abroad. A mystical figure known only by a chosen few and thought by the rest to be a too-temperamental genius or a charlatan who could not finish what he had begun. But to meet him is to see he is none of these things. He is neither remote nor exclusive, nor does a conversation leave any doubt that he was able to finish this multi-million dollar concept. He is able to talk without rancour of the schism between himself and the Minister for Public Works in the NSW Government, Davis Hughes. But it is clear that the building is as close to him as ever it was and that he still thinks of it as a living thing and his life's work.

Aside from his work, the 51-year-old Dane is, in fact, a very simple person. He is simple enough to believe that, on such a project, design and construction were his ultimate concern and external demands of little significance. He lives in isolation with his family in Hellebaek, just as he did away at Palm Beach in Sydney, not because he wishes to avoid people—he loves to talk—but because he needs his days to be uncluttered.

He is an acute observer of things as they naturally are, from the way leaves fall to shopping habits or a geometrical solution. The experiment that went into his famous solution to the shells construction (as segments of a single sphere, enabling the components to be mass-produced); and into the acoustic ceilings (which he based on the cylinder); and his bird's wing in plywood to support the soaring glass walls—he approached it all like a physicist and a philosopher, in search of a solution perfect in simplicity, both natural and aesthetic.

The first thing he makes clear is that his purpose in building the Opera House was characteristically simple amid the politics and polemics which raged over his head. He was building his Opera House not for the NSW Government, nor for Australian culture, nor for his own indulgence and certainly not as a monument to anyone; but for the ordinary people of Sydney, to express their life, the freedom and enterprise he found in them, their climate and the constantly changing, surprising and sometimes dangerous qualities of their harbour. The whole complex, as he described it, had a coherent philosophy which began with the life of the city and harbour and drew it towards the stage. There was not a light or a tile that did not have its place in that philosophy.

Since leaving Sydney he has received news of its construction only erratically. He knew practically nothing of the new plans for the interior, which depart radically from his own conception, and the news depressed him profoundly. Only the exterior has been completed according to his plans. Because of the individuality and complexity of the work, without him new designs have had to be made for the interiors. At present legal action is being taken by Utzon's lawyers against the NSW Government over the question of his designs for the interior. Utzon claims he handed them over. The Government claims they do not exist. In 1965 the final cost estimate under Utzon was $50 million and the estimated completion date 1968. Since then the costs have risen to $80 million and the completion date not before 1972.

His plans are now complete for the Zürich Schauspielhaus, for which he won a competition in 1965. In Zürich he is happier because he is protected from politics.

> They have a theatre company and know exactly what they want. And besides the theatre my job was to create a square in the centre of the town with traffic and a shopping area and restaurants. So it is a beautiful complex creating life day and night, not an empty monument. The planning is now successfully completed but before they can start building there must

be a public vote on the project. If the answer is 'yes' the money is there and there will be no political trouble. The method is slow but secure.

Utzon's unfinished symphony was planned to last a thousand years, as a cathedral does, but not as something to trap Australian culture in the mid-twentieth century. 'In order not to make it one man's work, a static thing, a monument', he said, 'I hope the decoration will be continuous, that new things will always be added to it, just as they are in all buildings of a great age. The architecture is so strong and simple, the structure is pure structure, pure function and you will be able to hang new things from its walls at any time, without risking that the heart is destroyed.'

Maybe the heart is not destroyed yet and in time it will again be known as Jørn Utzon's Opera House. Right now it is Davis Hughes' Opera House and, finally, he is more Australian than Utzon. Near enough is good enough. Casualness makes Australia one of the most pleasant countries to live it but it does not make for greatness.

At Hellebaek we talked first, nostalgically, about the way of life in Sydney among the people who liked the open air and were young enough to like a gamble. Nowhere else in the world, he said, would he have been able to embark on such a revolutionary idea. 'I could not make such a thing in Switzerland', he said.

> There the people are quite different. The Swiss are a conservative people. They like their intellectual life but they do not wish to be daring with it. That they leave for their mountain life. But in Sydney they admire daring very much. It was an absolutely perfect program I worked on. Every detail and space was planned according to the right proportions to the halls and this was based on many studies by people in Europe. The three halls and their size have been criticised and altered but they have arrived at nothing better—on the contrary something very much worse. It is very bad because what we were providing was a range of instruments. Theatre and concerts are simply meetings between artists and audience, and just as there are instruments—for instance the violin, 'cello and bass—which have a certain size and limitation for certain reasons, so the halls had their sizes and limitations for certain reasons.
>
> The size of the experimental theatre, with 400 seats, is the right size for small dramas that need intimate contact between actor and audience. You cannot get this in a bigger hall, nor can you use this kind of acting; so that even if you sit in the first row of a bigger hall the experience will be different because you will see a different kind of acting. A maximum

of 1,200 people is sensible for many bigger dramas, musicals and small operas. This is considered the right size in Europe and the maximum distance is important. There is a maximum for the last row and if you go beyond that the actor will again have to behave in a different way and the sexual appeal from him is lost if you go further out. The program for the Zürich Schauspielhaus was based on a report by the architect-playwright Max Frisch who is on the board.

Acoustics for music were the problem that determined the size of the major hall, planned as a dual opera-concert hall. After Utzon's departure the Minister dismissed his German acoustics firm; since then the problem has been pronounced insoluble and the major hall has been converted into a concert hall. The $3 million stage machinery housed in the tallest shell and providing the *raison d'être* for the shape of the Opera House, has now been discarded and the vast gap has become a cinema and waste space.

'Kramer and Gabler are the best concert hall experts you can find', said Utzon:

> They have made 35 halls in the last twenty years. They said: 'We can easily make a hall for 1,800, a beautiful concert hall; 2,500 is difficult; 3,500 very difficult but not hopeless.' I learnt from them what sound was and it is a curious matter. Their laboratories showed me how sound has direction and quality, that it depends on reflection. And I learnt how to build up surfaces to control the sound and how, in a hard room with 100 per cent reflection, to absorb the sound. But there is much more to it. My idea was to make the exterior a raincoat underneath which we would hang this cloud, the acoustic ceiling.

These were the challenges with which he began, not the elevations of the site nor size, shape and materials, but an environment and a desire to place his audiences in the best relationship to his stages to be in the right frame of mind for the performances. He wanted the exterior to astonish those who saw it but at the same time to belong to its surroundings. He wanted the walk from the entrance to gather in excitement as one moved towards the stage; and he wanted his structure strong but not dominating. Here is how he described this building he calls his symphony:

> It is typical Sydney. Because the site is one you go around and even sail around, the building needed to be a sculpture, so I spread the two theatres instead of putting them in a box and put sails over them to keep the feeling of being on the sea. Underneath I placed this big platform fitting beautifully on the peninsula, repeating the effect of walking on the heads

in Sydney. When you see a hill before you, you want to climb it, and so I put the wide steps in front of people leading into the foyer. The entrance into the foyer is low and suddenly you are in this soaring space, just as one comes upon the harbour suddenly through Sydney Heads. Over all we put these light sails, just giving a feeling of protection and no more.

If I had finished the building I would have carried through this sense of movement. It is treating space like music, almost non-existent today in architecture. But one has an architectural recollection just as one has a musical recollection. If you suddenly dive into a symphony you do not understand because you have not heard the start. In decoration I would have had everything concentrate upon and move towards the stage opening, in richness of colours and materials, even from the boiler rooms, which were grey, through the dressing rooms which were a little more refined and the same for the audience's entrance. So wherever you were in the building you were part of the movement. My lighting system was asymmetrical to draw people up the stairs and round the building. But it was not to be stronger than the dark harbour. The harbour was to dominate and ships passing by would be seen very strongly in the foyer.

The symphonic backbone was to be the visual structure over your head. Structure has disappeared in modern architecture for many reasons. Normally in a modern building you have a cardboard ceiling with all the piping and ducting up there, some columns sticking up, and you stand between two horizontal planes. You don't know whether you are on the tenth or the second floor and it doesn't matter. Here the span over your head is sacred; no installations can come through. That is very difficult, everything must be in the floor.

He went on to describe how the ribs and muscles of the vaulting had a shape and direction which again carried you up and through the building and how the bent plywood shapes of his acoustic ceilings would be:

like the autumn leaves outside my window, hanging free. You would see the secondary structure hanging on the big structure. And below the furniture would be of the same plywood with soft cushions and colour and suddenly it builds up almost like nature—and all of this lit by the beautiful light of Sydney Harbour, which is unreal sometimes and marvellous. You have seen its effect on the shells; if I had not made them shiny you would not have seen the reflections in the evening. The light it mirrors changes all the time and it's different again in the rain.

The battle of the Utzonites in Sydney has been lost and Davis Hughes, who was responsible for Utzon's resignation, has never flagged in his determination never to have the architect return to the project.

The building opened in 1973 and the final cost was $110 million. The experimental theatre became the Drama Theatre; 'the vast gap' that became 'a cinema and waste space', is now the Playhouse and Studio.

The original brief was for a hall holding 3,500 seats. The present concert hall holds 2,690 and the Opera Theatre 1,550. While the argument was conducted on reports of reverberation times and the differing needs of opera and orchestral music, there had also been powerful lobbying by the Australian Broadcasting Commission (as it then was) to reserve the hall for concerts. At the time the ABC had a waiting list for its symphony concert subscription series. Its rival, the fledgling Elizabethan Opera, had no subscriber base. The argument over the interior designs was laid to rest in 1994 when the Sydney Opera House and the State Library of NSW opened a retrospective exhibition, which included computer-generated reconstructions of Utzon's designs. In 2002 the Carr Labor Government in NSW invited Utzon and his son Jan to advise on the renovation of the Opera House interiors and provided $24.1 million for the purpose. Utzon, now in his 80s, accepted the brief but he has not returned to Sydney.

Utzon's plan for a new Zürich Schauspielhaus lost in the referendum following an adverse submission by the NSW Government.

Warsaw: Mind Plus Matter

Australian, 10 January 1970

It began with the Polish attaché in London saying rather shortly: 'We do have other directors, you know, besides Grotowski.'

And he's right, of course. I can think of no other city the size of Warsaw (population 1,300,000) which has such an aggregation of vivid directing talent or so many competitive, involved theatre companies.

The attaché's reproof was in reply to my exasperated complaint that in the long course of planning for a visit to the Polish theatres no one had told me that on the day I was due to leave London Jerzy Grotowski and his company would open a private season there. But here or not, the Laboratory Theatre of Wroclaw is very much at issue in the Polish theatre where his work is regarded with respect but by no means total approbation. 'He is not much thought of in this country. He is just one of the directors', was the first reference made. And it is true that as a prophet he and his followers have gained recognition in Poland only in the last two or three years—long after the recognition of his theories abroad, after the publication of his texts by his Italian disciple Eugenio Barba. And after many foreign actors and directors had made his tiny studio in the provincial city of Wroclaw the Mecca of a new messiah.

Jerzy Grotowski is at 36 already a myth in the theatre world. A graduate of the Kraków Theatre School, he worked as a director in Kraków and other provincial centres before beginning active research in Opole in 1959, which eventually became the Theatre Laboratory. In 1965, with an official government subsidy he moved to Wroclaw. He has never yet shown a production in Warsaw. The main reason for the mystique is that he is a teacher and research worker rather than a stage director and his concern is with his art and his profession, not with his public.

His reputation is that of a new kind of Stanislavsky whose theatre for a dozen actors and forty spectators is a holy ritual demanding vows of asceticism and discretion from the actors together with extraordinary physical and mental feats; and from the audience a shattering emotional participation. The 'poor theatre' he describes in his writings does without every luxury of illusion the theatre has acquired over the centuries and returns to the direct confrontation of the actor's body and mind with the audience. Further still, he excises all dramatic illusion from the text, taking Polish, Greek or English classics and removing all the poetic and visual elements until all that remains is a series of actions of which the text is the instrument.

The challenge he has made to the foundations of dramatic method has been revolutionary and far-reaching; and directors and actors both inside and outside Poland have been forced to recognise them. Inside Poland there is a natural ambivalence as there would be in any profession, among those involved with everyday commerce, towards a colleague who stands apart from the rough business world and who in any other era would never have been acclaimed in his own lifetime.

Inside Poland too, one quickly becomes aware of how Polish Grotowski's theories are; how serious and deeply romantic he is; how poetic in a neo-literary way and how his preoccupation with the spiritual resurrection of man through suffering is allied to the history of Polish theatre and Polish politics. 'Our people go to the theatre to think', one theatre manager said; and while this may be difficult to believe, it is true that in Poland's stormy and divided history the theatre has been a forum for political thought and nationalism. In times when the native language was banned in schools it was to be heard on the stage. Today the theatre is still taken very seriously by both the public and the government as an instrument of national oppression and dialectic, with both good and bad consequences for those involved in the creation.

The directors of Warsaw are proud of Grotowski, even though he is a thorny partner and it is impossible to discuss theatre with them without leading at some point to his theories. The main complaint against him—and it is a characteristic of the Polish theatre taken to an extreme—is his romantic seriousness. 'I believe that theatre should begin with a smile', said Professor Bohdan Korzeniewski, a friend and former teacher of Grotowski and one of Europe's most distinguished interpreters of Molière. 'Grotowski believes it should begin with a cry.'

'Grotowski's theatre is a police state', said Adam Hanuszkiewicz, the flamboyant young actor-manager of the Narodowy (National) Theatre. 'If someone laughs in a serious moment he is put out. His rehearsals are conducted in such silence and solemnity and with such exclusiveness. I am strongly against closed rehearsals and performances. Theatre is created for an audience. When people knock at the door of my rehearsals I say, "Come in", because they are part of the creation and help me create.'

What Hanuszkiewicz admires about Grotowski is his development of the whole of the actor as a means of expression. Polish directors, he said, were strongly divided between the extremes of literary and anti-literary interpretation. He belonged to the second division in that he believed that ideas bred their own forms and that one should play the form rather than package the text. He opposed Grotowski's distortion of the author's form and text to create a new form of his own. Grotowski, said Hanuszkiewicz, was the extreme of the anti-literary form and its advantage was that when his company travelled abroad they were understood in a way that literature was not. In relying totally on the actor and his body, however, Grotowski had created something that was neither pantomime nor theatre but was leading to an aesthetic of pantomime, not an aesthetic of theatre.

Hanuszkiewicz's own productions of the classics are as deeply personal as Grotowski's but at the other extreme of strong rhythms, visual extravagances, humour and incongruities—the nearest Warsaw has to total theatre.

Helmut Kajzar, a young director and playwright, is a former disciple of Grotowski who became disenchanted with his demands for a holy aesthetic and his humourlessness. He is equally disenchanted with the poetic nationalism with which the Polish classics tend to be celebrated and is working towards his own style of simple, directly-spoken satirical theatre, which he believes is more immediately a comment upon the life of today. His need for simplicity and direct meeting with the audience is, he admits, the result of Grotowski's work and the intimate proportions of his theatre; and he also admits that there are very few young directors in Poland whose work has not been affected by Grotowski's theories.

Erwin Axer, one of the directors best known abroad, is the leader among those to whom the text is the first and final criterion of the author's vision. But he was also the one to defend Grotowski's methods most strongly. For 22 years he has been head of the Wspólczesny (Contemporary) Theatre, in which he has created a distinctive style and ensemble of great modesty, economy and rationality.

'We have in our Polish theatre many different kinds of relation to the author', he said:

> Grotowski's experimental theatre is one in which through one or two years of work something is born and grows on stage. I would say that not only the acting but the play, if you can speak about a play with Grotowski—is his, not the author's. His is the most consequent and radical of our non-literary theatre. It is not without the spirit of a certain kind of literature or he would not name his productions *Apocalypse* or *Acropolis* after Wyspianski. But Wyspianski is only the source and not even the source of inspiration, only of material. Grotowski is a very special case. His kind of theatre is clean and original, entirely his own. But there are very few directors so great that they can supersede the author.

Asked if he thought a theatre had the right to choose so small an auditorium, he said:

> Grotowski calls his theatre an experimental school. He does not try to make a theatre. He tries to find new ways to develop the art of the actor. It is a kind of theatre I appreciate very much but which is very far from mine. He is a romantic and I am much more rationalist. But the influence of his experiments is very great in the English theatre and perhaps also in Poland. I see in the work of our young directors deep and interesting influences.

Grotowski is now in the United States, whither in November I shall pursue him.

From this point on Grotowski travelled abroad increasingly, preferring the life of the prophet outside his own country. He gave a lecture in Sydney for the Arts Council of Australia (NSW Division) which I reported on 7 July 1973; and the

Laboratory played a brief, exclusive season of *Apocalypsis cum Figuris* in the crypt of St Mary's Cathedral. I reviewed this on 8 April 1974. The work's physical and mental demands, its dark catholic mysticism and relentless pessimism, made a deep impression on its selected audience, largely from the theatre community, but was finally too alien to leave a lasting legacy. Grotowski's influence on Rex Cramphorn and the Performance Syndicate came principally from his published theories. Grotowski died in the United States in 1996, aged 65. Stanislaw Wyspianski (1869–1907) has been called the father of modern Polish theatre. His best-known play, *The Wedding* (1901) is a sharp satire on the society he knew.

New York: Stifled By Nakedness

Australian, 24 January 1970

Poor naked wretches, wheresoe'er you are: if you get up on stage you will certainly be stared at—but nobody will call it acting.

I did get round to seeing it, that famous nude show the Australian public has been promised, and I suppose I must tell you about it. That theatre critic's contribution to the dramatic art, *Oh, Calcutta!* I mean.

On my travels I have seen about as much naked flesh on stage as might be found in the nursery of a maternity hospital in a year—and making much the same kind of noise. And there is a place for nudity on the stage, there is no doubt about that. But the place is strictly limited, and the greatest limitation is that it hobbles the use of words and the other ordinary means of communication. One very soon reaches an impasse.

I did not find *Oh, Calcutta!* boring, as almost without exception the American critics did. I found it shocking. And I found it so not because of simple nakedness but because none of it was funny enough, clever enough or spectacular enough to turn us from a voyeur into a theatregoer. I could never get out of my mind the predicament of ten poor naked wretches up on stage saying out loud, unconvincingly, 'We believe in this show'. My only lasting memory of the evening was of the closing minutes in which the cast make fun of the audience and their motives for being there. These crumbled away into a panicky demand that the house manager confiscate a camera that had been clicking away in the front stalls all evening. The last words of the show, as far as I know it, are: 'Hand over that camera, your camera, your camera.'

If one is a voyeur, one behaves like a voyeur. The audience slipped away as quickly as they could. A man in front of me was explaining to his girlfriend: 'It was meant to be funny, Martha. It was a spoof.' But she was not to be moved. 'I just thought it was ugly', she said.

But I am being unfair. Much of it is funny and stays longer in the memory than one might have expected. And the show I saw did not have the original cast. There was a *joie de vivre* and genuine enjoyment about the early performances, New Yorkers tell me, which has over the months of grind and strip been lost.

The finished script is, of course, devised by Kenneth Tynan from sketches submitted by such well-known writers as Samuel Beckett, Jules Feiffer, John Lennon, Leonard Melfi, Sam Shepard and Dan Greenberg. But the best of the program is the score—penetrating, brassy hard rock quite as good as *Hair*. It sounds tremendous on record. And the title number, written and played by the Open Window group, has a compelling and witty nostalgia that stays on the brain. The coloured multi-film effects are impressive too, melting the three-dimensional bodies of the actors into giant reflections of themselves on moving screens. Another of the Open Window's numbers, called 'Much Too Soon', co-ordinates the multi-media with extraordinary effect to make it the big success of the evening.

But generally the impression is not of cohesion but of confusion. I found it difficult to enjoy the music because of the men and women taking their clothes off—and difficult to keep my attention on the strippers when there were much more sensual blow-ups of their more interesting angles occupying the backdrop behind them. The show lacks both coherence and a point of view. If one puts the best face on it, it is just fun. Beckett's contribution, for example—for which he enjoys top billing—is a 30-second view of a pile of trash containing a torso and a leg, and one or two emitted moans. Feiffer's, the only piece which could claim the title of wit, is a bedroom scene involving a wheelbarrow full of plastic equipment. 'We have seen into each other's souls', the man cries ecstatically out of the darkness. And then: 'Weren't you there, Jane? Don't say you missed it. Oh Jane, why weren't you there ... ?'

That is the best of them. Sam Shepard has a gutsily funny hillbilly Joe; the Lennon piece is too juvenile to describe; and others too sick. Tynan's contribution is a straight undergraduate dramatisation of a Victorian pornographic novel. The *pièce de resistance* is a rather pointless joke about the Masters and Johnson research at Kansas on sexual behaviour. What was intended as erotic is distracted by the idiotic crazy gang act that represents the medical profession, and what was intended as funny is distracted by the idiotic ditto. It is this kind of panic that makes the show neither one thing nor the other but tries to distract the audience from noticing anything too well—the kind of pornography that gives obscenity a bad name.

Oh, Calcutta!, if it is to tour the Lido circuit may perhaps elude the police as a club show—but if not, it is not the kind of show that can be defended on artistic grounds. It's an autograph book of midnight doodles by people who have been known for better things and that is the best part of the joke. The program could perhaps be defended as a public therapy session and there was a rather pleasantly conspiratorial air about the audience as they took their seats. As such, it would do no harm and might possibly do some good. But theatre it is not. If we attempt to explain why people find naked bodies boring on stage when we don't find them so on film, we come back to the fact that on stage, unless the lighting effects are very clever, it creates the atmosphere of a public bath.

As an art object some of the bodies were worth the money. But as soon as they open their mouths and let out their personalities one stops thinking in terms of Michelangelo or Botticelli and starts thinking one's next door neighbour caught in the nude doing something he shouldn't—or worse (oh horror) oneself. For a human being naked is to be totally vulnerable in a way that no actor can afford to be. And an actor can hold an illusion and a personality just so long as he reaches his audience's senses through the mind. His sex appeal is to know how to convey the tactile through sight and sound. By stripping them naked, we take away their power to choose either words or actions. The audience is not even looking at their faces any more. He is just a body, sadly over-exposed in the light of the bathroom mirror.

A happily unrepeatable example of the total uselessness of words in such a situation may be seen in a hippie play called *Che*, by Lennox Raphael, which has been running for over a year in an old warehouse in Greenwich Village. The main characters are Che Guevara, the U.S. President (clad only in tailcoat and top hat), the Ghost of Castro (female, in a topless bikini), a hermaphrodite who represents the machinery of war.

Allegedly it is an allegory about how politics and idealism rape each other—and while the free verse script rolled relentlessly on through lines like, 'Deliver me from this evil caress', the Sister of Mercy, whose duty it was to provide comfort with impartial plenitude, was raped almost eight times. Since everyone was pretty soon naked and acting aggressive, there was nothing much else to do.

The play is chiefly notorious for the fact that the cast was arrested soon after the opening on charges of indecent behaviour and corrupting a minor, and for having had actual sexual intercourse on stage. Later, however, the play was resumed in a more limp way—one critic suggested the limitations were a new political comment. But what I saw was a pretty humourless business and I am sure the audience did not hear one word of the script, certainly not its dialectic. Except for one line from the Sister of Mercy, which surfaced from one all-in pile-up: 'You remember how simple intercourse used to be?'

There are occasions when nudity can make a point, and the London and New York theatres have begun to emerge from the *succès de scandale* phase and look at what can be retained. One such is an incident in the Royal Shakespeare's production of *Troilus and Cressida*, in which a brief glimpse of Cressida's nakedness is used to express a lyrical quality in the young couple's newly-found love. Another occurred in *Stomp*, a performance nicknamed 'Son of Hair', off-off-Broadway, being given by a group of Texan hippies about their life and their parents' lack of understanding. A naked boy sits cross-legged in a spotlight being bombarded by his mother's threats over an amplifier. Neither he nor we more-than-half understand either her demands or his sins. This defencelessness—it stays with one.

But for erotica, the idea of having it in the theatre where one can take one's friends and feel both daring and respectable—it had to be tried. But I think it is better on the pornograph at home.

Stomp, which I saw at the Public Theatre in Greenwich Village, was described as 'a multimedia protest rock musical environment entertainment, the collective creation of a kibbutz-like group of 23 youngsters (most of them former students of the University of Texas) who call themselves "The Combine"'.

In January 1970 an attempt was made to present *Oh, Calcutta!* in Adelaide. Actors' Equity opposed it on grounds of exploitation and it was closed during rehearsal. A Melbourne production due to open on 21 February 1970 at the Lido Restaurant was prevented when the Attorney-General, Mr G. O. Reid, brought an injunction. The show was never seen in Australia.

Back in Australia, I visited the Adelaide Festival. The Royal Shakespeare Company's swinging 60s version of *The Winter's Tale* had arrived after a season in Melbourne. The cast wore the Carnaby Street look, flares and loose dresses, in white against a stark white set. The opening scene was a nursery, where the two kings, Leontes and Polixenes, rode a rocking horse. I had seen the play the previous June and had misconstrued the implications of the fashion industry's revolt against

English taste—in retrospect a signal of young Britain's decision to reject any grave responsibility for the sins of empire. Then I had dismissed this production as the nursery games of the RSC's infant prodigy, the 29-year-old Trevor Nunn.

The Winter's Tale: Adelaide's Magical Transformation

Australian, 16 March 1970

From time to time I begin seriously to doubt my capacity for being surprised by the theatre, but never again will I do so after seeing the Royal Shakespeare Company's production of *The Winter's Tale.* The performance has undergone a magical transformation since I saw it last June at Stratford-upon-Avon—maybe it is the sea change, certainly it is the transfer from the gloomy temple of art at Stratford to the friendly, almost Elizabethan actor–audience relationship of Adelaide's Her Majesty's Theatre. Or maybe the change is simply in myself.

Whatever the reason, what last year seemed a thing of thin contrivance aiming for a popular style at the expense of the play's meaning, has inarguably metamorphosed into one of the great stage performances of the world. It has in it all the virtues of this fine company, the chief of which is clarity, both of whole interpretation and individual meaning. This is marvellously aided by the raked thrust stage built out over the orchestra pit, which gently drops the words and action into the audience's laps as it if were especially for them.

The Winter's Tale is Shakespeare's great ecological play which shows us birth and maturation and returning to the earth, not as in the downfall of the tragedies but as the natural part of a continuous process of life. At Stratford the visual element of the play—the nursery toys, the Regency-cut suits, the ashram the court becomes during Leontes' sixteen years of retribution, clouded the larger world of which the king was a symbol. Polixenes' line, of the king's sudden jealousy: 'As his person's mighty must it be violent' seemed to have no meaning in a world of nursery squabbles. In the same way the country innocence of the shepherds seemed to have been twisted out of its meaning to make a pun of the line about making themselves 'all men of *Hair*'.

What the production has acquired over time is an overwhelming humanity. It puts those things in their place as tools to express not simply a rejection of the old world but a synthesis of the new socialist England which has retired from the tumult of wars and politics to seek a more gentle place in the afternoon sun. The clarity of Trevor Nunn and his cast's understanding and realisation of the play is breathtaking. It opens with the dangerous childishness of the boyhood friends Leontes and Polixenes, recapturing their lost time of irresponsibility at the expense of their kingdoms. We see how maturity ripens in the mother Hermione and how the canker of jealousy withers the immature king.

The opening of the second half demonstrates the sense of having Judi Dench play both Hermione and her daughter Perdita (despite the problem of the statue scene in which the whole family is reunited). In this Perdita and Polixenes' son Florizel replay the nursery idyll, this time not with mechanical toys but with the produce of the natural world of which they are part. Over this ritual of birth, death, the long winter of retribution and the resurrection and rebirth, the good witch Pauline presides like the Duke in *Measure for Measure*, the human hand of divine justice.

One of the contributions to the play's change of tone has been made by replacing Brenda Bruce's practical and witty Paulina with that exceptional actress, Elizabeth Spriggs. Miss Spriggs' outstanding quality is a kind of spiritual calm that gives to her women a mature grace as if there is nothing in nature they do not understand or cannot accept. Her Paulina is one of those miracles that extracts the meaning from Hermione's long hibernation and heals and restores the family in full time. When the play reaches the great moment when Leontes touches the statue of this lost Hermione and the whole play comes to life in that line brilliantly delivered by Barrie Ingham: 'Oh, she's warm', and Hermione, the two kings, and their son and daughter join hands and complete their circle of life, the release that comes has been the work of Paulina. Paulina is the handmaid of Apollo and an instrument of something greater, just as are the other children of nature, the comic characters—the shepherds and Autolycus the rogue.

Space prevents me from detailing the extraordinary performances by Judi Dench, Barrie Ingham as Leontes and Richard Pascoe as Polixenes; Sydney Bromley and Geoffrey Hutchings as the shepherds and Derek Smith as Autolycus. The RSC's philosophy is based on the speaking of Shakespeare and the conviction that there is a meaning to be found in every line; and this production is stunning evidence of their achievement.

The one interpretive criticism I have had of this company under its present direction has been a clinical quality, an attempt to capture perfection like a butterfly on a pin, which allowed no breath for the roughness of simply being alive. In the search for integration there seemed to be a cramping of life in the individual actor. But this is gone now. What is left is great maturity and taste and compassion. I hope those theatregoers who do not see this company during the rest of their tour regret it for the rest of their lives.

Hair had opened on Broadway in April 1968; and in Sydney, produced by Harry M. Miller and directed by Jim Sharman, in June 1969. It ran without protest and, as in the rest of world, attracted huge audiences. The show had a particular attraction for the young because Claude, one of the protagonists, is a draft dodger. In Australia and the United States young men were being called up to fight in the Vietnam War and this also resonated in Toronto since many young Americans had escaped the draft by fleeing to Canada.

Our *Hair* is Better than Most

Australian, 11 April 1970

My desk, as I write, is covered with what looks like plans for the decoration of a Chelsea salon. They are, in fact, programs from round the world of *Hair*, the musical Clive Barnes, critic of the *New York Times*, in a Boston magistrate's court recently called the greatest innovation in the American theatre since *Oklahoma!*. (That's a serious historical comment.)

The director of the Boston production that was being challenged in court for un-American activity, mainly concerning treatment of the United States flag, was Jim Sharman, the Sydney director who had already created the Sydney and Tokyo productions. He returned home a fortnight ago to whip up some action in the local cast and this week I went to see how this performance compared with others.

There was the German production, for example, which I saw in Hamburg. The foyer was decorated with dead-eyed, wire-haired window-dressers' dolls and the auditorium with ropes and aggressive pieces of junk. The Tribe sang the 'Age of *Wasserman*' in strict tempo. A huge Japanese called Minoru Terada played Berger as if he were Shintaro and there was a military efficiency in the way they dropped their clothes.

There is something about the German temperament which tends to make group allegiance a bit frightening and this performance was almost an assault. '*Mein Haar! Ich will es lang und liegend, fliegend,/ bursten-borstig,/ rabenhorstig,/ ruppig, schuppig, struppig, supfig*' etc. My German companions came away feeling angry at the ugliness of the younger generation and wishing once more that the theatre would stay in the era of Goethe *und* Schiller. I bought them the New York recording.

In Toronto I was fortunate enough to see the impact an opening night of *Hair* can have on a whole city. This was the first production directed by the authors, Gerome Ragni and James Rado—former New York actors who, because of certain incidents, are now forbidden to perform in America under penalty of a fine. That night they were prowling the crowded foyer like lions and the young producer, perspiring into his silver lamé caftan, had been hard put to prevent Ragni from stripping, he said later. His hero Claude's comment that he doesn't want to work, just to make a lot of money, had a certain relevance too.

The *Hair* organisation is efficient and each production is financed, managed and cast locally. Because of the special social problems involved this has proved enormously successful in creating the right kind of affinity between the show and the city, and the environment has certainly had much greater influence upon the show than the direction, which has tended, generally, to be a reproduction. In Toronto the theatre problems are peculiar. The city is the communications centre of North America and *Hair* has a special significance as an example of mass communication. Live theatre, especially locally-made, tends to be spasmodic because of the mass media domination; and there is strong feeling about being gobbled up by the United States.

Nudity was also a new issue in the city. These and other concerns all combined to make the opening feel like a revolution. This production differed in having some early songs restored to it by the authors and in being a much more personal statement about the kind of people the two leading characters, Berger and Claude, are.

But the Sydney production is different from the others too, in being probably the first conscious interpretation of the show in its environment since the musical's early days. Mr Sharman has in this production a freedom not allowed by the promoters in some other countries and there are some strikingly impressive elements. In particular Claude is played by Wayne Matthews not as a vulnerable young outsider but as an almost abstract, priest-like synthesis of the draft-age man's moral predicament. The Christ imagery that surrounds him, his ritual sacrifice to the war-governed society, and the final impassioned plea from the Tribe, 'Let the Sunshine In', make a remarkable piece of theatre. It brought to mind a statement made by an American drama student: 'We are the generation which has been deprived of a religion. I see the theatre as a means to restore it.'

Mr Sharman uses the technical equipment of his stage with great imagination and employs both the lighting and the elements of ritual in the script to greater effect than I have seen before. He also uses his bodies much more hedonistically, with an almost evangelistic pursuit of the pristine. The sex in the script is most carefully used as part of the energy and the drive through the whole production is quite distinctively Australian. It is also rather a relief to note that Australians are more used to wearing next-to-nothing than are most nations.

The cast, led, the night I saw it, by Reg Livermore as Berger, has enormous dynamic. In some cases the voices were not quite as good as I have heard elsewhere but there is great unity and spiritual fervour about the production and a beauty that America is unable to capture. The musical is a natural form of expression for the Australian performer. Our variety houses used to be real indigenous theatre and we can do American musicals way better than the British and the Europeans.

If we genuinely want to investigate the roots from which an Australian theatrical culture can grow we will find them in such ceremonies and forms of musical expression as you find in *Hair*. *Hair* has been so successful because it grew out of a recognisable culture with an attractive modern philosophy, and an appeal wider than the converts to hippiedom. We must find our own communities. The present form of *Hair* is already going out of fashion. Seeing it in San Francisco only a mile or two from Haight Ashbury, where the hippie movement began, it was like a glossy night-club entertainment, suddenly quite out of date. In New York one night I met Tom O'Horgan, the Greenwich Village director who took *Hair* from the small Public Theatre and blew it up into what it is today. He has done five productions and never wants to see another performance in his life. What he wanted to talk about was Ibsen.

On 24 May 1971 I reviewed the Melbourne opening, 'The new *Hair*: a great classic group creation', in which the non-professional, improvised quality achieved by Sharman by casting almost no professional singers, had given way to a much more structured production. The band was replaced by a theatre orchestra and the finale, 'Let the Sunshine In' was 'no longer a celebration but a plea'. The review ends: 'The result is a new mature look at the lasting qualities of *Hair* and shows it clearly as a great classic group creation. Take my word for it, its next place will be in the Sydney Opera House.'

This view was endorsed in a letter from the amiable Claudio Alcorso, chair of the Australian Opera, who I quoted on 29 May as writing: 'It is probably true that *Hair* is the most significant opera written in the 60s'. However, recent attempts at revival have not proved successful. Opera Australia has not attempted it.

Shintaro was a ninja hero of a popular Japanese cartoon TV series of the time.

PART III
THE TIDE TURNS
1970–71

In 1970 things began to move very quickly. The shock tactics died and the experiments in form gave way to individual voices demanding to be heard. In quick succession the Australian Performing Group in Melbourne and the Nimrod Street Theatre in Sydney became magnets for new writing. The La Mama playwrights Jack Hibberd, John Romeril and David Williamson, Sydney playwrights Alex Buzo and Ron Blair, and Perth playwright Dorothy Hewett, all began to push the boundaries. Pushing parallel with the Australian Council for the Arts' drive to establish companies of excellence, and the State Governments' determination to provide proud buildings in which to display them, the playwrights impatiently sought out their own makeshift venues on a more modest scale.

The Council also began to recruit staff. Temporary offices set up in the eastern capitals had been centralised in Walker Street, North Sydney. The special projects funding, initially dispensed by the Melbourne Theatre Company and the AETT, were restored to the Council and results were beginning to show.

In Melbourne the Australian Performing Group was in the process of formation at La Mama. La Mama, a 60-seat converted shirt factory in Faraday Street Carlton, had been opened by Betty Burstall in 1967, after visiting the La Mama Experimental Theatre in New York's lower east side, as a space for poets, playwrights and composers to try their work. La Mama survives and thrives today.

Investigating the Ethos
Australian, 30 May 1970

The theatre with the most potential as an investigation into the national ethos is the Australian Performing Group at the Café La Mama, Melbourne. Recognition of its steady output has been made by the Australian Council through its special project fund by a grant of $2,000 to the group. This week, after a tour of factories sponsored by the Amalgamated Engineering Union, it goes into recess for about four months to conduct a closed workshop in which eight actors, two playwrights and two musicians will be involved.

The work will be led by the group's chief moving spirit, Graeme Blundell, who is both actor and director; and the playwrights Jack Hibberd, chief writer at La Mama since long before the young spirits at the care resolved themselves into a combine; and John Romeril, whose work has also been consistently performed.

Last week I saw the group's production of Hibberd's *Customs and Excise*, a witty attack on censorship. The play is a series of anecdotes about the emotional deprivation of the average Australian couple and the blue movies that go round the back of their mind. What is most interesting about Hibberd's work is the use he makes of language. His plays are a dense forest of Australian clichés, prejudices and prevarications which make one gasp with laughter at the author's perception of the degree of our conformity. 'Christ was no intellectual', was one reason tossed off to the pair of book-burners trembling with dedication at their work.

The play does more than simply poke fun, but not much. It is characteristic of the young La Mama playwrights that their job so far has been to find ways of pointing to what we are. What has not begun to concern them yet is why we are what we are.

Joseph Heller's *We Bombed in New Haven*—or 'We Bombed in Sydney' as it might have been called by precedent—is a morality play which turns moralistic. It is an extended allegory by the author of *Catch-22* about the roles of the soldier and the actor based on the principles of The Games People Play, and as such contains a number of compelling ideas and images about the idiocy of modern warfare. But as a piece of theatre it is too much at odds with the nature of the dramatic medium to make its impact in the way the author intended, and its uneasy attitude to audience response makes one resistant to its satirical strengths.

The problems set by the author are not allayed by the production by Hayes Gordon at the Ensemble Theatre, Sydney, though the in-the-round shape is admirably suited to the dialectic style of the play.

The action is about a crew of airmen who have been conditioned to fly and die in response to their superior officers. All the vital questions are left unanswered—where the orders come from, what the purpose of the war is, whether there is a war at all—only the orders and the regulations are present realities. Their training is a series of allegorical games—games with toys and games of status. Some of the airmen are reasoning beings, some are clinical morons. The rebel is hounded by the system and murdered by it according to regulations. Parallel to this allegory is a comparative one between the theatre and the war game. It tries to relate the fact of knowing that a stage death is not a real death to the problem that war is unreal for these who do not actually witness it.

The play is symptomatic of a present trend in American theatre which is attempting to reassess the nature of the audience–actor relationship and to find new ways of involvement. But it misunderstands the power of the dramatic medium to suggest that because the theatre is not actual it is therefore not real. By demanding instead of seducing our involvement, the play creates its own resistance.

Given these problems, the cast does not do a bad job, although the production is a bit over-earnest and fails to make use of the one talent Heller has which is genuinely dramatic—his wit. Leaders of the cast are Max Cullen as Flight-Lieutenant Starkey; Reg Evans as a squadron leader; Reg Saunders as Henderson, the rebel; and Lorraine Bayly as Ruth, the Red Cross girl and the advocate for human attitudes.

The Legend of King O'Malley by Michael Boddy and Bob Ellis was a defining moment for me. I reviewed it three times. The search for an Australian style of theatre was ranging widely and *King O'Malley* was the signpost I had been seeking. Its influence can be seen in the article that ends Part III, 'Not Wrong—Just Different'. The play rediscovered the power of the outsider hero and affirmed a larrikin style that was taken up in the 'ocker' theatre of the 1970s. And its message was timely: the real King O'Malley also opposed conscription—and lost.

King O'Malley, the Larrikin Hero

Australian, 20 June 1970

When a second-year National Institute of Dramatic Art student volunteers to do a fire-eating act, and another allows a six-foot carpet snake to crawl up and down her net stockings, we begin to recognise that our theatrical horizons are extending way beyond what Mrs Worthington's daughter ever imagined. What is more, on this occasion these two performances were not even in the play.

They are part of four sideshow acts provided by NIDA students during the interval of *The Legend of King O'Malley* at present being given a try-out

Nico Lathouris as Mr Angel and John Paramor as King O'Malley in the NIDA / Jane Street production of *The Legend of King O'Malley*, 1970. (Photo: Robert Walker)

at the Jane Street Theatre in Sydney. It is the first of three new scripts being aired in the fourth annual Jane Street–Old Tote Australian play season.

The Legend of King O'Malley is a very special achievement, not exactly because it is a total tangible success as it stands but because, in the search process NIDA has established, it has leapt the first hurdle of recognising what they have been looking for. For me it has a particular pleasure because it synthesises so many of the elements which make up the Australian taste, for so long begging to be dramatised, and has used them to give us the first genuine larrikin-hero I can recall in our drama since the colonial theatre. And the real King O'Malley, of course, was American.

About 1893 he landed on the coast of North Queensland and was looked after for two years by an Aboriginal called Coowonga while he recovered from TB. He then walked from Rockhampton to Adelaide selling insurance, became a member of the South Australian State Parliament, then Tasmanian representative in the first Commonwealth Parliament and stayed in Canberra until 1917 when he resigned after losing the conscription issue to Prime Minister Billy Hughes. He was Minister for Home Affairs 1910–13 and 1915–16, was said to have founded the Commonwealth Bank and Canberra. He opened the Trans-Continental railway and was in the forefront of labour reform and social legislation. He died in 1953 aged 99. Such a hero is worthy of a country which so admires the outsider and is big enough to make its own rules.

What the co-authors of *The Legend of King O'Malley* have done—with their director John Bell, for this is a thorough group creation—is give us a man who is twice life-size through the ratbag language of the theatre.

Jane Street's little converted church hall, with its Gothic windows behind, is at home with the ramshackle revivalist meeting of the Waterlily Rockbound Church which is in progress as we enter the theatre. And it is natural that we should join in the community hymns and that the walls should shake with the music of the organ, tambourine and drums. King O'Malley (John Paramor) is in the centre conducting the service, assisted by his bad conscience, Brother Nick Angel (Nick Lathouris). We know it is all a fraud—and yet it has a truth of its own and I am tempted to put a nickel in the tambourine.

Nick Angel, the Mephistophelean figure whom O'Malley finally leaves on the shores of Queensland, and who becomes later just an ordinary member of Parliament, is a superbly funny idea, played with great appetite.

Lathouris' work gets better every time and his seemingly endless series of disguises give him scope in which he delights.

The second half is Roy Rene country, in which the Commonwealth Parliament is presented as a vaudeville. Andrew Fisher is there dressed as Harry Lauder. 'I say I say I say, a funny thing happened to me on the way to the hoose tonight ... I met a constituent.' And Billy Hughes is there— the Little Digger, scratching himself inside a lice-ridden uniform. But what is deeply disappointing about the second half is that when the play turns serious and returns to the word for strength, it has nothing really to say nor the power to say it. The portrait of Hughes is vicious without being considered, and we learn nothing of interest about our fathers of federation—even about O'Malley in his maturity. There is gossip, that's all. What saves the day are the authentic speeches of Hughes and O'Malley over the conscription question which give a startling picture of Hughes' myopia, and our first real insight into the humanity of O'Malley's liberalism. These speeches are the only moving moments in the play and show how, finally, the spoken word prevails.

My other reviews were 'A Sharper O'Malley' on 15 August and 'To be universal you must first be local' on 2 September.

O'Malley was followed at Jane Street by *10,000 Miles Away*, an improvisation based on a text by Willy Young (later William Yang, a photographer whose photo-performances have earned him an international reputation) and David Malouf. This was an early experiment in abstract form by the ensemble that became the Performance Syndicate, under the direction of Rex Cramphorn. *O'Malley*'s cast, David Cameron, Kate Fitzpatrick, Gillian Jones, Nick (later Nico) Lathouris, Robyn Nevin, Terry O'Brien, John Paramor and Willy Young—became the founders of the Syndicate while its director, John Bell and the authors, were moved to invent the Nimrod Street Theatre.

In Brisbane, the prudery I had perceived two years earlier (see p. 65) had become manifest to plague the founding director of the new Queensland Theatre Company, Alan Edwards. The new State Government Insurance Office Theatre had opened in October 1969 with Peter Shaffer's *Royal Hunt of the Sun* directed by Queensland director Bryan Nason; and in April 1970 had celebrated the Company's incorporation with *A Rum Do*, a musical about the life and times of Governor Macquarie by Rob Inglis and Robin Wood. In the teeth of early opposition, Edwards (1925–03) a skilful teacher, director and politician, successfully established the company. He retired in 1988.

The QTC: A Small Miracle of Efficiency

Australian, 15 July 1970

It is early days yet for predictions but a small miracle is occurring quietly in Brisbane called the Queensland Theatre Company. The company is at present performing at the SGIO Theatre only the second of its productions under the director, Alan Edwards. But already it has assumed a standard of ensemble playing and unobtrusive efficiency which one might reasonably have expected in two or three years.

The play is Brian Friel's charming Irish journey around a young man's mind, *Philadelphia Here I Come!* And in sensitivity, respect and understanding of this deceptively complex piece of entertainment, and technical accomplishment from the designer, the crew and the actors, this is equal to the very best Australia can produce.

But the truth is that so far Queenslanders are not taking the QTC to their hearts. This is partly because Brisbane has not before had a civic theatre company, and one suddenly imposed by law does not equally suddenly impose a taste for the theatre upon its citizens. The company has the odds stacked against it because of its artificial beginning, its high maintenance costs at a time when it can least afford it, and the imposition upon it of a too-public theatre building of which the public has had high but undefined expectations.

Despite this and the extra pressures associated with the end of its first financial year, there is no sense of panic inside the theatre. It gives all the appearances, in fact, of being a happy company with a fight on its hands. It seems undismayed at the task it has taken on and looks more with sorrow than anger upon the reactions of some of its audience.

Take, for example, this letter in a local paper, from Theatre-Lover, Geebung.

> I read that the Queensland Theatre Company belonged to the people of the state. I would like to dissociate myself from such a group after having seen the current production at the SGIO Theatre. Never have I heard so much blasphemy from beginning to end (I presume) as I walked out during the second act, as did many others. To give credit where credit is due, I must say the acting was very good, but this production could hardly be called 'entertainment'.

The play in question is a moving little study of an ignorant Irish-Catholic family, and in its brief life has saved the bank balance of a good many of the world's theatres, whose directors have recognised its qualities as popular

Frank Gallacher, Peter Lavery, Terry Bader, Robert Kingham and Don Batchelor in the Queensland Theatre Company production of *Philadelphia Here I Come*, 1970. (Photo: QPAC Museum Heritage Collection)

entertainment with a satisfying economy and sensitivity in the writing that makes it a pleasure for the actors. The hero is Gar O'Donnell (Don Batchelor), 25 years old and about to migrate to America, and the action covers the 48 hours before his departure. With the help of his private voice (Terry Bader) we roam widely over the circumstances of Gar's life and ambitions and the pressures which led to his decision. The comedy and the pathos in the script are derived largely through the contrast made by these two figures between what Gar finds himself able to say to his father, his friends and his girl, and what is inside his head to say.

Edwards' production is beautifully harmonious, full of lightnesses and gentle silences. He has assembled a fine, homogenous cast, led by the ebullient pair Batchelor and Bader: Bill Austin as the old man, sadly despaired into silence; and Hazel Howson as Madge, the housekeeper who hides her longing for affection behind a rough tongue.

Although Theatre-Lover, Geebung, is a single extreme voice, there does seem to be an ungrounded opposition by some Queenslanders to the QTC. Audiences in the past have been divided between the loyal supporters of the three strong amateur companies, and the occasional audiences of the commercial theatre. The QTC must find its place between the two, and that will not happen overnight.

The Old Tote, which I had previously dubbed a 'hot bed of conservatism', had its own tug of war. This rather touching conversation with its director, reveals a man caught between the need to develop his company at its own pace and an ambitious board pressing for expansion. Had the Trust Players (Lovejoy's previous company under the Australian Elizabethan Theatre Trust) remained together after 1961 and filled the place of the Tote, they might have been by 1970 in as strong a position as the Melbourne Theatre Company. Instead, in 1965 he took over the infant Old Tote Theatre Company with Tom Brown, director of NIDA. The insecurity of that early period never left him.

Robin Lovejoy: The Right to Make a Mistake
Australian, 8 August 1970

All my life I have felt that the theatre in Australia has been incomplete—inheriting plays from abroad as we do. It is like finding oneself in France, hearing the conversation, understanding the words and yet quite unable to take part because the subject is strange and it's not one's own language. Any play, except an Australian play, has always seemed to be not a complete dialogue. That is what theatre means to me, finally—a dialogue between audience and actor, or audience and playwright.

Robin Lovejoy, for seven years now director of the Old Tote Theatre Company, and still in his 40s, is already an old man of the Australian theatre, so many are the changes that have taken place since his first national success with *The Rivals* in 1955. He has spent a good part of his life fighting against the odds for some kind of native growth in an environment that found foreign plants more exotic.

His career of necessity has reflected this. The stamp of the Lovejoy production has been for most people the period play, with an emphasis on form rather than content. It was something born of the post-war yearning for colour and elegance inherited from the British theatre in the 40s and 50s. This view of the theatre, which ended abruptly in Britain in 1956, had a profound effect upon the machinery that set up subsidised theatre in Australia. It caught up with Lovejoy, who had already made a reputation as a designer—an exception at the time in preferring not to work abroad—and a favoured contender for the title of Australia's premier theatre director.

In 1958 he formed the Trust Players, who were to be Australia's first national theatre company, with headquarters at the Elizabethan Theatre in Sydney. But three happy years ended suddenly when the Australian Elizabethan Theatre Trust decided that the time was premature for such a project.

In 1961 he went to America and Britain on a Harkness travelling fellowship. In Dallas, Texas, a handful of actors are still clinging to his production of *The School for Scandal* as if it had been an evangelical mission. The costumes and sets are still in use in 1970 and the production has been revived some five times in nine years, handed on by the stage manager and the actors from the original cast. But somehow there has not been the opportunity for him to return there. It has never been easy to leave one's stake in the theatre profession, even briefly, without risking what one has built.

Increasingly he feels the need to go abroad again. Characteristically he is more attracted by the idea of studying the new forms and old non-western traditions of drama with the idea of placing Australia in its Asian context, than with the immediate needs of providing a repertory theatre with a marketable product.

The past seven years have been hard ones, steering a way for his theatre and the allied National Institute of Dramatic Art through the political network of the University of New South Wales, the Elizabethan Theatre Trust, the Old Tote board and latterly the Australian Council for the Arts. From being a playhouse for NIDA students, the Old Tote has grown and swept Robin Lovejoy along with it, not planning the route but shooting the rapids and fending off the present dangers. 'I am not one of those who can see five years ahead. I am not concerned with the future. I am concerned with the immediate. That is why I am in the theatre.'

The immediate which gives him the greatest satisfaction is NIDA's *The Legend of King O'Malley*, which transfers from the Jane Street experiment to the Old Tote on 12 August. His job, and that of the subsidised theatre, was to be the originator and second-stage developer of projects like this. 'I want it to have a commercial life. I think it would kill us [the Tote] dead if we were to become entrepreneurs. I want to be the developer, to give house-room. Profit royalties are another matter—that is something we legitimately earn. The Tote is paying NIDA profit royalties for this season.'

With Alexander Hay he directed the first Jane Street season in 1966 and his production of Rodney Milgate's *A Refined Look at Existence* is particularly dear to him. 'I enjoyed it almost more than anything I have done in my life. The play as been produced seven times since then. Being published by Methuen was a great help.' Like so many theatre projects this was another beginning for Lovejoy of which the end was out of his hands.

> What has held us back has been the lack of a permanent group. In the first season we did firstly three one-acters and the plays stayed pretty well the way they were on paper. By the next play, *Lucky Streak*, the group had been together three weeks and the play took something from them. By the time we came to *Refined Look* something really began to happen: the play that finally went on the stage bore about 40 per cent relationship to the original script. The other 60 per cent was entirely new, worked out by the playwright and the actors on the spot. But come the end of the season we have no group—it's gone and Jane Street doesn't even have an identity: it becomes just a lecture house again.

In 1968 they began again with *Terror Australis*:

> But there is no opportunity under these conditions for the life that has been invested in it really to flower. It needs great patience from the subsidising bodies … You can't force trees to grow—you can only feed and manure them and give them sunlight. You can't predict which way a tree will grow and you can't predict how people will use an opportunity. NIDA has in *O'Malley* that rare thing, a play that belongs to a group— the team spirit is one of its most potent forces; and this is what we must nurture.

His greatest fear, he said, was being criticised for not having coerced somebody into doing something to produce a tangible result. 'The only freedom I want out of life is the freedom to make a courageous mistake.'

> The terrible post-mortem influence is so heavy on our society that we really don't allow one another to dare to do anything. Not only are we unable to say: 'I was wrong', but worse than that, we lack the courage to say: 'I went wrong but the original premise was right'. By failing to recognise what is good in a failed experiment we send ourselves back into Limbo to start all over again.
>
> What I fear most is boards of control that finally coerce one into doing nothing, rather than lose something … 90 per cent of boards finally have the effect of coercing inertia. It's the old parable of the talents—bury them and then expect to get a pat on the back. That's why it is that nervous breakdowns loom all around idiot creatures like

me who try to be artists and businessmen at the same time. It's possible to be a businesslike artist—a craftsman if you like. Further than this I don't aim. To be an artistic businessman, that's not a life I want to inhabit.

Because he has been one of the pioneers in the field, Robin Lovejoy has found the burdens of greatness thrust upon him before the powers. Last year the Australian Council chose the Tote as recipient of one of two major grants to theatres—without a company, a permanent theatre or a workshop and in the face of armed resistance from rival theatres. He goes along with this because it is his job to do so but is frightened of so much building when so little trouble has been taken with the foundations. How can we talk about a national theatre, he says, when we don't even understand the parish?

> Thinking parochially—this has become a terrifying term of abuse in Australia. I refuse to accept this and say: No, I'm talking about regionalism and I don't believe you can be international until you are national; or national until you're regional. And perhaps you can't be regional until you're parochial. These are necessary growth stages and you can't mount one before the other—a sense of local identity. A really identifiable local culture is almost impossible if communication is too fast or too easy. Human beings being what they are, they absorb like sponges everything presented to them as package deals.

Looking at the genre of Australian plays, he was delighted, he said, to be moving away from imitation. We are beginning to see what is our own and finally, I think it doesn't much matter that the audience isn't getting the full value out of an Australian script. If the play is good enough and has made its local statement well enough, it will be saleable elsewhere.

> I can see quite a strong influence from *Refined Look* to *O'Malley*, in terms of form and production methods. Michael Boddy was right in the middle of *Refined Look* (he played a policeman) and in fact invented some of it because we did it as a kind of cast exercise. I can see that there has been a harbinger here and there—and on it will go. This is to me so important—to think that there is a connecting influence, even though the milestones are a long way apart.

Rodney Milgate's comedy *A Refined Look at Existence*, based roughly on the myth of Dionysus, received a second production at the Old Tote in 1968. *Terror Australis* was a group-devised satirical revue directed by Jim Sharman and it attracted Patrick White's attention to Sharman's talent. A decade later Sharman directed a revival of *A Cheery Soul* at the Opera House Drama Theatre, which set White on a return path to the theatre.

Robin Lovejoy resigned in 1974, following the Tote's move into the Drama Theatre of the Opera House. He became a freelance director and, later, was head of design at NIDA. He died in 1985, aged 62.

Within a few months of this conversation the Old Tote and Jane Street found themselves displaced as sources of new theatre. Thenceforward the Tote put its energies into its role as a quasi-national drama company, with an eclectic repertoire and grand touring productions. These ambitions were exemplified by Sir Tyrone Guthrie's splendid production of *Oedipus* which showed a company fulfilling the demands of a city rich in theatre-going tradition, and reflected its heritage as the offspring of the Elizabethan Theatre Trust. But the newly-fired younger minds were running in a different direction. The curious opening to my *Oedipus* review can be explained by new tensions in an audience accustomed to empathising with the attempts made by their actors in cut-down locations. Admired as it was, Sir Tyrone Guthrie's *Oedipus*, and his production of *All's Well That Ends Well* for the Melbourne Theatre Company, had few imitators and little lasting influence. This was one of his last productions. He died shortly after returning to Ireland.

Guthrie's *Oedipus*: Shedding the Temporal

Australian, 29 August 1970

The entrance to the Sir John Clancy Auditorium at the University of NSW, Sydney, is very like that of a grandstand; and though the spectators' dress on opening night was different from that common in grandstands, the expectations were very much the same. A thousand people, passing the steeply raked stand to the roof, were there to see whether, under its new international coach, our Australian team would win.

The game was called *Oedipus the King*; and the opponent was the author, Sophocles, via his new adapter and translator, John Lewin. But it was very quickly apparent that the equipment we audience had brought to such an occasion was not simply inadequate but irrelevant; for we were present at quite a different mystery. Accustomed as we are to having our theatre in battles and games reflect the assaults and divisions of our modern life, we were unprepared for the healing and unifying process the director was preoccupied with unfolding.

The fan shape of the auditorium concentrates the spectators' attention very well from the upper rows upon the half-moon stage. This was pierced by a number of looming rock towers, rough-hewn and Oriental in reference. There is a rising sound of drums and cymbals and clouds of incense in burning dishes as the libation bearers process through the auditorium to hear the king's message to his people. Thebes is under a curse; its people and cattle are dying. Creon comes with a message from the Delphic Oracle that the city must seek out the murderer of the former king, Laius. And so Oedipus embarks on the process of detection in which the guilty man proves to be himself.

This is the sixth production of *Oedipus* by its director, Sir Tyrone Guthrie, in Finland, Israel, Canada and the United States. And naturally he has been asked many times why he has chosen to work on it again. 'Inevitably, when you have done a play as often as I have done this', he said on one occasion, 'you begin to—I won't say "think you know what it means" but "think you know what it means to you".' This is the challenge this 2,500-year-old play offers. It is about the pursuit of human identity and in particular the pursuit of one's own identity—and how you like the play depends on what it means to you.

To Sir Tyrone, I believe, it is about the Fall of Man as the birth of self-awareness, in which Oedipus plays Adam in the Garden of Eden. His chorus, hugely masked and stiffly-robed, are half domestic animals, half children, in the trust of the king, their father. The principals are giant statues of the gods, marked by age and compassion, and they move inside their huge theatrical armour not with a show of physical strength but with a gentle spiritual power. The performance, curiously, is almost entirely without aggression. Teiresias, the blind prophet, comes to the palace not as an Old Testament Jeremiah but as a white bird, a still small voice, revealing Oedipus not to other people but to himself. The old Shepherd is a frightened silly sheep placed gently in the hands of the Good Shepherd.

And most radical of all in this new adaptation is the end of the play, in which the author leads Oedipus into a New Testament of *Oedipus at Colonus*. Opening his eyes to the truth at last, the king blinds himself with the brooches from the body of the dead Jocasta. But here it is Jocasta whose suffering is physical; it is her cries which echo round the Theban Palace. Oedipus' blindness and exile are not self-imposed in anger or revenge at the gods' injustice, but accepted gladly by a king whose strength increases with the weight of the sins of the world; whose journey into darkness had begun long before and will go on and on and carry with it its own light. Sir Tyrone's production is a deliberate search after a spiritual truth, and in it he has shed the temporal as far as it can be shed. At the same time it cannot be other than a very personal statement.

The standard of performance and mounting is way in advance of the

Old Tote Company's work for some time; but so personal is it to Guthrie with its swooping circular movements, its clouds of crowds, its musical phrasing, its extravagant designing, that one forgets the other contributions. Yoshi Tosa's designs are brilliantly moving, capturing power without ostentation; Ron Haddrick is transformed not only physically but vocally; and there is a unified strength in the whole cast, including Ruth Cracknell as Jocasta, James Condon as Creon, Ronald Falk as Teiresias and Barry Lovett as the Shepherd.

One of the features of Guthrie's production was an invitation to other directors to observe rehearsals. Many declined, but Bryan Nason of the Grin and Tonic Theatre Troupe based in Brisbane was one who accepted.

The Bacchoi in Brisbane

Australian, 30 September 1970

There was certainly a great sense of occasion about the opening performance in the new Sir Fred Schonell Memorial Theatre, Brisbane, last Thursday. But the kind of acclaim was not quite clear. Up on stage, and later in the foyer, the hairy, bare-footed cast of the students' pop version of Euripides' *The Bacchae*—retitled *The Bacchoi*—had one viewpoint. But the black-tie and glitter representatives of town and gown, most of whom had spent $8 a ticket, were not at all sure to whom their goodwill should be directed. Outside a small representation of radicals was handing out leaflets condemning the motives of the building.

The Schonell Theatre, well-equipped, seating 400, and with a harmonious, steeply-raked raw-brick, cloistered auditorium, is the most comprehensive student theatre project yet achieved in Australia. Costing $800,000, it has been the work of the student union at Queensland University and has been admirably designed as part of a recreation centre in which leisure activities are combined with restaurant and shopping facilities, creating a village for the isolated campus at St Lucia.

But right from the start the theatre was guided by the community ambitions of others, led by Sir Fred Schonell, who wanted the university to have a building of more consequence than the shabby, out-of-the-way Avalon Theatre, hitherto provided. The opposition elements claim they are being deprived of the Avalon, which was cheap to rent and where they could paint the walls and do what they liked. They say the rent of the new theatre ($35 a night to students), plus other costs and restrictions, will defeat them. However, last week the students were determined to claim their performance as their own, and *The Bacchoi* achieved a spectacular success through the shining evangelical fervour of the cast.

The adaptation has been made by Bryan Nason, who directed it with the dancer Keith Bain; and the music, which is the evening's chief pleasure, is by Ralph Tyrell, a composer of originality and distinction. It is probably disparaging to say that *Bacchoi* is a mixture of *Hair* and *Easy Rider* with overtones of the Guthrie *Oedipus* (at which Nason was an observer). It is a multi-media production of an ambitious technical complexity and the high standard of the performance in a new and barely finished theatre deserves admiration.

The performance is undeniably compelling, though more to the eye and the ear than to the mind. What is derivative in style reflects an unnecessary searching for support by Nason, and I found the original contributions to the text more attractive than the rather summary references to Euripides' text. Euripides' theme is the conflict between the intellect (Pentheus) and the passions (Dionysus, his half-brother); and this love-generation has adopted it as a popular theatrical ritual. The American Richard Schechner made his a force for sexual liberation in his nude *Dionysus 68;* the National Theatre of Britain did a man-eating, all-woman version called *Rites*, set in a women's lavatory; Ross Thompson—Dionysus in *Bacchoi*—has already played the role as a pop singer in Rodney Milgate's plea for freedom of self-expression, *A Refined Look at Existence.*

The Nason version is much more consciously innocent than any of these, and has adopted the love-and-sacrifice themes of *Hair* in the same terms of undress. There is no sense of violence and blood sacrifice, or even evil in the ritual murder of Pentheus by his mother, Agave, and the Bacchae, the followers of the god. The innocence is pursued even into the lament of Agave, splendidly played by Val South and accompanied by compelling slow-motion visuals of Agave's approaching figure. This is a memorable scene and the music and the cast make up for much that is missing in the text. The production deserves to be given growing room.

The Bacchoi will be followed in November by the Sydney production of *The Legend of King O'Malley*, now on a national tour. November, however, will also see the opening of the long-awaited Twelfth Night Theatre, situated closer to the city centre and with roughly the same facilities.

Sir Fred Schonell (1900–69) was Vice-Chancellor of the University of Queensland 1960–69. Of the productions mentioned, Schechner's at Harvard University and the National Theatre's in London were both from 1968 while Milgate's version was first produced by the Old Tote at Jane Street in 1966 and revived at the Parade in 1968.

The Bacchoi did receive growing room in June 1974 when the Nimrod directors in Sydney chose it to open their new premises at Belvoir Street, Surry Hills. But revisions to the text did not help. The problems inevitable in moving Nimrod from a tiny makeshift building to one with different demands told on the performance. I commented on a confusion of intention which conveyed itself from cast to audience; and the performers were not helped by elaborate architectural costumes that encumbered their movements. I voted it a disappointing evening.

Meanwhile in Melbourne the infant Australian Performing Group was moving from La Mama to its own space.

APG: Great New Start for Drama Group

Australian, 16 December 1970

Melbourne's Australian Performing Group has opened the doors on its new premises, called the Pram Factory, at 325 Drummond Street, Carlton. The opening production is a workshop performance of *Marvellous Melbourne*, a musical collage of Melbourne in the 1890s which has been collated by the company since it went into retreat last July assisted by a $2,000 grant from the Australian Council for the Arts.

No one quite knew what would happen when the group took time off from its Café La Mama performances, its street theatre and factory productions for the Australian Workers' Union. Under the guidance of its theatre historian, Margaret Williams, a PhD student at Monash University, members of the group have gone back to the origins of theatre in Victoria.

Marvellous Melbourne is based on a melodrama of the 1890s about the city scene and a royal visit. The group has used the play as the basis for improvisations on such aspects of city life as land-grabbing, police corruption, censorship, politicking, civic pride, union strikes and the imposition of English culture upon a rich but uneducated community.

The leading character is Sir Wallace Pork, the Chief Secretary (Bill Garner). Other vivid characters include Madame Suspendu (a brilliantly funny performance by Evelyn Krape), who runs a brothel for the city fathers at the top of Little Lon; the Duke and Duchess of York, the Mayor, a

Scottish puritan; the actor Alfred Dampier and two members of the Drury Lane Shakespeare Company; and a crowd of workers, starving unemployed and visitors to the Great Exhibition of 1888.

Because of a last-minute postponement of the first full performance, what I saw may have been altered since. But even in its rough state this show was obviously the beginning of something excitingly original, pungent and unmistakably Melbourne. Of the original script, many characters but only two scenes remain. The rest has been written by the APG and Jack Hibberd, with the help of their research into the public speeches, newspapers and cartoons of the time. The result is vividly evocative of the decade before Federation, but directed satirically at 1971.

The chief asset of the production, directed by Graeme Blundell, is the company. Technically they are amateurs: some are drama students and tutors from the Secondary Teachers College creative arts course; others are university students and staff, office workers etc. Most are waiting for the moment when they can give up their outside work and concentrate on the APG workshop. Until now the APG has not had a high technical standard. Its worth has been in its energy and support of its writers. Now with new two-storey premises, rough but extravagantly spacious, the group has released a fund of skills of a high order, in a fantasy of disciplined exuberance.

A large part of the wit comes from the jeans and sneakers of the cast, who play parliamentarians and strikers with only the aid of a hat. Their use of body and voice is excellently clever and I have a lasting memory of Miss Krape, teetering in high-heeled sandals, jeans, T-shirt, granny glasses and Afro-hair, quivering two pink ostrich feathers at the overweight Chief Secretary as she coaxes him in a mid-European Jewish accent.

Marvellous Melbourne is playing a brief workshop season before Christmas and will open in a more elaborate production at the end of January. I think it is going to be great.

The original *Marvellous Melbourne*, a five-act melodrama by Alfred Dampier and J. H. Wrangham, dated from 1889. As it turned out, I was disappointed in the finished production. It seemed to have added little and lacked the improvisatory energy of the try-out. Nevertheless the new space became, for a few years, the most fertile ground for new-style actors, writers and stage theory in the country. For a decade new venues like La Mama and the Pram Factory, Anthill and the Church in Melbourne, the two Nimrods, PACT, the Performance Space, and the Paris Theatre in Sydney, La Boite in Brisbane, Troupe's Red Shed in Adelaide, the

Hole in the Wall and the New Fortune in Perth, provided flexible breathing space for the imagination of our burgeoning writers.

Today only a few remain. Imagination, for the most part, is dictated by the new concrete palaces, and the programs such stages demand.

Like the Pram Factory, the Nimrod Theatre sprang up in promising soil and provided a home for what was to become the New Wave. My description here of a handsome theatre with a spacious foyer is coloured by my anticipation of events; early Nimrod was makeshift, offering hard benches, discomforting heat in summer and often barely-written, under-rehearsed performances. It was Leo Schofield, I think, who described the audience as battery hens. We, the audience, however, were not disappointed. We knew we were part of something. Later, backs were added to the benches and still later, when the Seaborn Broughton and Walford Foundation bought the building, the roof was raised, air-conditioning added and the pillar at the entrance to the triangular stage, an obstacle for actors and audience to negotiate, was removed. The building is now the SBW Stables, home of the Griffin Theatre. Though Nimrod is remembered as a pioneer of playwriting, and quickly became so following the success of *Biggles*, the repertoire proposed here is little different from the mainstream and the company returned to it towards the end of its life.

The Invincibility of Major Biggles

Australian, 12 December 1970

Sydney theatres are just now going through one of the worst periods probably since the war. All but a handful have burnt down, been pulled down, are being threatened with demolition or are facing bankruptcy or insubstantial promises of resurrection. But when the burdens seem the heaviest someone usually gets out from under and comes up smiling. In this case a new theatre has opened in Kings Cross which promises to update the face of Sydney theatre twenty years.

It is the Nimrod Theatre Club, a handsome, hundred-year-old former stables, which last week opened its doors with its *Biggles Show*. In its time it has been a gymnasium and the home of a cab company, both motorised and horse-drawn. It has been converted to contain a spacious foyer downstairs, to be used for exhibitions and other events, and an open space upstairs with tiered bench seating for 140. The Watters Gallery will hang a show of paintings downstairs which will change at each season.

The directors, John Bell and Ken Horler, have no shortage of ideas and hope in time to create a home style of a non-literary kind and to make

Clockwise from bottom left: Jacki Garland, Lance Tomlinson, Ken Horler, Ron Blair, Richard Wherrett, and Lilian Horler take a break at the Kings Cross Theatre. (Photo: Anthony Horler, from the Nimrod Theatre Collection, State Library of New South Wales)

their productions work in terms of their community and their public. Their immediate plans include a production of Beckett's *Endgame* upstairs and a baroque musical about Sir Robert Menzies; a reworking by John Bell of Shakespeare's *Henry IV Parts I and II;* and of George Farquhar's *The Recruiting Officer*, the first play known to have been presented in Sydney.

'Jim Sharman wants to do an environmental thing—50s milk bars and motor bikes up and down the streets. And there are openings for us to tour,' said Ken Horler. 'But this all depends on a permanent company of actors and at present we can only afford to hire actors from play to play.'

The Nimrod project has been a coincidence of Mr Horler's desire to set up a theatre for local writers and the experience of the team that created *The Legend of King O'Malley*. Chief writer at this stage is Michael Boddy, co-author of *O'Malley* (which was directed by Bell) and he and his partner Robert Ellis are the main contributors (with the actors) to *Biggles*. Mr Boddy also adds his own considerable weight to the cast as the multifarious villain against whom the legendary hero pits himself.

There is no point comparing *Biggles* with *O'Malley*. It is a much lighter, slighter show which sits very nicely in the temporary-looking space which the Nimrod provides. Major Biggles, for those who were not brought up on *Boys' Own* papers of the 1930s and 40s, was the intrepid British pilot invented by Captain W. E. Johns; as much a model of sublimated schoolboy fantasies as James Bond was of libidinous ones. In the Nimrod show Biggles' training in how to deal with the school bully sets the pattern for a lifetime of invincibility, accompanied by the never-failing loyalty of his chums Lord Bertie and Ginger. The trio is engagingly played by John Hargreaves, Peter Rowley and Drew Forsythe. The two versatile women are Jane Harders and Anna Volska.

The second half contains a splendid pastiche by Mr Boddy of an RSL club show to which the Biggles team—now an unchangingly youthful 65—have been invited as guest entertainers. It is a double satire against both the idea of personal invincibility today and the poverty of thought and taste which the club compere represents—and yet describing it like that makes it sound more serious than it is. It is a lampoon (and as such sometimes accurate, sometimes not-so-accurate) of those desiccated remnants of the 1940s which still hold sway in Australia, and an affectionate note of regret at the passing of a time when decisions and loyalties were clear-cut.

The Nimrod Theatre, 10 Nimrod Street, Kings Cross, is worth visiting, just because it is fun.

Endgame was produced at the St James Theatre when, after the opening season, Nimrod was abruptly closed as a fire risk. This no doubt also put paid to Sharman's 'environmental thing'. The Menzies musical and *The Recruiting Officer* never eventuated but the small theatre held productions of both *Macbeth* and *Hamlet*.

The conflated *Henry IV* had to wait until 1978 by which time the theatre had moved to a bigger venue in Surry Hills (now Belvoir St Theatre).

In Perth, the New Fortune Theatre was the inspiration that brought the poet Dorothy Hewett back to the theatre. A platform, configured in the dimensions of the Fortune Theatre of Shakespeare's day, had been built into a quadrangle within a university faculty building. Hewett's early play, *This Old Man Comes Rolling Home*, had made its debut there in 1966. This time around, the play's author and its heroine, both of whom subsequently became icons for young women in their struggle for self-expression, faced trouble before opening night. The play was publicly accused of immorality; and, because a journalist on the local newspaper was found to have the same name as her heroine, Hewett was forced to change Sally Thunder to Sally Banner.

The Chapel Perilous: Playwright's Perilous Journey

Australian, 27 January 1971

Zoe Caldwell once observed that the most essential aspect of theatre was a sense of danger shared by the actors with the audience. And more than one outsider has said of the Australian theatre that it would not come alive until our playwrights have something compulsive to say in dramatic language. Such a playwright is Dorothy Hewett, whose new play *The Chapel Perilous* set Perth by the ears when it opened at the New Fortune Theatre last weekend.

Miss Hewett is a poet whose compulsion to write plays about life as she knows it denies all caution, circumspection or nice arrangement of the mind. *The Chapel Perilous* is a play of vivid poetic imagination and awesome emotional memory; and the audacity of some of its ingredients left her audience gasping with laughter. For *The Chapel Perilous* is about Perth as so many in that audience remember it, from the 1930s to the 1970s.

It is about the education of Sally, a poet with an appetite for life which is given direction neither by her parents, her teachers, her lovers nor the causes with which she passionately aligns herself.

Poor Sally,
She never made it,
No matter how hard she tried.
She tried hard not to know it,
But she was a minor poet,
Until the day she died.

The title is taken from the journey of Sir Lancelot in Malory's *Morte d'Arthur* in which the knight endures a test of real and imagined dangers to claim a sword to arm him for his pilgrimages. Sally's chapel in literal terms is that of the school where she receives an education which offers no defence against life. As her teacher says in despair: 'I really cannot bear this much individuality'.

She becomes a precocious romantic poet, flings herself all the wrong ways into sex, attempts suicide, marries for the wrong reasons, joins the Communist Party and is expelled, goes through abortion and the birth and death of a child. Her actions are accompanied always by a chorus of derisive onlookers to whom Sally's capacity for living is incomprehensible—just as Sir Lancelot had 30 knights who 'grinned and gnashed at him', but proved powerless.

Sally's pilgrimage is towards a world in which life is comprehensible. Like so many of us Australians she is unable to embrace with realism her internal self, or to answer the repeated question: 'Who am I?'. So instead she does good works, gives a stained glass window to her school, is awarded an OBE, leaves her city in its state of self-mystification and is received into her chapel perilous.

It is a painful but not a sad journey because it is entertained with an outrageous, bawdy, embracing wit. There are musical and choreographic jokes as well as verbal ones; the chorus are consecutively schoolgirls, students, showground characters, unionists and jurors. Historical facts like the war and the Petrov Commission and rituals like the church litany are used to make judgments of Sally. Familiar objects like school hymns, quotations from the *Oxford Book of Modern Verse*, songs of the 40s, a housewives' radio program, are the witnesses of Sally's life. The play is as disorganised as Sally and it has the life and immediacy of the author's compulsion.

Aarne Neeme's production, driven by his entry into national service two days after the opening, has the same compulsion; and, blown up splendidly into the arena of the New Fortune, it reveals in Sally an imagination of Elizabethan proportions. Helen Neeme plays Sally with that painful innocence which makes her a very distinctive actress, and she delivers Miss Hewett's poetry exquisitely, with a kind of awe. The rest of the vast cast, led by Margaret Ford and Cliff Holden, Victor Marsh, Colin Nugent and Brian Blain, gave support in accord with their experience, as did the student chorus.

There are weaknesses in the second half, and much good in both halves

The New Fortune Theatre production of *The Chapel Perilous*, 1971.

which the weaker cast members were unable to clarify. But even in this early stage there is no doubt that Sally Banner (or Sally Thunder as she was called until two weeks ago when the Thunder family of Wembley threatened an injunction) is a memorable expression of the Australian's blind struggle towards emotional maturity. It places Miss Hewett with this, her third play, at the forefront of Australian playwriting.

Aarne Neeme's birth date had come up in the Vietnam War conscription lottery barrel. Two days after the play's opening, he reported for duty but soon found he could not deny his conscientious objections. He refused orders, was charged and finally released after being successfully defended by Ken Horler, barrister and co-founder of the Nimrod Theatre. At the time of his call-up Neeme was director of a promising company at the Octagon Theatre in Perth, which foundered on his departure.

Four years later Dorothy Hewett's former husband sued her, and her publisher Currency Press, for malicious libel in the portrayal of Tom, Sally's husband, with whom he identified certain incidents. The matter was settled out of court, one condition being that *The Chapel Perilous* be prevented from performance, or sale in book form, in Western Australia during his lifetime. The ban lasted until his death in 2004. Hewett died in 2002.

This was an expansionary period that encouraged many experiments, some successful, others ill-advised. My somewhat carping review below reveals the tension between the eagerness for revolution and a limited understanding of its complexities. In time such experiments played their part in the making of a new Australian theatre. Albert Barunga (c.1912–1977) was a traditional elder from the Prince Regent River, Kimberley, and an advocate for Aboriginal culture. He was a regional chair of the Aboriginal Theatre Foundation and an inaugural member of the Aboriginal Cultural Foundation and the Australia Council. His life has been celebrated in works by Jack Davis and Mary Durack.

Tribal Language, Vacant Gestures

Australian, 30 January 1971

Today we have two forests, one old, one ancient; one alien, one familiar. The first is a fashionable *fin-de-siècle* Forest of Arden in coloured leadlights where the Parade Theatre's youthquake is making its first rumbles in Sydney. The second is the bush setting of the Seddon Vincent Memorial Theatre at Parkerville, WA, which was opened last week with a performance of tribal dances from the north-west Kimberleys. The latter first.

The audience was quick to realise the service the theatre's owner, Mr John Joseph Jones, had done in providing a sympathetic surrounding with perfect acoustics for such an experiment. The dancers come chiefly from the Mowanjum Presbyterian mission at Derby, where for the past three years, with the help of Mrs Mary Selamark, the wife of an airline pilot, the elders have been reviving their dances and creating new ones. Last year the group received assistance from the Aboriginal Theatre Foundation and this performance has been backed with $7,000 from the Australian Council for the Arts.

There is a long way yet to go in finding a method of presentation and audience understanding before the dancers' and singers' art can communicate. But the scent of the gums and the creek, the noise of the frogs and the smoke of the campfires that pervaded the background did much to alleviate the sponsors' attempts at dramatic lighting and dramatic structure. These dances are not dramatic in that they are created for the pleasure of the participants and their initiates, not for the outsider; and the audience was aware of the intrusions made on the tribal traditions by attempts to attract the European eye. But it was the theatre itself that took charge, giving the boiling sound of the didgeridoo the sense of belonging, and the dancers a sense of not being strangers in their own country but hosts on their own ground.

This is a first step and it showed the way the work must go and how long the journey will be. The problem was admirably illustrated by Albert Barunga, the company's leader. After the Western Australian Minister for Education and Aboriginal Affairs, Mr Lewis, had opened his speech by saying that he had not actually done his homework so he would not say much, had repeated a joke about the 'fancy dress', painted a picture of Albert as a constant adviser, mentor and friend in his difficult task of communication (and then failing to recognise him under his ochre), Mr Barunga replied with great eloquence in his limited English, describing how he and his people were like the frogs in the pond: the earth was their life source and they must constantly dive back into it to support their life.

This at least they were able to convey to their audience without the aid of words. And this is the substance which in most circumstances is hidden from the white Australian. Tenuous as this relationship yet is, it is nothing like the yawning gap that lies between our theatre directors and the library of experience in their professional heritage.

As You Like It, as directed by Jim Sharman, would appear to a stranger to be a slight script with two good speeches in it, one about a motley fool and another about the seven ages of man, neither of which has anything much to do with the rest of the action. To overcome the slightness of the script and the actors' lack of comprehension, they have toys to handle, perhaps to keep our minds occupied. Tim Elliott's melancholy Jaques in the centre of these mumblings is more intensely alone than ever. He makes us listen as no one else on stage does and when we listen we catch a glimpse of a world behind the lines which makes our loss of it the keener. The worst aspect of the damage to Shakespeare's play is that the director does not seem to know what he has discarded.

First it is a play about game-playing. He takes this literally and yet fails to use his balloons and roller skates to elucidate the characters in any way. But the games of Rosalind and Orlando, Touchstone and Audrey, and the exiled Duke Senior playing at pastoral life in Arcadia, are there for a purpose. Through play and disguises, trial and error, the characters in Shakespeare's comedies arrive at an understanding of the way to live their lives, and with this a cloak of realism descends—light in the case of this play but disturbing nevertheless.

Second, the director and his designer Brian Thomson see Arden as a colouring book country of the mind where it is always summer. And very charming the designs are. But *King Lear* is to be Mr Sharman's next production and he must therefore know that the same wind that blows Lear's outlaws from an alien world blows through the Forest of Arden.

> Blow, blow, thou winter wind,
> Thou art not so unkind
> As man's ingratitude

To create a new state of mind out of an old play is a valuable thing to do, even an essential, but it must bear some relation to what the author has written. The strangers in Arden are there to find themselves and they do so in their own ways: Duke Senior through patience, Jaques through philosophy; Rosalind through role-playing (and Lear through humiliation). Mr Sharman's people remain in their slough of ignorance, discarding the warnings of Jaques, Touchstone, Corin and even Rosalind herself. They are as boring as ignorant people always are.

There are some things to be recommended, though, mostly visual and musical. The bad duke as a cigar-smoking powerbroker (but where was the fear such a man would create?). The silhouette of Jaques in bowler hat and moth-eaten umbrella walking a tightrope; the flurry of green silk over the audience's heads as the scene changes (Wizard of Oz–like) from the grey and white court to the painted Arden. The singing and dancing of the mod-magic masque of Hymen succeeded where many better productions have failed; as did the use of songs and Sandra McKenzie's electric music. These are the best things. With the yokels Mr Sharman shows familiarity and assurance. With the court, the good duke and the complex repartee he is at a loss. Against Mr Elliott, Darlene Johnson's

Rosalind is vulgar; Ken Shorter's Orlando is caddish, groaning at his lines as though they were as bad as Orlando's own verse. Touchstone, the wise fool, Peter Rowley delivers with a flippancy that makes him neither a good wise man nor a good fool. And few of the others made any meaning at all.

There were exceptions: Terry Bader and Diane Craig as Silvius and Phoebe drew their wit through the script as it should come. James Bowles offers a graceful Corin, which would be memorable if he could persuade the director to give away that ridiculous kangaroo hop and the toy traffic signs. Helen Morse as Celia makes better use of the verse than most and Garry McDonald's old servant Adam was second only to Mr Elliott in precision. But the whole is a motley thing and too often the director covers his shame like Autolychus, snapping up garments where he needs spirit, flesh and understanding. There is nothing wrong in adapting the ideas of his betters to his purpose: they come from a good school. But their substance, like that of the tribal dancers, lies not in the vacant outward gesture but in the fund of hard-learnt comprehension out of which the gesture springs.

Autolychus is the engaging petty thief in *The Winter's Tale*.

A month later, I took a second look at *As You Like It*. In this season, perhaps as a result of the apathetic public response to the elevated Guthrie *Oedipus*, the Old Tote joined the caravan moving towards a native theatre style. This article also introduces Richard Wherrett, who had returned from working in the United Kingdom and become, uneasily, associate director of the Tote. The following year he found his feet at Nimrod.

A Reign of Terror at the Parade

Australian, 3 March 1971

A palace revolution is underway inside the Old Tote Theatre Company, Sydney, and the time for it is long overdue. For years the Tote has been dabbling with one idea after another and underneath each has been the nervous feeling that youth, with all that energy—if one could only understand it—could discover the secret alchemy of success.

This year they have gone in boots and all with a young athletic company, first with a love-in (*As You Like It*) and now with a contemporary Chelsea-gear version of George Etheredge's Restoration masterpiece *The Man of Mode*. Revolutions are messy things and neither of these productions has made a coup. As yet it is more like a reign of terror.

Both these productions I frankly disliked, because they have taken great minds and turned them into trivial ones. But I like what they are trying to do almost better than anything I have seen at the Parade Theatre, and I am happy to endure the demolition and wait while they make ground and decide how to build afresh.

I went a second time to Jim Sharman's production of *As You Like It*, which despite critics like myself had a very successful season. And once I overcame familiarity with the play and the fact that almost no one on stage understood what they were saying, the production had a great conviction and certainly a great life of its own. It was a collage of part of the play, translated into sound and action, rather than the play itself. Had it been called *As I Like It*, I would have been well content.

The same problem arises with Richard Wherrett's production of *The Man of Mode*. The common verdict of the audience on opening night was 'a fine production of a trivial play'. The play is a rarity and from this production there is no reason to suspect otherwise. What point is there in my protesting that *The Man of Mode* is the most serious, bitter and complex dramatic character study in the Restoration theatre? What does the man who pays to be entertained care about the life of another country and another century? Both these productions have achieved a rhythm which is familiar to the audience, and this is a beginning of something our own— the end of which is much more important than acquiring a foreign acting skill. Shakespeare and Etheredge have survived worse indignities and worse directors. And they don't need to have their reputations defended.

The Man of Mode is an account of a long exhausting day in the life of a Restoration rake—Dorimant, allegedly the Earl of Rochester—a ruthless, heartless man of fashion with several concurrent mistresses. He humiliates one in public, bribes another to betray the first while at the same time wooing a third for her money. It is also about Sir Fopling Flutter, a would-be member of the in-set who is a butt of society because his income is not enough to buy him style.

This is a play about games, as *As You Like It* is; but in the latter the people make their own rules in order to discover themselves. Etheredge's characters play by their society's official rule book in order to hide and preserve their private selves. It is a game of survival and Dorimant is the master manipulator. He wins the women by the rules and discards them by the rules; and when the passionate Mrs Lovett makes the unforgivable error of breaking them with a show of true feeling, both he and the apparently pure-minded Harriet, whom Dorimant marries, demolish her with venom.

The amiable Ken Shorter, who wears his heart on his sleeve, is in every way the wrong actor for Dorimant. His face betrays Dorimant's every feeling. Where Etheredge's rake is stimulated by danger, Shorter is embarrassed by it. And at no point is he able to surmount the extravagance of his outfitters—as John Hargreaves, for example, does. Hargreaves, as Medley, Dorimant's confidant, has gone to some trouble to learn the rhythm of his lines. He speaks like a man of fashion and he walks like one—and this would have been so whatever he had been wearing.

Helen Morse's Harriet has been built to match Shorter. She is an engaging lady who makes her intentions clear; but she has little of the hard core of realism the role needs. Anne Haddy's formidable Mrs Lovett penetrates nearer the guts of the matter in her scenes with Dorimant than in any other part of the play. Garry McDonald plays Sir Fopling Flutter also with notable effect. The director's most witty and pointed contribution to the play is Sir Fopling's masquerade in which the company appears in Caroline–Restoration costume and makes a formal curtsy.

Richard Wherrett is right in many ways in attempting to show the parallels between the two insecure, permissive societies of the 1670s and the 1970s. It is true that they are periods of the peacock male and beautiful people still hide their faces behind their faces. And it is true that *The Man of Mode* is a play about style. But style is formal and the play is about a style of living on the knife-edge. A nearer parallel today than Wherrett's engaging in-group is probably the world of the power-game. But whatever the solution, Wherrett's people do not quite add up. They have no shape and no depth. They have lost their sense of locality and there are too many references, some up-dated, which jar on the mind, too many unexplained servants and too much unexplained idle time. And is not a play without a locality as trivial and remote as this play's origin? But that is a long way from its director's intention. Still, what we have is a beginning, a tiny beginning with the outer garments. Someday they will find a way of reaching the spirit. The Tote management must stick to its guns.

The very fact that I so overtly seek value in the demolition of two of my favourite plays is evidence of the sense of much to be gained, which at the time was almost evangelical. (I had, after all, been educated in the view that the British and European canon was a gift to be revered.)

I continued to rejoice at the growing confidence with which the new-wave theatre learned to interpret the classics. But it still causes anguish today—perhaps even more so—when a director, in pursuit of a personal 'vision', ignores or discards without reference the theatre history and social history that went into the making of that work. So often the mind of the author is more interesting than that of the interpreter.

Adelaide Company Shows its Strength

Australian, 17 March 1971

It is some months since I have seen the work of the South Australian Theatre Company and in that time a marked change has overtaken it. As a company the SATC has had a shaky history. It has never had a home of its own, nor has it ever been able to keep its actors in work for more than a few months at a run.

The people of Adelaide have never cared much because it has been a gypsy group, gathering its bread where it can and living on promises of a government-subsidised home. But the honour it has not gathered in its own state has fallen due to it on tour. Last month it took Peter Batey's production of *The Boors*, by the eighteenth century popular Venetian playwright Goldoni, to the Festival of Perth. Last week this production, and another of Ibsen's *The Master Builder*, drew the praise they deserved from audiences at the Playhouse in Canberra.

The sense of purpose necessary to the success of a play is often welded into a company by the condition imposed by a tour. But whatever the reason, these are two of the most mature productions I have seen from this group. Peter Batey is happy in his choice of Michael Meyer's translation of *The Master Builder*. It has a modern flow which reveals the many contemporary qualities in the play without too obtrusively taking it out of its context. Batey's production has followed this lead. The characters move easily in their nineteenth-century clothes without their distancing them from the central argument: the attraction between age and youth and the shaky line which divides reason from insanity.

The elements of Ibsen's whole philosophy are set out in *The Master Builder*. All his perjured, half-blind heroes are in Halvard Solness, the master who has lost his confidence and has begun to live parasitically upon the younger talent in his power. Both the wild duck and the unheeding Hedda Gabler are in the romantic–destructive young Hilde Wangel who comes to him out of the mountains to claim the castle he once promised her when she was a child. There is all the oppression of Ibsen's married women in Aline Solness, whose Protestant belief in duty and responsibility has stifled her life.

The play opens when Solness' life is breaking up. One valuable assistant is dying. His draughtsman is beginning to realise why he is being kept in subordination. Solness has made this assistant's fiancée fall in love with him in order to keep them both at his beck and call. His marriage has turned sterile after his baby sons died of pneumonia. His wife has chosen to suffer a lifelong penance for a supposed failing in her duty.

Into this, like Oswald and Regina in *Ghosts*, Hilde rushes, full of life, and becomes the lost life and the lost child of them both. She talks Solness into believing the strength of his youth can be restored, persuades him to climb the scaffolding of his tower and talk to God. And, of course, he falls to his death. Madness, destructive and divine, is equally present in all three characters, and this is admirably conveyed by Edwin Hodgemen as Solness, Daphne Grey as his wife and Roslyn de Winter as Hilde.

These three do equally well in quite different roles in *The Boors*, which is notable for an exceptional elegance that flows through the movement, the gracious expression of the lines, the comic timing and the excellent setting and costumes by Jennifer Carseldine.

Again Peter Batey has miraculously been able to convey the style of eighteenth-century Venetian comedy without at any point subordinating the characters to it. While the audiences took great delight in the skill of his figure-of-eight exits which wrapped and tied each part of the action so charmingly, it never detracted from their absorbed interest in the characters. These too, while being stock types from a long tradition, still retained their rounded human qualities to a compelling degree. This was by no means a cartoon production, despite the commedia dell'arte style of which it is a flowering. It is the realism underneath the flounces which is the strength of the performance.

Leonardo (Edwin Hodgeman) is a crusty old merchant with a bored second wife (Daphne Grey) and a pretty daughter (Julie Hamilton) whom he has betrothed to Filipetto (Peter Charlton) the son of an old friend. Out of pure contrariness he refuses to allow the young couple to meet before the marriage and so a plot is devised by a trio of dissatisfied wives to smuggle the boy into the house. The wives get their way in the end, the old boors agree to allow their wives more freedom to amuse themselves, and the young couple is well satisfied with the match.

There is nothing original in this, though there is much wit to be made of the lines and much credit is due to the director and his cast for one of the happiest evenings the theatre has offered for a long time.

Not Wrong—Just Different

Australian, 20 March 1971

There are plenty of things wrong with this country and we take a masochistic delight in inviting distinguished foreigners and expatriate countrymen to expound them. We have always felt that outsiders know best because our standards have come from outside. For so long we have conformed first to British and then to American standards that it is from their distance that we call ourselves wrong.

But there is much left, thank heaven, in Australia that is neither British nor American. Let us call it—not wrong, just different.

What has been stifling the Australian theatre is exactly this desire to conform to foreign standards. This reforming zeal which took over the Australian spirit in the 1930s is historically probably the most damaging single element in the Australian theatre. While it kept the theatre alive during wars and depressions when commercial ventures faltered, it drew it so far from the necessities of Australian life towards a belief that the world's good theatre was medicine for an ailing society, that those who felt themselves not in the least ailing fled as far as possible from the bitter dose.

Because it is an expression of the moment, the theatre has always been a useful barometer of what people really think of themselves. And the Australian theatre reflects on quite a subtle level the world about us—the quality of our education system, our paradoxical contempt for authority and politics, our over-governed society, our preoccupation with sport, our distaste for the public expression of ambition or emotion.

For a long time the theatre has been an expression of how we would like to be; or of how those embarrassed about being Australian would like us to be. And so it has not been a popular theatre. Classical and foreign plays were—and many still are—interpreted not with personal enthusiasm but as an approximation of productions abroad. Local writing in the 1940s, 50s and 60s, except for the popular successes like *Rusty Bugles* and *Summer of the Seventeenth Doll,* tended to take a didactic line; to teach the audience acceptable attitudes rather than commit themselves to a personal view. An example of this was Alan Hopgood's *Private Yuk Objects* (1966) which effectively presented the prevailing attitudes to the Vietnam War without committing the author.

The Australian theatre has been guilty of much deception, partly by wishing our country could grow up faster than it has and partly through a lack of courage to back one's own judgment and one's own taste. But behind the apparent inefficiency the indigenous theatre is extremely vigorous. I would go so far as to say that the next five years will see a burgeoning of talent such as we have not seen since the last century. It has been among us for some time and gone unrecognised.

The theatre of colonial Australia began with the First Fleet and has been lively from the very beginning. Theatres came and went, fortunes were won and lost at the same rate as they were in the goldfields. And at the same rate they are gambled on the stock exchange today. The men who ran our theatre were as ratbag a mob as any of our heroes have been. They presented their own rewrites of plays they remembered from London, they presented new shows from abroad with surprising swiftness, they did classics with a burlesque afterpiece to make sure the audience would come. They did opera on a rumbustious scale, variety and vaudeville. All this was dictated by the taste of the roving actor manager and his audience. The critics sighed and swore and doused them with invective. But the men in the cabbage-tree hats paid their money and were content. When they were not their discontent was heard loud from the gallery.

In the latter part of the century the gold strikes brought a sudden affluence to Australia and with it a surging nationalistic pride. And the theatre shared largely in this affluence. But with money there was no equal burgeoning of sophistication either in the actors or the audience. It was a working man's taste into which no abstract standards from abroad intruded. This was a much more united audience than we have had since, despite the class distinctions that existed and the authoritarianism. And we still are—and this is only beginning to be recognised and even acclaimed by the average Australian—the inheritors of that essentially vulgar and working-class society, founded by a population of convicts and work-evaders, militarists and opportunists, with the vitality, impudence, disorderliness and ignorance that goes with these things.

This era ended with World War I and this first encounter with the centres of civilisation left us for the first time self-conscious of our roots, of our uncouth appearance at the international conference table. Our standards had been shaken and the following half-century expressed our defensiveness in fierce jingoism and a conscious yearning for a myth—Gallipoli, the great primary industry, 'Land of Hope and Glory', 'Clancy of the Overflow'. And yet our education in its entirety, was directed towards the centre of knowledge and taste in which we really believed—that rash of red on the world map, the British Empire.

The theatre reflected all this. Wars and depressions battered and divided the business; the strong tradition of vaudeville went into the Tivoli Circuit. The opera went to J. C. Williamson's operettas and the luminous career of Gladys Moncrieff. These popular forms hung on to the mainstream of the public and our folklore was adopted by our new film industry and radio comedies.

But a new influence began to grow with a power quite out of proportion to its capacities: that of the amateur theatre. Amateur theatres in all states kept the legitimate theatre alive for 40 years. These people had quite a different purpose and a different taste from that of the old actor-managers. Largely white-collar workers, some with standards brought home from abroad, they aimed at putting the theatre on a more elevated level; to study the classics and to introduce the lasting values of dramatic tradition to an audience as yet unaware. This desire to improve has been inherited by the majority of our professional theatres and has dominated our attitude to government subsidy. But its legacy is an unease of mind both in the writers and their audience and in the directors and their actors who wish to please their public but no longer know who their public is.

What I find so interesting, now that we are entering the 1970s, is that discussion of what our environment means is taking a new and more realistic look into our beginnings as a nation. Parallel with this, in its more outrageous aspects, the theatre is beginning, just beginning, to take a realistic look at what we are; and audiences are responding in recognition of that view.

Our playwrights have begun to look back at the days when our theatre was popular. They have found, not surprisingly, that it was most popular when it was least respectable. The earliest evidence of this new practical attitude was the setting up of the first Music Hall Restaurant, at Neutral Bay, Sydney, in 1960. At first this was determinedly disowned by the greater part of the legitimate theatre. But whether the theatre liked it or not, the music hall restaurant was beginning to develop a style which was more comfortable to audiences than the more refined form other theatres were offering.

Gradually and inevitably this style has begun to creep into the serious theatre. This broad, loud, extremely agile and all-enveloping theatricality is reaching out into the theatres which have protected themselves from it for so long, bringing a vitality which is totally Australian, for the first time since the death of Roy Rene. The chief example of this kind of play is *The Legend of King O'Malley*. But signs may be seen in earlier plays, some of which have not been so successful but which all emphasise the kind of impressionist writing that depends much more on rhythm—the rhythms of Australian life and its speech—than on theme or construction.

It is to be found in the plays of Rodney Milgate, Jack Hibberd, Alexander Buzo, John Romeril, Dorothy Hewett, Rob Inglis; and Stanley Walsh of the Sydney Music Hall. They are rorty, wasteful, intensely colloquial scripts and they make one realise how foreign to us are clever construction, eloquence and precision. They also show, to an awesome degree, how rich, vivid and accurate our colloquial tongue is. For years we have called ourselves inarticulate because we do not as a nation speak the tongue that Sir Robert Menzies speaks.

The style is also beginning to surge into production—it is being imposed upon such classics as *As You Like It*, at the Parade Theatre, Sydney, in February; it came unselfconsciously out of Bryan Nason's rewriting of Euripides' *The Bacchae*, at the Schonell Theatre, Brisbane, last August. It has been consciously reproduced in the Australian Performing Group's *Marvellous Melbourne*, at the Pram Factory, Melbourne.

There is also a common sympathy in the themes this new, popular form of theatre is adopting. It tends to deal with maverick characters, outlaw heroes who by their very existence impress upon us the extreme conformity of Australian society. They tend to reflect the oldest conflict in our history—that between the convicts and the soldiers—and to be violently anti-authoritarian in attitude, and strongly on the side of survival.

A third theme is that Dead Heart at the back of our history; the kind of sterility that comes from a vacant centre in our past and of which most Australians feel the loss. Such themes are very strong in Rodney Milgate's *At Least You Get Something Out Of That* (1968) which attempts to excoriate suburban living with the myth of Aphrodite and Ares. In Colin Free's *Cannonade of Bells* (1967), an embezzler who has carved a convict empire out of a dry creek-bed dreams of the green hills of Tennysonian England; and his mistress mixes the hard experience of life with the manners of Jane Austen, whose books have been her education.

In *The Legend Of King O'Malley* (1970) a confidence man turned imaginative idealist is crushed by short-sighted conformists who disguise shabby thinking under the name of practical reality. In Robert Wales' *The Cell* (1966) a non-conformist nun is punished and stifled because she wanted to behave in sympathy with the Redfern delinquents whose language and behaviour she understood better than the rigid discipline of the convent.

In Thomas Keneally's drama of early colonisation, *Halloran's Little Boat* (1966), two Irish innocents are hanged for their innocence by a corrupt, repressed Protestant authority. Alexander Buzo's *Norm and Ahmed* (1967) places Australia in its Asian context and reveals both the Australian and the Pakistani student as aliens. His *The Front Room Boys* (1970) satirises the extreme conformity of office routine in a purely rhythmical form. Wacka, the old Anzac in Alan Seymour's *The One Day of the Year* (1960) deflates the Gallipoli myth.

> When we went in there we was nobody. When we came out we was famous. Anzacs. Ballyhoo. Photos in the papers. Famous. Not worth a crumpet.

In Dorothy Hewett's new play *The Chapel Perilous* (1971) a woman for the first time examines this Gargantuan appetite for life and waste of ill-directed energy. Frederick Folkard's *The Sound of Frogs*, in workshop with the Melbourne Theatre Company, takes us back to the First Fleet and shows in comic terms how the convicts got the best of the soldiers. How the quick-witted survived and how ignorant authority upholding British rules in an alien land had to choose between oppression and defeat.

There is much more to be discovered yet and one of the first tasks must be to teach our actors to speak their native language. The theatre is, slowly, coming out of the cocoon with which it has protected itself for so long. The world of illusion behind the footlights is beginning to be seen as nothing more than an illusion and those in the industry who still believe in it are going to lose out.

Years later, when I selected Alan Hopgood's *Private Yuk Objects* for publication, I saw that the author's perspective on the warring stances was clear and balanced, though tempered by an element of country comedy that sat uneasily with the political argument.

PART IV
THE NEW WAVE ROLLS
1971–72

Part IV projects a rising assurance in direction and performance and the playwrights of the New Wave begin to show their mettle. New forms, a fresh encounter with our own language and new informal venues dictating their own forms, all contribute to the mix. The major companies demonstrate the benefits of larger resources and clearer direction; and begin to acknowledge the rising talent.

My reviews at this time still appeared mid-week on the leader page, sharing the space in turn with the art, film and music critics. On Saturdays a general review section allowed greater space and the opportunity for features. The amount of performance was expanding and increasingly I was jamming multiple reviews into the standard wordage. I have therefore been even more selective in what I have reproduced here from my columns. The New Wave artists who had been taking second place in my columns were now assuming the better part.

The Philanthropist: **The Heart on the Anatomist's Slab**
Australian, 7 April 1971

Every now and then the determined ballet-goer has the privilege of seeing that magical thing, a performance that sweeps away the memory of so much flailing energy and gives a glimpse of the metaphysics to which so much repetitious struggle has been directed. Now and then it happens in the theatre too, and the effect is the more astonishing because the familiar, indiscriminate bushfire energy is so often an end in itself. But there is another power that burns from within—and rare the play that has it—a still cold flame that can eat through steel.

Such a play is *The Philanthropist* by Christopher Hampton, the Royal Court Theatre's prodigy who had his first play in London's West End at 18 and even now is only 25. It comes as a gift out of the blue from the

Melbourne Theatre Company, awesomely anatomised by George Ogilvie; and the phenomenon is the greater because at first glance its fabric seems so dry, foreign and unpromising.

The setting is an English university college, probably Oxford, where the hero, Phillip, teaches philology. Words are his joy and preoccupation; and his tragedy that he is unable to feel the effect of their meaning. He and those around him are desiccated, their springs of feeling lost below the surface long ago. They struggle and protest a little and settle for what is, after all, bearable. The structure has a classical formality which stems from Molière's *Le Misanthrope*—on which not the play but the idea of the play, has been structured. Molière argues that society cannot stand the unvarnished truth. Hampton mourns the personal tragedy of losing the power to speak from the heart.

Like Molière's misanthropist, Phillip appears transparently truthful. He has an unlimited capacity for liking everything and wanting to say so, but it springs not from a misguided evangelism but from a profound inability to respond to human feeling. At the same time he is acutely sensitive to the cocoon which isolates him from the human heart and to the devastating effect his simplicity has upon the vanity and affection of his friends. Each of his well-intentioned bombshells brings disaster, the chief of which is the breaking of his engagement to Celia. In the riveting last ten minutes of the play the life of terror inside our hero surfaces quite suddenly and, in his panic-stricken pursuit of the precise weapon with which to drown the hallucination, he spews at the audience an image of life as a traffic roundabout on which he is trapped, with no exits and no stopping or turning—only an increased frenzy as he reaches closer and closer to the vortex.

There are two moments of violence in the play, sudden and shocking, which show the pent-up energy beneath the surface. The play is vocal, with that luminous mannered wit at which the English excel. Words circulate in patterns through the dialogue as they do in Phillip's mind, almost as if for their own sake. Movement, both physical and dramatic, is minimal. Verbalised action, by contrast, is dizzying—a series of Grand Guignol jokes about the machine-gunning of the parliamentary front bench and the assassination of prominent literary figures.

Ogilvie and his leading actor, Neil Fitzpatrick, have brought off together an extraordinary dissection. Phillip and his microscopic world are laid out on the slide, white and clinical. But the most memorable thing about the production is the intensity of its starkness. Richard Prins' set has achieved the feat of putting an idea into three dimensions without obscuring it with a life of its own. Made of rough oak and milk glass, the objects in the room, part college-gothic, part Molière Restoration, are dead of imagination, and in their over-life-size swallow up Phillip and his life and seem to leave the room always empty.

With the same sensitivity to the central thought, Fitzpatrick sets his character study. The mood is comic and the pain latent, only very slowly understood. His movements are of the slightest but he draws his audience toward each of them. And when, at final curtain, he takes his first decisive step, he grips the audience by the throat as though their world were falling in ruins along with his.

The style extends also to the other characters whose qualities as people do not in themselves account for our compulsive attention. In particular John Allen, as Don, supports this core of realism with a kind of humane cynicism. Alison Bird makes a vulnerable Celia, defending herself with words; and Simon Chilvers' Braham manages somehow to be both satirical of a particularly English literary cleverness and an appallingly recognisable person.

Ogilvie does not seem to have a signature to his productions, as other directors do. Where others add he exorcises and excoriates; his vision comes directly through the actors. Sometimes when he and the author diverge such methods can cut the lifeline; but in Hampton he has found a writer with the same clinical wit and together they have probed into the light a life which has devoted all its energy to hiding from it. 'There, but for the grace of God go I', say the audience. The result is a rare work indeed.

John Bell's Arturo Ui: Today America, Tomorrow the World

Australian, 15 May 1971

We must say thank you to the Old Tote Theatre Company for engineering the return of John Bell the actor to the Australian stage in a role that gives him a range for his exceptional mental and physical talents. Last weekend the company opened at the Parade Theatre, Sydney, in the first Australian production of a minor but arresting play by Bertolt Brecht, chiefly memorable for a leading role of idiosyncratic splendour: *The Resistible Rise of Arturo Ui.*

The play is a funny-terrible satire on the rise of Hitler and the Third

Reich. The setting is Chicago in the 1930s where Arturo (Al Capone) and his gang are petty criminals awaiting their big chance to set up a protection racket inside the vegetable markets. The parallel between Hitler's ministers and Arturo's gang is direct: the little Givola and the overstuffed, overdressed Giri are Goebbels and Göring; the gunman Ernie Roma is the police chief Ernst Röhm. Dogsborough, head of the Cauliflower Trust, is Von Hindenburg, President of Germany.

The action of the play, involving arson, corruption of the judicial system, standover tactics, murder and enforced capitulation, approximately covers events both in Germany and Chicago in the 1930s; and the author's purpose is straightforward: to present Hitler in a new proportion and remind us how small criminals can grow into big ones.

'The great political criminals must by all means be exposed, and preferably to ridicule', wrote Brecht,

> for they are not so much great political criminals as the perpetrators of great political crimes, which is altogether different ... The ruling classes of a modern society are in the habit of enlisting rather mediocre people for their enterprises. No special talent is required even in the all-important field of economic exploitation. Industrial giants, such as the IG Farben, show no particular intelligence, except in so far as they exploit intelligent people. [unsourced quote from the program]

Brecht is asking us, in this play, to look at our own backyards and keep our eyes open. And we do not have to look very far to find candidates for his 'field of economic exploitation' or political interference in civil rights and freedom of speech.

Richard Wherrett's production is very funny and Bell's rodent-like Ui, with hunched shoulders and quick, sawing arms, is masterly. The famous acting lesson, in which he emerges under the tuition of an old classical actor into the public figure of the Führer is one of the greatest pieces of theatrical writing in Brecht. If for no other reason, Bell's virtuoso performance in this scene is worth the price of a ticket.

What I did find disappointing about the production is the almost total absence of any political sense. The play is witty and delights with its audacious mixture of fun-fare, gangster movies, Goethe's *Faust* and Shakespeare's *Richard III*. And the director has been quick to grasp these opportunities. But the play has a core of terror. Without this it is no more than a collage of pastiches. Wherrett's production is local in its affection for the vaudeville. His gangsters are caricatures of Jimmy Cagney and

Edward G. Robinson; his Reich a *Hogan's Heroes* view of the Gestapo. There is little outspoken grim reality behind the cut-out characters and the cut-out sets (except at the opening); perhaps it is a reflection on our lucky country that Chicago hoodlums have no more reality outside television than the house painter turned Führer.

There have been alterations to the text somewhere along the line which do some damage. The opening exposition has been cut, making the politics of the gangsters and the Cauliflower Trust difficult to follow. And the wounded woman who crawls in crying for help and vengeance at the end of the play after Ui has made his triumphant address to the crowds: 'Today America! Tomorrow the World!' has been tucked away into an earlier scene. In short, it is a most reassuring production.

Perhaps I am carping, but if one does not seek substance for Brecht's claim that the elements that contrived the rise of Hitler are still 'in heat' today, if the St Valentine's Day massacre (Chicago 1928) is a fiction of the movies; if the notorious Reichstag Fire Trial (1933) or the murder by the Gestapo of the Austrian Ambassador to Germany (1934) are simply notes for the record, then surely Brecht's play is now old-fashioned?

The Old Tote's excellent program (would that more theatres were so informative) does show an awareness of these things. It names some big criminals safely distant from our shores. What about some of the petty sins closer at home? Given the premise, though, that *The Resistible Rise of Arturo Ui* is simply an entertainment, there is still much to recommend it, including performances by Ron Falk as Roma, Terry Bader and Tom Dysart as Givola and Giri; and John Trenaman as Dogsborough.

Hands Down Gourds: Inexplicable Evening

Australian, 29 May 1971

Last weekend, in a kind of afterglow of *Hair*, I spent a most entrancing and inexplicable evening at La Mama in Carlton, hypnotised by a new play by Syd Clayton, called *Hands Down Gourds*. Play is not exactly the word for it. Its form, says Clayton, is based on the shape and variations of a Bartok quartet and it is more like a composition for four voices than a play with a logical theme.

The floor of the wooden hut which is La Mama was covered thickly with dead maple leaves. There is a narrow cupboard with four doors and no back, surmounted by a cinema sign: TONIGHT. Inside is a black figure with a luxuriance of flame-colour hair, reading a comic. Enter the author in white face. Silently he swishes a broom through the leaves. Leisurely he paints out the TONIGHT sign. Then he retires to his orchestra loft up in the rafters, with a conglomeration of percussion instruments, including cymbals, bells and a copper washtub.

The real action begins with the arrival of Don White, bumping down the stairs dressed in ragged black with a white face and yellow motor cycle glasses. He delivers himself spreadeagled among the dead leaves, and, contemplating cheerfully on the slowness of travel in 1872, propels himself on his back among the leaves with a quite extraordinary sensation of luxury. White's role is a sort of comic allegretto with a touch of the bassoon. He has splendid recitatives with refrains like 'Dog owners! Dog thieves may be discouraged by having your pet painlessly tattooed!' He invents spontaneous games of violence and derring-do, like Charlie Brown's Snoopy.

The two female characters are Faith Rosa (Val Gordon), the black girl with a necklace of bones and a moon lunacy; and Sunlight (Jan Cornall) with a gypsy dress and a tambourine. The trio play at a series of games of life and death. There is a firm and deliberate disintegration of logical motivation.

If you ask me what it was about you are asking the wrong question. What it offered was a strangely invigorating delight in sounds and colours and variations of mood. Externally it bears a strong resemblance to the French Absurdists and *Waiting for Godot*, in that their form is an external orchestration of sounds, pictures and ideas to demonstrate what a junk-heap of a world it really is. Syd Clayton's world is much more optimistic. He clowns with the fragments because for him they cohere into part of the same world. The work has the same hopeful, realistic synthesising mind behind the celebration of confusion which so pleased me about the new production of *Hair*. And it was also quite remarkably well performed for such a difficult score.

The Melbourne production of *Hair* had opened that week. I had reviewed it enthusiastically on 24 May.

White with Wire Wheels: The Valiant and the Avenging Angel

Australian, 16 June 1971

Sydney is having a first opportunity to see Jack Hibberd's first full-length play, *White with Wire Wheels* at the Wayside Chapel, Kings Cross. It is an important play for this time, if not a major one. It was first performed at the Prince Philip Theatre, University of Melbourne, in 1967, when Hibberd was what might be called honorary resident playwright at the Café La Mama. It has since had a production by the Australian Performing Group, which was taken to the Festival of Perth. Now it is receiving a production by Sean Surplus for the Head and Hand Theatre Company, which consolidated the good qualities in the script; and no one in Sydney who is interested in what makes our current playwrights different from their colleagues overseas should miss the opportunity of seeing this performance.

The play is a character study, in compelling slang, of three ambitious young executives who share a flat. They have their women—Rod has a mistress of three years; Mal makes a show of never letting a relationship last over three months; Simon doesn't really know where he is. But their real conversational obsessions are cars and beer. These are their true virility symbols and Hibberd makes a close comic comparison between their collection and abuse of cars and of girlfriends.

He reinforces this point by having one actress play in turn all the women, including Helen, the new ideal conquest who teaches them all a lesson. Helen is partly a real doll who, invited in to be introduced, finds herself superseded by a lyrical paean on a new white Valiant with wire wheels. And she is partly a maternal and avenging angel who haunts their dreams and their hidden emotions. In a half-comic, half-sad dream sequence they offer their most precious possessions to her as a kind of Mother Kali, and when she jilts them they bolt back into their well-lined hole of hearty mateship, car-racing and getting drunk.

What makes the play less than it might have been is that the investigation goes no further than this statement about the emotional poverty of Australian men; but it does realise the proposition in a most vivid and witty way. And it is always a pleasure to feel an audience filling in the background associations and warming to the familiar. Such occasions are a reminder of how large a gap plays from unfamiliar contexts have to leap. The production has a good young cast, notably Paul Creevey as Rod, offset by Rod Williams, Gerard Bonk and Sandi Young.

This is Hibberd month, by the diary. His short *Customs and Excise*, a satire on censorship and middle-class morality, is due to open at the Nimrod Theatre, Sydney, at the end of the month, along with Alexander Buzo's one-act parody of a TV sports commentator, *The Roy Murphy Show*. On 29 June his new work *Aorta* (described as a sanguinary play) will be presented by Ormond College as part of a trio by Melbourne writers at Melbourne

University Union. The first, John Romeril's *200 Years*, had a season last month, and the second, *Sideshow*, a ballad opera by Leonard Radic on the events and songs of Gallipoli, will play Wednesday to Saturday this week.

Chicago, Chicago: Our Underground Talent Breaks to the Surface

Australian, 30 June 1971

The most remarkable play yet to come from the hand of one of our younger playwrights is now available in one of the Australian Performing Group's best performances yet, at the Pram Factory, Drummond Street, Carlton, Melbourne. I say this advisedly because though the mainstream of the theatre industry has not yet publicly allowed the thought to interrupt its flow, there is an underground current of dramatic talent which will not for much longer permit itself to go unrecognised.

The play in question is *Chicago, Chicago* by John Romeril, and its quality combines the mastery of a radical new form and a searing capacity to put the subliminal into dramatic expression. The script is a series of fragments about the Man, an ordinary person who is at first a convention delegate, then an alcoholic, then the inmate of an asylum, the victim of gangsters. The situations differ but the pressures are the same—a weight of immutable automated authority.

It is a witty play. The Man, inside his cold motel room, blunders from one idiotic but recognisable situation to another, facing the imaginary demands the world is making of him, failing in imaginary tests, breaking into manic and futile protests. The first half concentrates on the personal predicament, the second upon what the author calls the American madness.

Outside the room they are holding marches and throwing stones; a lunatic American president bursts into his room to broadcast a speech on the state of the union; the Man finds himself humiliated before millions as he loses a TV contest; an art critic talks about electronic environmental art as her exhibit ingests its spectators like an amoeba. All this is played against Chris Berkman's illuminated Coca-Cola and war memorial window while two masked members of the audience, George and Lilian, dispute the popular arguments on sociology and culture from the opposing views of Carlton and the suburbs.

John Romeril has never been to the United States and certainly not Chicago; nor is the play an objective study of the city. Rather it is an emotional illumination of what we as a people fear most about America—and Chicago as a distillation of that fear—from Al Capone and James Cagney to the Chicago Seven. Graeme Blundell gives a first-rate performance as the Man and is supported in varying roles by ten members of the company, including Meg Clancy, Yvonne Marini, Evelyn Krape and Martin Brennan. The production is by Max Gillies.

Chicago, Chicago was first performed in a different version in 1969 and has had extensive rewriting before reaching its present form.

The Chicago Seven were anti-Vietnam War protesters at the 1968 Chicago Democratic Convention, whose famous trial lasted five months and led to wider protests across the country. Varying guilty verdicts were overturned on appeal.

A debate in London on the role of the art critic provoked me into writing a partisan manifesto urging fellow reviewers to put their shoulders to the wheel and become creative participants in our developing arts.

The Critic as Advocate
Australian, 10 July 1971

You have told me many strange things tonight, Gilbert. You have told me that it is more difficult to talk about a thing than to do it, and that to do nothing at all is the most difficult thing in the world.

You have told me that all art is immoral and all thought dangerous; that criticism is more creative than creation, and that the highest criticism is that which reveals in the work of art what the artist had not put there; that it is exactly because a man cannot do a thing that he is the proper judge of it; and that the critic is unfair, insincere and not rational. My friend, you are a dreamer.

Oscar Wilde's literary dialogue, *The Critic as Artist* (1890) which Charles Marowitz has adapted for the stage in London—part of which appeared on this page last Saturday—is a complex piece in its entirety and presumes a much higher respect for both critic and artist than obtains in this country.

His arguments are paradoxes but in their essence unassailable. He deplores the fact that most modern popular criticism is mediocre; he claims that the true critic uses the artist's work as the basis for a true creation of his own; that all criticism is subjective just as all art is subjective.

He says all art is immoral because 'emotion for the sake of emotion is the aim of art, and emotion for the sake of action is the aim of life, and of that practical organisation of life that we call society'. Fairness and sincerity, he says, are 'if not actually moral at least on the borderland of morals and the first condition of criticism is that the critic should be able to recognise that the sphere of art and the sphere of ethics are absolutely distinct and separate'.

Let me rephrase in journalistic terms three propositions which Wilde's essay would support:

1. The good critic is as creative as the good artist.
2. The quality and (where necessary) the virulence of critical writing in the Press is in proportion to the quality and vitality of the creative activity.
3. The task of the critic as artist is to be an advocate for the artist.

A fourth point needs to be added. The critic today has largely lost the personal contact he had with the artist in Wilde's day. The appreciation of beauty is no longer enough and the contemplative life no longer possible.

When Hazlitt and Shaw were writing on the theatre their issues were clear—what they took theatrical excitement to be, what they thought the writer or actor had to offer, what they took life to be about. They were entitled to their personal bias; personal assault drew personal retaliation. And when they wrote about the work of Mrs Siddons or Henry Irving, the high respect in which their public held these artists was never placed in question.

It is still true of the great critics and great artists today and it is true in most European capitals where the theatre still remains a matter in the public interest. The toughest adverse theatre criticism in the world is written today in West Germany and this is not because the West German theatre is worse than any other theatre but because its purpose is held in higher regard by its audience.

But the theatre and its relations with the critics have suffered from the natural processes of economic growth like everything else. The specialist is an invention of this century. The technological expert, the medical specialist and the theatre director are all inventions of this century. The artist has very little dignity and his audience very little concern in the newer cultures like Australia and America. Rapid material development has brought with it divisive specialisation and our arts have become insulated and fragmented. It is therefore here more strikingly than anywhere that the critic must be the synthesiser, interpreter and expert eye for the audience.

He must be much more inventive, more sure of the standards, more awake to opportunity than in other countries. The German critic has acquired 400 years of Goethe, Schiller, Dürer and the Bauhaus handed down at his christening.

Our heritage is still awaiting discovery. It demands work and thought. As Oscar Wilde says, the critic must draw into his account a wide context of which even the artist may not be aware, if he is to find the real significance of which he is to write. He is a pattern maker. It is of the utmost importance that a critic has a clearly defined philosophy behind his writing. If he has learned to see his art steadily and see it whole, then constantly the work that he deals with will offer him evidence in support of that philosophy.

'It is criticism', says Wilde,

> that by concentration makes culture possible. It takes the cumbersome mass of creative work and distils it into a finer essence. Who that desires to retain any sense of form could struggle through the monstrous multitudinous books that the world has produced, books in which thought stammers or ignorance brawls? The thread that is to guide us across the wearisome labyrinth is in the hands of criticism.
>
> Nor is this all. It is criticism that, recognising no position as final, and refusing to bond itself by the shallow shibboleths of any sect or school, creates that serene philosophic temper which loves truth for its own sake, and loves it not the less because it knows it to be unattainable. How little we have of this temper in England, and how much we need it!

Not to mention Australia.

The great weakness of criticism in Australia is that it is not in itself a profession. Journalism is a profession. But to be a critic is to write a column in one's spare time. The amount of irresponsible criticism on current affairs, politics and the arts in Australia in the Press and the other media can be laid to the fact that full-time professional skills are not brought to these options. Very few of our critical columnists have taken up the challenge of their changing role or the opportunities that lie behind a simple discussion of a work. Most of them have another job—usually a journalistic or academic one—at which they earn their real living; and a visit to an exhibition or a performance is a diversion of their weekly routine.

This is not entirely their fault but that of the conditions under which they work. The critic, like the rest of the world, is so pressured by the immediate that he is seldom allowed the luxury of remembering the larger issues or the space in which to explain them. His is no longer the contemplative life Wilde prescribed for him. Nor does his reader have the leisure to contemplate his views. He has, more often than not, become a notemaker, an inspector doing spot-checks and awarding the good housekeeping seal where he can. And even at the elementary level of daily reviewing this familiar world has been shifting under his feet.

Many of the plays the theatre critic sees come from distant origin, created for an audience by actors he has never seen. His leading actor may have flown in last week and be facing an audience in this town for the first time. The critic may dislike the set, not because the design is poor but because it was first designed for some theatre he has never seen. The language may sound wrong because it is half Australian and half foreign.

In trying to clarify for the reader this complex and often mangled matter, it is no longer enough for a critic to be well-read in the classics, sensitive to the medium and conversant with the work of the artists in the local industry. He must know the reasoning behind the evidence. And yet there is an old-fashioned and mistaken belief, which obtains not only in this country but Britain and other countries which should know better, that the critic should have nothing to do with the processes of the artist's creation. He should know nothing about the financial stresses, the private dilemmas, the public demands, that go into the creation of a play. Many critics believe such knowledge will influence them. Of course it will influence them. Of course it will do away with objectivity. As Wilde says: 'The man who sees both sides of the question is a man who sees absolutely nothing at all.'

The artist is a truth-teller and if a critic is an artist he is concerned to create the truth. Truth from someone who has remained objectively aloof from the whole industry on which he depends is another word for ignorance. Ignorance is the real destructive force in criticism. The harsh word in the Press which puts an actor out of work is not often written because the critic is concerned for the creative work, because he believes the actor capable of better; but because the critic's mind is preoccupied with the immediate pressure upon himself. Judgments are never as simple in context as they seem in isolation, nor are incidental disasters as bad or important in the long view as they seem in isolation.

If the critics in this country are to be the creative public relations men for the arts they need to be, then they must learn to think in a wider context than they at present do. The critic as journalist has a primary duty to be read: whether he is right or not matters very much less than whether he is read. If the critic has no reader, then he is powerless.

William Hazlitt (1778–1830) was the first great English drama critic. G. B. Shaw (1856–1950) published music and drama criticism between 1888 and 1898. Sarah Siddons (1755–1831) and Sir Henry Irving (1838–1903) were two giants of the English stage.

Cramphorne's *Orestes*: A New Dramatic Language
Australian, 18 August 1971

A partnership of actors, writer and director has been formed in Sydney to continue its members' previous experiments in new forms of dramatic language, and already it is giving impressive evidence of the seriousness of its innovation. Calling itself the Performance Syndicate and working under strictly laboratory conditions, it has opened its doors to the public for this week and next at the Arts Factory, 158 Goulburn Street, Surry Hills, Sydney, with a dance-tragedy, *Orestes* (The Arts Factory, incidentally, is a converted warehouse space which has been taken over as a try-out venue for the pop scene.)

The director of the syndicate is Rex Cramphorne, arts graduate from the University of Queensland, production graduate of the National Institute of Dramatic Art, director of the recent *The Dutch Courtesan* at the Parade Theatre, and former theatre critic of the *Bulletin*. He has for some years been drawn to the Asian performing arts, the disciplines of yoga and the asceticism of the Polish dramatic theorist Jerzy Grotowski. His first experiment in the use of these devices was the performance at the Jane Street Theatre last year of *10,000 Miles Away*, an investigation of the idea of space travel as an expression of the mind.

The *Orestes*, written by Willy Young, is a considerable advance and much more outward; it is precise both in its intention and expression, and for much of the time extremely beautiful to look at. The story, of the last son of the House of Atreus, who avenges his father's murder by killing his mother at the instigation of his sister, and who then goes mad with guilt, is taken from Greek tragedy. It is used here in the Greek way as a statement, rather than a dramatisation, of human emotion.

The choice of three male actors—Clytamnestra, the mother (Andrew Siman), Electra the sister (Nick Lathouris) and Orestes the son (Terry O'Brien)—is also taken from the Greek; and the ritualistic properties are retained in a way extraordinary in a modern production. Lathouris, quivering like a bird, wearing white-face and speaking in a kind of whistling melody, has a peculiar androgynous quality which is neither male nor female but symbolic in a pitiful way of both. Siman, black-hearted and wearing a voluminous parachute cloak which at times rises like the wings of a butterfly, is much more like the military chiefs of the Chinese and Japanese classical drama. His role of the fierce and possessive mother is as much of the earth as Lathouris' is of the spirit. The whole adds up to the beginnings of something quite individual.

What Cramphorne has done is to reverse the dramatic process. He does not ask his actors to create the illusion of emotion and to shape the history of a conflict; he has in rehearsal built up a state of mind, which the actors carry with them and which the performance restates in bare, careful words and movements. The statement, though emotionless in itself, remains a statement about emotion, as it must always remain in the theatre. Cramphorne is after a new language—and to have demanded and received already so much from three actors is a remarkable achievement in itself.

The more so when one compares it with that phenomenon *Man–Child* inside a nylon bubble at the Sydney Showground. (The production was halted temporarily when the bubble was flattened on Monday.) This show was made by a group of teenagers led by a young composer, Chris Neal, and is entitled 'a musical odyssey in search of truth'. Whatever the truth is they certainly have not found it, or if they have they have kept the secret to themselves.

Man–Child breaks the two unfailing rules of show business, firstly in making claims to the public which it had no hope of fulfilling, and secondly in not understanding that enthusiasm and general good intentions are not enough in the business of communication.

Rex Cramphorn dropped the final 'e' from his surname shortly after this time and, as I've already pointed out, Willy Young is now known as William Yang and Nick Lathouris as Nico Lathouris.

Burke's Company: The Marks of Isolation
Australian, 21 August 1971

Reinforced by four months of popular comedy-drama, the Queensland Theatre Company has chosen to pit its resources behind one of the toughest, most unrelenting plays to have been taken up by our repertory companies. Looking back, it stands almost alone in a stark, undramatic prospect against a host of comic, iconoclastic contemporaries, emerging as the last of the poetic plays which rose through radio in the 1940s, and 50s, not the first in a renaissance with which its first performance coincided early in 1968.

The play is *Burke's Company*, by Bill Reed, a study of the last weeks in the life of the explorers Burke and Wills, who attempted to ride north to the Gulf of Carpentaria from Melbourne in 1861. The play covers their separated party as they blunder between the rescue camp at Cooper's Creek, the base camp at Menindie and Burke's fatal attempt to walk to Mount Hopeless.

Mr Reed presents the expedition's predicament through the mind of Brahe, the indecisive, harmless man left at the rescue camp while Burke, Wills and the 22-year-old John King press farther into the centre. Brahe it was who, his companion dying, his leaders long overdue, despair setting in, made the decision to abandon camp only five hours before the exhausted trio returned. By the time Brahe returned to the rescue camp, Burke and Wills had gone again. The romantic, handsomely-equipped expedition, led by a dreaming Irishman with more physical courage than acuteness, was a muddle of wrong decisions made in the merciless heat of the central desert where decisions either way were fatal.

Burke's Company goes a good way towards conveying this scene of futility and harshness—Brahe turning over and over his responsibility for the deaths of his leaders; Burke turning over and over his own similar responsibilities. And history's record remaining in the mind all the while. But it is this which, finally, makes the play undramatic—the awareness of history that accompanies it. It is a lyrical and poetic evocation of events long past which made hardly a mark on the immutable face of the landscape.

Those who have presented the play in Melbourne, in Adelaide—and Brisbane is no exception—have done a great deal to inject dramatic immediacy into the play's multi-levels. The SGIO Theatre stage, infinitely wider than the others, gives the director, Alan Edwards, the advantage in separating the tangible reality of Brahe's camp from the emotional memory of the others' journeys, and he is assisted by a good set from Cliff Simcox. Strands of the play become clearer in this production than others had made them.

At the same time it also reveals a thinness of texture, a repetitive single-mindedness which is unnecessarily tiring to the audience, and a want of human complexity. It is motivated by a preoccupation with a myth, as our painters have been, not with the ordinary material out of which myths are created. The present QTC company is a young one and is led by Tony Thurbon, who does very well as Brahe. The others show their mettle as an ensemble more truly than as individuals and do not yet have the experience to carry the characters further than the author has taken them—as George Whaley did as Burke in the Melbourne Theatre Company production.

The decision to present the play derives partly from the QTC's tours of Queensland, which have taken them as far as Mount Isa. They clearly have an affection for the work and a feeling for the land which carries them a far distance towards success. The real trouble is that events have overtaken the play since it was written ten years ago. We have reached the point where most of our plays are now created in the theatre. *Burke's Company* bears the marks of that isolation from which our dramatic literature for too long suffered.

Don's Party: Study of Inertia

Australian, 11 September 1971

Don's Party, by David Williamson, which finished its season on Sunday at the Pram Factory, Melbourne, as the Australian Performing Group's best box office play to date, takes this group for the first time into the neglected field of suburban living. It also pushes in a new direction a characteristic of our own particular enjoyment, the pleasure of watching activity without compulsion.

In *Don's Party* nothing happens, in the way that one might say nothing happens in *Who's Afraid of Virginia Woolf?*. The subject matter is the same: a party to which unwelcome and unsuitable guests are invited and who, as the evening progresses, tear each other's lives to pieces out of apparent malice. But Williamson's play is nothing like so tightly or so deeply bound as Albee's. His room has no claustrophobic feeling of couples locked in mortal combat. The doors of this room are open, the conversation loose and trivial and the guests come and go out of sheer inertia. The comparison is not intended as an invidious one between one of the great men of the American theatre and a very new Australian playwright. It is rather to help illuminate the fascinating sense of locality Williamson has. He is peculiarly a Melbourne writer. His subject matter might be drawn from any city but there is something in his form of expression, even the form of the bad language, which defines the locale.

Don Henderson, a not-very successful writer and his wife Kath, give an election-night party for five of his former university friends and their partners. It is ten years since they graduated and none of them have fulfilled their early promise in business or marriage. They still carry the torches

Rod Moore (centre) as Cooley with the cast of the APG production of *Don's Party*, 1971. (Photo: Ian McKenzie)

and hang-ups of ten years ago but have begun what the author calls a 'social change of life'. Their disillusionment is expressed in much anatomical discussion, attempts at wife-swapping, intermittent marital squabbling and financial grieving all mixed up with social pleasantries and politics. There is no sadism, passion or determination, as you get in Albee, and no accuracy. The tone is instead facetious, the jibes that hit the mark do so by accident.

Because the script is so formless the APG was taken by surprise by its popularity. But it is the familiarity of the characters that startles and captures the audience, not any dramatic contrivance by the writer. The shock of familiarity is still a novelty on our stages.

The play has received the Pram Factory's most elaborate production. Don's house occupied most of the floor space and a two-storey façade leading to the bedrooms. The cast was led by Wilfred Last and Evelyn Krape, and only some of the other actors did the play the service done by these two. More structure is obviously needed if the play is to receive a less environmental production; but at this first performance it is still an impressively original piece of documentary drama. Direction was by Graeme Blundell.

For this production the audience sat around the walls of the Pram Factory and the actors occupied the centre of the floor. The following year the Old Tote Theatre Company presented a revised version of the play at Jane Street. The play had been restructured for an end-stage theatre, so that fragmented conversations heard by Melbourne audiences as the partygoers circled the auditorium became tight consecutive scenes of confession and confrontation (see p. 210).

Meanwhile Williamson's *The Removalists* had opened at La Mama in July 1971 and had quickly been taken up by Nimrod—their first script from another group. I had reviewed it briefly in Melbourne, calling it a 'promising try-out' and commenting: 'The women and their family relationships have not been drawn closely enough yet to call it a complete play but the two constables who dominate the action are a riveting pair, particularly as played by Peter Cummins and Bruce Spence; and the whole play is expressive of that peculiar cauldron of repression, prurience and authoritarianism which is too recognisable in us and too commonly boils over into acts of violence.' ['Caste in the Theatre', *Australian*, 7 August 1971]

The Removalists: The Psychology of Assault
Australian, 23 October 1971

The enterprising Nimrod Theatre, Sydney, which has spent its first year proving that entertainment is more than a polished script and that audiences are susceptible to a new idea, have with their newest play assumed a more serious task. They have brought from the Café La Mama experimental theatre in Melbourne, the work of a new young playwright who, with four plays, a screenplay and some revues and sketches behind him, is proving to be a writer of very remarkable talent indeed.

He is David Williamson and *The Removalists* is probably the best of his plays. The principal characters are a middle-aged police sergeant— prejudiced, repressed and an expert bludger—and a 21-year-old recruit on his first day in the force. The Sergeant's skills lie in showing how to evade work and how to punch where the bruises do not show. Into the station come two sisters who reflect the same leader-and-led relationship. The elder sister, Kate, has come to complain about Fiona's husband who has allegedly beaten her up. Over Fiona's head a separation is agreed upon by sister and sergeant; and a removalist is ordered for the family furniture. The four go to the flat where Fiona's husband, Kenny, in his singlet, is drinking canned beer and watching the midday movie. When Kenny protests, he is punched, at first jocularly, then in handcuffs and finally in an orgy of violence.

Williamson's writing is about violence, not always overt, but capturing with quite extraordinary emotional recall the peculiar aggressive defensive nature of so much of our social behaviour. This unacknowledged violence is in our literature—*Wake in Fright*, for example—but it has so far escaped analysis in our drama, partly because we have wanted to see ourselves differently, partly because we have wanted to place the blame on outsiders—the bosses, the migrants, Uncle Sam. But *The Removalists* shows how much of this uncertainty is in ourselves. The play gives us three authority figures: Sergeant Simmonds, Kate Mason and the Removalist. The first two are pompous and hollow and they are turned inside out by the end of the play. The Removalist, who goes on with his job, cares about nobody and dismisses the pleas of the handcuffed Kenny as none of his business, is unshaken by the events.

The cast, under the direction of John Bell, enjoy the opportunity of dealing for the first time in some depth with the Australian character. As a team they balance the status games with skill and handle with wit the fine comic qualities of the language. Don Crosby and Max Phipps play the policemen as an equal duel making the end almost unbearable. Carole Skinner and Jacki Weaver play the sisters, and Chris Haywood gives a wonderfully awful, accurate performance as the Removalist.

Martin Harris (Kenny) is an actor of great individual talent. In the standard repertoire, what is special about him has lain hidden. This year in a series of local scripts—as a Parramatta recidivist in *The Chocolate Frog* and as Clarrie the sports commentator in *The Roy Murphy Show*—he has been given the opportunity to show where his talents really lie. Now in *The Removalists* he gives a really gut-tearing performance of a fighter with the courage to come up smiling. It is probably the best work he has ever done.

There are still weaknesses in the area of the women's portraits and the Kenny–Fiona household. But the rest remains enough to shake Sydney audiences with the talent of the first realist among the new wave of Melbourne playwrights.

As a curtain-raiser, the Nimrod has chosen Tom Stoppard's *After Magritte*, a funny surrealist play in which Jacki Weaver plays a tuba-playing grandmother. It serves both to define our kind of verbal extravagance by comparison with the most intellectual of the younger English word merchants; and to compare an English parody on British respect for the law with an Australian study of our contempt. Lively direction by Larry Eastwood.

At this stage *The Removalists* ran about 90 minutes. When Harry M. Miller bought the rights to transfer the production to his Sydney Playbox, he asked for an interval and a new scene between Fiona and Kenny to open the second half. The film of Kenneth Cook's novel, *Wake in Fright*, was released in 1971.

The new Prime Minister, William McMahon, had appointed Peter Howson as Minister for Arts, Aborigines and the Environment. Howson's first act was to defer for twelve months a decision, on moves Prime Minister Gorton had begun, to set up a national film and television school. This led to a massive outcry and Howson was dubbed 'Minister for Odds and Sods' and 'A pain in the arts' in the Press. The unstable nature of the Federal Government since Robert Menzies' retirement in 1967 contributed greatly to the arts' rocky road at this time, as Dr Coombs' vision was passed from Holt to Gorton to McMahon and in December 1972 to Labor's Gough Whitlam. Although the arts were now confident enough to be asserting the right to autonomy, it was 1975 before the Council became a statutory body as the Australia Council for the Arts.

Putting the Arts in the Environment

Australian, 23 October 1971

> In the leaner years of the past, in the face of hardship and a little encouragement, young Australians have risen to fame and brought distinction to their country over a wide range of cultural activity. Given the support of governments, federal and state, and the backing of the people, I am sure the talent is there for us to rise to new heights and give our people a growing pleasure and satisfaction.

This general hope for good, which usually attends our cultural attainment, was the last word from the Prime Minister, Harold Holt, announcing the decision to establish an Australian Council for the Arts. Since then, in the face of hardship and a little encouragement, the whole aspect of the performing arts in Australia has changed. And the credit for this is largely due to the work of the Australian Council.

But having embarked on a growth policy, the artists have in three years taken over the development far faster than the specified rate of growth for government departments. This, now coinciding with a budget squeeze, has made the position of the Council critical. This year's rise of $700,000, of which $400,000 was earmarked by the Minister for the Arts for the Australian Opera, has left the Council barely able to meet the year's increased costs of work already under way. Grants to the smaller capitals and the special projects fund, the most important of the council's original work, have been cut to almost nothing. And now the storm of the postponement of the National Film School has visibly shaken the unsteady relationship of the Council to the Federal Government. The backlash on all the arts may well be much more serious than is yet apparent.

The achievement of the Australian Council, both tangibly and intangibly, has been phenomenal in the short space of three years. In that time federal money for the arts has increased from $1 million to $4.5 million. This money has hastened the process by which the Australian Ballet, the Australian Opera, the Melbourne Theatre Company and the Old Tote Theatre Company have become cultural institutions of quality. But far more important, the Council's largesse has shown that there is more to culture than money can buy. The effects of the very existence of the Council have been far reaching upon the whole composition of the Australian outlook to the arts—far beyond the effects which can be explained away in terms of money.

To face its new challenge efficiently the Australian Council needs to be a statutory, autonomous body, free to make its own decisions, quickly and with its own priorities. The Council sees its film program as crucial to its existence, not simply because of the film industry but because the medium was their centre for a cross-fertilisation of the arts. 'The film', says one spokesman, 'is the young people's natural form of expression. This is where the exciting thinking is coming, where the rules are being broken and the unexpected is happening. The results are relating to education, to the visual arts, to all kinds of fields.'

The rise in standards in the past three years has meant an expansion in the quality of original thought. The talent has, as Mr Holt hoped, risen to new heights and is now demanding attention. But while the artist has found the courage to break the rules, the Treasury is imposing new ones. Corners are being chipped off the Council's program, which must affect the appearance of the whole plan. The challenge now before the Council is that of nurturing an entirely original new culture for which no precedent has been laid down in government policy. At the outset no broad financial base for a dynamic policy was provided (as with the Canada Council) to cover such an eventuality. And it is all turning out quite differently from what we had expected.

Mr Peter Howson's multiple portfolio, Environment, Aborigines and the Arts, has been the target for much embittered public hilarity. It has been implied that their peremptory lumping together reflects the

Government's contempt for all three. And so far there has been little to show that the Minister has taken grasp of the problems. But do not the three belong together?

Like our form of government and our television programs, our culture, for the most part, has been imposed upon the face of the country arbitrarily and without thought for meaning or use. It has been acquired in a way typical of an acquisitive society and with as little originality. Our visual arts are way ahead on this count. Our painters were the first to take pleasure in the shape and scale of the country and to see us as part of a great Asian complex. But the performing arts, which have come to depend on government money, have with only the occasional notable exception, clung to the harbour of the old precedents.

But what other purpose can art have than that of expressing our outlook and our environment? New artists and craftsmen are moving as fast as they can out of the department of museums and opera houses and into the department of the environment, and if the Minister had the perception to see this he would find ways of helping the Australian Council to increase this ground-breaking work.

Then again, Australians tend to be too dependent upon government aid. The result of the National Film School row is that private enterprise is now looking into the need. If a school could be privately funded and set up as an attachment to a university or technical school, then it might very well be a better and more efficient project than the original objective. The subsidy squeeze introduced at a time when the performing arts are moving forward so rapidly might also be put to some effect.

One of the startling facts about the boards of the regional theatres is that, with only the smallest exceptions, none has ever made a proper attempt to raise its own private subsidy. This has been a direct reflection of their private judgment of the value of their artists' work. The Friends of the Opera are setting the pace in the best European tradition. What the performing arts really need is more European–American finance and more indigenous, Aboriginal environment.

A bill to establish the film school was passed in 1973 and the Australian Film, Television and Radio School became an adjunct of Macquarie University. In 2005, the university gave it notice to vacate the premises. Film, including an experimental film fund, was part of the Australian Council's brief until the responsibility was transferred to the Australian Film Commission in 1976.

The Australian Performing Group: Raising the Banner

Australian, 4 December 1971

Theatres thrive on crisis. No one ever asks for a theatre to be started, but once it is there, try to take it away. The Australian Performing Group at the Pram Factory, Carlton, is no exception. With the ideas buzzing, the playwrights writing and not enough energy to carry out what is filling their heads, the APG has been teetering on the edge of catastrophe for a year now. And at the moment when, to the public at least, *The Feet of Daniel Mannix* seemed to be putting them on their own feet, they have closed their doors and called for help.

And help has indeed come spontaneously. The publisher Lloyd O'Neil and a group of interested citizens have responded by forming a committee to take care of the administration.

> We are just people who feel a deep concern that we might lose what we believe to be the most important experimental theatre in Australia at the moment. Our job will be entirely behind the scenes. We shall not interfere with the structure of the APG, which at present is a cooperative; but we shall find ways to enable them to continue doing their work in the way they wish. My interest is simply that of a theatregoer in danger of losing his favourite theatre. I take my children there and I think it a most exciting theatre group.

Mannix closed from exhaustion, said the company secretary, Rod Moore, at a time when the company was doing capacity business. Bruce Spence (who plays the title role) had another commitment; and the rest of the cast, who were working at other jobs during the day, were too tired to conceive of continuing without him. 'If we had enough to pay these actors not to work elsewhere, then we could really have done as well as the play deserves.' He and the company are delighted at the thought of having someone to 'organise us a bit better' and to take a lot of the responsibility from their shoulders. They have a long way to go and a lot of expensive plumbing yet to lay, but it looks as if at the point of exhaustion APG is better off than it has ever been.

Footnote: The Nimrod theatre, Sydney's Australian Performing Group, celebrated its first birthday on Monday with a charity night to pay off the $1,000 worth of equipment, much of it borrowed, which went in a recent burglary. The Nimrod, while it does pay its actors adequately, has followed the same pattern of penury, health regulation problems and neighbourhood complaints; and this week, while enjoying its best box office ever with *The Removalists*, by the APG playwright David Williamson, is having to close the season because of the cast's more lucrative commitments.

I had reviewed *The Feet of Daniel Mannix* on 30 October 1971. It was a rumbustious satirical comedy by Barry Oakley about the fiery Irish Archbishop who blurred the bounds of church and state in Melbourne from 1917 until his death in 1963. I described it as 'in many ways a second edition of *Marvellous Melbourne*, bringing up to date the APG's history of religion, corruption and gullibility, as they see it'. Mannix variously appears first from the heavens bearing a wrench and a tube of Tarzan's grip, then befriending the 'gentleman and hoodlum', in a boxing ring with Billy Hughes over World War I conscription, and in the 1950s splitting the Labor Party.

At the other end of the theatrical spectrum, a concert version of the much-anticipated *Jesus Christ Superstar* produced by Harry M. Miller, directed by Jim Sharman and designed by Brian Thomson was presented at the 1972 Adelaide Festival as a warm-up for the full production, which opened at Sydney's Capitol Theatre, later that year. Even more than *Hair*, *Jesus Christ Superstar* was receiving the kind of saturation promotion that later came to be associated with the Cameron Macintosh organisation. My over-the-top assault was, in retrospect, a response to the unreal expectations the show had aroused.

Jesus Christ Superstar: **Strictly Secular Miracles**
Australian, 23 March 1972

> God, forgive them, they don't know what they're doing.
> Who is my mother? Where is my mother?
> My God, My God, why have you forgotten me?
> Father, into your hands I commend my spirit.

What really is *Jesus Christ Superstar* all about?

So many expectations from so many people; and a notoriety that has ensured that the 8,000 seats are filled every night at Memorial Drive Park, Adelaide, come what may. The promised brain-snapping experience is a rock concert with a light show which runs one-and-a-half hours without an interval.

Visually there is nothing extraordinary or unexpected in the performance, except that the audience is a much wider cross-section than a differently promoted rock concert would attract. What is new and worth the money is the stupendous 50-piece orchestra, directed with immaculate clarity by Patrick Flynn. The composition is computer accurate, with styles and pastiches slotted into each other like a jig-saw puzzle to make a dazzling, multi-coloured picture. It is a performance of miracles and none of them—this must be made clear—is by Jesus Christ.

Let me describe the history of *JCS* as clearly as I can. Once there was a little single recording released by a highly-trained and academic young musician called Andrew Lloyd Webber and a dropout singer with a pop group called Tim Rice. The record grew into a double LP, and from thence into a concert and was played through Europe and America. Then along came a prince of Broadway called Tom O'Horgan who, having dabbled in Christian imagery in *Hair*, said: 'Let's make of this a real traffic-stopping blockbuster'. And so he chewed up the LP and turned it into bubble gum and he blew and blew until it became a castle in the middle of Broadway, the like of which had never been seen by Sodom and Gomorrah. But the man who was put to live in that castle was still the same little saint who once inhabited one side of a record.

The authors say that *JCS* is about Jesus as a man. In fact, it is an endeavour to express in contemporary terms what those around Jesus felt about him. In this it is singularly successful. The big moments are Mary Magdalene's songs of reassurance, the screaming confusion of Judas in his betrayal of Christ and his penitence; and those scenes showing the aggressive authority of Pontius Pilate and the pitiless Herod.

The great highpoint of the music and action is the scourging scene, in which the fortissimo brass and tympani and the full chorus raise the conflict of political pressure, public recrimination and the private agony to a cataclysmic disaster. Robin Ramsay, in black leather, whipping the air with his microphone lead, is having the most stupendous time on stage since he played Fagin in *Oliver*. The role of Pilate always seems to bring out the best in an actor.

Seriously, though, *Superstar* has the makings of a fine show. It is certainly a blockbuster. What it fails to do entirely is to explain in the least degree what Jesus is trying to do and why so innocent a creature is to be subjected to so violent a death. As a person, Jesus Christ might as well not be there.

Dramatically (and I am sure this was discussed in some detail by the shrewd minds behind *Superstar*) there is well-founded sense in basing a musical upon a popular myth. But if you are going to invite an audience to come and see its favourite story, then you must also at some point surprise them with its newness. In this case the music is surprising in the context, from King Herod's strip rhythm: 'So you are the Christ (*boom*), you're the great Jesus Christ' (*boom*) to Magdalene's rock lullaby: 'Everything's all right, yes everything's fine', and Judas, the despairing revolutionary: 'You sad pathetic man, see where you've brought us to. Our ideas die around us all because of you'.

The show is not blasphemous. There is no intentional denial of the Christ. It is a quite sincere attempt to interpret what happens to a person of Christian qualities in the nasty, brutish materialistic world of today. What the show needs, to lift us out of this brassy amplified rubbish heap into a world of more lasting values, is a superstar. Perhaps it is a reflection on more than the authors of *JCS* that this opera is quite incapable of providing one.

The vacancy at the heart of the show that I perceived in the concert version was magnified in the full production by the extravagant mounting and the enormous expectations. Such was the anticipation, I was required to write an overnight review and, due to a last-minute breakdown of the mechanics on which the show depended, I left the theatre before the final apotheosis. Harry Miller found this difficult to forgive in a critic. The review appeared on 15 May 1972 under the heading, 'Jesus—a triumph of engineering', and was the last overnight review I ever wrote.

The faulty TV monitors that delayed *Jesus Christ Superstar* for an hour in Sydney last night were symptomatic. When, finally, that long-promised, too-long awaited show exploded in a cloud of steam upon a tumultuous and impatient audience, there it was, revealed in all its power, a triumph of mechanical engineering.

There was Jesus, packed in a monolith for the primates to wonder at like the opening scene of *2001 Space Odyssey*. There was Jim Sharman revealed as the Stanley Kubrick of the musical and his designer Brian Thomson as Australia's Sean Kenny, the wizard of Las Vegas. The Australian theatre has seen nothing like it since the real fountains and Venetian canals disappeared from our stages. This is the busiest, most hysterical, most mind-blasting—to use the producer's phrase—show in living memory.

Hair was people. This is mechanics—mass-produced, clinical, mindless kitsch. The show itself is not as bad as it appears and there survive from the concert version beautiful things from Michele Fawdon as Mary Magdalene and Robin Ramsay as Pontius Pilate. And as Herod Joseph

Dicker's baiting of Jesus has a real vulgarity that is true to today's image of the Christian dilemma. But the problem is transparent and insuperable.

Jesus Christ Superstar is a genuinely simple, troubled, mannerist expression of today's questioning of the Christian religion by those who would like to believe. It has been blown up into a huge, baroque Stanley Kubrick, pussy-not-feel-well-in-the-pit-of-the-stomach affirmation of the Godhead for those who can only feel when they are kicked in the guts. Jesus is held up to admiration in a glory of triumphant mechanics that drown in amplification the painful private doubts the poor souls are trying to make understood through the hubbub.

Some feeling comes through; occasionally one is allowed to hear the chorus away from the microphone. The costumes one must salvage as being one of the few interpretations of what I take it the authors are trying to say. In itself the designing is superb—transparent tubes descend from the flies enclosing the tormented apostles and the guilt-ridden Judas. A Leonardo-style Last Supper hangs in space. Pilate's cloak covers half the stage behind him. But the effects tear into each other, pushing aside the chance to study them, in a kind of fever of fear that we might want to hear what the cast is trying to say. What is left is frightening in its shallow contrivance—so much attention and so little to say.

But there it is and there are more than enough people who would rather be hit in the stomach and pretend it is religion than put two thoughts together. But for me it was a heartless exploitation of the best talent in the business and something beautiful spoiled. I would rather Loreto Convent, Kirribilli, had had the rights.

The show was, of course, a huge box-office hit. The composers liked it so much they chose Sharman and Thomson to present the London production, which ran for eight years. Loreto Convent had been in the news for having applied for, and been refused, the rights to perform a concert version.

A Stretch of the Imagination: Taking Interest in the Bare, Forked Animal

Australian, 31 March 1972

Jack Hibberd, the Melbourne playwright who back in the 1960s set the style and started the modern movement in Australian playwriting, has for a little time been wandering in the wilderness. His rich, inventive language has become part of the general theatre scene, his confused, iconoclastic

Peter Cummins as Monk O'Neill in the APG production of *Stretch of the Imagination*, 1972.

style has been expanded by the new developmental groups. Now at last we have the debut of a new Hibberd, a piece of splendid quality and a new sane maturity which contains all the splendours of the Hibberd style inside a feat of self-imposed discipline.

The play, *A Stretch of the Imagination*, opened last week at the Pram Factory, Melbourne, directed by the author. The task he has set himself is for the first time to create a rounded humane character. In the past he has been more concerned with causes and dramatic technique than he has with the minutiae of behaviour. In *A Stretch of the Imagination* he has drawn the portrait of an 80-year-old invalid pensioner with loving care and a sense of wonder at the resilience of the human spirit.

This is a new Hibberd altogether and it puts him once more ahead of his fellows as a playwright not only of vitality and originality but of range and depth. He has also set himself the extraordinary—one might even say unnecessary—discipline of writing a play for a single actor; and accomplishes it with ease. This play is not a one-man show; it is a play in which the single character peoples the stage with a vivid population of lives and loves.

Monk O'Neill, played with great tact, humour and gentleness by Peter Cummins, lives alone in a galvanised iron hut on a barren scrap of earth called One Tree Hill. There was a moment at the beginning, when he crawled out from the hut and stretched his arthritic limbs to face the day, when I thought a little sinkingly of Samuel Beckett. But the thought was unworthy. For this is not a play about barrenness, nor survival, nor does it moralise on our neglect of old people. On the contrary, it reflects the author's wonder at the riches of such a plot to a contented soul. Monk, we discover, is a man who has had three wives and many mistresses, who has travelled widely and had money—or so he would have us believe. And he has failed in every material sense. He relives all this not because he cannot face the present but because the past and the present are equally vivid. The memories are not painful or to be mourned. He looks at the world with a childlike wonder and a humorous shrug of resilience that forestalls pity. Death he welcomes with the same friendliness with which he receives life.

The play in Peter Cummins' hands is effortless to watch, a balm to the spirit and a new and promising departure into naturalism for the Australian Performing Group.

The play has continued to be compared with the work of Samuel Beckett and most of the many productions have been darker than this one. In retrospect I think I did not take sufficient account of the contribution made by the amiable Peter Cummins' interpretation of Monk to making the play 'effortless to watch, a balm to the spirit'. In February 1973 the production toured to Sydney, where on 8 February I reviewed it in tandem with a Viennese comedy from the 20s, *By Candlelight*, by Siegfried Geyer, playing at the Community theatre, Killara (Headed 'Strange Bedfellows—but both in need of more style'). Of the APG's style I wrote:

The Australian Performing Group (on its first visit to Sydney to play at the Australian Theatre, Newtown) is being judged for the first time for standards of professionalism similar to the Community or Parade theatres. Precision of detail has never worried the APG and its authors very much. It has attracted an audience by its enthusiasm, its daring and has used a close, almost physical, contact with its audience to stretch their imagination. It has, for this reason, eschewed what it calls ornamental acting, the summit of which is the kind of elaborately confected, wholly conscious, style designed for a play like *By Candlelight*. It has wanted to create a kind of acting that is warts and all.

Cummins' style is a sensitive one that invites you gently into his confidence. Watched from a distance of a few feet it has much compassion and integrity. But it does not have precision, projection and vocal range. Questions of the shape of the play, the shape of the sequences within it, the precise timing of the hundreds of jokes dotted through the text, would appear from the production not to have entered the consideration of the author-director. The Carlton complex has won brilliantly a long battle to recognise the Australian playwright and an indigenous style, and it is now facing the Goliath of professionalism. It is a matter of great regret that the Australian Council for the Arts turned down the group's application for a grant large enough to put the full collective on salary to work on this very problem. It is crucial at this point of maturity that a method be established for this madness at present called Aussie acting. As one well-known actress described it: 'A man must be capable of playing Macbeth to play a role like this'.

The APG writers have reached the point now where they must develop their plays outside the group or be left behind by the rest of the world.

Alex Buzo was the first of the New Wave to gain attention abroad when a production of *Rooted* by the Hartford Stage Company, Hartford, Connecticut in January 1972 attracted the attention of the American press. It was followed in 1973 by a production at the Hampstead Theatre Club, London, and a season of his play *Tom* by the Arena Stage in Washington, DC.

Also reviewed here are *Sonia's Knee and Thigh Show*, a reference to Sonia McMahon, wife of the then Prime Minister William McMahon, who had worn a revealing dress, with a side-split to the thigh, to a state dinner in Washington; and Rex Cramphorn's *The Tempest*, for the Old Tote's schools program. In the latter, the cast sat on the rim of the stage when not taking part in the action and provided music and sound effects. They also spoke Ariel's lines.

Rooted: Comic Flowering of the Buzo Genius
Australian, 18 April 1972

Alexander Buzo's comedy, *Rooted*, which earlier this year made its American debut with some critical success, is now to be seen at the Claremont Theatre Centre, Melbourne, and next month at the Nimrod Theatre, Sydney. It is an ingenious and witty indictment of the shaky foundations of Aussie mateship and the way the little man submits to the system—in fact, of the accepted rituals and unstable standards of judgment with which most of us guide our lives. 'You must have a point of reference', Bentley keeps saying as his world crumbles round him.

We first meet Bentley, a public servant in his twenties, in a nice little home unit at Bondi, packed with status symbols of mechanical luxury. His wife, Sandy, is clearly bored with him. That worse things are to come is soon apparent: from a vantage-point offstage Simmo, a former schoolmate, has begun to take over his friend, his wife and—the last insult—his home unit. Simmo is a composite of all those people who have ever got the better of us: the school hero, the football captain, the bully, the seducer, the one who beats us to promotion.

Simmo is unseen through the play—as are Bentley's other legendary boyhood mates Hammo and Davo—but he mushrooms like the body in Ionesco's *Amédeé* until there is no room in this little world for Bentley.

It is easy to see why *Rooted* has attracted the American taste. Not only is this a popular capitalistic nightmare, but it introduces the first flowering of Buzo's verbal comedy—which is both firmly linked to American gag style and exotically, juicily Australian. The play has much in common with the comedy of Neil Simon or Woody Allen, who combine hair-rasing verbal feats with a central comic character in an appalling position of defeat. Bentley is a wonderful creation in the tradition of all the great sad comics, pitting his feeble strength uselessly against superhuman forces and remaining desperately optimistic in the face of defeat.

The other battle Buzo takes on is those ambivalent male relationships established by years of proximity in school, bars and gatherings around the keg. The members of Buzo's hearty school gang, now in their twenties, protest their pleasure in each other's company, their reliability, their fidelity. But the edifice crumbles the minute pressure is applied. Buzo is at his best in pointing out the cracks—failure to recognise each other, shared memories gone, jokes at each other's expense.

Kevin Howard at the Claremont Theatre deals with both sides of Bentley splendidly; and the scenes with Bruce Kerr, as his friend Richard, are the best in the play. Some of the other characters are less successful. Sandy is a fiendish role for any actress and Sue Kerr has not yet found a way to tackle her. The complications of the play tend to be exaggerated by the small stage, despite the neat and pertinent design; and Leila Blake's production, while it does cope very well with many of the difficulties has a staginess which tends to emphasise others.

But the play is not an easy one for a director, nor is it faultless. The peripheral characters depend too heavily on allegory and comic turns; and the mythical power of Simmo, by remaining unexplained, has, by the end of the play, become an extended joke. Buzo, like Pinter and Ionesco, with whom he has been compared, depends for the success of his enormities on a convincing and serious ordinariness. To this necessity I would add a drifting rhythm that is tightly woven into Buzo's writing and brings him close to us.

Satire of another kind is available in the Australian Performing Group's revue, *Sonia's Knee and Thigh Show*. The material is a heartily scurrilous collection of sketches by the APG's writers on matters such as the Melbourne City Council's urban renewal plans, conscription, American ownership of Australian companies, the pressures of being a successful wife and career woman, and the Prime Minister's virility. Some of it is good, some not. All of it is dictated by a general but ill-defined libertarianism. The best pieces are those in which some sense of character is developed—a devastating near-verbatim account of Mrs Sonia McMahon's Washington press conference, an Italian greengrocer and wife describing the projected demolition of the Victoria Markets, the redevelopment plan for Carlton, a Vietnam veteran and a pair of Catholic public servants discussing sex. The final blow is the tale of a prime minister with a Pinocchio complex. This will no doubt receive notoriety beyond its deserts, but it is really much funnier as an idea than a performance.

Rex Cramphorne, who has already shown us he can do remarkable things with Shakespeare, has devised a production of *The Tempest* with a cast of seven, for performance in Sydney schools. Much of the interpretation is stunning, most particularly the conception of Prospero as a magician, drawing his characters into a magic circle and conjuring up the spirit of Ariel through his wand and a magic ribbon. Dazzling also is the chanting, particularly of Miranda and Ferdinand, as they are drawn innocently and inexorably together; and the musical accompaniment which evokes the magical powers of music in Shakespeare's verse.

But there are problems which had not been overcome at the time I saw it—the chief being that many of the lines were inaudible, especially those of Nick Lathouris' Prospero. Cramphorne has David Cameron play both Ferdinand and Caliban, which ingeniously defines the spiritual network of Prospero's world; but dramatically it has not been properly devised.

As a whole, Cramphorne's investigation into the text of *The Tempest* is not quite as thorough as it was for *Pericles*, and his intention at the close defeated me entirely. Prospero for much of the time seemed too much under the influence of his magic mushroom to dictate the action; and I simply could not see how Shakespeare's vision of benison was being incorporated into Lathouris' interpretation. Gillian Jones' Miranda, however, was a small—no, a large—miracle.

In Eugene Ionesco's *Amédeé* or *How to get rid of it* (1954), a couple's house is consumed by a swelling corpse.

A Royal Requiem

Australian, 13 May 1972

Balloons, streamers and tears were shed on the stage of Sydney's Theatre Royal late last month as the curtain came down for the last time on that site since it first rose in 1863 [actually 1875]. Timothy West, leader of Britain's Prospect Theatre Company, which has been performing *Love's Labour's Lost*, read a prologue referring to the future of drama in this country from the opening of the Sydney's first Theatre Royal. And he mourned the loss of—words that in a week have already become a catchphrase—'this fine, this historic, this useful theatre'.

The Theatre Royal was sold some two-and-a-half years ago to Lend Lease Corporation as part of a larger site including the Hotel Australia in Castlereagh Street. The sale passed with some, but no concerted protest, except from the lessees, J. C. Williamson's Ltd; and the repeated deferral of the death-knock lulled the murmurs into silence.

So that it was only recently that the hard fact began to knock on the consciousness of the general public and the acting profession that Sydney was about to lose its last example of the Victorian proscenium-arch theatre. For more than a hundred years a theatre has stood on that site, in the throbbing centre of Sydney, housing artists like Dion Boucicault, Sarah Bernhardt, Nellie Melba, George Rignold, J. C. Williamson, Gladys Moncrieff, Madge Elliott and Cyril Ritchard. Its further historical importance is enhanced by evidence that it was designed by Edmund Blacket [actually J. P. Hilly].

And so a protest began three weeks ago when members of the theatre profession taking part in a Peter Summerton Foundation seminar with directors of the Prospect Theatre Company, formed a last-ditch save the

Theatre Royal committee. They have received telegrams of support from all over the world from eminent guest artists to expatriate Australians and supporters within the country. Supporters include John Grey Gorton, Gough Whitlam, Don Dunstan and Gladys Moncrieff.

Two weeks ago, faced with a highly vocal protest meeting at the AMP Theatre, chaired with becoming partiality by Mr Justice Martin Hardy of the Land and Valuation Court, the chairman of directors of Lend Lease, Mr G. J. Dusseldorp, made two concessions: first to postpone the auction of contents scheduled for last Thursday and secondly to entertain a committee of professional men to investigate the feasibility of saving the building. He did that, he said, in the knowledge that such a committee would come to the same conclusion as he, that the problems were insuperable. They were: making the theatre comply with health and safety requirements, surviving two railway tunnels bisecting the foundations, and building, as had been suggested, a shell over it to take a high-rise block.

The building was in a dilapidated state, he said. The air-conditioning and ventilation had packed up, the condition of the seating and carpets was bad and the backstage facilities obsolete. He could build a new theatre for the price of renovation. He added that the new complex would contain a 500-seat 'experimental' theatre which would be offered free of charge to theatre groups; and he offered also to include a new theatre of similar size to the Theatre Royal on the old Tivoli Theatre site. As a result of the meeting Lend Lease revised its plans and announced it would build a 1,000-seat theatre to replace the Theatre Royal.

Three years ago, Lend Lease had, in fact, promised Sydney it would replace the Tivoli Theatre; plans had gone some distance and J. C. Williamson's were to have leased it. But when it was realised just how far behind office-space rental theatre-space rental was, the project was quickly dropped. It is obvious that no theatre building can survive on the land values of the city area. Because of this, Sydney has a crippling lack of large theatres. It has lost three in the past four years and the Theatre Royal will be the last of its kind. But if Mr Dusseldorp can give Sydney two new theatres for the price of one, can the preservation of the Theatre Royal be justified?

The present Adam-style decoration and proscenium arch (much larger than the original) date from 1921. Modern construction could enable the removal of the supporting posts in the auditorium that obscured a view of the stage and architects and theatre people agree that the building would be improved by restoring the Blacket [Hilly] proscenium. The two most cogent arguments in favour of retention came from the environmentalists, led by Mr Justice Hardy and Mr Jack Mundey, president of the Builders Labourers' Federation; and from Mr Toby Robertson, director of the Prospect Theatre Company. 'Sydney is like a bombed city', Mr Hardy said fiercely. 'The developers are tearing the heart out of the centre. By demolishing such a building they are creating a city that dies at the end of the day. By doing such a thing they will lose in goodwill and in public relations so much it will not be worth their while.'

Mr Mundey's view was a down-to-earth one. 'All Australians have a right to decide what is to be retained and what destroyed.' The Congregational Church in Pitt Street, he said mildly, had been saved by industrial action. He would wait for a public report from the expert committee and if, in the light of this, it was felt that Lend Lease's actions were not in the public interest, he would not stand in the way of a black ban by his union. As a tradesman he was concerned, he said, that the city was becoming a canyon of glass and concrete, most of it architecturally bankrupt.

Toby Robertson, whose company depends for its livelihood upon such large old theatres in Britain and Europe, said that the useful qualities of the building could not be reproduced by a modern architect. The Theatre Royal had the capacity to take plays from the early seventeenth century to the present day.

Mr Justice Hardy pointed to a weakness in the Local Government Act which placed restrictions on new development but none on demolition. Alderman Leo Port described the floor space ratio bonuses available to developers who wished to provide amenities, and pointed out that it was possible to transfer to another site the bonuses acquired by preserving a building. In the case of the Congregational Church the church authorities had been permitted to add floors to their adjacent building. Mr Dusseldorp, he said, could transfer bonuses from the Theatre Royal site to the Tivoli site.

It is difficult for a builder like Mr Dusseldorp to conceive that modern architects might not be capable of providing better buildings than the Victorians. He spoke with feeling of old buildings as rabbit warrens and death traps. But people once knew what they wanted from theatre buildings much better than they do now. Mr Robertson has an irrefutable argument:

that no modern architect anywhere has tried or succeeded in reproducing the actor–audience relationship of the Victorian and Georgian theatres. If we are to continue to be hosts to touring companies like his own, we must be able to provide a practical house. Scenery from a normal touring company could not be used in the Opera House, he said. It would have to be specially made. 'To work in, the Georgian theatre just is better than any other theatre yet invented.'

'They are taking away all the places we loved', mourned the president of the Housewives' Association. 'They are turning the city from a place to live, into a place to exist in. We cried when they pulled down the Hotel Australia.'

What chance does the Save the Theatre Royal Committee have? Mr Dusseldorp has dealt with such committees before. But to judge by the public's growing impatience with development it would appear to be quite good. The Minister for Local Government, Mr Morton, has assumed power to act in the matter; the City Council and the Labor Opposition view the matter as one of 'grave concern'. On the other hand Mr Dusseldorp's principals are in Holland and are not concerned with the interests of the people in Sydney. The committee's major task now is to find ways and means and this will involve money and the powers of all these authorities. If a way can be found to save the Theatre Royal, then I suspect that the simple builder's labourer, as he calls himself, Mr Jack Mundey, may have the last word.

I say the curtain first rose in 1863, but in fact the first theatre on the site, the Prince of Wales, opened its doors in 1855. The Theatre Royal, which opened in 1875, was the third theatre on the site. Both it, and its predecessor, the second Prince of Wales (1863) were designed by the architect J. P. Hilly, in his time considered a better architect than the more celebrated Edmund Blacket. On 19 May 1972, I continued the story under the heading 'When the public gets up and asserts itself':

An accumulation of events over the past week, culminating in a public meeting at the Town Hall on Monday night, has sealed the fate of Sydney's Theatre Royal. The Lend Lease Corporation's plans for their centre-city block, examined by a committee of architects and engineers, showed that, because of the underground railway under construction which bisects the block, the only area on which a 780-foot tower could be erected was on the site of the Theatre Royal.

In his report to the meeting, the architect and theatre historian Ross Thorne said that Lend Lease's plan relied heavily on space-ratio bonuses and the tower was necessary to make the whole complex economically feasible. Retaining the old theatre required a new concept for the whole block; and two years after work had begun was too late for such radical rethinking.

He said that it would be easy to provide a new 1,000-seat theatre that would comply with the Chief Secretary's regulations, be well-raked and give a less interrupted view of the stage than the present theatre. The only way of retaining the theatre appeared to be to buy it for some $5 to $10 million. In view of the evidence, he said the committee felt there were very few rational arguments for retaining the present theatre.

The chairman of Lend Lease (Mr G. J. Dusseldorp) agreed, upon a resolution of the meeting, to enter an agreement with the Save the Theatre Royal Committee to ensure that the new theatre 'conform at least to the performing standards and quality of environment of the existing Theatre Royal'. And that the building be available for live theatre at an economic rent, have a seating capacity of no less than 1,000 and that certain features of the present building be maintained.

The meeting, led by the president of the Builders Labourers' Federation (Mr Jack Mundey) passed a further resolution to establish an enlarged vigilante committee to prevent further demolitions of buildings of architectural or public value until the government enacts suitable legislation.

The Theatre Royal row has served two purposes. It has awakened the public to the fact that Mr Mundey, who has taken industrial action on previous occasions to prevent the demolition of historical buildings, is serious in his concern for the environment and buildings in which we take pleasure. And it has drawn attention to the fact that the ordinary citizen can be effective in preventing disasters of this kind. But the dangers concerning the Theatre Royal are by no means past. In fact they are just beginning. A new theatre that will not only incorporate the advantages of the present building but eliminate the disadvantages, sounds a fine idea. And after all, it will be the fourth theatre on that site. The fact is that new theatre buildings with proscenium arches that actually work for both actor and audience are very rare indeed. They certainly do not exist in this country. Some are passable from the audience's point of view. None have less than one major problem for the artist. And, as was pointed out at the meeting, in most cases backstage facilities have been whittled away in construction as building costs mounted. A theatre plan already drawn up by the architect of the Lend Lease project, Mr Harry Seidler, will clearly not do, despite the fact that it has been passed for approval by the Minister for Local Government (Mr Morton) apparently in an effort to conclude the dispute.

To build a theatre that actually works requires a great deal of hidden space with no rent return; and Lend Lease have already dealt with this problem on the site of the old Tivoli. Here they are embarking on the second stage of a building complex under an agreement with the City Council to build public amenities including a cinema, a theatre, a licensed restaurant and attendant entertainment amenities. For this they received the concession of ground rent from the city commissioners of $1 per year for a period of two to three years. This amounts to $150,000 in local subsidy for public facilities.

The City Council claims that Lend Lease's conduct has been 'most unsatisfactory'. The theatre originally was to be a thrust-stage building to seat 1,300, with a throw to the back of the gallery of 65 feet. And it was to have been leased by J. C. Williamson's Ltd. But over the months the building space was whittled away. To quote the JCW manager, Mr Sydney Irving: 'Finally we were offered a one-level theatre suitable for a third-rate cinema and at an enormous rent'. They were also required to fit out the building as a theatre. Clearly the time has come for public demand to be demonstrated about favourite public buildings of every kind before sins are committed that later we will wish undone.

On Wednesday the Theatre Royal committee, now called the Save Sydney Committee, signed a lengthy agreement with Mr Dusseldorp on the new theatre. Besides the points agreed on Monday, the substance of the agreement is that both the original design and all amendments thereto will be discussed with the committee before being submitted to the City Council. A theatre consultant will be employed and every effort will be made to have the theatre ready for use before the end of 1973.

Though I don't mention his name, the prime mover in this campaign was the theatre director John Tasker, who used his Labor Party connections to engage the interest of the Builders Labourers' Federation. The vendors were the descendants of Gustave Ramaciotti, J. C. Williamson's partner 1904–11, who had bought the theatre in 1897. The developers Lend Lease were also developers of the Tivoli site.

The present Theatre Royal, which faces onto King Street, was opened in 1976.

The original review said it was the fourth Theatre Royal on the site, but in fact the first two theatres were called Prince of Wales. The new theatre was designed by Harry Seidler and seats 1,000. The old theatre seated 1,292. Seidler's theatre is practical, has better backstage facilities and has been important in providing Sydney with musicals since the demise of J. C. Williamson's but it does not have the grace of the old theatre. To me it is like sitting inside a bandbox. While some items were saved from auction and many of the decorative features of the old theatre were conserved during the demolition, none found their way into the new building.

The Tivoli in Castlereagh Street, Haymarket, opened in 1911 as the Adelphi, was designed by Henry E. White and seated 2,500. It was demolished in 1969 and no replacement theatre was provided on the site. It was replaced with an office block. The nearest Sydney has to a theatre of that size is the Sydney Opera House concert hall which holds 2679 including behind the orchestra. The renovated Capitol Theatre holds 2,000.

By this time Philip and I had founded Currency Press and begun publishing in an amateur way the plays of the New Wave. Our first play, Alex Buzo's *Macquarie*, had been launched in January 1972. In the light of this, I began to assign some reviewing to others and at times changed the approach I took myself.

The Sound of Our Own Voice

Australian, 27 May 1972

To be seen in Sydney a new comedy by Peter Kenna at the Independent Theatre called *Listen Closely;* and at the Nimrod Theatre Alexander Buzo's *Rooted*. Being closely associated with both writers as a promoter of new playwriting, I am not in a position to write with disinterest about the productions. Instead I want to interpret as nearly as I can the kind of writing they are attempting and the challenges it sets.

The new production of *Rooted* raises a number of interesting questions. It is a good production, better by a way than the Melbourne one, with fine performances particularly from Max Phipps, Helen Morse and Serge Lazareff; and it tackles head-on in a firmly naturalistic manner the problems raised by this totally original style.

I have written often about Buzo's verbal style, his dedication to the task of exhuming the rich variety of our lingo ('Diane nearly went off her brain') and to hold it up to the light. *Rooted* was his first exercise in extending this examination into a full-length play. And in it he has tackled a vital task remaining to be solved by the new vernacular school. This is how to extract the inner Aussie man from his carapace of jargon. (It is a fairly new problem. Kenna seems never to have faced it. The characters in his work are always articulate.)

The first challenge for the new writers has been to capture the vernacular for the stage. With this they have been able to people the stage with a range of recognisable types and to make judgments about them. This is what Buzo has done in *Rooted*. Bentley, the central character, is a typical public servant with a mouthful of pedantic jokes and phrases. His wife is everyone's nightmare of a teenage go-getter sexpot; their friends cover the chunderous surfland, the art world, business and so on.

At one level we have a complete cartoon of the world of the young middle-class Sydney man. On another we have the author's criticism of it; on still another the familiar persecution nightmare which at some time has enveloped all of us. As punishment for being so boring, acquisitive and pathetic, Bentley has everything taken from him, bit by bit—his home unit, his wife, his status. The last we see of him is in a borrowed blanket being thrown out the door.

It is a very witty play and the audiences who are packing it are in ecstasies of joy over the code language. But there are problems which neither the Melbourne nor Sydney productions have solved and which are leading me to the belief that a whole new approach to the treatment of plays like this is needed.

At the time when *The Legend of King O'Malley* burst on the scene in 1970 I wrote about how the rhythm of Australian life was at last being defined on the stage without reference to the conventions. Of how extravagant and lazy we were in our expression and how we would prefer to use an expletive as a blanket adjective than to take time to choose the appropriate word. Twelve months of exuberance in the theatre served the purpose of hitting the public on the head with the fact that our playwrights were no longer prepared to be ignored.

Under the tumult there has been a steady consolidation. Buzo has not in his early plays solved all the problems of style which he has set himself but there is a precision in the rhythm of the writing which demands a new approach to orchestration. Behind the apparently rambling scenes there is a backbone of formality. For example, there are two almost identical scenes in which two unexpected guests catch Bentley at a disadvantage. When embarrassment reaches its height the couple hastily make their departure incanting over the unfortunate Bentley a liturgy of aphorisms. In the Melbourne production this was done formally, in the Sydney production naturalistically. Neither really worked because the emphasis was placed on the situation rather than the words. Phrases such as 'Don't let it get you down; live it up; have a bash; play it cool' are only approximations of language. We are not used to listening to them. What writers like Buzo and Kenna are doing so well is to make us listen. But we will only listen if the actor shows us how.

Kenna's new play, *Listen Closely* is a petit bourgeois comedy of manners in just the way *Tartuffe* is. It is set in a country pub to which Henry is being dragged to celebrate his eighteenth birthday. The town's tradition determines that on this occasion every boy in the town must get drunk with his father and lay the barmaid, Flora. The plot is disrupted by Henry's tyrannical mother and his fiancée Lesley who between them bring the pub almost to the ground.

On the surface the play is a conventional three-act domestic comedy, an entertaining light piece in the style of *Saturday Night at the Crown*. But two things make it a more substantial play. One is the strongly imaginative poetic image in the construction, a comic vision of Aphrodite and Artemis fighting over the young Apollo until the temple crumbles. The other is the almost celebratory quality of the language. Carole Skinner as Flora the barmaid gives a fine performance and the rhythms come to her naturally. As the mother Judi Farr, who usually does so well in this kind of dominant role, seems to keep slipping out of focus. The answer is not in her conception of the role but, again, in her orchestration of the language.

Kenna, having made his name in the 1950s can, though still only 42, be regarded as one of our older writers. He began writing at a time when the three-act format was obligatory and plays that discarded it tended to fail. But within that framework he has built characters more solidly real than those who followed him have managed. He stands almost alone, too, as a playwright for women. Except for Dorothy Hewett's Sally, whom Melbourne saw this month, there are almost no good women's roles in the contemporary writing. The central character in all but one of Kenna's plays is a motherly, striking woman and his insight is unusual in its compassion.

The Independent production has relied very largely on situation for its effect and this does emphasise the conventional qualities in the play. It is a play not for looking but for listening, as the title suggests, and this is beginning to apply to almost all our new plays. It does not come as easily to us as looking. *Listen Closely* is a difficult mandate for a country which has never been very proud of the sound of its own voice.

My review of Robin Lovejoy's Old Tote production of Molière's *Tartuffe*, with John Gaden in the title role, preceded this one; *Saturday Night at the Crown* was a Lancashire comedy by Walter Greenwood, starring Thora Hird, which I had reviewed on 19 February 1972.

Don's Party: An Ecstatic New Comedy Finds an Audience

Australian, 6 July 1972

David Williamson's *Don's Party*, the second play in the Jane Street Theatre's 1972 Australian season is nothing short of a triumph—a rare and startling combination of cast, production and script in the right place at the right time. In my review of the last Jane Street play, Tom Keneally's *An Awful Rose*, I made curt note that, with so many untried playwrights looking for a nursery, Jane Street chose to bet on a certainty by selecting the playwright of the year {Williamson}, and a play which had already proved itself in Melbourne. But times change and many nurseries have sprung up since Jane Street first opened its doors in 1966. And the road to success is still a complex one for the theatre writer. What John Clark has done so admirably in his production of this rorty comedy-drama is to turn a good play into a good marketable play.

Such a director our young playwrights have long been yearning for— not someone who competently gets the play on, or one who mauls it into conformity for a preconceived but problematical audience. I mean someone with respect for the writer who presents his qualities in clever and attractive packaging. No other Australian theatre director has yet done this so effectively and those who follow will look back on this production as a new step toward our cultural maturity. This is Williamson's year indeed: two Awgie awards, the George Devine Award, the film *Stork*, *The Removalists* opening at the Playbox on 10 August, his new play *Jugglers Three* at the Russell Street Theatre on 17 July; and now this new surprise which will transfer to the Parade Theatre in September.

Don's Party is Williamson's second full-length play and is set in a Brighton (Melbourne) house on election night, 1969. Don has invited the mates of his university days, fellow Labor men, to celebrate the projected Whitlam victory. It is ten years since their graduation and they don't have all that much in common any more. Their women have almost nothing.

One man is an industrial psychologist compensating for his

dissatisfactions by ignoring his wife and overspending on his home. Another is a dentist with a too-attractive wife who likes to freely exercise her artistic libido; a third an advertising man who takes pornographic photos of his wife because he is 'curious'. And there is the inimitable Cooley, a lawyer still on the carnal knowledge round, to the admiration and despair of his marriage-trapped friends.

Don's Party was first performed at the Café La Mama in Melbourne and last year had a season at the Pram Factory. There it was presented in the round over a large area and at such close quarters the audience was made a part of the play. It was also played without an interval, was apparently formless and had an impelling acceleration which continued through the whole evening. The language was wild, the air bohemian, the standard of performance erratic. The most distinctive thing about it was the wit and the acute, observant sense of the Melbourne locality. If there is one thing I regret in the transfer it is that this Melburnian quality has been sacrificed to a wider context.

At Jane Street the play has been remodelled, set in Sydney and given an interval. The speed and emphasis has changed. There is none of the desperation of the Melbourne production and almost none of the viciousness. In its place is an assured emphasis upon the dialogue, which reveals not only the stunning wit but a great warmth which has not before emerged from Williamson's work. Unlike most of his contemporaries he is not a satirist but writes with an almost unshockable compassion. This motley group of people at the watershed of middle age have inevitability and face not defeat, but reconciliation to age which the older cast at Jane Street understands. The voting counts, which crackle from the television throughout the evening, capture in a single image the author's compassionate view of these friends; he shares with them their hopes, their fiery façade, their faded radicalism. None of us can alter the passage of time and we all know that the Labor Party did not win the 1969 election.

On the surface Don's is a party like any other. In fact the action is full of shocks; the comedy is a gag a line. But the sheer joy of the play lies in the people themselves: familiar, funny and real. And this is where John Clark has it all over the Australian Performing Group, and where we find a different play. Martin Harris, John Ewart, James H. Bowles: I have seen them do nothing better. The men on the whole have the edge over the women's roles.

Don's Party has now become a disciplined comedy of character designed to attract the young with its wildness and the shockable middle-aged with its truth. The production combines all the attractions of commercial comedy with the lasting elements of serious comedy. Exchanges like that between Mack and Cooley over the qualities of certain photographs; Cooley's account of Mal the psychologist as an encyclopaedia salesman—this is comedy at its purest. *Don's Party* cannot fail to go on playing to a wide, ecstatic audience for a very long time.

As indeed it did. The mentoring David Williamson received during this production set him on the path of the 'Williamson play' as we know it today.

Inside an Intricate Web of Dependence

Australian, 8 September 1972

This week I paid my first visit to the Brisbane Repertory's new La Boite Theatre in the round, which opened in July. The opening production was Rodney Milgate's massive allegorical account of the life of a pop singer, *A Refined Look at Existence*, which in the intimate proportions of La Boite became a participatory pop concert and had great popularity. This was followed by Arthur Miller's four-hand drama *The Price*, to be succeeded by the racy jibe at RSL Clubs and childhood heroes, *Biggles*, which opened the Nimrod Theatre two years ago.

The variety of styles is part of an experiment to discover the uses of the theatre's space; and an interesting space it is. The new building increases the auditorium capacity from 70 to 200 and is literally a 'box'. The arena is square, with steeply raked seating and gives a satisfying feeling of being enclosed in the same space as the characters and their problems, while at the same time being securely above them. This makes for an excellent play-audience relationship.

The Price, which I saw performed, gains greatly from the architecture. It is a beautifully constructed play, low-keyed enough to lose some of its vibrations behind a proscenium arch. The cast—John Dwyer, Claire Crowther, Edward Thompson and Neil Woodgate, with director Jane Atkins—did not give a technically polished performance but they played comfortably at close quarters with the audience. The play, in these circumstances, emerged more purely than it has in some more glamorous productions I have seen. Miller has drawn a most intricate web of dependence between four people—two brothers who have not met in sixteen years, one wife and the old Jewish furniture dealer whose presence among the possessions of their dead father is the excuse for the central situation. The play opens by tying all of them together in a tight knot of frustration and yearning and gently unbinds until it becomes clear to each of them in turn that no one else can be made responsible for the direction of one's own life.

The Nimrod Theatre, Sydney, has discovered a play with an oddly similar anatomical attraction, the same examination of the false interdependence of lives, the same acute observation of the beneath-the-surface world. It is *The Sweatproof Boy*, by a New Zealander, Alma De Groen, married to the Sydney painter Geoffrey De Groen and at present living in Canada. Mrs De Groen is not a comfortable writer. *The Sweatproof Boy* is her first full-length play—an examination of the aridity of a prosperous suburban couple and a remarkable study from a writer, at the time only 25-years-old, of the pain of middle age.

She followed this play with a short, violent piece first performed last year by the Stratford (Ontario) Festival Theatre workshop, *The Joss Adams Show*, which Melbourne will see soon at the Pram Factory. *Joss Adams* is the study of the state of mind of a young woman who batters her baby to death. Together with her portrait of Olivia in *The Sweatproof Boy*, they make an important addition to the new theatre; writing with a deep and uncanny insight into the female psyche at all ages, beginning among the nightmares of the subconscious and rising unerringly into the light of recognition.

This is a characteristic shared by a handful of New Zealand writers whose work I have read recently. On the surface lie an apparent calm and at the same time a tension, as if a lid were pressing down on those troubled volcanic geysers. The force is vertical, in direct contrast to the extravagant horizontal sweep of the Australians; and they are almost all without comedy of any significance. It is a pretty gloomy, repressed, sadistic existence they are choosing to uncover.

Mrs De Groen, however, has written about Sydney and sets her play in Vaucluse. Charles and Olivia are a childless, dehydrated couple who let a room in their expensive harbour-view house in order to have a third person sit between them at breakfast. Charles has a children's radio program and is beginning to lose his touch. He is cold, prim; she is timid and childlike; both of them have never had much of the flesh about them. They married young and have preserved their immaturity in formalin.

Into this unhappy household comes Sam, a young, beautiful and fleshly satyr, a gigolo of the arts world, one who has made a career of his instinct for what this dried-out middle-aged world needs; and he unbuttons Olivia, partly from impudence, partly from compassion.

Alma De Groen and the producer between them capture with dazzling precision the knowingness, selfishness and innocent brutality of youth; Sam is played with splendid insolence by Joe Hasham. Equally absorbing are the other two characters, particularly Olivia; a menopausal figure familiar in literature but rarely to be found in our drama outside Seymour and Kenna. Rilla Scott, returning to the stage after ten years, plays her most movingly and the pair are equally matched by John Morris as Charles. His performance on roller skates to the strains of 'Abide with Me' is a moment of real joy.

The production by Richard Wherrett is beautifully understated, the best production yet I have seen of his. Altogether the evening is a most compelling one, full of surprises, different from anything the Nimrod has offered before. They have clearly chosen the right moment to make the change.

After this production Alma De Groen suppressed this play. She used some of the material to create a brief work called *Perfectly All Right.*

The Chocolate Frog: Laughter without Bitterness from a Prison Cell

Australian, 11 August 1972

The author was not in the audience on Monday when the Melbourne Theatre Company presented his two pieces of evidence, a timely comment on the Pentridge Inquiry. Jim McNeil is in Parramatta Gaol serving the last two years of a sentence for shooting a policeman.

Presenting a prisoner's eye view to the general public is not that easy from inside Parramatta and McNeil has found a way. He has written two plays, *The Chocolate Frog* first performed outside gaol by the Q Theatre in Sydney, and *The Old Familiar Juice.* Both plays have been introduced to Melbourne audiences at the MTC by the director Malcolm Robertson, who discovered McNeil in a prison drama class. It is odd, and perhaps a tribute to the truth-telling of the emergent plays, that McNeil has been able, with such apparent ease, to have his name joined with the new stream of writing while cut off not only from his fellow artists but from the very world to which his work is a communique.

The setting for the two plays is a three-bed prison cell. In the first the arrival of a young first-offender gives two old lags the chance to explain their stern Old Testament view of justice, the system of honour among thieves and their strong sense of belonging to the prison. The aspect most splendid about McNeil's writing is its sane, balanced assessment of the world he knows. He does not rail against the prison system. He merely points out the absurdities of depending for justice and mercy upon innocent nuns, crusty old-fashioned magistrates and illiterate, underpaid and bullying officers. And in confining convicted criminals to their own company: 'While we are inside training to rob', says Shirker in *The Chocolate Frog*. And Bulla in *The Old Familiar Juice* describes the Second World War as servicemen 'out there fighting for our prison system'. It is forceful but not bitter writing and will have the more influence for that. The gift of making people laugh at fear has always had a more lasting effect than tirades of despair.

The Old Familiar Juice is about the way an ill-suited trio rub along together: a talkative unhappy bully, a resigned wino and a youngster. The pointless routine of their day is brightened by the chance to steal yeast from the bakery, which, mixed with sugar and water in a slops bucket and allowed to ferment, makes a fiery and acceptable booze.

I first saw the play inside Parramatta, performed in a confined space by members of the Resurgents Debating Society. Seeing it and the other play on a larger stage and in less emotive surroundings makes one aware of some thinness in the writing, of much that is left unsaid. This is inevitable, in the circumstances, and what is there leaves one in no doubt that McNeil is a natural dramatist of great wit and charm. *The Old Familiar Juice* is, technically, an advance on his first play; but his full capacities will be seen only when he has the same freedom to work as other writers. May that day be hastened.

Malcolm Robertson's productions seemed to be suffering from hasty preparation; the cast on opening night were finding the rhythms of the plays difficult. John Clayton, from the original Sydney cast, has a grasp of the McNeil vernacular and he held the work well, but his natural slow style needs a foil he is not yet getting from his colleague.

Pentridge Prison in Coburg, Victoria dated from 1850. It was progressively closed to prisoners and opened to tourists from 1994.

Shirker's lines are: 'Here we are with the squareheads payin' for our tucker, while we're strainin' to get out and rob them again. And the genius 'ere reckons it's all necessary. Haw!' And Bulla of the old man: 'All the *men* went orf to fight fer our prisons system but 'e stayed behind to hold the walls up.'

The Resurgents Debating Society was an elite prisoners' group that debated teams from outside prison.

Bon-bons and Roses for Dolly

Australian, 16 October 1972

> My sister and I played the adapted plots of movies all day in my grandmother's sleepout, dressed up in her ostrich feathers, black jet beads and yellowing Victorian petticoats. Under the corrugated iron we played our torrid love dramas while the temperature outside in the paddocks was 112 degrees [44 degrees Celsius]. That was where I got my theatrical training—at the movies.

So writes Dorothy Hewett in the program note to her new musical play, *Bon-bons and Roses for Dolly*, which has its premiere at the Perth Playhouse. Audiences in Perth are looking sideways at the play, as well they might, because Miss Hewett is a deeply Western Australian writer who uncomfortably likes to disinter, even to dwell upon, aspects of its life about which there is a conspiracy of silence.

The play is set in a cinema, the Crystal Palace, opened in 1933. It has been built out of the life and dreams of Dolly's grandparents and parents, who each in their own way have failed to touch more than the borders of their potential and who readily substitute for life their dream factory, the Hollywood movies. Dolly, fifteen years old when she walks down the turkey-carpeted stairs in her green crepe-de-chine gown, is the direct product of those dreams. Love in her small life has been replaced by the spurious celluloid pleasures of Eddie Cantor, Hedy Lamarr and Jane Russell.

Bon-bons is about the absence of love—not the loss of it but the realisation that it never existed. Deprived of any real preparation for life, any belief or experience on which to make sane judgment, Dolly seeks her consolation, and places her faith and her life, upon the altar of Hollywood. The dream fades and one day she finds herself middle-aged, searching desperately in the blackened mirror of the old suburban fleapit for the ghost of the girl in the green dress. A diet of sex and dreams, says Miss Hewett, is not a substitute for love, and today's pornographic society is Dolly's legacy.

The figures in Miss Hewett's play are (as one might guess by the theme) less substantial than in her previous plays. The work is more an evocation of memory—and memory of something which even at the time did not exist—than it is a drama in the true sense. What characterises the play so particularly is the total absence of dramatic conflict. Faced with the truth about themselves and the world about them, they gently crumble, as the dashing Ned Corker, known as the Silver Fox, crumbles. Faced with the choice between his family and drink, he surrenders without a struggle, without a word. This is something particularly evocative of Perth. It is the same struggle one finds in Tom Keneally's new play, *An Awful Rose*, in which the family ties are knit by the same conspiracy of silence.

As a play, the script still has deficiencies which come from the very fragility of her theme. Dolly and her family flicker past and are never caught in the kind of substance the audience would wish—which is the author's point. But fragility gives way to thinness at certain moments, particularly towards the end of the play. One of the weaknesses of the construction is lack of substructure to support the latter half.

Another problem is that the play is almost entirely without wit—even cynical wit, the saving grace of the hopeless. The play has two splendid characters, Mr Ortabee, the organist, and Ollie, a middle-aged gossip, marvellously played by David Clendinning and Margaret Ford. They sum up Miss Hewett's cutting analysis of the real duplicity underneath the dream: uppermost the yearning for life to be different and below the nasty private actuality.

The director, Raymond Omodei, achieves a great deal with the fragile text, aided by the designer, Bill Dowd. John Williamson's music recalls the period lovingly, especially as sung by Clendinning. The whole production has been done simply and neatly and with great credit to the Playhouse. But the full flavour of the play still demands, like Miss Hewett, to be noticed; and it will in time demand a larger stage, an orchestra and the extravagance of the tinsel which was once—ah me—Hollywood.

The original cinema, built by Dorothy Hewett's grandfather, is now restored as the Regal Theatre, Subiaco. The play caused some scandal after a member of the public tore down the production photographs in the foyer and stuffed them down the toilet. The cause of this outburst was thought to have been a monologue in which Ollie describes to her husband (represented by a rag doll) a knitting-needle abortion and a menstrual flooding.

Meeting Our Blacks

Australian, 4 November 1972

By coincidence both the Melbourne Pram Factory and the Sydney Nimrod Street Theatre have this week opened their first full-length programs in combination with black theatre groups. In Melbourne the Australian Performing Group has been associated informally for some months with the Nindethana Theatre; its founder Jack Charles was last seen at the Pram Factory in John Romeril's *Bastardy*. This week the two groups have combined to present Katharine Susannah Prichard's 45-year-old classic set in the Pilbara region, *Brumby Innes*, which includes a corroboree prologue. The majority of the cast are Aboriginal. (Barrie Watts reviewed this from Melbourne.)

The Sydney production, a revue entitled *Basically Black*, has been initiated by Bob Maza, co-founder of Nindethana, who received a special project grant from the Australian Council for the Arts to work with Nimrod on the creation of black theatre. Firstly let me say that it is an enjoyable, completely unpolished evening to be recommended to everyone. To describe it is not so easy.

It aims to present the black view of Australia and the material, as one would expect, deals chiefly with the Aboriginal embassy and figures like Lionel Rose, Lionel Brockman, Evonne Goolagong, Mervyn Eades, Neville Bonner, Bennelong and Lord Vestey. Most of the material has been scripted by white writers. There is some dialectic, some passion at injustice and some celebration of the black power salute; the seriousness of many of the statements by no means escapes the audience. But the real character of the actors, which makes them different from white actors and shows the direction in which a national black theatre will inevitably grow, lies in their humour and playfulness.

Gary Foley, the 22-year-old co-founder of the Aboriginal Legal Service, has written a sketch involving an aggressive white labourer and a black industrial designer in a bar. The exchange ends with a stoush and the Aboriginal, after being beaten and kicked half to death, is arrested for assault. While the action is clearly angry, it is not anger which makes the point but Foley's own comic performance as the labourer. A feat of appalling accuracy.

There are other small triumphs—Bindi Williams in scarlet dress uniform acting John Macarthur. Bob Maza as Bennelong in a gilded cage ('Good tucker, boss') stepping out to show the eighteenth-century gentlemen that the savage can outdo them all at the minuet. There is great charm in a scene in which two Aboriginals try to make a kamikaze pilot, crashed on Melville Island, feel at home—and more of the like from Aileen Corpus and Zac Martin.

Interestingly, the rhythms of Australian life, and in particular comedy (of which I have written so much) are more apparent in the work of this group than they are in much of the white writing. It gives a glimpse of the common area on which work might begin; and it shows how sound is the Australian capacity to laugh in the face of adversity.

The theatrical medium is a useful one for those who have something to say; and the national black theatre will, I hope, continue to use it as such a platform. But at this early stage of black and white relations the real value is a social one. In the ready convention of the Nimrod the white audience is offered the chance of discovering its fellow Australians in a freer situation than can easily be achieved socially between strangers— one in which each party can be himself.

Rose, Brockman, Goolagong and Eades were sporting heroes, Bonner the first Aboriginal to enter Federal Parliament, Bennelong was Captain Arthur Phillip's friend; and Lord Vestey the British owner of the Wave Hill Station, subject of the first strike, in 1966, by Aboriginal workers and instrumental in launching the modern land rights movement. In 1972 Gary Foley was one of the leaders of a group of activists who set up an Aboriginal Tent Embassy in the grounds of Parliament House. Various attempts were made to remove it but it remains today outside what is now Old Parliament House, and provides cultural information to visitors.

PART V
INTO THE MAINSTREAM
1973–74

Section V begins after the election of the Whitlam Government on 2 December 1972. The sudden announcement of a new and vastly enlarged structure for the Australian Council for the Arts was one of the new government's first actions, along with orders to return troops from Vietnam and diplomatic recognition of China. These things came as successive shocks in the heady early days of Labor in power after 23 years. For the arts, news of a ready-restructured Council came as an unpleasant shock and dashed the hopes of many who had contributed to shadow Arts Minister Susan Ryan's arts policy. It was seen as a further betrayal that on winning government she quickly moved to a Cabinet portfolio. These events galvanised practitioners into action and the companies begin to articulate their responsibilities. Just as the tone of political debate changed, so my reviews change as I become less tolerant of the larrikin vogue and urge a more substantial contribution from the New Wave.

In July and August 1973 I visited the American National Playwrights' Conference in New London, Connecticut, and wrote some columns from New York and Washington. I also went to the opening night of *The Removalists* in London at the Royal Court Theatre. That year both the Adelaide Festival Centre and the Drama Theatre of the Sydney Opera House opened, and with these edifices came fresh empire building.

By October 1974 the task of covering theatre over the whole of Australia was unsustainable and other reviewers had been introduced. My private role as drama publisher was also creating a perceived conflict of interest. A proposal to retain the national perspective by confining my articles to overviews was rejected by my editors and I resigned. I was replaced by a team of state reviewers.

Actors' Equity Takes a Stand

Australian, 15 December 1972

Employees in the entertainment industry had the best news this week since the establishment of the Australian Council for the Arts. That timid doormouse, the Australian Actors' and Announcers' Equity Association, supported by the Musicians' Union, the Theatrical Employees' Association and the Australian Writers' Guild, is to bite the hand that feeds it so frugally.

At a lively meeting at the Musicians' Club in Sydney the president of Actors' Equity, Hal Lashwood, announced the results of two years' lobbying—a union ban on the wholesale import of performers. A new 'Make-it-Australian' policy, covering stage, clubs, film and television will come into operation on 31 January. From that time all productions made or part-made in Australia (and this includes all those English and American-backed films) must be cast from the existing membership of the Australian Actors' Equity.

Any management that wishes to import a performer must first satisfy Equity that the job cannot be done by an Australian and then ensure a reciprocal agreement for an Australian with the country in question. The new ruling does not cover theatre directors, who may still be freely imported; but affiliated unions have offered in principle their support for a ban here too. Among those affected most severely will be the entrepreneur Michael Edgley and his companies, recently parted from J. C. Williamson's Ltd, to run dance companies from Europe. It was through his intervention that the Australian Ballet was invited to Moscow and he has assured Equity that he will make every endeavour to arrange performances by Australian artists abroad.

However, Edgley said yesterday in Perth that the decision would not affect his operations. He had conducted discussions with Equity before the announcement and had made a separate agreement. 'This type of culture is too valuable to the country for it to be affected.' Other companies include Col Joye Enterprises, which manages pop groups and soloists; and are the agents for the NSW clubs circuit. All managements will be affected to an extent by contracts already entered into with foreign stars. The opening program of the Sydney Opera House will also come under this ban. Lashwood said it was unfortunate that during Australia's adolescence we had borrowed so heavily from English-speaking cultures. It had long been a policy of Australian managements to bring out overseas performers in the belief they would draw the public. This had forced local talent to take second place or go abroad.

The change of heart inside Actors' Equity has been part of a gradual process over the past two years and involved a change of council. Strikes have never been part of Actors' Equity tradition. Only one, in fact, has taken place, against J. C. Williamson's in 1944, when Equity members in Melbourne and Sydney refused to work with non-members. It lasted three weeks and ended when all joined Equity. As a result JCW has since employed only Equity members. It was clear, said Lashwood, that the hoped-for new deal promised the profession by the Edgley–Williamson merger was not going to change the status quo. It was up to the actors to do something. Those foreign performers receiving work permits in future would be allowed to work only at the job contracted and not accept extra work while inside the country.

The ruling is long overdue. Australia for years has been almost alone in its failure to provide job protection for its artists. British and American unions, facing increasing unemployment which has now reached 90 per cent (the Australian figure is 60 per cent) have been understandably militant. With the United States our position has been doubly critical because, in a limited quota of permits for performers, Australia was regarded as 'part of Britain'.

Under a reciprocal agreement it is now hypothetically possible that *The Removalists*, which was to have been presented in New York with an American cast because of union regulation, could wind up with an Australian cast in exchange for say, Lauren Bacall in *Applause*. Approaches were being made at a federal level, Lashwood said, for a proper cultural exchange treaty with major foreign countries to allow for the export of Australian artists.

This is the most significant aspect of the new equity militancy— management will be forced to put back what they take out. It will mean a greater concentration on original work as material for an export market, a chance to stop being copyists. The onus is on the performers now to see that their rulings are kept.

Edgley briefly became managing director of J. C. Williamson's in 1971 in an attempt to save the dying company. Bacall did visit Australia in 1973 in the Broadway musical, *Applause*, but the United States production of *The Removalists* had an American cast and was greeted largely with incomprehension.

The ruling led to many disputes, especially within the (then tenuous) film industry that today still depends on casting known international actors in order to gain overseas distribution. The ruling still prevails but its impact has lessened over the years as stage, film, opera and dance practitioners gained in reputation; and the state-government sponsored festivals (excepted from the ruling) proliferated and assisted Australians to join the international circuit.

On Australia Day 1973 Prime Minister Gough Whitlam unexpectedly issued a press release announcing (quaintly) 'New Government arrangements for the arts'. It came as an enormous shock to the arts community, who had pinned great hopes on a change of government and had contributed very publicly to the Labor Party's 'It's Time' election campaign. The announcement elicited a stormy response. Here I accuse Dr Coombs, probably unfairly, of responsibility for the new Council structure. In retrospect almost nothing—except funding—survived of his original proposal to the Government and it is unlikely he would have approved the Whitlam plan. I also attack the Opera House architect Peter Hall, whose appointment to the Theatre Board was doubly contentious. The majority of the arts community had supported the return of Utzon to the Opera House project and Hall's solutions to its interior had not been widely admired. In the event, his Theatre Board did a good job.

Amateur Hour in the Arts World

Australian, 16 February 1973

The dismissal of the Australian Council for the Arts, the Commonwealth Art Advisory Board, the Commonwealth Literary Fund, the Committee for Commonwealth Assistance to Australian Composers and the Interim Council for a National Film and Television School—just when they were finding ways in which they could be useful—has caused growing amazement as its implications have emerged. When the Attorney-General wants to get the divorce laws cleaned up he puts a conference of jurists onto it; when governments want information on foreign monopolies or rural relief, they have an inquiry. When it comes to the arts, though, some amateur always knows best.

In 1968, Dr Coombs, then chairman of the newly-formed Council for the Arts, spoke with some fervour against monolithic organisations. The way to maximum individual freedom, he argued, was to have a variety of autonomous bureaucratic structures. If an individual found one door closed there were others to try. One often ended up getting more money that way. Dr Coombs is a pragmatist. He has now built the biggest monolithic pyramid the arts in Australia have ever had.

One is struck by the enormity of it. There are 24 members on the new council—professors, public servants, businessmen, all the usual people whose opinions are most sought on the subject—rubbing shoulders and dividing budgets with a tiny minority of specialist artists. Below them—and apparently where the real work will be done—will be seven boards, each with its own area of artistic competence and each subject to the main council. Their chairmen have already been chosen, presumably by the Prime Minister or Dr Coombs, who is Mr Whitlam's adviser in these matters. Appointments to the boards are expected to be announced today, after the first meeting of the new council. That's about all that those who work in the arts know about it.

Members of the former council, the art board and the CLF were given no notice of their dismissal. Practitioners of the arts have not been consulted to any wide extent. The specialist advisers inside the present council know only as much as they have read in the newspapers. Those involved understand in a general way that Mr Whitlam has at last set in motion for the first time the basis of a system of statutory autonomy for the arts. Many people fought hard for this and its importance cannot be over-emphasised. But who is now to wield that autonomy?

The new formula looks frighteningly like the bad old days of the Australian Elizabethan Theatre Trust when the performing arts were designed and managed not by the artists but by the spectators. Even Mr Whitlam, who makes much of the democratic nature of the Labor Party, is elected to his position. His colleagues are elected by their peers. Why can't our painters, writers and performers be asked to show what the real needs are in their own areas? The performing arts have never been allowed to speak for themselves at government level.

The Chifley Government ignored the advice it itself asked from the late Tyrone Guthrie on setting up a national theatre. John Allen's UNESCO report was buried. The Arts Council and others were rejected when they asked for an inquiry into the needs of the profession before the now-superseded Council for the Arts was set up. The Council for the Arts had a group of first-rate field workers who knew the working arts and their problems; but their opinion was not sought.

Take the Theatre Board as an example, by far the biggest and most contentious of the seven. The chairman is Mr Peter Hall. It is no reflection on his professionalism to say that Mr Hall did not make a name in any of the theatre arts, as have those whose future now depends on him. He is a government architect who completed the Sydney Opera House, the most famous and controversial building in Australia. The other boards at least have chairmen with some expertise in their area. It is an insult to the performing arts that nobody in the theatre seemed capable, to the Government, of being a fair, informed chairman. Apart from this, the new formula—a combination of part-time attention in an increased committee system—seems highly ineffective.

It is instructive to put the situation in terms Mr Whitlam might understand. The boards are equivalent to cabinets. The theatre cabinet is led not by a man who knows from experience the people and pressures that put him there, but by an outsider appointed by a secret caucus. He is not a career politician but the secret caucus thinks he is as good as one because, since he knows very little about the subject, he should be impartial. The big budget portfolios in this cabinet are the Australian Opera, the Australian Ballet and the Melbourne Theatre Company. There are smaller ones, covering such matters as research, education and rural relief. At the bottom are the no-account ones like modern dance and local opera composition and the development of an Australian comic-strip culture—portfolios about as important as Aboriginals, the Environment and the Arts in the previous Federal Government. Yet people like David Williamson, Mr Whitlam's favourite playwright, come from this group. It is in such obscure corners that the miracles are discovered. Today's obscene play may be tomorrow's Broadway hit; today's Narrabri songstress may be tomorrow's Joan Sutherland. Equally they might just be a dirty play and an amateur singer. Who decides? Being able to finish an opera house does not qualify Mr Hall to make an opera; the judge cannot necessarily build the courthouse. It looks as though Mr Whitlam and his advisers are more concerned with the outward appearance of the arts than in stimulating the skills without which the arts cannot survive.

The Chifley Government fell shortly after the *Guthrie Report* report was delivered in 1949. The recommendations were poorly received by the public; but it raised debate which led to the establishment of the Australian Elizabethan Theatre Trust. I can find no record of John Allen's UNESCO report.

The shock of a de facto new institution galvanised the arts community and led to the formation of an Arts Action Committee and a Film Industry Action Committee aimed at achieving a more democratic outcome. By now the hierarchy was growing.

The Australian Council for the Arts: A Progress Report

Speech to a public meeting called by the Arts Action Committee at the Independent Theatre, Sydney 8 April 1973

I have been asked to talk tonight about how the structure of the new Theatre Board of the Australian Council for the Arts could affect those who come under its care. And it is widely conceded that the Theatre Board is the least satisfactory of the seven boards, that its mandate is too wide. Every kind of performance has been made the responsibility of this board. This may seem a tidy idea but to those more closely involved the differences between the needs and the skills of the various fields are wider than their similarities. Something of this has been acknowledged: at the last meeting of the Theatre Board opera was seconded to the Music Board.

A great many things are wrong with the present structure as we now see it. But the issues that concern me go much deeper and wider, and cannot be resolved by legislation. What I want to urge tonight is a fundamental change of heart by both the government officers and our artists. Only by making the Council for the Arts a community of artists in the service of artists prepared to invade the community, will this come about.

The first Council dealt simply with the performing arts and the single subject under discussion was money. In the years that followed a great deal of money was pumped into the Old Tote and the major companies and this money has enabled them to increase the staff and efficiency. It has enabled them to mount, in particular, classics in the style to which European theatre has long been accustomed. And we now have at the top a small but respectable representation of the arts that can hold its head up with similar companies anywhere in the world.

Beyond these large subsidies the Council had a small budget to spend on experimental and training work. And it has had the courage to give some of our more advanced thinkers the chance to stay alive and work. The present blossoming of Australian playwriting owes a great deal to the Council, not because of many sensitive artistic judgements made by it but because the Council's self-help policy was an encouragement.

Not all the Council plans have worked out ideally, and there have been constant and irritating delays between the announcement of a grant and the arrival of the cheque. And in some areas there has come to be an unnecessary dependence on government aid. But the fact remains that the existence of the Australian Council has been a reassurance to our artists. They have lost the old feeling of battling alone in an alien climate that playwrights like Vance Palmer and Louis Esson suffered back in the 1920s. Such artists are not alone any more. But they have a price on their head. In 1973 they are worth $4,055,600 to the taxpayer. The question we must now ask is: Are they worth anything more to the community?

Today unquestionably there is a new value placed on the arts to which the Council has contributed, but for which it is not solely responsible, nor must it ever seek to be. It is part of a changing climate that is also responsible for putting our Labor Government in power; and which has encouraged us to shed our dependence upon great and powerful friends. So that the decisions now to be made in the arts in 1973 are much more complex than they were in 1968; and the problems the Theatre Board faces will be very different. It is no longer simply a question of money. What we need now is a reassessment of the nature and value of the arts. If the Council is to be of real value, then it must find a means of facing such fundamental questions.

Now the arts have been very much a part of the Australian Labor Party platform. There are those in Federal Parliament who believe strongly that the arts have a contribution to make to the quality of our lives. What this small group is demanding is not $16 tickets at the Opera House but the kind of arts that will help us all live our lives more pleasurably and to understand better both ourselves and the world about us. But this is a big demand.

Increasingly, the boards of the new Council are going to be faced with radical plans to investigate our lives. There are going to be schemes for drama training in primary schools, teacher-training, yoga training, psycho-drama and oriental studies; there are going to be black theatres, political arts, travel itineraries to gurus in obscure corners of the world, and applications for moog synthesisers from country schools. The question of public obscenity will have to be faced again and again. Already, in the past two or three years, the Council's officers have been involved in questions of training and development; and the façade of impartiality has deceived nobody. There has been sharp interference on artistic questions. In some cases subsidies have been withdrawn. So long as there continues to be insufficient money for everybody the choice must remain an artistic one. This is why practising artists must influence that choice.

There has long been an embarrassed belief such boards should be, like Caesar's wife, above suspicion. Again and again there have been desperate searches for people who know all about the arts and yet have no allegiances. In the arts people with no qualifications can rise to the top as patrons and administrators; and where political and social advantage can be had, free from political pressure. Can you imagine recommending someone professionally who is not a qualified lawyer but as good as one? Or not a chartered accountant but better? The choice of spokesperson for the arts, of course, has inevitably been a compromise; and a tradition of paternalism has by default grown up.

In his statements of 26 January, Mr Whitlam took the first step towards the recognition of this new self-assurance in announcing his intention of establishing the Council for the Arts as a statutory body. 'We believe', he said, 'that public support is best provided through a body established independently of government. Vitality in the arts is frequently accompanied by innovation, by controversy and by challenge to established conventions of taste, beliefs and behaviour.' Autonomy for the Council is something for which the majority of artists have long worked. But, Mr Whitlam went on to say: 'Artists need protection from unnecessary restraint and governments should be able to resist pressures from those who are disturbed by controversy and challenge'.

And there's the crunch. It is true that artists like anyone else need protection from interference with their work, but the old idea that artists are primitives incapable of running their own affairs is long gone. If they do not know how to run their own affairs in government, it's time they learnt, because this is a vital part of the hubbub of living which it is the artist's duty and pleasure to interpret. So far the new Council has already been marred by haste and undignified wrangles over territory, together with a very clear determination by the leaders of the Council itself to retain control rigidly in its own hands. I would remind you all that the Council for the Arts does not exist for the sake of its own administration, that those appointed by the Government are public servants, whose job it is to provide a service to our artists. If, on the other hand, the administrator continues to believe that he or she knows best and that 'protection from unnecessary restraint' means systematising the artists into the kind of order the Treasury and the public service demand, then we shall get the kind of art the Government deserves.

The artists themselves in this country have a long way to go; but the time is right for them to find their own way. A first step could be to seek active, constructive and democratic government of their own affairs.

The Council boards at this time were: Aboriginal Arts, Crafts, Film and Television, Literature, Music, Theatre and Visual Arts. The irritating delay between the announcement of a grant and the cheque that I mention here is mirrored today by an equally contentious delay between the deadline of applications and advice of the result.

Opening Tonight in the Athens of the South
Australian, 2 June 1973

The refreshing thing about Adelaide's Festival Centre, the major hall of which will be opened tonight by the Prime Minister, is that it has such a human scale. The overall seating of the proposed complex is only slightly less than that of the Sydney Opera House—the Festival Theatre holds 2,000, the Playhouse 650, the open-air amphitheatre 1,200 and the Space (experimental theatre) 350. Despite the 10,000 yards of red carpet, designed, like the stage curtains, by the Adelaide artist John Dallwitz, the building and its surroundings are the kind in which you would not be ashamed to eat a meat pie.

No one has yet claimed, blessedly, that it is the biggest and best in the southern hemisphere. But they do claim that it will work to suit the needs of Adelaide. And very likely they are right. Built on a site behind Parliament House, it overlooks the River Torrens and Elder Park. Its three-tiered roofs and extensive plaza, its huge windows that invite the parkland into the building, seem already to belong to the Sunday promenades and garden fetes which make up the life of Elder Park.

The Festival Theatre, however, has not been achieved without drama. In 1960 at the first Adelaide Festival, it became clear that if the festival were to be a recurring event, the city would need a Festival Hall worthy of its international guests. From then on the disputes began among the Festival Board, the City Council and the State Government over the site, shape and purpose of such a hall. Particularly the site.

Three sites had their vocal supporters. Carclew, in North Adelaide, a nineteenth-century property overlooking the city; vacant land behind Government House; and the present site. Arguments in favour of Carclew were that it provided parking and avoided city congestion; against, that a public pleasure palace should be centrally located. The Government House site was taken more seriously and was firmly supported by the Labor Party.

The ghost of the Sydney Opera House budgets has haunted the Adelaide Festival Centre since its beginnings. With the complex three-quarters built so far, the estimated cost is $15 million—a good deal more than Premier

Dunstan's figure of $4 million quoted from the Thomas DeGaetani feasibility study in 1968. But $15 million barely covered the foundation costs of the Sydney Opera House.

The action groups and the South Australian people, who together for nine years prevented the go-ahead, are now united in their pleasure at the success of their final choice and the achievement of the architect, Colin Hassell, and the theatre consultant Tom Brown. The architecture is comfortable, with a pleasant feeling of good proportion, but not ostentatiously luxurious. It looks and is a good practical building of stout timber and concrete, aimed at reducing maintenance costs and using as much natural material as possible. The theatre seating, for example, cost $30 a unit, instead of $300 at the Opera House, and the upholstery is reversible for double wear.

The luxury—and this again is unique in such a public building—is chiefly where the public will not see it. The carpet, for example, stretches right to the dressing rooms. But more importantly the backstage of the Festival Theatre is the largest in Australia and equipped with a spacious fly gallery. The orchestra pit has a capacity for 90 musicians and a floor that can be raised to stage level when required. There are adequate workshops underground to provide the mounting for plays on the site, though storage space is limited. All the theatres have complex light and sound systems, closed circuit television and in the larger theatre a translation system for international conventions.

The Festival Theatre will be used in its dual-purpose capacity for tonight's gala opening—a program of divertissements in opera and orchestral music. The first season will begin on Tuesday when the Royal Shakespeare Company opens its season of Peter Brook's famous production of *A Midsummer Night's Dream*. The theatre will make, without a doubt, a welcome improvement in the performing arts available to South Australia. Since the Theatre Royal was knocked down in the 1960s to make way for a car park, Adelaide has had only Her Majesty's Theatre to accommodate touring companies and the Town Hall for concerts. The braver companies made use of less satisfactory venues and during the festival visitors have been all too aware of the spartan comforts offered by the Athens of the South. Now impresarios are lining up to make use of the new building and the chief problem—the job of Mr Anthony Steel, the general manager—is that of scheduling.

The Festival Centre is the latest in a number of projects throughout the world seeking to bridge the gap between the people and the performing arts. The Adelaide Festival itself has been attempting this for twelve years with only moderate success. But the city's long argument over the hall has in the end given the architect the benefit of hindsight, and the City Council, the Festival Centre Trust members, the South Australian Theatre Company and the SA Government a chance to consider what Adelaide needs in a building like this.

The Festival Theatre has been erected in three years and now it is to be put to work. To the general public the simplest idea in the whole planning may prove the key to making it the community arts centre the Premier had in mind—the acre of promenade around the building with its trees, benches and Barbara Hepworth sculpture, restaurants and amphitheatre on the river bank. In all, the theatre is another rung in the slow and steady climb down by Adelaide from the cultural establishment to the social workshop.

The Festival Centre beat the Opera House to opening night by four months. Carclew is now a youth performing arts centre.

Summer of the Seventeenth Doll: A Paean for an Old-fashioned Playwright

Australian, 6 September 1973

Only rarely does one chance an entirely satisfying evening in the theatre; but such an evening in the makeshift surroundings of the Village theatre in Paddington, Sydney, is the Nimrod Street Theatre's production of *Summer of the Seventeenth Doll*. It is a play clearly due for such a revival. Having been on the school study lists for so long and had frequent amateur performances it has never actually faded from our consciousness but it had acquired a shop-worn reputation with our repertory companies.

Richard Wherrett's outstanding production draws attention to qualities that have outlasted the years. The production has come at a moment when the mood is moving towards maturer and more considered work; and the *Doll*'s qualities are solidly three-dimensional. I watched the performance with a sense of relief at the security of the writing—the rightness of the structure, the formality of the three-act frame, the strong domestic detail and the joyous familiarity of the characters. Everything comes in cycles and the very revolution against the regimen of convention under which the *Doll* was written can now by default display those conventions to advantage.

Summer of the Seventeenth Doll, written by Ray Lawler in 1955, is about a pair of cane-cutters who spend seven months of their year in heavy work in North Queensland and five months in light play with two barmaids in Carlton. Today that run-down, companionable corner of Melbourne has changed in nature and cane-cutters have changed their jobs; but Lawler's study of these people and his dissection of marriage remains in its wider implications as surprising and recognisably true as ever. The integration of form and meaning is brilliant.

The play opens with Olive awaiting the arrival of Roo and Barney at the beginning of the seventeenth lay-off. With her is Pearl, a tight-lipped barmaid lured there to replace Nancy who, after sixteen years, has invested in marriage to a bookseller. Olive cannot understand Nancy's choice and in inspired language persuades us that a love relationship can be more fully realised in a concentrated form five months of the year than in full-time marriage.

But this lay-off proves to be different and in it we see the final disintegration of their youth. With deep sympathy and humour, Lawler pulls the threadbare fabric apart and shows how little strength was in the threads, how childish and narrow have been Olive's sixteen golden summers. Old Emma, Olive's mother, who provides the comedy, is also the means whereby Roo and Barney come to realise their middle-age and try to salvage what they still have.

Richard Wherrett's production exploits the play's levels, orchestrates beautifully the sound, shape and pace of the play. It is also brilliantly cast. Reg Gorman looks and is a splendid Barney. Bill Hunter, perhaps physically not a heavyweight, gives a warmly solid, serious performance as Roo. Melissa Jaffer's Olive is movingly real in its portrait of a faded little girl, as are Rosalie Fletcher, the young Olive in miniature as Bubba; Marion Johns exploiting the irrepressible comedy as Emma; and Dennis Grosvenor as Johnnie Dowd, the new pack leader, tempting Bubba gently in a seductive North Queensland cadence.

But the real find in this not-so-familiar cast is Maggie Blinco as Pearl, in her black crepe dress and her bang hairdo. Mrs Blinco is not only a masterly comic actress in a style kept on ice for fifteen years, but she recalls, in her shifting emphasis on Pearl's longing to be daring and passion for respectability, so much of Australia in that period when convention's greatest weapon was the fear of being found out.

The production's only aberration is Larry Eastwood's fairy-floss set, which looks as if Olive had brought the whole Luna Park to Carlton.

At this time Ray Lawler lived in Ireland, where he had settled since going abroad in 1957 with the cast of the *Doll*. He returned to the Melbourne Theatre Company In 1975 and wrote two further plays about the *Doll*'s characters, which in 1977 became *The Doll Trilogy* (see p. 256).

You've Got to Make Something Happen
Australian, 11 September 1973

'The Australian Council's attitude to date has been that most of the regional theatre companies are training grounds for the two major companies, the Melbourne Theatre Company and the Old Tote', said Aarne Neeme, gritting his teeth. 'This is just not good enough. Australians in all states have a right to good entertainment and in a place like Perth, where there are no perks for actors, good pay is essential.'

'You've got to make something happen', is his motto. He has never waited for work to come to him.

Born in Germany of Estonian parentage, Neeme migrated to Melbourne in 1949 with his family. Since then he has made his way first as a dancer and choreographer, stage manager and actor. In the 1960s, as a student at the University of New South Wales he became a director, formed his own company and with them moved into the professional theatre. In 1969 he transferred his MA studies to the University of Western Australia in order to become director of the Octagon Theatre. There with a young company partly recruited from his Sydney group, he developed a centre for classical theatre.

His eighteen months work was cut short by the call-up.

After four weeks he decided army life was not for him. So he took off his uniform, reported to the officers' mess. He then returned to his hut where he went without food and water for three days (except for the assistance of his friends). He was driven to the outskirts of Sydney and told he would need time to prepare his defence. After a hearing and an appeal the case was finally dropped. He then settled back in Sydney working as a freelance, chiefly for the Nimrod Street Theatre. Now at 29 he has succeeded Edgar Metcalfe as director of the Perth Playhouse.

In his manifesto to the Playhouse he has made his intentions clear. 'Our theatre must be established as a vital part of its community. Our art must be a reflection of the life around us. We must teach and be taught by our audience. The kind of theatre Perth is getting now is what it once years ago thought it wanted. It now knows what it does not want but it has not been offered an alternative.' Because of a severe shortage of actors, the Playhouse had for years taken the easy way out by importing English actors through the immigration scheme. The result had been a matter of pot luck. For years the Playhouse company had been 75 per cent English.

Neeme's immediate plans for the Playhouse are to play two plays a week in repertoire, opening a new one each three weeks; to revise the work being done in education and to abolish cut-rate country touring. He had been impressed, he said, by the work instituted by the South Australian Theatre Company and he believed with them that work in schools and in the country should not be itinerant performances but community teaching programs. He planned, he said, to build up a company of 15 or 16 actors, of which between six and twelve would be available to take part in educational programs. He is also planning a cooperative venture with a commercial television station.

'Perth's isolation has a number of advantages. People here are almost desperately progressive. There is a much stronger cultural awareness than in the bigger capitals. It is still possible to be noticed in a city the size of Perth. It is not possible to contribute to the community in a big city the way you can in a small one. Having come through the little theatre, I welcome the opportunity at the Playhouse to practise what we have preached. It is too easy to sit back and know what is right and wrong. You've got to get your feet dirty and make something happen.'

The Australian Theatre in Sydney is now playing a revival of Arthur Adams' 1910 comedy *The Wasters*. Adams was a prolific writer who, as literary secretary to J. C. Williamson, wrote a large number of plays, most of which were claimed by his employer as work done in office time.

The theme is similar to that of Ibsen's *A Doll's House*, except that Adams' sympathies lie with the husband. A successful department store owner, John Dangar (Charles Thorne) finds his son has been embezzling company funds and falls into the hands of a blackmailer who proves to be his wife's former lover. The plot is an excuse to show the flighty preoccupations of women and reaffirm the status quo by demonstrating that through men.

The basic material is thin and reflects the pace at which Adams wrote his farces but it has the virtue of much of the writing of the time—of being written directly for the actor. Each character in turn has opportunity for histrionics centre stage and a skilled cast could still today make the play a showstopper. The Australian cast is not particularly well equipped for a task as delicate as this (with the exception of Jill Pratton in an inventive performance as a salesgirl) but they do give us some feeling for this rare play.

The Australian plans to do other productions from the archives and could become a most useful adjunct to our theatre in researching a neglected field.

Aarne Neeme was director of the National Theatre at the Playhouse 1973–77. In 1972 George Ogilvie had been appointed director of the SATC and had announced he would form an ensemble to work for a year before appearing in public. His appointment of Helmut Bakaitis as director of youth activities had a far-reaching effect. Bakaitis founded the theatre-in-education company, Magpie, the Carclew Arts Centre and the Come Out youth festival. South Australia remains the national leader in young people's theatre.

Neeme introduced the work of the New Wave to Perth theatregoers in what was a period of the greatest intensity for the company, creating an attic theatre, the Greenroom, and touring extensively. He received a Churchill Fellowship in 1978 and following his departure the theatre returned to the popular English repertoire to which audiences had been accustomed. It went into liquidation in 1984, since when the life of a quasi-state company has been hazardous.

The Australian Theatre, in Australia Street, Newtown, was a short-lived venture by Amy McGrath, who was a co-founder of the Australian National Playwrights' Conference and who for some years conducted Sunday readings, with her husband, Judge Frank McGrath, at their Mews Playhouse in the grounds of their Centennial Park home.

On 2 October 1973, the Sydney Opera House Drama Theatre opened amid high hopes but did not live up to expectations as my unkind review of the long-awaited opening production no doubt captures. The stage, with its great width and low-hung proscenium arch, divides the audience's focus and has proved an intransigent space for designers and directors. In the full glare of public expectation Robin Lovejoy was the first to carry the responsibility of making it work; and to bear the disappointment. My review, by drawing attention to the style of his body of work, may have contributed to his decision the following year to retire from his post as artistic director.

Richard II: The Time for Temporising is Over

Australian, 4 October 1973

In Act III scene three of Shakespeare's *King Richard II* Henry Bolingbroke confronts for the first time his treason against king and country. Unjustly banished by Richard, Henry has returned with a force backed by the Duke of Brittany, has gathered to his side most of the English power, and now comes to Flint Castle to face Richard with the Earl of Northumberland as his ambassador. It is a sobering moment for Henry; Richard on his battlements is at his most gracious. A crucial moment in the play.

In Robin Lovejoy's production, which opened the Drama Theatre at the Sydney Opera House on Tuesday, it was more like an encounter in Carpetland. The pair, in Shakespeare's imagination, darting royal thunderbolts, tentatively peek around a mountain of green Wilton and retire, impotent.

The production is decorative to the point of suffocation. Even the conventions are old-fashioned enough to have gone out of use. The court is immaculate, the product of the best dressmakers; the set is weighty, making more than full use of the new turntable and looking like real wood. (I was relieved to find out at last what that unlikely buttress was for that everybody had to negotiate.) The result was stultifying.

The first thing that needs to be done is to remove from the stage everyone who has nothing immediate to say. With this distraction relieved, the audience might concentrate on the essential action. Secondly, if those in conversation with each other could actually approach close enough to make human contact credible, the audience might begin to listen. Pamela Stephenson's predicament as the Queen was the worst. The effect of her actions was chiefly to immobilise herself as far as possible from those she addressed and then to signal by semaphore.

In fairness to Mr Lovejoy, he has a serious problem with the Drama Theatre stage, which has an aperture like a letterbox. I reserve my comments on the theatre until I have seen the other two plays in the season.

Thirdly we need to recognise that this is a great play breeding great thought, with great lines that for centuries have been spoken by great actors. John Gaden as Richard did at moments manage to capture our attention in his contemplative speeches, though never at the moments of command. Gaden's performance is charmless—and this I can only blame on the production, because Gaden is not an actor without charm. I could not, in fact, gather from his Richard any real personality, other than an irritating stupidity. Perhaps he could do without his royalty and his halo, perhaps he could be represented as a rather dowdy leader of the conservative party whom nobody is sorry to see go. But he cannot bore us—and that is what this production does.

George Whaley managed better as Bolingbroke. It is his part, through and through. I can think of no Australian actor better equipped for this role. And yet he too suffered from the weight and immobility of the production, a heavy burden for so restlessly active a character. Henry's are the driving temporal virtues and vices as Richard's are the spiritual; and each in this performance diminished the other.

What the Opera House now demands, remorselessly, is greatness, and for this also the careers of these actors have not prepared them. These are roles for two actors locked in mortal combat to dominate the stage. What Mr Lovejoy offers us is a game of shuttlecock. The Opera House is a battleground for great ideas and *Richard* is a great play, a treasury of ideas on the nature of politics and political domination, on the nature of art, freedom, God, the vanity of the world, democracy, loyalty… Mr Lovejoy's crime against Shakespeare is to take all those disturbing ideas and render them harmless. The actors are rendered harmless also.

It was not always so. Mr Lovejoy's contribution to the classical theatre was to teach us the excitement of style at a time when we badly wanted to know about it; and his work in the 40s and 50s is still remembered. But the theatre has taken other turnings since then, found other preoccupations, seen new dangers. Now that this company has assumed control of a corner in one of the world's great buildings the time for temporising is over. Our interpretation of the classics must be more penetrating and our approach to performance more serious. Nothing less than a new, magnanimous vision at the head of this theatre now will engage it from the stage of the Opera House in intercourse with the world.

One actor of the 32 in *King Richard II* escapes the net. Ronald Falk as the Earl of Northumberland possessed the stage in a way that gave me real consolation. He and John Walton as young Hotspur were a true, flesh and blood father and son in this arid, dusty museum world.

The Marsh King's Daughter: Complexity in Simplicity

Australian, 13 October 1973

A mile away and a world away from the Sydney Opera House is the Nimrod Street Theatre and *The Marsh King's Daughter*. The performance has grown stage by stage over more than a year. A version was presented under otherworldly conditions at St Martin's Theatre, Melbourne earlier this year. Now a new company, led by the beautiful actress Gillian Jones (who has been with the group from its foundation in 1970) and two former members of the cast of the Royal Shakespeare Company's *A Midsummer Night's Dream* is presenting the third stage of growth.

The syndicate's work under the director Rex Cramphorne has developed peripatetically over four years. It is not directly experiment for the theatre. It goes further than that: it uses the theatre as a crucible in which to investigate the nature of the creative impulse. Cramphorne's work does not depend on its audience, nor is it ever complete in the sense the audience understands this. The audience is there to serve the actors, for the creative act is not complete until the thing created is acknowledged.

Cramphorne's preoccupation is with the myths that are the source and product of the creative impulse. In his first experiment, *10,000 Miles Away* (1971) he examined the idea of the voyage of the mind and the body. In the *Orestes* later that year he combined the myth of blood ties, sin and expiation, with further experiments to the body as an instrument of expression. These discoveries he then applied to *Pericles* and *The Tempest*; in these he managed in a curious way to dive under the text into the impulse which generated the composition and to bring this fleetingly into the light. This is perhaps a large statement for what were not in any sense perfect works; but myth is something which draws together the great and the small minds, the creator and his audience, because it evolves out of the common experience of birth, growth, ripeness and death.

In *The Marsh King's Daughter* the company's experiment is to tell a narrative in such a way that its mythic force might convey itself most vividly. Cramphorne in this abandons a dramatic text in order to examine separately the dramatic impulse behind the simple narrative. As he explains in his program notes, the first stage of their work was to dramatise the story. The second stage retained the narrative form, illustrating the narration with mime and music. The third and present stage is more complex; it pulls apart the elements of the story and presents them sometimes in music, sometimes in narrative, sometimes in dramatic form.

The Marsh King's Daughter is ideal material for such an experiment combining as it does a transparent simplicity with a profound acknowledgment of the Christian myth. It is a tale told by two storks who live in the chimney of a Viking's home in Denmark. In the autumn they fly south to Egypt, where they nest at the palace of the king. One day in Denmark they see three swans alight on the marsh. One discards her feathers, revealing that she is the Princess of Egypt, and dives into the water in search of a flower. Her two swan-sisters tear her feathers and leave her to drown. But the next autumn a water lily grows in the marsh and inside it is a child, daughter of the princess and the Marsh King. The child is reared by the Vikings; by day she is beautiful but cruel; at night she is kind and loving but her body is that of a frog. One day the Viking returns with a priest as prisoner. Through him the girl Helga is rid of her evil spirit and united with her family; and through him she attains sanctity and an end to her journey, which is the opening of the doors of perception and knowledge.

The style of the group is roughly Indian; there is an occasional use of a Hindu gesture and the costumes are Indian. But Cramphorne and his actors are not, as I understand it, attempting to adopt another culture. Rather they find certain qualities useful. One is the use of music, another is the imaginative demands some kinds of oriental theatre place on the audience, as early open-stage theatre in other countries has done.

The actors in *The Marsh King's Daughter* do not act their roles (the daughter, in fact, is played by Ralph Cotterill, who also plays the mother stork). Instead they convey the elements in a purified form by their use of gesture and expression to musical accompaniment. Cotterill's performance is particularly remarkable—as Helga nothing in his performance attempts to imitate femininity or adolescence; rather it presents the spiritual and emotional qualities which spring out of youth and femininity (and demonic possession) and give expression to the universal rather than the particular. I can remember seeing something like this only once before, in Ronald Pickup's performance as Rosalind in a Royal Shakespeare Company *As You Like It*. By being in no way feminine the actor became a neutral vessel in which the text was distilled, and from which it emerged the more transparent.

The Performance Syndicate is a laboratory theatre and as such is to do with the development of our theatre profession, not with the development of audiences It is by far the most advanced developmental program we have in Australia now, the only one wholly concerned with the source of the theatre and not with the end product. It is essential to our growth because only by aiming as deep as Cramphorne can our drama grow the strength to give it lasting greatness.

If I have made the experience of seeing *The Marsh King's Daughter* sound formidable it was not my intention. My companions at the theatre were my children, aged ten and twelve, for whom the departures from the old ways and the exercise of the imagination were things to be taken for granted. What has gone into this experiment has been much thought, research, exercise and emotional discipline. Its ultimate end is simplicity.

The long-term influences of the writings of Peter Brook and Jerzy Grotowski upon the work of Rex Cramphorn were distilled in this production. The work began development in late 1972 when the foundering St Martin's Theatre in Melbourne had invited the Performance Syndicate to be resident artists. But the demands of an orthodox theatre schedule defeated them and they disbanded at the end of that year. Peter Brook's famous production of *A Midsummer Night's Dream* (which I reviewed on 9 June 1973) had ended its world tour in Sydney in July 1973 and two of its cast, Ralph Cotterill and Hugh Keays-Byrne, remained in Sydney and began to work with Cramphorn. Cramphorn later worked with Grotowski and his company when they visited Australia in June 1974.

Clifton Pugh and the Rising Bureaucracy

Australian, 11 January 1974

The intrepid painter Clifton Pugh has spoken out again against the public service silence and the snowballing administration costs of the Australian Council for the Arts. His views have much in them of the feelings more privately expressed by those from the Australian Council and those who are involved with their dispensation.

'It is becoming increasingly apparent that there are serious differences within the Council as to its policy attitudes', writes Mr Pugh.

It seems to me that in the area in which I deal, the stumbling block is a total lack of policy. It is the major problem with which the new chairman will have to contend. Open government is one of the Prime Minister's prized policies and one that could with benefit be applied to the Council. As it is, because of the official silence, the Council's head is surrounded by a swarm of gossip, some of it more unfavourable than with more public consultation it would be.

To each of the boards hundreds of applications are submitted each meeting. The members of the boards are volunteers, men and women with busy professional lives who spend their time, like Mr Pugh, in the hope of giving help where it is needed. Each board has different problems, some more complex than others, and some involving more people than others. And some have more policy than others.

Taking the theatre board as an example, most of the members do not have the time to research the applications. Each application naturally puts the best face on it and the member has the choice of taking it at face value or relying upon the advice of his or her fellows, friends or the Council's staff. This is what Mr Pugh means by élitist. Prejudice and hearsay come into play despite the wishes of the board, who at each meeting must feel like the miller's daughter in *Rumpelstiltskin,* being asked to spin a roomful of straw into gold.

A public row developed early last year, led by Clifton Pugh, over the new Whitlam format for the Council; and following this an advisory committee was set up under the theatre board, consisting more directly of theatre professionals and intended to formulate a policy. Since then the committee's time has been similarly taken up with the study of individual applications, duplicating the burden of the board. On some occasions the research officers and consultants on staff have not been able to attend meetings to give factual information.

The Council's boards and committees are further aggravated by two facts: one, that it is policy to give no official reason for an application's refusal; and two, that their decisions may be overruled by others within the administration. When a rejection slip arrives the applicant usually finds out as best he can the reason for the refusal. Then, if he is persistent, he submits a new application. All this is exasperatingly inefficient and time-consuming. When organisations say they are going to put in an application for a salary for someone to fill in applications forms, they are no longer joking.

The Australian Council is also too centralist. Despite the high airfare budget the outlying States still feel neglected and the voluntary board members who visit for meetings do not have the time or means for proper research. Their schedules are often interpreted locally as uncaring and arrogant. It is unfair to them and makes bad public relations for the Council.

The Senate committee investigating the Council would do well to consider an alternative structure. That the boards and committees meet less frequently and the bulk of the travel budget be diverted to the setting up of regional offices. That the board and committee members cease their battle against paperwork and draw up a statement declaring their understanding of the immediate needs and setting out a three-year plan of action. Having done so, that the officers of the Council should sift through the applications, discard those that do not accord with the policy, and make recommendations to the boards in the light of an approved plan. This would also enable the arts organisations to develop their own work in the shadow of this plan. And it would enable those who disagree with the plan to state their reasons and request a revision.

There is no question that the arts have burgeoned as a result of government aid. But those charged with the responsibility of Treasury money are reaching the point of shuddering at new projects and watching, awed, the growth of such Gargantuas as the National Gallery, the Australian Opera and the Australian Ballet. There comes a point at which growth is no longer useful. The paper work in the Council has reached a point of absurdity. A friendly understanding of conditions by regional officers could eliminate a big slice of the task of writing and reading applications. There must be other solutions; and a different solution for each board.

Meanwhile, Mr Pugh's criticism is thoughtful and valid and reflects the exasperation too often to be heard in the voices of the board and committee members. They feel they are being asked to make decisions for which they are not competent and are not being asked to do those things for which they are admirably chosen.

At the start the Council had offices in both Melbourne and Sydney and project officers travelled regularly to other states. Today the boards rotate their meetings around the capitals and staff travel is largely confined to these occasions.

Clifton Pugh had been an activist in the Victorian ALP. In 1971 he was elected with others by the State Council of the ALP to formulate a democratic structure for support of the arts. Their report recommended a structure for an Australia Council, which was submitted to Gough Whitlam while he was still in Opposition. Pugh accepted a position on the new Council in 1973 but regarded the autocratic way it was imposed as 'a betrayal'. He and a wide representation of the arts community campaigned for greater participation by artists in the decision-making. Dr Coombs had resigned from the new-form Council to take up the issue of Aboriginal rights; and was replaced in June 1974 by Professor Peter Karmel, foundation Vice-

Chancellor of Flinders University and author of the Karmel Report into Education for the Federal Government.

Since the Freedom of Information Act (1982) was passed records of opinion are no longer kept by the Council.

One Hundred Years of What?

Australian, 30 July 1974

J. C. Williamson Theatres Ltd have launched their centenary celebrations (official date is tomorrow) with a visit from the theatre critic of the *New York Times*, Clive Barnes, and his wife. It is a high-pressure, flying visit to most states to show him the extent of this largest and oldest private-enterprise theatrical management in the world. And Mr Barnes has shown himself at his most affable: an excellent after-dinner speaker and a persuasive advocate for the axiom that a critic has to be a tough journalist and nutty about the subject to put up with the demands made upon him and the slanders made against him.

His visit has done well what it set out to do—to draw our attention to the occasion. There has been wide opportunity for public talk; not a lot for listening. And some of the talk has been pretty depressing.

One such dismal occasion was a press dinner in Sydney, at which the recently appointed managing director of the Firm, Mr Alistair Mitchell, was the introductory speaker. Prologue to the dinner had been a preview of the ABC TV film of the history of JCW, a bland production with some interesting material from the early years, some entertaining and revealing anecdotes from the luminaries who have graced the JCW stages and no reference whatever to the Firm's rowdy business relationships. The Tait family, for example, is not mentioned, nor John McCallum, nor Michael Edgley.

Mr Mitchell, himself a Tait offspring, did nothing to redress the balance. His speech contained nothing of the company's achievement. He talked expansively about their failure to receive the favour of the Australian Council for the Arts and his failure to achieve a position on the Theatre Board. And how the Firm would die within five years if it did not get help from somewhere. Then he went on to talk about plans for expansion.

The Firm proposes, for example, to start an artists' agency to protect performers from the shark's teeth of the established agents. Had it not occurred to him, we asked, that JCW's 100-year-old career had been subsidised by meagre wages and that agents and unions had grown up to defend performers from such managements? JCW would also run a centenary contest with a $5,000 prize for a 'commercial' play or musical. (This will be the richest prize ever offered in Australia. Entries close 28 February.) 'Would they produce the winner?', we asked eagerly. 'Not if it is not commercial', said Mr Mitchell. We were not sure how the script would be judged commercial without it being produced.

So the speech went on, its audience listening in growing amazement as the speaker shifted uneasily from one foot to another.

JCW's contribution to the development of the theatre industry has not been impressive, except in terms of employment. Their total list of local scripts presented amounts to about twenty, of which most have been lost. If one compares this list with the English and American work which has taken up most of the 100 years, the former is no worse than the bulk of imported material: it is simply less well exploited.

Far and away the freshest, most original, forward-looking, purely entertaining show JCW have presented in a generation is the current production of *Irene*. It has been entirely devised and designed in Sydney and shows that JCW can beat its rivals anywhere in the world when their artists and administrators together put their minds to it. But most of the thought behind JCW for many years has been tired and imitative. Through good luck and good casting it has had successes before, like *Fiddler on the Roof*, *Man of La Mancha* and the post-war musicals and a lot more that have paid their way. The efficiency of the JCW backstage machine is something that has always impressed the visiting performer; but since the death of the Tait brothers no one with the eye for a commercial property has been given the authority to exploit it.

The Firm is famous for its private strife and its public unity and this has been part of its strength. Crisis is part of the JCW way of life, like every other theatrical management. That's show biz. The latest of the many retirements is that of Sidney Irving, Sydney manager of JCW—and I write this with regret. It was Mr Irving who oversaw the building of Her Majesty's Theatre, which opened last year, and demonstrated inspiring calm and attention to the needs of those who work in the theatre. An admirable achievement in the shadow of the Opera House opening.

Clive Barnes has supported Mr Mitchell's claim that the Firm will die without government subsidy, by reporting that Broadway has only five years to live and that London's Shaftesbury Avenue is also under sentence of death. One of the journalists at the Barnes dinner asked Mr Mitchell why, if he felt the subsidised theatre was undermining the commercial theatre, he didn't join them? But no real answer came.

Mr Barnes claims that subsidy would buy time for a commercial management, a chance to experiment and to fail in the cause of growth. Admirable reason and the one which has for years been applied to our subsidised theatre. But the job of the commercial theatre is not to experiment—we have other theatres for that and JCW is simply not equipped for the job—but to pick up and exploit talent and make a fortune out of it. If the Firm had truly followed in the footsteps of its founder we should have been exporting musicals to Broadway for 50 years.

We have in Australia today the most promising climate for new theatre in the English-speaking world. We have a big export market waiting to be exploited. But we do not yet have the actors and directors with the sheer craft skills that count in the great white ways of the world. And J. C. Williamson's must bear a great responsibility for that. There is still time, if the Firm is not so keen on emulating Broadway that it wants to commit suicide with her. A clever commercial management would make the subsidised theatre work for it. It is paid to fail and it is infinitely corruptible by the thought of success.

Our biggest commercial success yet must surely be Jack Hibberd's *Dimboola*. There's a show old JCW would have approved of. It must have made a couple of million by now and reportedly is being carved up for exploitation in the United States, Europe and Britain. That's what one would call a 'commercial' play but it was around for a good long time being un-commercial.

Ah well, Happy Birthday J. C. Williamson's. Here's to the next 100 years.

JCW's production division closed in 1976 (see p. 274). The musical comedy *Irene* (1919) starred the untried Julie Anthony in the title role and began for her an international career when the production was remounted in London. *Dimboola* (1969) written by Jack Hibberd is a wedding-reception farce in which the audience participates and which had popular success in theatre restaurants.

The Floating World: Unruly Masterpiece
Australian, 14 August 1974

For the tiny number of people who have seen John Romeril's earlier plays, *Chicago, Chicago, I Don't Know Who to Feel Sorry For, Bastardy* and *He Can Swagger Sitting Down*, his new one will come as no surprise. For those who haven't seen them, a viewing of *The Floating World*, produced by the Australian Performing Group of the Pram Factory, should restore Romeril to his rightful place as one of the best playwrights we have.

In his earlier days, Romeril's concern with the interaction of politics and madness somehow lacked a depth of feeling that would allow an understanding of how social change might be achieved in the face of his pessimistic analysis. Later on Romeril adopted a sort of naturalism in *Bastardy* and continued experiments with revue-style material, street theatre and attempts at directly political plays. In *The Floating World* we have a synthesis of his past work in a framework of plot and myth that has resulted in a major work, one that will be considered one of the unruly masterpieces of Australian theatre.

It deals with Les Harding, ex-AIF private and POW (Bruce Spence) who is reluctantly on the 1974 *Women's Weekly* Cherry Blossom Cruise to Japan. Les's wife Irene (Jane Clifton) is with him and meets a retired vice-admiral of the British Navy, Herbert Robinson (Robert Meldrum). The only other real people on the boat seem to be the Comic (the entertainment officer played by Peter Cummins) a steward, a bald professor (both performed by Carol Porter) and Mr Williams, another passenger (Wilfred Last).

As the voyage progresses, however, Les falls apart. He has conversations with the imaginary McLeod (Wilfred Last) who was at the fall of Singapore and in the prison camps afterwards. The waiter becomes a Japanese soldier who is selling, or instructing in the use of, dippy-birds. The routines of the Comic become weirder and Les imagines him to be an AIF officer.

His not-so-hot marriage cools off. Irene has an affair with Robinson, and the steward tries to seduce her. Scenes from prison camps, and horrific stories of what happened to Australian soldiers there are acted out. And at the end, in a magnificent mad soliloquy that lasts for twenty minutes, Les in a straitjacket rants and attacks the Japanese nation. He thinks he's back in the camps but perhaps he's in hospital, an example of the Australian paranoid.

What the play really deals with is the effect of World War Two on its victims and, as a corollary, how Australia views racial issues and especially Japan. It is one of the virtues of the play that the background to imperialism is never directly stated or forced, but rather is implied by the ubiquitous dippy-birds. The detailed dissection of Les's mind, his dreams and fantasies on this ship of fools is presented so sympathetically as to be almost an argument in his favour. He battles with his alter ego McLeod about whether or not the war is over, and with Robinson about whose fault it was that so much suffering was inflicted on soldiers sold out by the officers in charge. Les's madness is Australia's madness, and a logical extension of the historical xenophobia of the *Bulletin* and the Australian Labor Party.

The play is not all serious and tragic; it is, for the most part, extremely funny. It is written in a filmic sort of way with fast cuts from one scene to the next, and directed by Lindzee Smith at a very speedy pace. Bruce Spence's Les shows once again that he is a fine actor in both comic and serious roles. His physical work in the final monologue is precisely what is needed to counterpoint the poetry; and his ability to switch from either edge of madness is a delight to watch. In fact the weird undercurrents in the sub-text are brought out with ease by the whole cast. Even in the comedy of Peter Cummins there is an unnerving uneasiness. I kept wondering why this man was laughing at me. Cummins invests really ancient gags with a new energy and shows again that he is an actor of consequence. The rest of the cast is slightly overshadowed by these two, but put in unquestionably right performances.

The necessary complexity of the play is simplified by the bright, intimate design of Peter Corrigan. The audience and the actors are confined inside a big wire cage, with a boat-like protuberance at one end and a curtained stage for the Comic at the other.

The only quibble I have with *The Floating World* is with a series of statements that are spoken by Harry the Drummer during Les' final speech. Harry (Eddie van Roosendael) is used to provide the percussive background for sections of the play that are almost chanted. This hasn't been made to work yet and the effect, when he interrupts Les's flow with some really banal things about changing the world, is terrible. Sometimes, too, the focus of the action is lost by having a few things happen at once, but on the whole Lindzee Smith's direction is fine and Romeril will undoubtedly revise the play now he can see it in performance. *The Floating World* is one of the most important plays to come from an Australian and should in no circumstances be missed.

Because of the sympathetic dissection of Les, the play was, in fact, accused of racism in its early days. Harry the Drummer's statements with which I take issue were later excised.

PART VI
CONSOLIDATION
1976–85

In October 1974 I left the *Australian*. I returned for a short period in the late 1970s to write Sydney reviews but the conditions were disappointing. By now the arts editor and the publicist were entrenched, reviews were assembled onto an arts page and the reviewer no longer had the mandate to report news, range over subject matter or, indeed, influence newspaper coverage in any way. The task no longer held any joy.

The pieces that follow I wrote for journals like *Theatre Australia* and the *National Times*, where I regained that freedom. The style differed: they were occasional pieces, and of greater length, which offered the opportunity to be more descriptive, ruminative and to provide a broader perspective. In them I note the arrival in 1975 of the Australia Council, the demise in 1978 of the Old Tote, the birth in 1979 of the Sydney Theatre Company, and the death in 1981 of the Australian Performing Group. I was only an occasional reviewer for *Theatre Australia* and my reviews were confined to Sydney but I continued to seek a national perspective to the extent I could.

The awareness that the arts must become a business if they were to survive became evident from 1976, which saw the Industries Assistance Commission Inquiry propose the phasing out of subsidy and a Treasury cutback in the generous funding of the Whitlam years. The failing light of the Old Tote empowered a rapid brightening of the Nimrod Theatre which from 1976 made a brief bid to become Australia's national theatre company. But by 1982 it too was in turmoil.

The end of this section is redolent of rising bureaucracy, domination by the new arts centres and a stasis in creative drive. My calls for renewal went unheard and our theatre reinvented itself in yet another way.

A Toast to Melba

Theatre Australia, November–December 1976

There are two particular pleasures for me in the Parade Theatre's production of *A Toast to Melba*. One is that its popularity here as elsewhere confirms Jack Hibberd's long-held view—and that of the Australian Performing Group—that popular theatre can be contrived out of our daily rituals and our vaudeville tradition. The other is that Hibberd has found a director and a cast able to do real justice to the inventive raw material of the text.

While I cannot be categorical about productions of Hibberd's plays—and certainly about many productions of *Dimboola*, for example—I have long wished to see a really luxurious performance of his work with actors vocally better qualified than those common in the Australian Performing Group. Hibberd's work has never been as successful outside the Pram Factory as it has been in it, and the chief reason has been a lack of the precision which more formal environments demand. At the Parade Theatre under Mick Rodger's direction the Hibberd style comes into full bloom in a splendid amalgam of elegance and vulgarity.

'Popular theatre in general', writes Hibberd in the introduction to the printed text, 'suggests for me a theatre of accessibility that is above all Australian in theme and substance, a theatre for the populace that deals with legendary figures and events, perennial and idiosyncratic rituals, mythically implanted in the nation's consciousness'. It is a tall order and one he has been searching to satisfy since he first emerged as a playwright in 1967. *A Toast to Melba*, which places our most legendary lady in a context of sublime Italian music and ribald larrikin burlesque, is his most triumphant experiment to date. And in artistic terms his most successful.

The play is an account—a lively and fairly objective one—of Melba's life as those who knew her have recorded it. We see her first as a child practising the piano and swimming naked in the Yarra; and follow her through training to triumph, through her marriage and love affairs to maturity and the gradual loss of her powers. Seven actors play a gallery of miniatures: her teacher Madame Marchesi, Oscar Wilde, Enrico Caruso, Neville Cardus, John Norton, and so on. The script gives splendid opportunity to the imaginative resources of director and actors and the cast is impeccable. John Allen's time with the Neutral Bay Music Hall stands him in fine stead as, in particular, Nellie's lifelong friend. Ralph Cotterill gives four immaculately devised vignettes of which my favourite was Maestro Cecchi; and Drew Forsythe, whose work continues to astonish, goes from the extremes of Treacle O'Kane, Mackay pineapple farmer, to Shaw, Wedekind, Sir Thomas Beecham and the Duc d'Orléans. Anne Grigg is especially endearing as a 13-year-old streetwalker and as Gladys Moncrieff in duet with Melba; and Christine Collins' roles included the Lady Fairfax of Covent Garden in the 1890s, Lady de Grey. Jovially at the piano all evening as Gottlieb is Mario Merino.

As Melba herself the Old Tote has been blessed in Jennifer McGregor, who not only sings with great charm but as an actress has a warmth that makes a real bridge between the audience and the woman Melba. Ms McGregor's Melba is vastly different from that of the APG's Evelyn Krape; and Mick Rodger's production takes a different slant from Hibberd's own production as I saw it in Adelaide. Ms Krape is an excellent comic actress and she concentrated upon the burlesque and the bitterness. She has a pleasant trained singing voice but did not attempt to reproduce Melba at the height of her powers, making use instead of the nostalgia inherent in the recordings. Hibberd stays nearer to the text as published by Outback Press than Mick Rodger, who takes a number of liberties, which diminish the touches of cruelty in the writing—and indeed in the personality as it has come down to us. The message I took away from Adelaide was that the killer instinct could make the creative genius a right bastard.

Melba's treatment of her fellow characters was more ruthless in Adelaide and historically probably truer. Its drawback was that without a fuller exploration the audience was not always inclined to empathise. In other words I found Ms Krape's Melba a pretty unlikable character and I needed more to justify my attention. Ms McGregor's Melba, on the contrary, is engaging at every point and her voice, if not exactly in Melba's class, has more importantly a moving warmth—in, for example, the mad scene from *Lucia di Lammermoor*, which opens the second half. One can forgive her everything. But this is not without cost to Hibberd's text. So much of her eccentricity, as he sees it, is played down that there is nothing much to forgive. And when in the last line the words of Mimi's farewell are quoted, '*Addio senza rancore*', they express not a lifelong struggle accomplished but a life lived without bitterness and in Ms Krape's terms, without passion.

The critics greeted *A Toast to Melba* with enthusiastic praise at the last Adelaide Festival. At the time it struck me as odd that the festival productions of *Coriolanus* and Tennessee Williams' *Kingdom of Earth* should be knocked so savagely in the process of giving *Melba* its accolade. For the challenges set by each are incomparable.

But the answer to the riddle lies in Hibberd's own aim: *A Toast to Melba*'s great quality is its accessibility. After the hothouse sexuality of Williams' imaginary world and the cold power politics of Rome, the world of Melba was, literally, a coming home. Such a homecoming is not to be undervalued and already thousands of Australians are confirming its value. But here lies my serious reservation. To present a ritual in the theatre is not enough: the author must also interpret it. *A Toast to Melba* gives us a theatrical account of Melba's life—and that is certainly an education. But it takes the examination no further. It sheds little light on those fascinating questions of what an artist is or what it is that artists share. We are not asked to reach out to Melba: to pity her, or admire or even disapprove of her. To be aroused to any kind of emotion, in fact, which will hold her in our memory.

This seems to me, finally, a fatal flaw in *A Toast to Melba*. But more serious than that, in the context of Hibberd's other work, I see pessimism at the root which can only be destructive. The play stops when Melba dies. The last comments are a few bars of *Ave Maria*, an account of the funeral and her epitaph, 'Farewell without bitterness'. 'Is that all?' one asks. 'That is all', is his reply. The serious implication for his work, at least in my view, is that for Hibberd life is not without bitterness but is without faith and without hope. And, lacking these two, it must inevitably follow, without charity.

During 1975 Labor's accelerating economic problems, brought about by rapid expansion and galloping inflation, led to the Senate blocking supply and to the notorious Dismissal of the Federal Government on 11 November. One of Labor's last acts was to legislate for the creation of a statutory body to be called the Australia Council for the Arts. On 13 December 1975 the Liberal–National Party won a landslide victory in the federal election. In the aftermath of Labor's perceived profligacy Prime Minister Malcolm Fraser and the expenditure committee set about cutting costs. These housekeepers came to be known as the Razor Gang.

Rookery Nook / Here Comes the Nigger
Theatre Australia, December 1976

It has been one of those weeks. The Prime Minister, Mr Fraser, had been seen to turn his stony gaze towards those areas of free expression known as the performing arts and the media. The newly-formed Media Workers' Council was sternly raising forces to save the ABC. The Theatre Board of the Australia Council had been sitting and news of its cutbacks was beginning to seep through. Finding itself with a poorly furnished Christmas stocking and too many vociferous orphans crying for it, the Theatre Board had apparently made the choice of putting performance before development—meaning by that to save the livelihood of those at present in the profession. A worthy aim in a crisis.

Inevitably, however, the money must end up going to the big theatre companies stuck on their treadmill of yearly repertoire, never mind the progress which only risk can achieve. I don't blame the Theatre Board. We are all reaping a whirlwind today and the hard thinking it brings is no bad thing. Just as has happened in the ABC, in the shipbuilding industry, in uranium mining and elsewhere, the time is fast arriving in the theatre when we shall have to put our jobs on the line and declare what, in Churchill's words, up with which we will not put.

It was with the hard luck stories of the disappointed applicants in mind, and the militant proposals of the National Playwrights' Conference executive (the ANPC had its entire $20,000 application refused for the first time) that I attended two plays that could not be more divergent. At the Old Tote's Parade Theatre at the University of NSW was Ben Travers' *Rookery Nook*; and at the Black Theatre, behind the railway in Redfern, G. L. Bostock's *Here Comes the Nigger. Rookery Nook* is an example of the kind of theatre which is to be saved: a 1920s farce, not very well done and—to judge by the mood of the audience the night I saw it— sadly out of time and place. Mindless rubbish, one might fairly call it, if one chose.

But it is, of course, not the Old Tote's only current offering. At the Opera House Drama Theatre we have the rare joy of seeing Patrick White being performed again—something only a company with the Tote's resources could undertake so successfully. With *The Season at Sarsaparilla* at one theatre, why not *Rookery Nook* at the other? No good reason at all. Though, oddly, it is the White play that is occupying the more commercial of the two theatres.

I am not condemning *Rookery Nook* as a Christmas show: how many times has it been so, in its lifetime? What condemns it for me is that the audience found it unfunny and effete. It is charmingly designed by Allan Lees and has an experienced comedy cast led by Neil Fitzpatrick, Ronald Falk, Judi Farr and Edgar Metcalfe. But they were all working too hard, tying themselves in knots where the text calls for only the simplest gesture.

With the exception of Lynette Curran, whose Rhoda, an innocent pyjama girl who seeks refuge from her fearsome stepfather with a newly-married man, was like the lightest of lemon meringues, the cast puffed around as though they lacked any atom of faith in the play.

Bill Redmond is unquestionably capable of directing the play for our enjoyment. The fact remains that all these actors have done better work elsewhere. In short, the play was out of sorts with its theatre, and that, for a farce, is fatal.

Here Comes the Nigger, on the other hand, grows out of a theatre on survival rations, and the material of the play is, accordingly, basic necessity. It may lack elegance but it does have passion and the great advantage this group have over the Tote in this case is that they care; because it is their own basic needs, their own immediate experience they wish to express in this play. The result is rough theatre but it had us, its all-white audience, sitting on the edge of our seats for reasons other than comfort.

The Black Theatre has advanced since *The Cake Man* a year ago. *Here Comes the Nigger* is directed with confidence by Jack Charles who now has the support of black actors of growing experience like Athol Compton and Marcia Langton, and gutsy young white actors like Julie McGregor and Bryan Brown.

The hero is Sam (Athol Compton) a blind Aboriginal who makes leather belts and is studying for the Higher School Certificate. The play opens as he is about to meet a new tutor, Odette (Julie McGregor) a sociology student on a part-time job. Odette takes up with Sam with enthusiasm, partly from attraction, partly from curiosity and admiration, and soon finds herself at a storm centre of prejudice both from Sam's black colleagues and from her brother Neil (Bryan Brown), a violent, racist Vietnam veteran.

The first half is an amiable study of the lifestyle of the urban Aboriginal in Redfern, touching on domestic habits, money worries, black power, the condition of families on the reservations. Most of all it sends up whites, particularly the liberal white trying to understand. It is a sharp slap in the face for us whites and its blunt speaking is honestly refreshing.

In the second half from the time Neil explodes on the scene the play moves out of that casual reality into tragic mode, Jacobean in flavour. That it goes too far is due to the author's inexperience and the influence of the European drama; but at this point that is unimportant. What one retains is that sense of danger and honest passion, of something exciting about to happen—maybe not tonight or tomorrow but not too far ahead, And in retrospect that makes *Rookery Nook* an even sadder object.

So what price our development programs?

At this point a third play raises a particularly tricky problem. This is the recent season in Canberra of Roger Pulvers' *Drop Drill* in the as-yet-unfinished Australian National University Arts Centre. This was directed with great clarity and ingenuity by Ralph Wilson and performed with skill and a conviction similar to that of the Black Theatre, by actors including Ann Grey, David Bennett, Marguerite Wells and Ewa Czajor. Mr Pulvers, an American-Polish, now-naturalised Australian, who lectures in Japanese at the ANU, writes in a style which reflects both the Polish and the Japanese theatre and is totally foreign to the average Australian audience. I myself do not understand Pulvers' work but its quality is self-evident.

Drop Drill is an allegory about the conditioning human beings suffer, the rituals that have lost their meaning and the ways people find to survive. The characters include a woman prime minister and her attaché, foreign powers, and a family of several generations. The setting, roughly, is an Asian desert in which the prime minister for a time is lost. There is a deal of mime, often very witty. To give you some inkling, one of the early scenes is a summit talk conducted by parties who exchange views by playing a variety of instruments, sometimes in harmony and sometimes in embarrassing discord.

Theatrically, the play works very well and is certainly no more strange than the work of Peter Handke who recently had some vogue in our theatres. But when life is tough, as it is just now, what place is there in our theatre for such radical originality? Then again, when life is tough, should not this be the very time to decide our priorities?

To return to Patrick White's *The Season at Sarsaparilla*. For all its brilliance no one can deny that it also contains structural and technical problems which Jim Sharman's fine production did not solve. One cannot help ruminating that had the climate of the theatre in the early 60s been more mature, more progressive, more of those things we like to think we look for now, we might today have greeted this revival without reservation.

Developmental work is by its nature continuous and changing, and essential to authors, actors and audience in a wide variety of ways. The alternative to change and variety is stagnation and monotony and if we don't take time off from the present pressing financial pressures to get our priorities straight, the danger is we shall be stuck with not-very-good performances of *Rookery Nook*.

Bill Redmond, an Australian-born director whose career had been in Britain, succeeded Robin Lovejoy as artistic director of the Old Tote 1975–78.

The Cakeman by Robert Merritt was first presented at the Black Theatre in 1975, and at the Bondi Pavilion in 1977. It was the first Aboriginal play to be professionally performed. It was filmed for television and received acclaim at the World Theater Festival in Denver, Colorado in 1982.

The Late Flowering of Ray Lawler
Bulletin, 19 March 1977

I suppose that in every profession just now and then—perhaps even once in a lifetime—we are present at an event we know to be a moment in the history of that profession. In the theatre this is certainly true and in my seventeen years as a theatre critic I have been privileged to observe a few such occasions.

It is not the good performance and the exciting moment I mean. Such events as I describe may not, objectively, have been good performances. But they contained something that exceeded the acting and writing: an empathy between the giver and the receiver in which the actor and the writer became the medium. And we knew that our view of the world had shifted and would never be the same again.

Back in 1957 an expedition to the Nottingham Playhouse to see the touring company of *Summer of the Seventeenth Doll* defined something unique for me about the Australian psyche and sent me, tears streaming, to the nearest shipping agent to book my passage home. In 1962 at Stratford-upon-Avon, Paul Scofield's anti-heroic King Lear, a response to that generation's experience of modern genocidal warfare, made many more than myself radically rethink our approach to Shakespeare. In 1970 a rumbustious performance of *The Legend of King O'Malley* at the tiny Jane Street Theatre in a flash cleared a trail others had been blindly hacking. I remember that same presentiment as I read three drafts brought to me by a gangling young man to the Melbourne bureau of the *Australian: The Coming of Stork, Don's Party* and *The Removalists*.

Such an awesome experience—not, in this case, of seeing the future flashing before my eyes but of seeing the past reaffirmed and reassessed—

was a Saturday performance in Melbourne last month of Ray Lawler's *The Doll Trilogy*.

The plays had been seen before. The first one, *Kid Stakes,* had been on a national tour last year. The second play, *Other Times,* recently completed and set a decade later, had had a run-in season in Melbourne. Neither play had been received ecstatically by the critics or the public, so that, looked at coldly, the idea of a twelve-and-a-half hour stretch at the Russell Street Theatre was not all that appealing. And yet something was working for Lawler. Not exactly curiosity—people had their expectations. More a yearning to confirm a faith in ourselves.

The feeling, oddly enough, I found echoed in a profile of Lawler, then 36, published by the *Observer*, London, on 8 September 1957, as it commented upon his success.

> With £60,000 in his pocket for the film rights of *Summer of the Seventeenth Doll*, with American tourists pouring into St Martin's Lane every night to see his play before it goes to Broadway, and with weekly acclaim from theatrical people of the calibre of [Noel] Coward and T. S. Eliot, it might be supposed that Ray Lawler, who left school at thirteen, would now be enjoying the sweet smell of success.
>
> He is, and he isn't. He really wrote *The Doll* for himself, trying to express something wholly private about Australia. The fact that Europeans understand his meaning so readily makes him think he must have come up with something less Australian than he had supposed.

And indeed so deeply does *Summer of the Seventeenth Doll* penetrate the privacy of the ordinary Australian's consciousness that the event of the trilogy was for the audience as much a private need to confirm the stature of our past as an expectation of any new discovery.

The trilogy will not be repeated in other capitals. Maybe that is wise for the moment. Lawler belongs to Melbourne and to those who were present at those two performances it was a coming home at last for Australia's number one playwright. For all of us it was a confirmation of that simple fact. That he remains number one.

Not that such titles matter and they are based in most cases on a single play. There are other contenders: Alan Seymour for *The One Day of the Year,* Peter Kenna for *A Hard God,* David Williamson for *The Removalists*, still his most famous play. These are all plays with a dimension beyond that of their dramatic quality—firstly because they make discoveries of a wider implication that reach into our history and that of humanity. *The Doll* is, however, the one that overcame the national barriers to carry the message of our self-recognition abroad. It bears on its back those first timid assertions of national pride in ourselves since Federation. The *Observer* notes that:

> Hitherto Australia has made its impact on England chiefly through its soldiers and sportsmen. The idea that it has anything cultural to contribute is only just getting round, with its singers taking some of the best jobs in the opera houses of Europe, with its painters such as Sidney Nolan and its writers such as Lawler. Lawler, in a way, is the most significant: by accident an Australian is doing for the Australian character what Synge did for the Irish and Tennessee Williams for the Deep South. Lawler says he feels as if he were involved in the early days of the Abbey Theatre in Dublin, and the analogy is very close.
>
> Irishmen attacked the Abbey because it exposed things about Ireland they did not want the outside world to know. Similarly Australians were extremely doubtful about allowing *The Doll* to come to England on the ground that it should simply confirm the English belief that their country is entirely populated by low-class people leading rather unimportant lives in violent conditions. That Lawler has exposed representative Australians before West End audiences, has actually exploited the Australian accent instead of disguising it; and that this has moved English people to respect rather than to sneer, may well be a boost to the growing Australian inclination to create their own standards instead of relying on those in Europe.
>
> Lawler can thus stand for a whole rising Australian generation which, unlike its predecessor, has no instinctive respect for England as 'home', and prefers the look of the Australian future to that of anywhere else.

That was twenty years ago. The dream of self-assertion faded quickly for Australia's Synge and the years that followed were painful. He returned to Australia in 1959 for the J. C. Williamson season of *The Piccadilly Bushman*, a play which carried the hurt and confusion of the artist made afraid of his own country by success abroad. Australian audiences were not ready for his sharp satirical attacks on our imitations of British manners; and his portrait of a 'real' Australian as a kind of Rolf Harris did not appeal to the following *The Doll* had gained. His play *The Unshaven Cheek* failed at the Edinburgh Festival in 1963, after which he refused to have it performed elsewhere. He retired to Ireland, working as a script-writer, from whence he was not winkled until the 1970s by his faithful friend, John Sumner. For Sumner, Lawler wrote a play about Governor Bligh, *The Man Who Shot the Albatross*, which toured Australia in 1971. In the starring role Leo

Elspeth Ballantyne as Olive and Sandy Gore as Nancy in the Melbourne Theatre Company production of *Kid Stakes*, 1975. (Photo: David Parker)

McKern made a massive personal comeback to his old country; but the writing itself was too televisual, and too remote from the radical changes in Australian life inherent in the turn of the 70s, to contain that density that marked *The Doll* as unique.

The trilogy is a return to the personal. On the eve of *Kid Stakes*' opening in Melbourne Lawler remarked to the journalist John Hurst: 'I would dearly love it to be a success because I am fond of the people in the play and it is the most personal statement I have ever made in my writing. For that reason I would hate to think it has no meaning' [*Australian*, 5 December 1975]. *Kid Stakes* does, of course, have meaning; and with its crackling pace and laughter, its bursting youth and frivolity, probably comes off best of the three plays in the trilogy performance, at least the day I saw it. But what the performance did for all three plays on that occasion was to put them, for me and for others, in perspective. *Kid Stakes*—'nothing to win and nothing to lose'—introduces us in the summer of 1937 to Olive and Nancy, two young milliners, in the boarding house of Olive's mother,

Emma Leech. Dickie Pouncett, a good boy and window dresser at their department store, is courting Olive, not very successfully, and he is soon bowled out by the arrival of Roo and Barney, skylarking in pretence of being convalescent in the hope Emma will take them in as boarders. The joyful summer ripens as the couples commit themselves. Barney is caught out with two illegitimate sons in Makarandi; Emma succumbs to the irrevocable. Here is the spoiling and at the same time the confirmation of youth, laying down the rules by which the quartet will conduct their lives—a golden play which with refined craftsmanship plants the seeds of that destruction which makes up *The Doll*. For *Doll* lovers *Kid Stakes* is like a treasure hunt.

Other Times changes mood sharply. It is 1945 and the air is full of discord. Barney and Roo in an alien winter climate are awaiting their discharge. All of them are uneasy and impatient. Gone are the golden eagles flying south as Olive describes their lost youth in *Summer of the Seventeenth Doll*. In their place are two privates at the butt end of six years' life-denying ordinance. Roo receives his discharge: coming home drunk, bloody and half-mad, he builds a bonfire and burns his uniform. Olive, obdurately possessive of her romantic dream, dismisses the wasted years and embarks on a peacetime plan to restore her girlhood. But the fun is over already. In its place are petty racketeering, survival tactics. Nancy, the wise one, turning alcoholic, watches the changes, the growing gap between the men, the happy larrikin in Barney hardening into callousness. A Jewish immigrant, interned during the war, becomes the catalyst for further revelations of Barney's insensitivity. He and Nancy laugh together but the laughter is no longer shared.

By the time the curtain rises on *Summer of the Seventeenth Doll*, much of the ground in the first act has been covered. This changes our approach to the play: the dramatic progress of discovery is now the material of old rituals that add a poignancy to Olive's single-mindedness; and the short references to the absent Nancy reverberate with the ghostly presence of Sandy Gore's vibrant realisation. Repeated incidents, like the gifts of peppermint sticks from Bubba Ryan, ache with the passage of time; and the new year toast at the end of Act Two scene one: 'Happy days and glamorous nights', attains the dignity of tragedy as the balding Barney raises his glass to Pearl, Nancy's commonplace substitute.

The shape of *The Doll* is semi-circular. Hopes rise as we share Olive's romanticism, admiring the life force that the dark little Carlton House has so long contained. Slowly they fall again with the passing of youth, on which the trio have gambled all and lost.

Lawler's achievement in writing the trilogy is a triumph much greater than the three plays themselves. He has expanded that semicircle to enclose the trilogy, a triumphant web of construction, each intricate part of which reverberates upon the others. *The Doll*'s initial success lay in the fact that the characters struck a deep chord in the Australian psyche. The trilogy confirms that note and makes a monumental orchestration of it. The shattering ending to *The Doll* is the greater now because of what we have witnessed before; the arch is wider, higher and deeper. That is why his audience stood weeping and cheering Lawler and his cast. Nothing of this dimension has occurred before in our dramatic literature. Such an achievement is rare in any culture.

In style there remains a clear distinction between *The Doll* and its companion plays. The first two are period pieces, written with a conscious emotional memory. They draw conclusions about that remembered life, but *The Doll* is the stuff of that life itself. *The Doll* is a contemporary piece, dense with the psychic context of the 1950s. The love and understanding, the transparent truth of it, then and now, makes it grow in dimension when placed beside its sister plays.

This rare perspective upon Lawler's work, artificially created, forces us to see Lawler—his apparently old-fashioned well-made style, too neat in contemporary terms, perhaps; too sentimental, too elegantly conscious of the curtain line and the nice business and the upstage exit—to see him on his own terms, shed of the comparisons with rougher, tougher and smarter minds in the 1970s. It is a triumphant coup for the Melbourne Theatre Company, its director John Sumner and his cast, Bruce Myles and Sandy Gore, Carole Skinner and Peter Curtin, Irene Inescort, David Downer and Christine Amor.

At 55, Ray Lawler has ended the painful long road home. From now on, whether or not he writes another play, there will no longer be the need to compete. His place as a dramatist is affirmed. And that in our 200-year history of youthful hopes and defeated old age, has never happened before to one of our playwrights.

Peter Brook's production of *King Lear* with Paul Scofield was inspired by the theories of the Polish critic Jan Kott, author of *Shakespeare Our Contemporary*. The gangling young man with scripts in 1971 was, of course, David Williamson.

Lawler's trilogy was in fact revived jointly by the Melbourne and Sydney Theatre Companies in 1985 and performed at the Victorian Arts Centre and the Sydney Opera House. The director was Rodney Fisher. The *Observer*'s reference to the Abbey Theatre is interesting. The Abbey had repeatedly been raised as a model for Australia in the development of a literary theatre, from Louis Esson and the Pioneer Players who invoked it early in the 20th century to the historian Leslie Rees in the 1950s and Hugh Hunt, first director of Australian Elizabethan Theatre Trust.

Nimrod's *Much Ado About Nothing*

Theatre Australia, August 1977

There can be no question of the success of the current Shakespeare season at the Nimrod Theatre. John Bell's productions of *Twelfth Night* and *Much Ado About Nothing* make him arguably the best director of Shakespeare we have in the 1970s.

Inevitably they have aroused controversy. The casting of a boy in the role of Viola, for example, disturbed many people's sensitivities. What these offer—and audiences have responded to it—is not correctitude but that same audacity, that same confrontation with the flesh and blood of the actor, that first brought John Bell to our attention as a director in 1970 with *The Legend of King O'Malley*.

The location of *Much Ado About Nothing* is Messina. In this production, a revision of the successful 1975 one with Anna Volska as Beatrice and Peter Carroll as Benedick, Bell has capitalised upon the Mediterranean setting both in vivid colour and a strong sense of the clan structure which frames that society. Within this structure the blood conspiracies, the protection of women and the preservation of honour, the elaborate rituals of the vendetta—all sit comfortably. The period is vague—Tony Llewellyn-Jones' Don John is a little Napoleon, out of his time; others might be drawn from the present day. As originally conceived, Larry Eastwood's set was a circus tent in which Leonato, Governor of Messina, oddly stowed his family and entertained the Prince of Arragon and his train.

Kim Carpenter's costumes expand this sense of a congregation of peasants and clowns. The bunting in the new production is still there, there is a new two-level set made over from *Twelfth Night* and painted primary colours. The present set adds little to the design of the play's action, rather it adds a permanence: no longer the circus—Luna Park, perhaps. It matters little to the audience; enveloped in bunting and Sandra

McKenzie's circus music they find themselves in jolly, outgoing company at a family party.

The point of controversy in this production, however, is not the vaudeville visual style but the greengrocer accents. 'Can one possibly justify', one asks oneself, 'a jewel of the English language being played in such an accent?' Unless, of course, they are a company of Italian greengrocers. And again: 'Is it distracting? Is the meaning obscured? Is it incongruous? Or does it, in fact, assist the audience's comprehension?' All the evidence, of course—the packed houses, the laughter, the bubbling interval, the hooting enjoyment of the schoolboys who surrounded me in the audience—point to the production being an even more resounding success than its premiere season in 1975.

Perhaps it was the expectation, this time. I admit that first time round I found some of the accents distracting and obscuring and they tended to pale after the first scene or two. In this new production that dialect seems more deliberate, consistent and painstaking in its care of the text. It reflects a general concentration on detail, particularly of the externals—the timing of business, the pointing of implications—that characterises the present production.

The reason I liked the accent was a simple one: that it provided a communal reality within which the actors could work and a bridge over which the audience might approach the play without timidity or reverence. The problems involved in trying to find something in common between Shakespeare and the modern Australian are, of course, legion. Aristocracy, in particular, is something that makes us uneasy. We have no sense of natural hierarchy and the intrigues of the nobility would seem remote to our experience of life. That is why the study of Shakespeare so often becomes an effort of will, instead of an enlightening experience. John Bell's production of *Much Ado About Nothing* knocks the stuffing out of such uncomprehending reverence and focuses the audience's attention and affection directly on the people and events on stage.

The chief beneficiaries of the technique are Beatrice and Benedick, Claudio and Hero. Peter Carroll's rough, amiable soldier, part-clown, part-hero, engaging with the audience at every opportunity, is paired with the swinging peasant liberality of Anna Volska's Beatrice. They make of their affair a public circus in which their mutual affection, transparent from the first, is blasted in happy salvos across the arena. This Benedick vies with his role in *The Christian Brothers* to be Carroll's best performance yet. Anna

Volska's Beatrice is equally a landmark in her career. In this role and her Olivia she has discovered a warmth and affability behind her elegance which gives a new quality to her acting.

Bell is, of course, right in exploiting the Sicilian blood to explain the vindictive behaviour of the villain, Don John, and the gullibility of Claudio. A veteran at arms, Claudio is naïve in matters of human nature. He falls in love with the first girl he meets on leave, precipitates her into marriage, does a quick reverse after falling for a crude trick to dishonour his bride and an about-turn when ordeal by death proves her innocent. He then takes the next partner offered him, does a full circle and ends up with the resurrected Hero as if nothing had happened since the beginning of the dance. Shakespeare makes a point of tripping up his characters when they attempt a too-hasty marriage. Claudio's marriage looks doomed. The real marriage in the play is that of Beatrice and Benedick, born of long testing and tolerance.

The one reservation I have is the interpretation of Hero. The young women among Shakespeare's lovers have a way of being more level-headed than their men and more courageous. The direction of Deborah Kennedy's Hero as a half-grown schoolgirl is at odds with the dialogue and Miss Kennedy's potential in the role. As Claudio, Tony Sheldon is splendid—a difficult feat to follow John Walton's memorable performance last time. Also new in the cast is Gordon McDougall, who makes a genial democratic Leonato, at home in this barn of a house. Drew Forsythe's audience-stopper, Dogberry, returns, complete with banister brush and police whistle, fighting a pitched battle with his malapropisms. A genuine original. Others who make up the ensemble include Maggie Blinco, replacing Melissa Jaffer as Ursula, the dependable Alan Tobin as the Friar and Verges, and Robert Alexander and Dennis Scott as Don John's conspirators.

Tony Llewellyn-Jones, who plays Don John as a sinister spoilsport, a Carabosse peeved at not being invited to the party, is now one of our most considerable actors. He demonstrated his promise early and the work of the years that followed is now bearing fruit in a repertoire of wide range and perception. In August he will undertake his biggest challenge yet when he undertakes the title role in the trilogy, *The Norman Conquests*.

Ivar Kants' Don Pedro is also a remarkable performance, holding the centre of the play with a relaxed authority that brings harmony to the old hierarchical world from which Shakespeare's characters sprang and the new hospitality John Bell's production offers them.

Much Ado About Nothing is not the most difficult of Shakespeare's plays to perform; its principal characters captivate their audiences and the play has a long stage history of popular success. The pleasure of this production lies not in new twists to an old theme, though they are there, but in the rare confidence of the production, which takes the play by the forelock as though such had never been done before. It is a confidence not of youth and ignorance but of a slowly maturing realisation that the shadows of history should not be permitted to fall between a director and his playwright, even if that playwright is Shakespeare.

This production has remained in popular memory as a defining moment in our interpretation of Shakespeare and the genesis of the approach that became a trademark of Bell Shakespeare Company. It toured widely after the Sydney season.

The Christian Brothers (1975) by Ron Blair is a solo piece that became a personal triumph for Peter Carroll and in which he toured national and internationally. He revived the role in 2003.

Outside the cities, the expansionary aims encouraged by theatre subsidy brought to the surface a deep-seated division between the aspirations of the profession and those of the community from whom they sought their audience.

A Tale of Two Cities

National Times, 8–13 August 1977

Among the dockyard workers, the shift workers and the seasonal workers, some of the 12,000 out-of-work winding their way to the Newcastle Department of Social Security a young woman stopped short her interviewer. The exchange went something like this:

'I'm an actress.'

'Oh. And how do you earn your living?'

'I act.'

'You earn your living at it? Here in Newcastle?'

'Yes.'

'Have you always earned your living by acting?'

'Yes.'

'You've never done anything else?'

'No.'

'Oh.'

Pat Bishop, one of Sydney's best-known stage actresses, who threw in her lot earlier this year with the troubled Hunter Valley Theatre Company, was the first of the group to apply for the dole last month. The fact that her profession was outside the experience of the dole clerk is an indication of the communication gap that has plagued the company since its inception 20 months ago. Too large a theatre and too small a box office have eaten up this year's budget. The company retrenched its actors in June after a public meeting at which the board of directors called for a moratorium to take a fresh look at company policy.

The actors could have removed to the greener fields of Sydney; instead they opposed the board's decision to take a six-month break in favour of two months, determined to show Newcastle they wanted to belong. The time expires on 14 August. Meanwhile they have got up a music-hall revue at the Tavern in Hunter Street, which is doing thriving business.

Such is the present predicament of the Hunter Valley Theatre Company, a small tremor in the crisis-ridden city with one of the highest unemployment rates in the country. If the company dies, as it may next month, it will deal another blow to decentralisation and the first brave experiment in establishing subsidised theatre in a regional city. The problem, which is basically one of money, is also one of local acceptance, which in itself is a way of generating money.

The root of the problem goes back to the manner of, and the motives behind, the establishment of the HVTC. It was set up in 1975 as a fully-operating theatre company on the initiative of the Arts Council of NSW and the Joint Coal Board. But these motives again raise the larger problem of how in a largely working-class town preoccupied with industrial and economic problems and with no tradition of theatre-going, a theatre company can tackle the task of contributing to the quality of leisure time and to the imaginative life of its citizens.

This article looks at two companies of actors who face this challenge and take very different stands upon it. The motives that inspired the HVTC were the Arts Council's concern at the inadequacy and expense of touring as a method of serving country areas, and local citizens' desire to provide a new city-style facility for Australia's largest regional city. Similarly, the Q Theatre late last year deserted its comfortable AMP Theatre at Sydney's Circular Quay and moved to Penrith, at the foot of the Blue Mountains, to serve Sydney's West.

The venues for both companies were chosen with care: Newcastle for its population, its substantial following for music and its thriving amateur theatre; and Penrith, in the words of the director Doreen Warburton, 'because it had a definite feeling about it, quite different from other places—a community spirit. You could feel it in the audience's reaction'.

Both companies rely heavily on subsidy for survival, from the state and federal governments, both make use of local talent and work widely in non-profit making community programs. The major aim of both companies is to produce good theatrical, energetic work that will develop the theatre-going habit and the discriminating taste of its theatregoers. They employ people of good standing in the profession—of the two the HVTC's is the bigger: its standards have been equal to, and often better than, Sydney's.

Why then is the Q Theatre venture being looked upon as a success and the HVTC as a failure? The answer lies in the ambitions and the point of view. Both companies recently presented Joe Orton's comedy *What the Butler Saw* to similar-sized audiences. For the Q in its 90 and 150-seat theatres it was a tremendous success; for the HVTC in the 1,200-seat Hunter Theatre it was a disaster.

No one involved in the Newcastle dispute would now deny that to graft a fully-operating theatre company onto the unsuspecting city was not the wisest way of going about it. For very soon both the Arts Council and the Joint Coal Board found themselves in no position to give continuing support. So far no assistance has been received from BHP, on which about 20 per cent of the town is dependent, and almost nothing from the City Council. Director Terence Clarke is frank about the fact that it should not have happened—though he is not sorry, he said. 'The only theatre companies that have sprung full-grown from the loins of their creators are those that have been set up by statute', he said. But he is determined to preserve the high professional standing the company has achieved. Asked if it might not have been wiser to develop a professional company out of the community theatre, he said: 'That is an invidious question which I cannot answer because I would not have applied for the job, nor would most of the present company have come. It would have been a different kind of project.'

It is not, however, true that Newcastle did not want professional theatre. In the words of John Robson, head of drama at the Newcastle College of Advanced Education, himself a long-time aficionado and a member of the HVTC board:

I don't think it is true to say that the idea came from the Arts Council. People in Newcastle have been hoping for and trying to get professional theatre here for many years. It goes right back to my childhood. It so happened that the initiative came from the Arts Council in this instance; but I don't think that has any bearing on the fortunes of the HVTC.

Mr Robson believes that money can cure the problems, the chief of which is to find a home. He himself is actively involved in that search. The company's first year was spent at the University's Arts Drama Theatre—pleasant and a good modest size but formidably difficult to reach, being out of town and off the public transport route. And the campus site only reinforced the essentially middle-class face the company presented, with its Arts Council–appointed board of academics, lawyers, accountants and businessmen. No election has yet been held by members. A recent attempt to have a trade union representative appointed to the board has for the moment been quashed. This year, after every other effort to find a suitable theatre building had failed the HVTC took over the echoing Hunter Theatre—a graveyard, the actors called it and so it proved to be.

But from the start the company has been grossly under-capitalised. The board and the company refused to see the present troubles as failure, simply as deficit—and they are right, of course. On paper the company's attendance looks good. The national average of theatregoers is 2 per cent of the adult population. A recent market survey conducted by the HVTC put the figure of supporters at 7 per cent. As the chairman, David Wood, said: 'Even if half those people never come to the theatre, 3.5 per cent is still a good figure.'

John Robson put the case more subtly:

> Sydney has approximately ten times the population we have in Newcastle. On top of that they have established over the years quite a large theatre-going public. They have a much larger educated middle class—probably twenty times our theatre-going population. Now we can draw in some 3,000 to 3,500 people in quite unfavourable conditions—a far higher proportion of our population than either the Old Tote or Nimrod—probably more than they do combined. So really our level of subsidy is too low for the conditions in which we have to operate.

The company battled through last year, living from hand to mouth. David Wood, a city accountant drawn in only last year as auditor and now chairman, admits that when $40,000 was granted in subsidy for the 1977 season the board relaxed and were caught unawares by the new crisis.

> One of the main issues seems to be that the most successful companies operated at first by paying far lower than award wages and obtaining a great deal of voluntary and student help. We came in fully professional

but tried to do it on an amateur budget. It just doesn't pay. One of the greatest mistakes we made in our funding application for 1977 was not to stick to Terry's original estimate of $104,000 deficit.

The Q Theatre has no deficit. 'We haven't had a deficit in 15 years', said the ample actress who is prime mover in the present venture. 'We cannot afford a deficit because we don't have a board to bail us out.' Neither does she have any magic formula for survival. But listening to the Q's story of struggle one is aware of one perceptible difference in emphasis. Where the HVTC talks of numbers, Doreen Warburton talks about people.

She can quote numbers: they are part of the armoury with which she enlists the support of councils, Rotary Clubs, Red Cross branches, teachers and community aid programs. She knows the crime rate in the area and the number out of work.

> As the result of automation, 20 per cent of the kids now unemployed around here will never work in their lives, according to the latest statistics. So leisure time is going to become more and more important. We run classes, all kind of classes, for kids who have nothing to do—anything to get them out of this desperation.

She added an anecdote about a 17-year-old who got the job he longed for as a fork-lift driver after a short involvement with the company had boosted his self-confidence. 'I don't say we were responsible but we helped', and then, as if to excuse the story, 'well, one person's important'.

It is this ratio of one to one which is getting the Q on its way. Before moving to Penrith the Q had spent four or five years performing for the West's audiences, running ten-week classes, giving lunch-hour theatre. In that time councils had given their halls rent-free, ladies' auxiliaries had made coffee and sandwiches. In short the Q had become a familiar and friendly institution. An active support group now provides much of the labour behind the actors, who on Ms Warburton's insistence have settled in the area. 'We have to, it's part of the commitment. People have to see us shopping in the supermarket if we are going to belong.'

The theatre's home is also a familiar place:

> Everyone knows the Railway Institute in Penrith. People used to play pool there and go to dances. One man said to me, 'I haven't been here since I was a bodgie.' So when we were converting it people walking by would come in to see what we were doing. The Council gave us the building—they weren't going to give us any money for the conversion until they saw us working our guts out. In the end they got excited too.

What the Q have done, in fact, is deliberately set out across those quicksands which have put fear into every pioneering theatre venture in this country (and which the HVTC set-up was designed to avert)—the accusation of amateurism. In fact all the older theatres in Australia (commercial theatres aside) were once amateur, which is one way of saying they grew out of a community need; and in some cases the painful journey towards professionalism has left scars that have never healed. Professionals dislike the word amateur because they regard it as meaning unprofessional in work standards. But equally it can simply mean that the work earns little or no pay.

The Q Theatre employs nine theatre people who earn a flat $150 per week. Their production of *A Hard God*, which I saw at the Marsden Rehabilitation Centre at Parramatta may have been makeshift in get up but the performance was as good as I have seen anywhere. The two teenage boys, who control a third of the play, gave performances deeply rooted in the suburbia from which the play derived. It is Ms Warburton's ambition that in time such young people will become the nucleus of the company. 'I knew if we were coming out here the only true way to work would be as ensemble. We don't pretend to be individually brilliant but we feel that together we might be able to achieve something. We want to have energy, we want to have a different style.'

Doreen Warburton's involvement with the community does not mean inviting the amateur on stage but exploring and knowing the leisure activities of her new home. Her respect for people, her concern for the desperation behind the rows of houses in Bankstown and Mt Druitt, her ambition to build a genuine working-class style of theatre, she caught at the age of 17 touring the mining towns of England with Joan Littlewood's radical ensemble troupe. These are things which will set that 'different style' though it may not make anyone rich. In the theatre every person is important and, as David Wood has shown, can very quickly affect the statistics.

The Hunter Valley Theatre Company has not met its audience on the Q's intimate terms. While they had a busy community program which took theatre to the dockyard, the factories, the gaols, they have never encouraged a support group—of which local citizens like Malcolm Barnes, who when he abandoned his own amateur theatre gave all his equipment to the HVTC, is openly critical. Given the pressures of a company in full performance from the start, there has been little time or energy for the Q's style of groundwork and the company is now reaping the consequences.

The problem of repertoire has been another vexed question. In the amateur theatre there has been a history of popular entertainment and the HVTC's greatest success has been the pantomime *Hamlet on Ice*. On the other hand is the evangelistic view of board members like John Robson: 'Newcastle is a theatrically unsophisticated city. If we are to introduce plays that respect the modern world then we have to expect at this stage a fair number of offended people at the box office. But I think it is a path we have to follow. We cannot keep Newcastle isolated from what is happening in the world forever.'

Looking at the box office patterns, however, it is clear that vested interests have a healthy influence upon audience appeal. The Hunter Valley's second most successful play was the premiere of *A Happy and Holy Occasion* by John O'Donoghue, a teacher at the Newcastle CAE, about a Catholic family in Mayfield, a Newcastle suburb in smoke-haze distance from the BHP steelworks. Intrinsically a good, funny and sad play, its appeal to Newcastle audience was clearly the novelty of self-recognition. The touring Nimrod season of Jennifer Compton's *Crossfire*, co-winner of a Newcastle drama competition, received heavy local promotion and support, which the next Nimrod show did not. On the other hand Jack Hibberd's *The Les Darcy Show*, presented recently in the clubs of Maitland and Newcastle by the HVTC, along with Alex Buzo's *The Roy Murphy Show*, ran into choppy waves of local allegiances and foundered. More than money, this proprietorial sense is, finally, what will make or break the HVTC. The company is exhausted and needs help. The initial refusal to go away (Terry Clarke, for example, turned down a comfortable job as regional theatre director in another state to remain in Newcastle) is their most overt demonstration of commitment to the city—that they are not there because 'they can't get work in Sydney'. But it may be that even two months is too long a period of stagnation. Actors must go where the work is and they all have agents to keep. Pat Bishop has accepted a job with the Queensland Theatre Company. Meanwhile the board of businessmen, academics and accountants are doing a quick two-month course in theatre administration and the actors are back rehearsing a new play—just in case—as they await the outcome of 14 August.

Les Darcy (1895–1917), Australia's favourite lightweight boxing champion, grew up in Maitland and the controversy surrounding his early death is still an issue there.

The company disbanded. Local pressure resulted in the Civic Playhouse being built within the wintergarden of the Civic Theatre. It opened in 1979 under the direction of Ross McGregor. The company has continued a chequered existence under a variety of directors and hazardous levels of funding. In 1999 BHP, who had dominated Newcastle's economy for a century, closed their Newcastle steel mills. Since then Newcastle has transformed itself into a university town with a diverse economy. Following the 2003 state election Premier Bob Carr promised funding for a 400-seat theatre for the Hunter School of Performing Arts. It has now been designed and tenders called but construction has not yet begun. The Civic Theatre received a refurbishment in 2004.

The Q Theatre in Railway Street, Penrith, continues to be a regional theatre. Its company is now the Railway Street Theatre Company, created in 1998 by a merger between the Q and the New England Theatre Company for the purpose of country touring. The theatre closed for demolition in August 2005 and the company moved to the Joan Sutherland Performing Arts Centre at Penrith.

Many theatres went to the wall in the 1970s as the pecking order for subsidy was established. Not the least of these was the 100-year-old institution, J. C. Williamson's, which closed its entrepreneurial arm in 1976, after failing to gain help from government. Those surviving, hit by the Razor Gang cuts, scrambled to fill JCW's vacuum by hiring second venues. The Industries Assistance Commission inquiry was treated with horror and bemusement; in retrospect its comments quoted here amount almost to a motherhood statement.

Round Up 1977: The IAC Inquiry

Theatre Australia, February 1978

There has been evidence of radical and far-reaching change in the Australian theatre over the last twelve months—or at least a change of thinking with far-reaching implications. The old barrier between art and commerce is breaking down. Inevitably, it has not happened by the commercial theatres becoming more cultural but by the art theatre becoming more commercial: but this time at least the art theatres have something to be commercial about.

The timely origin of this upheaval, in October 1976, was the Industries Assistance Commission's Draft Report on assistance to the performing arts.

The draft, when it appeared, sent a ripple of horror through the performing arts. It sent the Australian Opera flying to the Utah Mining Company and made boards of directors at every level look again at their policy and progress. The cause of the panic was not so much the report itself but the summary that took the headlines. At the top was the recommendation that subsidy be phased out over five years at the rate of 20 per cent a year.

In the resulting storm Prime Minister Fraser made a hasty rejection of the idea and things calmed down a bit. But from the results we have seen this year the thought that survival might depend eventually on sources other than government subsidy has taken root. Long-term thinking is perhaps putting too fine a point on it: let us say, rather, that our theatre companies decided that in 1977 they had better find ways of making money.

The Draft Report and the Report that was delivered to the Prime Minister in April were much more considerable documents than the daily press made out. In the final report the idea of phasing out subsidy was modified but the premise on which it was based is argued through cogently. And that is that culture is not the privilege of the few. Our culture, it points out, is our national character and not what we should like to be or what we should like others to think of us.

What the IAC did was to challenge the foundation on which the Australia Council's policy—and that of the Australian Elizabethan Theatre Trust before it—was based: the pursuit of excellence, or as the report calls it, 'the flagship approach'. I quote from the introduction:

> The flagship approach involves three inherent elements of discrimination—towards a few selected art forms, towards a few favoured companies and towards live performances. This discrimination, it was argued, is justifiable on the grounds that these arts bestow the greatest cultural benefits; the selected companies are the most advanced in the 'pursuit of excellence'; and live performances represent the essence of the performing arts by providing a measure of immediacy or interpersonal empathy between performers and audiences which cannot be achieved otherwise.
>
> But the very nature of culture is such that no particular performing art or activity can be shown to generate more benefits to the community as a whole than any other. For example, there was no evidence that, within music, opera is more 'cultural' or more publicly beneficial than, say, chamber music or a whole range of other dance forms. As is shown later in this report, the 'pursuit of excellence'—while desirable—is not in itself an automatic justification for public assistance... The alternative philosophy, which underlies the assistance measures proposed by the

Commission, is that embodied in the IAC Act. It reflects the community values and broader, more even-handed approach being applied to assistance policies for activities in all sectors of the economy. Inherent in this approach is assistance that is equitable to the community as a whole and thus requires assessments of the benefits which the performing arts provide, or have the potential to provide, to that community. [IAC, 'Draft report on Assistance to the Performing Arts', p. 4]

When the Theatre Board laid down a policy in 1968 the establishment of 'flagships'—that is, regional theatre companies of the first quality—was the first priority. In the list drawn up for that purpose of existing theatres in Australia, the chain of commercial theatres was excluded. It has remained excluded ever since—and it was, in fact, this creeping doubt about such exclusion that led to the IAC inquiry.

The first result of the IAC Report was the setting up of a Community Arts Board. The second is foreshadowed in an aggressive new commercialism within our subsidised theatre companies. The collapse of the J. C. Williamson's production arm following the IAC's refusal to recommend subsidy was no more than a delayed inevitability. In its place new entrepreneurs are springing up with new tastes and a fresh eye for a bargain. The obvious example is *The Elocution of Benjamin Franklin*, in which pie a remarkable number of producers have had their fingers. And it is not without interest that the Melbourne and Sydney productions of David Williamson's *The Club* were scheduled for transfer and tours before the play opened. (*The Club*, now playing at Nimrod, goes to the Theatre Royal this month.)

The Melbourne Theatre Company has expanded into the Athenaeum with a program of popular classics. The Old Tote has moved into the Seymour Centre firstly with that comedy industry called *The Norman Conquests* to be followed by a program from those attention-getters Jim Sharman and Rex Cramphorn. And the Tote has taken up touring again: *Big Toys* to Melbourne and *Mothers and Fathers* to Adelaide in January.

There have been smaller tours this year too, like the Australian Performing Group's *The Hills Family Show*, which as a by-product enabled Sydney theatregoers to see Max Gillies' distinctive performance in *A Stretch of the Imagination*. And Nimrod's season of *Much Ado About Nothing* toured to Adelaide. In the commercial field Parachute Productions have opened the Playbox in Melbourne again to popularity and in Perth have had an unbroken record of success with their resuscitation of the old Regal Theatre.

All this is just a sample of the kind of movement at last beginning to occur apparently spontaneously among theatres.

Perth, Hobart, Brisbane and to a lesser extent Adelaide, are still isolated and too little remains known in the bigger cities of their theatre work. But at least there are openings. Gone at last is the door kept so obdurately shut for so long by the J. C. Williamson's monopoly against the idea of a commercial product of our own.

Appendix F of the IAC Report makes a sad obituary for JCW. Considering the effects of the Government's refusal to assist the chain in the short term the Commission found the major effect would be the presentation of fewer attractions 'during the next six or nine months' and the displacement of some 58 technicians whose skills were in demand by other theatres. As it turned out, those six or nine months have been an opportunity for others and the JCW influence upon the theatre over a hundred years has in 1977 already become history.

I don't want in this article to single out performances in anything more than a personal way because I do not travel as much as I used to and my theatre-going is highly selective. For me the most memorable day in the theatre in 1977 was unquestionably the performance of *The Doll Trilogy* at the Russell Street Theatre last February. Another warmly sentimental occasion was John Gaden's benefit at Nimrod before he left for New York, at which again I saw a rare performance. This and the return of Patrick White to the theatre late last year and the resultant birth of *Big Toys* makes me feel—an illusion, perhaps—that we are beginning to learn how to value our artists in the theatre at last.

On the downside this year I also mourned the death of George Landen Dann in Queensland, one of our neglected playwrights who deserved better from his country. His parting was alleviated a little by the touching performance of *In Beauty it is Finished* at La Boite Theatre in April only weeks before he died.

Maxim Gorky's *The Lower Depths* at the Opera House, marathon as it was, has set a new standard of classical production for the Tote in which the Romanian director Liviu Ciulei drew new qualities from the actors. My disappointment of the year in terms of expectations raised was *Chorus Line*. My favourite all-round production was Rodney Fisher's no-nonsense direction of *The Club* for the Melbourne Theatre Company—and the most endearingly theatrical performance that of Frank Wilson as Jock. He vies with the sheer glow of Sandy Gore as Nancy in *Kid Stakes* and the concentrated tenacity of Tony Sheldon in *Inner Voices* at Nimrod for the performances I look back on with greatest affection. It has been a good year, on the whole, that has done a lot of stirring; and one of the most valuable aids to the new circulation has been *Theatre Australia* itself. Long may it grow and prosper.

Theatre Australia, a national journal of record founded by Robert Page, Lucy Wagner and Bruce Knappett, was published from August 1976 to May 1982. Its seesaw relationship with the Theatre Board of the Australia Council finally led to its demise. The Athenaeum Theatre in Collins Street seated 880. The expanding MTC leased it pending its move to the Victorian Arts Centre in 1984. Perth's Regal Theatre was a former cinema in Subiaco. The Playbox Theatre in Exhibition Street was taken over by Hoopla Productions in 1978 which became the Playbox Theatre Company. The theatre burnt down in 1984 and the company built a new complex in Southbank, known as the Malthouse, on the site of an old brewery donated by Carlton United Breweries. Playbox changed its name to Malthouse Theatre at the end of 2004.

The Industries Assistance Commission or IAC report, entitled 'Draft report on Assistance to the Performing Arts', was published in Canberra in October 1976. The final report was dated 30 November 1976.

The benefit for John Gaden helped him to spend six months in New York studying voice.

Among the plays mentioned, *The Elocution of Benjamin Franklin,* a play for a solo performer by Steve J. Spears, was created by Gordon Chater and premiered at Nimrod Downstairs on 28 August 1976, directed by Richard Wherrett. It transferred to the New Arts Theatre in Glebe with the help of Harry M. Miller and then went on a national tour. Several international managements expressed interest before the London entrepreneur James Hammerstein bought the world rights and presented the production successfully in London and off-Broadway.

The Norman Conquests, a three-way, three-play family comedy by Alan Ayckbourn at the Seymour Centre, was a last-ditch attempt by Robert Quentin to save the Old Tote. It was to have been followed by a season of large-scale new work directed by Sharman and Cramphorn. But the Tote was sinking under debt and that program was cancelled. It went into liquidation in 1978. The following year the pair presented two commissioned plays, Hewett's *Pandora's Cross* and Louis Nowra's *Visions* at their converted Paris Theatre but the venture folded. A third play, Patrick White's *A Cheery Soul*, was presented by the team at the Opera House in 1979 (see 'An Exultant Debut', *TA*, March 1979).

Big Toys is a Mozartian attack on upper-class preoccupations by Patrick White;

and *Mothers and Fathers* a farce about surrogate motherhood by New Zealand playwright Joseph Musaphia. George Landen Dann (1904–1977) was the author of many award-winning plays, all of which, until 1977, were produced by amateur theatres. He lived a solitary life at Noosa where I visited him in 1976 and wrote a piece for the *National Times* headed 'Playwright Victim of an Engineered Scandal' (21–26 March 1977, p.50). His play *Fountains Beyond* (1942) was presented by the Queensland Theatre Company in 2001. A State Premier's award for playwriting has been named after him.

In the midst of the turmoil about the death of NSW's first state theatre company, signalling the souring of our early hopes for a vital new world of performing arts, news came of the death at 49 of one of the greatest and best-loved figures from the old world.

Goodbye Gloria

Australian, 6 April 1978

When the theatre paid a grand farewell to Gloria Dawn at the Church of the Sacred Heart in Sydney's Darlinghurst on Tuesday it was farewell to a kind of actress Australia is not likely to see again.

Gloria Dawn was brought up in variety as a part of the razzamatazz of the Tivoli era and in her latter years she brought that same vitality, toughness and single-minded professionalism to the legitimate theatre—sometimes to its consternation. She was never stagestruck and never in her own mind a star. She was in the business because she was born to it and knew nothing else.

She was born Gloria Dawn Evans in Melbourne in 1929. Her mother, Zilla Weatherley, was a contortionist of the Weatherley circus family. One of her acts was to be folded away in a suitcase by a magician. Later with her sisters Toots and Gaga she went into variety. Gloria's father, Bill Andross, was a paper-tearer and all-round variety performer. Gloria joined her parents' act at the age of two and by four was bringing the house down with the line: 'I would like to do my impression of a very young girl singing a song'.

The family moved from town to town with variety shows and her education was snatched week by week at the local convents. Sometimes she was punished for arriving at school with last night's greasepaint still staining her face. Sometimes she had to leave mid-morning to do a community concert. When Shirley Temple became popular she was employed doing impersonations at the cinemas. At 10 she joined the Tivoli as a child actress and by 13 had become a soubrette. (A soubrette is an all-round utility performer who can sing, dance, play characters and feed lines to the comics.) It was not an easy life for a child and she never forgot or forgave those early hardships.

Her parents separated and at 16 she escaped into marriage with Frank Cleary, a juggler and variety artist, with whom she had four children. But the necessity to work pursued her and after her first child, Peter, was born she could be seen at rehearsals doing her dance routines with the baby on her hip. In the 1950s, when variety took a nosedive following the arrival of television, she began to work the clubs and went into musical comedy. Her first show was *Little Nelly Kelly*, with Will Mahoney at the Cremorne Theatre, Brisbane.

But it was Garnet Carroll's production of *Once upon a Mattress* in partnership with the new Australian Elizabethan Theatre Trust that established her national reputation as a musical comedy actress. Somehow Carroll, who had known her since childhood, had dug her out of a country town in Victoria, where she was looking after children in a caravan and Frank was selling army disposals.

It was typical that she should have been winkled out in that way. By her own confession she was never ambitious, there was never a role she yearned to play or an actress she wanted to emulate. She never liked the theatre or the world in which she worked but she needed her audience for the reassurances they gave her. 'I've always had that need to have that bit of encouragement behind me all the time. I've got to be reassured in every show that I'm good. I haven't got that thing in me that knows I'm capable. I want them to like me.'

And again: 'Whenever I am approached with a part I always say I'm interested. I think I can't be too bad if they want me.' But she never knew why.

Other musicals, like *The Sentimental Bloke*, followed and variety shows with imported stars. Then in 1965 she joined the Phillip Theatre in Sydney in the long-running success *A Cup of Tea, a Bex and a Good Lie Down* by John McKellar. When it ended McKellar wrote another for her: *Hail Gloria Fitzpatrick*. It was during this period that she settled in her modest little house in Rosebery, Sydney—the first home she had ever known.

It has been said that the most eccentric thing about Gloria Dawn was her ordinariness. Her home was the centre of her later life. She never arrived at the theatre until half an hour before curtain—there was no feeling herself into the part for her. And she left immediately after the curtain to catch the late movie on television. She was a TV addict and once had three TVs in her house so she could watch while doing the housework. And she slept with a radio beside her. That was her education as a performer, how she knew, as one friend put it, 'every song that was ever written'.

The secret of her craft was not feeling inside herself but mimicry. She was a brilliant mimic and would begin the creation of a character first with the physical appearance and then by copying people she knew. Her memorable role as Aggie in Peter Kenna's *A Hard God*, which he wrote for her, was a mixture of 'a landlady I once lived with and my mother'.

It was Kenna, a long-time friend, who in 1972 made her a 'legitimate' actress by persuading her to play Oola, the buxom retired madam, in a revival of his comedy *The Slaughter of St Teresa's Day* for the Marian Street (then the Community) Theatre in Sydney. It was the first time she had ever learned a script. The experiment established a new career as a serious actress and earned her an immediate contract to play Brecht's Mother Courage at the Princess Theatre, Melbourne, for the Melbourne Theatre Company.

There are many stories about Gloria at rehearsal. She would never take a note from the director but would sit knitting. Aarne Neeme, the director of *Slaughter*, recalls the horror of finding her script at the end of rehearsal as pristine as at the beginning. But she remembered everything. Kenna says of her: 'Gloria had a totally retentive memory. She was like a sponge. She was also absolutely unproducable:

> She had her own way of doing things and never did it the same way twice. While she would appear to give a lot in rehearsal it was only in front of an audience that she came alive. Actors learned to make allowances for Gloria's performance being twice the size on opening night.

It was her vaudeville training, he said. Variety artists were always afraid of others stealing their jokes and it was not done to watch other performers from the wings. He recalled how after a rehearsal at the Opera House for *The Threepenny Opera*, in which she played Mrs Peacham, she had said: 'I did a bad thing today', because in response to a successful gesture the director, Jim Sharman, had adopted it for the whole cast. Rehearsals, she confided, were nothing but an embarrassment. Her real practice came with the audience.

But my favourite Gloria Dawn story was of a rehearsal of *Mother Courage*. The German Brecht expert Joachim Tenschert, imported as director, had

Gloria Dawn as Aggie in the ABC production of *A Hard God*, 1974.

been giving her a lecture on Brecht. She sat knitting and listening to his academic English until finally she looked up and said: 'Fair crack of the whip, what are you driving at?'. But she did what he wanted just the same.

Having little education, she was nervous of intellectuals or talk about her art. She may not have understood her playwrights but she understood her audience—which one had dropped his program, which corner of the theatre was losing contact. She knew how to place a laugh better than any Australian actress I can think of—and how to make them cry, too. She had only one caveat: 'I don't work blue'.

It was that very common-earth quality which she shared in private with her audiences from the dormitory suburbs, that occupation with vacuum cleaners and televisions sets and the sale at DJs (which she admits thinking of during performance) that gave her acting a unique vitality. With one gesture she could set aside all that is precious and exclusive in our concept of dramatic culture and make us look afresh at a commonplace object suddenly grown great before our eyes. Of such is pop art.

Sadly, by the time Gloria Dawn opened in *Gypsy*, the first symptoms of her cancer were upon her. She was ill for some months after leaving the cast and then appeared for a short season at the Nimrod Theatre in *Young Mo*. Her last season was playing variety at the Music Loft, Manly. She died in Sydney's King George Hospital on Saturday.

Today two memorials remain: a gentle performance as Geraldine Fitzgerald's housekeeper in the film *The Mango Tree*, currently showing; and the character of Doris, the motherly, sad actress in *Furtive Love*, the second play in Kenna's trilogy *The Cassidy Album*. Kenna wrote the trilogy, which begins with *A Hard God* for her; and Doris, he says, is based on herself and the late Neva Carr Glyn. A long reminiscence in which Doris describes her hard career as a performer and life as a part to which she has not been invited, was, says Kenna, life as Gloria told it to him.

The Cassidy Album, from the Adelaide Festival, opened in Sydney with Maggie Kirkpatrick in the roles of Aggie and Doris in the week Gloria Dawn died. Its author was the last friend at her bedside.

The most spectacular by-product of the Old Tote's spectacular fall was the Paris Theatre Company, with which the Sydney profession launched their anger at the rising restrictions on their work.

Paris Theatre: An Act of Faith

Weekend Australian Magazine, 24–25 June 1978

The Paris Theatre Company, which comes out fighting on Thursday, may in time just prove to be one of the indirect victors of the knock-out championship rounds in which official theatre in Sydney has lately been engaged. The Paris Company, which will open with the new musical

Pandora's Cross, by Dorothy Hewett and Ralph Tyrell, is headed by a group who, ten years ago, were the luminous young stars of the Australian theatre. Today they are frankly tired of their profession being run by accountants, boards and managers and are after a new—or rather old—style of theatre in which the performers make the decisions. They have chosen a timely moment to make their protest.

'We don't have any ready ideals for this theatre', Jim Sharman said this week. 'For the company, many of them had reached the point in their careers when it was this or a plane ticket out.'

Sharman understands the feeling, having worked all this life alternately here and abroad, and admits to such thoughts on reading the very mixed reviews of his new movie, *The Night the Prowler,* from the Patrick White screenplay. He had finished editing it only just in time to open the Sydney Film Festival before starting rehearsals for *Pandora's Cross.*

'If I took notice of the knockers I'd have put a bullet through my head five years ago', he said. 'Australian critics are constantly on the lookout for losers. Australians are obsessed with approval.' The film will be released commercially in Australia at Christmas.

Sharman and Rex Cramphorn, who have launched the Paris Company, are not looking for approval but for dynamic. And they know what they want. 'The actors are Jennifer Claire, Arthur Dignam, Robyn Nevin, John Gaden, Kate Fitzpatrick, Neil Redfern, Julie McGregor and Bryan Brown. Set, costume and lighting designers are Brian Thomson, Luciana Arrighi and David Read. An impressive line-up of people now in their prime at the top of the profession, who have thrown in their lot with the Paris for the sake of job satisfaction they have not found elsewhere.

The choice is not without sacrifice. The company is under-capitalised: all members are working without salary to opening night. They are employed under conditions which normally apply to those doing their apprenticeship. But as Robyn Nevin remarked: 'Here I am once again starting out, working for little money, living on hopes. But all of us in the company have reached the age where we are tired of standing up there on stage, taking the knocks for decisions over which we have no artistic control. We have the knowledge and the skills and it is time we used them the way they are meant to be used.'

The Paris Company was born out of the sudden deprivation of hope. Last year its program and its actors were a part of the Old Tote's plans for 1978—and indeed made a substantial contribution to its successful application for government subsidy. Cramphorn and Sharman were contracted to take over the Seymour Centre with a season of five plays: *Pandora's Cross*, Louis Nowra's *Visions*, Patrick White's *A Cheery Soul*, Edward Bond's *The Fool* and Sam Shepard's *Angel City*. Late last year, however, the Tote's financial crisis reached the point where the board was forced to relinquish the Seymour. In late December the two directors resigned.

In their letter of resignation, commenting on the board's compromise offer of two plays at the Parade Theatre, they wrote: 'This final revision has eroded the original conception to a point where to accept it would be to embrace the status quo we so enthusiastically set out to change.' So now, determinedly, they are setting out to change the status quo on their own, with the avowed aims: to tell the story of our times; to give the tellers responsibility for the way it is told; to make the story worth the price of a ticket.

Asked why they took on the task, Jim Sharman said:

> We both felt a responsibility to the two playwrights—Hewett and Nowra—who had written plays at our instigation, not only to present their work but to do it in an exciting and stimulating manner. I'm very much concerned with the situation of the writer in this country. If I'm to remain here I want to work with writers who reveal society to itself in the most imaginative way. This is not something one necessarily gets thanked for, as the reviews of my work on *Big Toys* and *The Night the Prowler* showed. But good theatre can only come from good writers.

('No', Cramphorn added firmly. 'From a good company.')

All the plays chosen, Sharman went on, had a quality in common—richly imaginative writing, breaking away from realism. *Pandora's Cross* would be followed by *Visions* and *A Cheery Soul* and at Christmas by a pantomime by Norman Gunston's writer Bill Harding. Did they think a theatre today could run on its box office? 'That', he said disarmingly, 'is what we are going to find out'.

> We are asking a lot, opening with a quite demanding selection of plays like this in an 800-seat theatre, but we believe in a form of theatre that excites and stimulates the imagination. Dorothy Hewett's play has this. On the one hand it has all the razzamatazz of a musical set in the heart of Kings Cross. On the other it uses the story of the fictitious Ern Malley and his sister Ethel to explore the realm of the artist in society. On the one hand popular, on the other very complex. The production is one of the most challenging things I have had to do in my life.

It is no secret the company is treading a tightrope. They have taken a lease of the Paris Theatre, a cinema by Sydney's Hyde Park, designed by Walter Burley Griffin in 1913 and owned by the Sydney City Council. The bill for converting the stage and updating the building—$40,000—has been picked up by the council; but the work is being carried out by the Paris Company. It now has a bank account of $20,000, of which $7,000 was raised by an art auction. They still need a further $5,000 to see them through their first season: the future of the venture is very much dependent upon the public reception of their first production.

But what concerns Cramphorn and Sharman most is that they should survive long enough to see their 'alternative way of thinking about the theatre' grow. 'The difficulty we have at the moment', Cramphorn said,

> is trying to solve all the problems at once. What we are trying to accomplish really has to be seen as a long-term operation. We have plunged in at the deep end, having to renovate a theatre as well as set up management and produce a new play. What we are after is a new way of working and developing a company. How it will finally be will only emerge in time. It won't all pop out like a rabbit out of a hat on June 29.

Time, in his theatre career, Cramphorn has seldom had. And he has dedicated most of it to new ways of working and developing a company. With his Performance Syndicate in the early 70s, Cramphorn produced some of the most memorable and penetrating investigations of the dramatic medium ever conducted in this country; but his methods, because they are alternative, have never married well with the structure of established companies.

Sharman, who immediately formed his own acting company upon leaving the National Institute of Dramatic Art in the 60s, has been a maverick director, has dared his way to an international reputation by breaking the barriers of his youth, his ambitions and his background. His success with *Hair*, *Jesus Christ Superstar* and *The Rocky Horror Show* were only the most showy areas of a career which has forced established thought at every level to rethink its basic premises.

In the present partnership, his job is to choose the repertoire and form the outward-going policy of the company. Cramphorn is responsible for the company and its development. Two teams of thought, they call it, which coexist and collide to advantage.

There is a lot hanging on those terms of thought, not only for this company but for the Australia Council and those who depend on it. It has long been contended on one hand that artists need administration: and on the other hand that artists need to be free of administration. If the Paris Company can make a go of it on their own terms and without a board of management, it will set a precedent which will have a reverberating effect upon government subsidy to the arts. If not, then a lot of old prejudices will be confirmed.

Sadly, they were confirmed. The company lasted eight weeks and presented only two productions, the Nowra and the Hewett. *A Cheery Soul* became the Paris's contribution to the Sydney Theatre Company's inaugural season at the Opera House Drama Theatre.

The Cassidy Album

Theatre Australia, May 1978

It is inevitable that *The Cassidy Album* be compared to *The Doll Trilogy*, since by some curious coincidence our two senior playwrights have come up with similar projects. (Has Patrick White thought of autumn and winter in Sarsaparilla?) But in fact the one experience bears no relation to the other except in the fact that they challenge us to reassess these two playwrights as dramatists.

The two have another similarity: and that is that the authors have found in the task a means of working their way back into their Australian psyche after long absence. Both works are reassessments of the past from the perspective of middle age. But while Lawler's task has been to travel backwards to the beginning, the end predestined from the start, *The Cassidy Album* is a journey forward into darkness, an unsure, experimental, brave and personal voyage of discovery in which the author himself examines, Oedipus-like, the causes of his own self-destruction.

Summer of the Seventeenth Doll remains the masterpiece of *The Doll Trilogy*. *Kid Stakes* and *Other Times*, while handsome plays in their own right, serve to expand a familiar story and enlarge the emotional force behind the demolition of that doll's house of seventeen years. *A Hard God* will remain the major work of *The Cassidy Album*. It lays down not the direction of the journey but the ground roots of the other two plays—the rich soil of neurosis and sterility which has created Joe Cassidy, a hero who, again like Oedipus, is not bad but—in Joe's own word—'trivial'.

I suppose it is impertinent to compare Kenna with Sophocles, especially since we think of the Greek as the most perfect interpreter of universal truth. *The Cassidy Album* is a not-altogether-satisfactory account of a half-successful writer whose life and potential death hardly touch those around him—certainly not in the way Oedipus' life is bound to the life of the people of Thebes. I suppose the parallel has occurred to me because a season of Sophocles was playing concurrently at the Adelaide Festival.

And yet the authors do have a common theme—a human's defiance of God; and Kenna sees his hero's life not as affecting but as reflecting his environment. Joe Cassidy's journey, if one cares to see it that way, is a challenge to self-determination in the teeth of a hard and apparently incomprehensible deity. It is a working out of that conflict between the flesh and the moral beliefs which guide our lives and which ends in acceptance and a hard-won endurance—but not, as in Sophocles' case, understanding.

The three plays were conceived from the beginning as a trilogy and were written, in fact, before Lawler's, though not performed in their entirety till now. At the time Kenna was suffering chronic kidney disease and his life prognosis was limited. He was living, as he describes it, a kind of half-life; and the backward-looking sources of his work can be traced to his recollection of learning how to live.

And yet the weakness of the trilogy as a totality is that Joe Cassidy's life, which forms the backbone, is never firmly at the centre. In *A Hard God* Joe's brief love affair with Jack Shannon hovers in the darkness like the guilty thing it is, and yet it implicitly parallels Aggie Cassidy's defiance of God at the end of the play, as though his action had dictated hers. A whole field of Irish Catholic Australians is ploughed for us in this play, and the barrenness of the stories that follow is its harvest of empty husks. *A Hard God* is rich in comedy and tragedy. John Tasker's fine production with Maggie Kirkpatrick as an earthy and uncomprehending Aggie, had the audience sobbing audibly in the gallery at the end of the play.

Kenna is as much concerned with form and time as means of expression; the second play is daring and to his audience puzzling. It is a decade later and Joe, now an actor and the author of a touring play, is one of the company on the point of disbanding. Here we have a new set of characters; and a new style of play altogether.

The theme of *Furtive Love* is identity. A group of vacant-minded actors, diverting themselves with various sexual aspirations, transform into real flesh as they act out the roles Joe has given them. These roles, in turn, represent the lives of the Cassidy sisters as Joe remembers them. Deprived of these identities by the last performance the group falls apart, leaving only a photograph and a shabby autograph book to remind them of something already forgotten. Doris, whose itinerant life was imposed by her parents, goes from play to play, resenting a condition which has deprived her of living. Ned's memory is going and, fearful of losing himself, he keeps his biography from the theatre program in his breast pocket. Tom is a closet bisexual, conspiring against himself, and has become a pompous bore. And Joe, the observer, torn between his homosexual nature and his faith in a moral order, in the end opts for his sexuality out of fear of never coming to terms with life.

Furtive Love is a startling contrast to *A Hard God*, both in its episodic form, the mirror images of life it imposes one upon another, and the complex clues to the Cassidy family album which are sprinkled through it. The play within a play has, I think, some of the best writing Kenna has done. But there are still bugs in the structure, which left me frustrated. I would like, for example, some discussion of the Cassidy sisters by Joe and the cast to elucidate the facts; more importantly Joe is over-pompous and the point that his sisters' affairs were a crucial cause of his own tensions is not made clear in the text. Nevertheless the fact that these inconsequential people held my attention for two hours makes me feel that in time this play will prove better than I think it is now.

An Eager Hope, the last play, returns to safe ground in the Cassidy living room, with Aggie. Joe is now in his 30s, mature and self-determined, doggedly but unsuccessfully fighting off kidney failure. While Joe's wheel of fortune is relentlessly on the downturn, that of his charming but irresponsible brother Francis reaches its zenith. Having deserted both wife and mistress, Francis is now being happily pampered by his aging mother. Francis is a hollow man, irresistible but hollow. This is Francis' moment, not Joe's. My time is not now, he says at the end of the play, but it will come.

It is a triumph for John Tasker and Peter Kenna to have succeeded in mounting such a project for a week at the Adelaide Festival; and their faith has been rewarded in a transfer to Sydney. As Joe, Tony Sheldon also contributes immeasurably, as he realises with conviction and assurance a personality at three stages of growth and in three environments. It is a splendid performance.

Not all the cast manage three roles so well. *An Eager Hope* is Francis' play and Ray Meagher is not a big enough actor for such a role, though his cowardly Paddy in *A Hard God* was delightful. It was a huge undertaking for a cast not all that well prepared by experience. That they succeeded as well as they did is due to the director and the deeply felt performances of Sheldon and that fine actress Maggie Kirkpatrick.

The NSW Government established a Sydney Theatre Company by statute after the demise of the Old Tote. During 1979, under the management of John Clark and Elizabeth Butcher of NIDA and the actor Tony Llewellyn-Jones, the new entity mounted a year-long season of plays presented by the theatres of Sydney.

A Cheery Soul: Exultant Debut

Theatre Australia, March 1979

The World Play Season at the Sydney Theatre Company which this year replaces the Old Tote Theatre Company at the Sydney Opera House, has had an exultant debut with Jim Sharman's production of Patrick White's *A Cheery Soul*. It brings a fresh sense of occasion and of stature to the Drama Theatre. It projects, not the familiar assertion of 'world standards' but the relaxed confidence of work that takes its quality for granted. The kind of evening that makes us wonder, unkindly, why we tolerated the Old Tote for so long.

There is no question that *A Cheery Soul* is a difficult play—a confronting one, as Sharman says. Its structure is picaresque, literary and in places over-explains without clarifying. In the production some of the performances do not make the grade. But at no point does the whole fall from the level of extraordinary. With all its sins it is the most serious and commanding performance Sydney has seen since Liviu Ciulei's *The Lower Depths* in 1977; and for my money the finest production Jim Sharman has ever done.

Firstly, let us talk about the play. It opens upon the warm, homely kitchen of Mr and Mrs Custance, a contented middle-aged couple who take life for granted and rub along without much imagination. In a kind of assuaging gesture ('I wonder if it's right to be always happy', she remarks innocently, in the wake of tales of careless death and destruction), the couple invite Miss Docker, a homeless pensioner, to share their all. She arrives—launches herself, one should say, upon the unprepared innocents. Like the tallboy and the rocking chair that accompany her, her huge impertinence strains their accommodation.

Miss Docker does good. No one in Sarsaparilla does as much good as Miss Docker. People are beneficiaries of Miss Docker's goodness whether they like it or not. In no time her presence invades every corner of the

Custances' lives and the old fiend is bundled off to the Sundown Home for Old People. So much for the first act. When the curtain rises on Act II, we have left the cosy fireside. The play opens out into an expressionist universe where old women in black dresses, like the relatives in *The Ham Funeral*, nurse their memories and form a chorus of silhouettes against our heroine's journey towards the light.

Miss Docker has already invaded Sundown Home. She is omnipresent as she was in the Custance household. As Mrs Hibble says: 'She's only been here a couple of days and her name beats in my head like a gong'. She encounters Millie Lillie, a statuesque tragedy queen whose seductive but spendthrift husband Miss Docker nursed ruthlessly into the grave. Memories revive—we see his death, his funeral and the awful incident when Miss Docker, after momentarily descending from the cortège, is deserted on the road as car after car, bearing a train of those to whom she has done good in her time, leave her in the dust.

This is the turning point of her indomitable spirit. It is followed by a poignant short scene in which the old woman with her shoebox of photographs asks: 'Will anybody recognise the true portrait of Little Me?'

MRS HIBBLE: I never saw such an enormous baby.

MISS PERRY: Lovely rug.

MRS HIBBLE: You look as though you'd swallowed the world.

Sharman captures the appalling image in the high point of the production as the astonishing Robyn Nevin, who has stamped through two acts like an omnivorous Raggedy Ann, cracks open the case of her bitter candy heart in a raucous revelation of her beginnings. As the curtain falls we are left with the caricature, legs and arms flailing, of a vulnerable old woman turned baby, braying for love.

The third act is occupied with recognition of that need for love. The chorus's vision of spring is followed by Miss Docker's confessions of girlish passion, firstly for the butcher and then for the Rev. Wakeman. Her devotion to Mr Wakeman leads to a heart-to-heart about his shortcomings as a preacher; he reproves her: 'The truth we know already is always the hardest to bear'.

Mr Wakeman brings his condemnation of militant virtue to his Sunday sermon. The message drives Miss Docker to attack, to strike down the Rev. Wakeman with her lightning. She takes on the role of God and pulls her armour of prayer around her like a warm cardigan. But her message is for herself alone: 'Oh, I could tell, if I could tell! All of you! But failure is not failure if it is sent to humble. The only failure is not to realise…'. There are echoes of *King Lear* in these words of impotent rage:

> I will do such things—
> What they are yet I know not; but they shall be
> The terrors of the earth.

The scene ends with the exalted old woman, confronted with the body of the dead minister, crying: 'My thoughts could light a fire! I could breathe love into the dead… If only they was willing…'.

The play leaves her on her storm-tossed heath, in the company of jeering children, a swaggie and a mangy dog who pisses on her leg. In her last words she draws dejectedly upon her lost faith. For her there is neither death nor love and only the beginnings of humility, for consolation.

That Patrick White should have written *A Cheery Soul* is remarkable enough. That it should have been produced in Australia in 1963 is more remarkable still. Expressionist drama may by that time have been fifty years old but here it was relatively unknown. Brecht was not popularised in English-speaking countries virtually until the 50s, and writers like Wedekind not until much later.

Since the 1960s Australian audiences may not have become much more sophisticated, but they have become accustomed to a variety of styles in the theatre, to being surprised, in fact. And that is an advance. A further advance lies in a greater willingness to listen to the message of Patrick White's burnt ones, to his recognition of great heart and barren landscape. The country has begun to catch up at last to White's environmentalism and in the theatre he is more today's playwright than he ever was.

The beauty of Sharman's production and Brian Thomson's design which works in harmony with it, is that it takes on unflinchingly the problems of interpretation imposed by the mixture of realism and caricature. From curtain rise, with the characters planted like puppets motionless about the stage; from the moment Robyn Nevin explodes down the aisle in all-too-audible laughter, to the final moment when she twists in our direction, emitting a silent scream, we know this is a production the like of which we may never see again.

The play is a comedy, though a black one, and Miss Docker is a comic character. The Custances are funny in their suburban complacency, the old women in their second childhood. But the production never oversteps the hard truth. Miss Docker may be a cruel figure of fun but White opens her up like a fresh wound as an object of pity and warning.

Robyn Nevin's performance, as I have said, is extraordinary. This tiny actress, still in her 30s, is transformed into a shapeless ball of ancient but indomitable flesh, all too capable of mowing the minister's lawn on Thursdays. Flat-footed, enveloped in cardigans and drooping lisle stockings, she contains a voice that booms like thunder. Miss Nevin's gait, her limbs spread as though her body were too big for her, is both cartoon-like and touching, denying at each moment the indestructibility her voice commands. Her shuffling feet and swinging arms as she telephones her admired butcher, will remain for me one of the true comic moments in the theatre.

Finally, I think Harry Kippax was right when he called the performance an impersonation, rather than a characterisation. Miss Nevin is still too young an actress to bring off the Lear-like pain of spirit that transforms the last act. In the attempt, however, she was in part prevented by the cruel miscasting of John Paramor as Rev. Wakeman, on whom the building of Miss Docker's tragic stature at this point depends. Paramor, unable to cope with prayer, replaces simplicity with emotionalism. The result seriously damaged the final scenes.

There were other faults. Thomson's attempt to unify the domestic style of the first act with the grandeur of the rest diminished that sense of a cosy nest being split open by a gigantic cuckoo. (Mr Custance really needs his tomato plants.) Nevertheless Peter Carroll and Pat Bishop make a touching pair—Miss Bishop's careful kindness is masterly. It is a good cast; in the second act the brooding figure of Maggie Kirkpatrick as Mrs Lillie is splendid.

A confronting evening, certainly. It marks a new level in the work of Jim Sharman and Robyn Nevin—and in the contribution of Patrick White to our theatre. Let us hope it sets the standard for the new Sydney Theatre Company.

Raggedy Ann, the creation of Johnny Gruelle, was a rag doll who yearned for a heart and was given a candy heart by her mistress, Marcella. The Raggedy Ann and Raggedy Andy stories were first published in Chicago in the 1920s.

The climate was changing and the arts were becoming hard-nosed as we entered the 1980s. In 1981, I received an offer from David Marr, newly-appointed editor of the weekly *National Times* to write the fortnightly overview of the arts' role in politics and business as well as aesthetics that I had wanted to do for the *Australian*. It lasted about 18 months, until Marr was summarily dismissed for exposing the 'bottom of the harbour' tax scam. My job went with him.

Melbourne Stasis

National Times, 22 July 1981

One of the challenges about professional theatre-going is to define what makes one city different from another. The theatre is, after all, only a matter of taste; and one great advance the local drama has made is to exploit nationally regional difference we had not been aware of ourselves. The traditional rivalry between Melbourne and Sydney has, in the theatre, expressed itself in the claim that what succeeds in one city will fail in the other.

In Sydney the theatre companies have undergone an upheaval over the past three years, which has introduced new managers, changing tastes and a fresh approach. Change in Melbourne does not come so easily; the upheaval that will come with the $180 million Victoria Arts Centre complex—now looking expectant but still roofless in St Kilda Road—recedes by the month. 'I used to joke that I'd retire when we made the move into the Arts Centre', said the Melbourne Theatre Company's administrator John Sumner, looking back on the first sod dug in 1968. 'Now it looks like being a reality.'

The stasis in Melbourne is increasingly the concern of the Theatre Board of the Australia Council and of the Victorian Ministry of the Arts. The MTC is as firmly established as ever but at the Pram Factory, to go under the wreckers' hammer before the end of the year, the last play is now in rehearsal. 'Our greatest concern in Melbourne is venues', said the director of the ministry, Paul Clarkson. 'There are simply not enough to provide alternatives to the MTC.'

On offer to audiences is the Playbox in Exhibition Street, which has a 300-seat theatre downstairs and an upstairs holding 80—not economic seating for a permanent theatre company. The Universal Theatre in Fitzroy has a capacious open stage auditorium and a cinema in a rambling Pram Factory–style building, and should be a buzzing centre but somehow never is. La Mama is still alive and well with its tiny space and special coterie. The St Martin's Theatre, South Yarra, home of the St Martin's Youth Theatre, is being rebuilt into two auditoria, the larger of which will be available for hire at times. But apart from the big shows at Her Majesty's and the Comedy, and the too-occasional use of the Princess, the hard core theatre-goers of Melbourne are the subscribers to the MTC.

It is, in fact, quite difficult to tell the difference between a success and a failure at Russell Street or the Athenaeum. Both theatres are packed to the gunnels and charter buses from distant places queue outside the entrance. But audiences are not always demonstrative. It may be Melbourne's Presbyterian past that leaves one wondering how much the expectation of enjoyment has to do with the decision to go to the theatre.

The exception to all this, of course, is *An Evening's Intercourse with Barry Humphries*, which was booked out before the season opened at Her Majesty's. Humphries' performance is a must for Melburnians and the reason, as they express it, has more to do with the fact that Humphries belongs to Melbourne than the assurance that it will be a nice night's entertainment.

The show has mellowed greatly since moving from the alien corn of Sydney. This is particularly evident in the second half in which Edna tortures a handful of people from the front rows and drags them, half-shoeless, limping like Quasimodo, onto the stage where they prepare a barbecue. Of the scene Leonard Radic in the *Age* wrote: 'She has lost most of her waspishness. The dame is now a warm, friendly, affectionate and mum-like character, at pains to emphasise her "caring sharing quality".'

Sydney readers will not recognise this description and Edna is, of course, as monstrously self-opinionated as ever. But there is something of a shared secret between her and her Melbourne following, a closer understanding of the definitions of suburban life, the finer points of brick veneer and natives in the garden—and who to watch on TV—which she can never quite maintain in Sydney. There she is a brash parvenue who has clawed her way to the top and mixes with the Hungarians of Double Bay while pretending contempt. In Melbourne her chatter is not of Toorak society but of the greyer suburbs out of which she grew.

She is rude to her audience, it is true, but it is also true that she contrives to elicit from her unfortunate victims, as they sit around a garden table making salad and buttering bread, a scene of complacent domesticity. She wins from them a silent assent, that they stand for a recognised group to which both they and Edna belong.

When I saw the show last week, every seat tight packed and roaring with laughter, it was like a grand final: a barracking for the home team with the coach out front screaming insults for their own good. At the National Press Club recently Humphries said, in answer to a question about expatriates, that he was not an Australian, he was a Melburnian. He calls himself a 'regional monologuist'.

Across the road is *The Dresser*, at the Comedy, with Warren Mitchell and Gordon Chater, both with reputations solidly Sydney-side. Mitchell, now in the top ten of British stage actors, has made Sydney his second home, though he has appeared on the legitimate stage there only once. Elsewhere he is making a fortune in the RSL clubs as Alf Garnett. Alf must have plenty to say about Britain today.

Gordon Chater, who plays Sir, the aged Shakespearean actor, has long been one of Sydney's favourite comedy actors until he settled in New York three years ago after touring *The Elocution of Benjamin Franklin*. Though a figure in Sydney for over twenty years he has rarely been seen in Melbourne, except on TV, just as Frank Thring, Melbourne's heavyweight, has only once in recent memory been invited to Sydney.

It is a matter of wonder that, despite the enormous investment of funds since 1968, the theatre has remained such a cottage industry. Each city has its admired faces: in Melbourne actors like Patricia Kennedy, Monica Maughan, Simon Chilvers and Bruce Myles; in Adelaide Les Dayman, Daphne Grey, Edwin Hodgeman; in Perth Margaret Ford, Edgar Metcalfe, James Beattie—and so on. A few, like Neil Fitzpatrick, have gained a wider following by keeping moving. Most build their national reputations in film and TV. The television industry has a hungry maw which gobbles up actors and not many are seen on stage again.

A visitor in search of entertainment wants something different from their home town and it follows that what is local should be distinctively regional. Even more so in Melbourne where each theatre seems to exist in its own territory. Nowhere can there be two theatres more different and apart than the MTC and the APG.

So what does Melbourne have to offer?

For one thing, springing from its roots of religious and political conservatism, Melbourne is the only city which produces political satire. It has created its own brand of theatre restaurant revue—a mixture of low comedy, repartee and circus acts in a deceptively loose style which owes nothing to the 'professionalism' of the TV-style revue.

The Australian Performing Group, once a flag-waver for the Carlton intellectual, has been foundering. Their current show, *Thank God it's Not Christmas*, by Malcolm Frawley, who won the award for best play in a recent APG competition, is a bedroom farce. The script has good one-liners but it's a one-joke play, hard to sustain, and in any case is a vehicle that needs all the fuel of the commercial theatre. It is curious that it was submitted to this once-Marxist theatre, and even more curious that it was selected. Time changes all things. The play is on at the Universal, presented by the APG.

A local group that looks promising is the Australian Nouveau Theatre, run by Jean-Pierre Mignon. It recently leased the Rechabites' Hall in South Melbourne after touring for a year. Through Mignon it has a strong European belief in a 'thinking theatre' and early productions have included Beckett, Handke and Artaud. It is hoped the theatre will become a community centre and a host to overseas performers. This is what we look to Melbourne to provide; but the group, like the APG, has structural and dialectic changes to make which may yet bring it down. Administrative decisions, according to the theatre manager, John Moore, are achieved by a process of 'controlled anarchy'—a philosophical position at which only a Melburnian could arrive.

The play I saw was *Exiles* by the writer-in-residence Alex Miller, a play originally the property of the APG. It is a promising post-expressionist piece not unlike the work of La Mama writers like Kris Hemensley; and is about loneliness and oppression in a bureaucratic society. There is a particularly telling scene by Julie Forsyth and William Gluth about a mother attempting to persuade an ineffectual psychiatrist to return her child.

Another version of bureaucracy is Harold Pinter's *The Hothouse* now playing at Russell Street. It is interesting only because it is early Pinter, with all his hallmarks: the unspoken threat, the sub-text at cross-purposes to the dialogue, and the characters are locked in an enigmatic institution (in this case a psychiatric hospital). The director needs the experience with later Pinter to make the play work and this production did not reveal it. But it was good to see Ray Lawler (a truly regional figure) back on stage as the Hothouse chief.

The MTC is doing its best to be innovative, as the current word is. After Keith Michell's Australian *Peer Gynt* comes a production by Bruce Myles of *The Good Person of Setzuan* in modern dress, set in some city Chinatown, with the gods played as Canberra politicians. The clarity of the text and the unselfconscious performance by Sally McKenzie as Shen Te, the good woman whom poverty will not allow to be good, is admirable. Under the punk hairdo she gave us a performance that drove home with great simplicity the message of moral bankruptcy—a fine contrast to the many over-decorated productions of Brecht which our state theatres have mounted in the last decade.

The last play I chose to see was Doreen Clarke's comedy *Farewell Brisbane Ladies*, about two Queensland prostitutes trying to change their ways. The production comes from South Australia, with Melbourne actress Monica Maughan and Sydney actress Maggie Kirkpatrick, so it has nothing much to do with regionalism. But fine acting has its own justification and these two all-or-nothing actors have taken a rather contrived plot and made a show I enjoyed immensely. It is not doing great business, as it should, though. As someone said: 'The Playbox has not had a GP play for a long time'.

Which gets back to Melbourne's difficulty in promoting the idea of something just for fun. Only Barry Humphries seems to know how to do it. Or is it just the moral chastisement that attracts them?

The sense conveyed in this article that the performing arts had stalled, was typical of the turning point into the 1980s. Huge strides had been made in the arts, but as the assets grew, so did public responsibility. The death of the Old Tote and the Paris Theatre in Sydney was a lesson in people's minds; several of the old pro-amateur groups around the country had already gone to the wall. The stagnation was particularly noticeable in Melbourne, still waiting for its promised Arts Centre. The search was on for a new direction.

Alf Garnett was Mitchell's alter ego, the bundle of Pommy prejudices in the classic British TV comedy, *Till Death Us Do Part*.

Australian Nouveau Theatre, more widely known as ANT or Anthill Theatre, survived until 1994 when state funding was withheld. During its time it introduced many European authors to Melbourne audiences and built up a group of performers with a distinctive style.

Arts Come Out Fighting
National Times, 1–7 November 1981

The Victorian Ministry for the Arts has been the first government department to come out fighting in response to the federal cutbacks. In a new self-help drive it convened a seminar on private support for the arts at the Grant Street Theatre, Melbourne, on 17 October, for over 200 recipients of state arts grants. And announced the establishment of an arts resources-and-planning unit under the directorship of Donna Greaves, to assist the arts in alternative funding. Nobody pulled their punches that day.

'Two things are apparent to me', said the director of the Ministry, Paul Clarkson. 'The arts have done a lamentable job in selling themselves and their benefit to the community; and they have had a generally negative media. We never put a positive viewpoint—the impact on tourism, for example. The Minister's problem is getting money out of the Treasury. The arts could help by presenting themselves better. Don't accept that funding has reached its plateau and is gone forever.'

The seminar speakers were high-powered and tough. 'There must be substantial and effective cutbacks and things are unlikely to change in the future', said the Victorian Minister, Norman Lacy, opening the day. 'The Ministry needs your help in making an irresistible case for the arts, not only with the private sector but with Government.'

'There have got to be cuts', said the new chairman of the Australia Council, Dr Timothy Pascoe. 'There will be hardship. The Council must work closely, amicably and comfortably with the state teams. We all have to get together to lobby government. We need massive help.'

'Fundraising is part of being a general manager', said Patrick Veitch of the Australian Opera. 'Private funding is a desirable form of funding, not just a necessary evil. In the first place you can control it. In the second it is continuous. Fools can fill out application forms—some even get grants. But it takes skill to present a case to the private sector.' His advice to board members was 'the three Gs—give, get or get off the board'.

'It's not the taxpayer's money, it's private company money', according to Tony Maine, BP Australia manager, Government and Public Affairs. 'There's got to be something the company can get out of it.'

'Seeking private donors is an important move', said Robert Perrier, director of the Murray River Performing Group, 'but we would be foolish not to recognise the limitations. They are not going to fund vision and process.'

Six clear messages come through the dispute.

1. In Patrick Veitch's words, 'those who help themselves will be rewarded. Others will be left to struggle unaided'.

2. Small community groups can succeed as well as national institutions, if they use their ingenuity. The secret is to believe in the work you are doing.

3. Attracting private sponsorship is a skill all administrators will have to acquire and vulnerable groups will need government help.

4. United we stand, divided we fall—and this applies to all the arts at all levels.

5. Donor involvement has political advantages and provides loyal support in hard times.

6. If the Federal Government is to push the arts into the arms of private enterprise then the Australia Council will have to pick up the tab for developmental projects and disregard the inevitable commercial exploitation that will follow its nurturing.

Since this meeting the Council has already taken steps in this direction. The Theatre Board has withdrawn grants to eight middle-grade theatre companies, and some community and youth theatres; and cut the state company grants by 20 per cent. Top priority goes to dance and young people's theatre, and other grass roots projects.

Two successful case histories were outlined in the seminar. Hugh Morgan, a trustee of the National Gallery of Victoria and executive director of Western Mining Holdings, described how the Art Foundation of Victoria raised $6 million as an acquisition fund for the gallery, providing an annual income of $400,000, and with it 'created a new family'. Robert Perrier showed how his group got 54 children to a festival of children's theatre in Vancouver and 'achieved delivery from regional obscurity'.

The parallel nature of the two stories, one among big business and the privileged, the other among small business, workers and the self-employed, was what gave most heart to the day's labours and to those practitioners feeling most desolated by the challenge to survival.

The Art Foundation raised their target with a $10,000 promotional film, and business lunches presided over by the Premier and other dignitaries. The Murray River Performing Group did it by showing their work and talking about it in the ex-service clubs. It was only the scale of the enterprise that varied.

The Art Foundation campaign was launched by the Queen in 1976 and was an outcome of the trustees facing the fact that the gallery no longer had the funds to keep up a major arts purchasing program. The plan was élitist in the extreme and this was the secret of its success. Donations were graded from $100,000 to a minimum of $2,000. But each level was equally eligible for membership of the board, for a period of three years. This, said Morgan, gave each the opportunity to participate in the affairs of the gallery.

Money was raised through the personal approaches of the fundraising committee and promotional lunches. But the great achievement of the campaign, he said, was the establishment of a new family for the gallery.

Many donors had never been near the place before.

> We now get from them regular interaction and comment—adverse at times—about the running of the gallery and the choice of acquisitions. We have been accused of élitism and we answer that in this way. Requests were made at every level of society. And we have a gallery society with 11,000 members at a subscription rate of $20 a year. But we wanted also to establish a group to take responsibility for the gallery, which meant providing a continuing service of information and personal contact. We could not have done that for a large number of small donors.

Art patronage is, of course, by its nature élitist; and, as Morgan admitted, galleries have it all over the performing arts in being able to provide a tangible acquisition and a brass plate. And access thereafter is free (or almost free) to all. So the battles are worth the heat. As was proved with the recent pre-Columbian collection presented by a syndicate to the gallery, which got the donors into hot water with the Tax Department. The Treasurer is now moving to close a loophole on the evaluation of works of art in the income tax legislation. But as one curator at the seminar commented: 'We still have the collection and we have no doubts about its value.'

From the rarified world of corporation lawyers and tax deduction schemes we moved to a country town, population 60,000. The Murray River Performing Group from Albury–Wodonga was established in 1979 with joint funds from Victoria and NSW under the federal 'sunset' scheme of three-year funding to enable it to establish itself in a region.

'We are a community theatre company. Our job is to create a link between the artist and community', said Robert Perrier.

> We feel we are responsible for the next major development in the Australian theatre. It was with this idealism and at the same time panic that we launched into the Flying Fruitfly Circus project. It started as a means by which we could gain direct involvement with local kids. So far we have 250. Mastering a skill gives you a sense of confidence, and there are many skills involved in making a circus. It amounts to a kind of alternative education. Neither the kids nor their parents had had anything to do with the performing arts before; and all the training we offered was free. Worthwhile as it was, it was an incredibly expensive operation. It was costing $30,000 for a season of one or two weeks. So we decided to make the product good enough to tour beyond the district. This is how we achieved delivery from regional obscurity.

The opportunity arose for the circus to attend the Vancouver Festival. The fares would cost $40,000. But they decided to go. 'We thought that if we got there and were well-received then maybe we would be noticed in our own country.' The Australia Council, the Department of Foreign Affairs and the Albury–Wodonga Development Corporation came good with $15,000. Next they organised a circus tour of the surrounding area to raise funds; and a team of guest speakers at the local service clubs.

> We now made contacts that cut our costs by 40 per cent. Those people began to understand that they were serving the community and so were we. The connection was unmistakable. Benefits flowed from then on. There were also the parents of the kids—plumbers, dressmakers and so on. After six months we had the contacts through which we would ask assistance—in cash, in kind, in manpower and know-how. It was a direct involvement by the business community. When news come from Canada about what a fantastic reception we had had, the community got a lot of satisfaction.

The end of the story was that following the Canadian tour the troupe did a Melbourne season in the August holidays which, with the help of Michael Edgley International made enough money to work off the 18-month deficit and make the circus a self-sufficient part of the MRPG. Performance development is Perrier's first priority and he has been able to turn down a $60,000 offer from the Sydney and Adelaide festivals next summer to keep the children in training at home. 'So we are now seen as a company that is fairly aggressive. Seeking private donors is an important move, but the development of a national cultural event is a delicate process. Governments will have to rearrange their priorities so that they are more and more serving the source—writers and artists—and to help source organisation tap into important resources.'

A 'view from HQ' from Tony Maine outlined the guidelines of BP's arts policy, which at present was giving its chief assistance to modern dance and publishing projects. In the main they were: that the body should be Australian; that its work should have national effect; that patronage should be on-going with a minimum of three years; that they would not compete with other sponsors; that there would be some opportunity for BP workers' participation; that the administration be demonstrably competent; and the work should be a developing rather than already recognised form.

'We try to take the initiative in creating sponsorship. I really believe we are doing something for the development of dance in this country (they are sponsors of the Australian Dance Company and the Sydney Dance

Company) and we are also doing something for my company's image.' Maine spoke in detail about the ways of presenting an application and of the pros and cons from the company's point of view. 'I can honestly say in the three years I have been in the job only one application has been impeccable.'

It was a salutary and sobering day and it gave warning of the battles to come. Perrier had summed it up in his opening remarks: 'Subsidy is like the races with different entrants all vying for part of the prize; the maidens, the improvers, the performers—and there is another class, retired and expensive studs.' Jon Hawkes, of Circus Oz, voiced the fears of the younger classes who 'had made it plain that they were not equipped to make the proper approach to private sponsors. I find the whole approach of the seminar disturbing', he said. 'Private sponsorship will only be given if there are tangible benefits. I don't see it as the arts' job to give tangible benefits to the private sector. Benefits to government are very different. If Patrick Veitch really believes the approaches to government and the private sector are the same, I find the whole thing terrifying.'

He was not alone.

But he now has one cause of satisfaction: the maidens have won in the current Theatre Board stakes. The Board has given top priority to what Robert Perrier called 'vision and process'—the developmental programs that are especially vulnerable. It looks as though the Australia Council's heart is in the right place. It is asking the arts to unite behind it.

The appointment of Dr Timothy Pascoe as both chairman and chief executive of the Australia Council (1981–84) was symptomatic of the direction in which government was pushing the arts. He is chiefly remembered for having restructured the council from individual boards into five units based on administration rather than art form. This was immensely unpopular and soon disbanded. At the time of publication the article below created some controversy and the suggestion that I had 'sold out' in presenting his views. Today they appear so generally accepted it is hard to recall the cause of dispute.

Dr Pascoe's Business

National Times, week ending 10 November 1981

The last couple of weeks have been heady ones for the arts. The Theatre Board of the Australia Council have given the chop to eight middle-grade companies. The general manager of the Australian Opera, faced with a

$700,000 deficit, has retrenched 22 employees and is under notice of industrial action. The strike by dancers of the Australian Ballet has hardened into a year of attrition. The board of the Australian Gallery Directors' Council has recommended liquidation, abandoning debts of $200,000.

Last weekend the Prime Minister told the South Australian Liberal Party Council that 'Australia in the 80s is one of the most vibrant and vital countries in the world in a cultural sense, one of the most harmonious, free and stable countries in a political sense'. He wanted to lay the ghost, he said, of the idea that the health of the arts was due to the good nursing of the Whitlam Government.

What is happening to the arts, of course, is much the same as what has happened to Medibank since 1975—being legislated into the private sector. Given the Prime Minister's premise that the present state of the arts is a tribute to his government; and that the last official word on their status was from the Industries Assistance Commission inquiry in 1976, I thought a word with the new man in charge of this new heal-yourself service, Dr Timothy Pascoe, chairman of the Australia Council, might help me understand about our vibrancy and vitality.

Dr Pascoe proved not without resources and determined that to be disadvantaged should not be the only criterion for free health care. Dr Pascoe (42), Adelaide University graduate in civil engineering and economics, Cambridge graduate in operational researches, and a graduate of Harvard Business School, has close ties with the Coalition Government. He was federal director of the Liberal Party and secretary to the shadow cabinet 1974–75; and is a close friend of Tony Eggleton, whom he met at Harvard. Since 1975 he has run his own arts administration consultancy, Arts Research, Training and Support Ltd; and is the author of handbooks on private sponsorship and the responsibilities of arts boards and administrators.

The word from the IAC Commissioner, Richard Boyer, back in 1976 had been that federal funding should be phased out in five years. Here it is five years on and it looks as though Treasurer John Howard might be planning just that. Boyer's question: 'Why should the arts be subsidised?' was not answered to his satisfaction at the time and still remained to be answered. So I asked Dr Pascoe.

He was not unprepared for the question and answered in five points:

1. *The majority of the arts are not subsidised.* If you look at the totality and include pop music, popular crafts, television and so on, only a limited

range is subsidised. 'People forget that. They think of it as a hand-out industry', he said.

2. *If they were not subsidised either you wouldn't have them at all or access would be limited even more than it is already.* 'That takes us to the question of what is the merit of having them. I think there are external benefits which go beyond the immediate consumer and relate to things like the national identity, our own social values. You need things within a society which cause you to look at the way you have traditionally done things. Theatre quite often has that role. It forces you to think again about conventional wisdom.'

3. *The subsided arts supply resources to a wide area.* 'Without the theatre and the allied arts we would not have a film industry or an advertising industry. The whole visual arts world supplies the visual language that goes into advertising. What is avant-garde today on exhibition at Frank Watters' gallery in a couple of years will show up in commercial packaging.'

4. *Another role is the maintenance of history and tradition.* 'Obviously this is a decision which society makes as to whether it wants to keep its traditions. But we must keep our arts in use if we want to keep them alive—and this requires subsidy. There are also points where the user-pays principle falls down. Put a piece of sculpture in a public place. You cannot charge the beneficiary. You cannot even identify him or her.'

5. *Finally is the question of national pride.* 'Someone like Joan Sutherland is a cause of national pride just as a great sportsperson is. The Council commissioned a survey into attitudes to the arts and a substantial proportion of people who did not go to opera, for example, were totally in favour of subsidy, partly from the view that if they wanted to go it would be there; and partly the feeling that the arts are part of the kind of society we want.'

Dr Pascoe made it clear he believed financing growth was the responsibility of governments; but that private enterprise could help. He saw no conflict between artistic excellence and private patronage. It was a question of allocating responsibility.

It was the job of management, not the artist, to balance the books; and boards of management in particular were letting the side down. 'I would find it very hard to deny', he said, 'that a great number of boards of arts organisations have not been good about carrying out their responsibilities. They do not apply the vigilance they would to their own companies. They fail to ask the questions: Are we clear about our objectives and priorities?

Do we have the right staff? Are we giving them clear guidelines? Are we evaluating performance? Do we have proper cost control?'

> Some boards evaluate performance only as they would a commercial organisation—the profit and loss account. But with an arts organisation your actual product cannot be measured in financial terms. Some boards give insufficient attention to monitoring the quality of the product. I am not saying the board should in any way decide artistic policy; but it should determine whether what is being delivered artistically fits with the organisation's objectives. In a very real sense the employees are the product. Like the Australian Ballet—the dancers are the product.

We discussed the ballet crisis. There have been disputes within the Australian Ballet ever since the appointment of the administrator Peter Bahen in 1966, through a succession of artistic directors. Standards have declined, discipline also; there has been a move towards spectacle, not developmental work, a resentment of press criticism, a cutting back of classes and rest periods; and now a demotion of principals to the rank of soloist, obliging them to perform longer hours for less pay. Recently the administrator announced a plan to import principals from abroad. Some 29 dancers have resigned.

'It's not a dispute about money or about too many performances', said Michael Crosby, secretary of Actors' Equity. 'It's about the whole relationship with Bahen, his treatment of the dancers. He has been quoted as saying he doesn't even know their names. I'm quite worried about the future of the company. Some of the dancers have said that if Bahen is there in 1982 they won't be. It is almost a joke within Equity how much punishment they have put up with. If it had been the Opera...'. Ironically, the Australian Ballet is probably the only performing arts organisation not in debt but has a healthy surplus. Is this what we must expect of the new commercial outlook on the arts?

Dr Pascoe was quick to deny this. 'Peter Bahen's attitude is a very different thing from seeking sponsorship in the private sector', he said. 'Let us be clear about the difference. One can go after excellence and also seek sponsorship in certain areas. I see that as neither a degrading of artistic standards nor necessarily a cop-out for government. On the other hand one can go after commercial product, as the ballet has done. The Australian Ballet has never sought or obtained much sponsorship—unlike the Australian Opera, which receives between half and three quarters of a million a year.'

He does have a point. But how to do it?

Firstly, said Pascoe, developmental work and the avant-garde were the responsibility of government:

> It is up to the Australia Council to make it clear that it supports the cutting edge, and why. We must have clearly defined priorities and policies. Just as this year there has been a reorientation towards individual creativity. The Council has taken a very good step towards coming to grips with the problems.
>
> All the same, I think a lot of what we are doing today says more about how we got here than where we ought to be going. And that is one of the things we must do. I know Council itself wants to reappraise what it is doing, not only because there is less money but because, if we want to do exciting things, we've got to be able to shift resources.

Secondly, he believed all arts organisations should start to think comprehensively. Experimental seasons were unlikely to gain private sponsorship but he saw no reason why more conventional areas of that same company's work should not raise the funds for experiment. And equally why one area of the arts should not assist another in the same way.

A lover of theatre and dance—'I have been a theatre-goer since I was six'—with a preference for 'work which is confronting rather than conventional', he is a strong advocate of self-help. 'One reason the corporations keep away from the avant-garde—and not all of them do— is that they feel out of their depth. It is not just that they feel it might be socially confronting or anarchic. You must remember that they are going out of their depth in moving into the arts at all.' People often try and argue that the arts are different from business. My answer is that they are not different, simply more difficult. The basic principles are in most cases the same. It is just that you are up against additional aspects which make the job very complex. Profit isn't your only motive: you've also got the question of artistic standards. In the arts you don't have the financial reserves to fall back on.'

The Australian Gallery Directors' Council is a case in point. It began as an industry association and more recently has become an exhibitions promoter, sometimes having as many as 70 exhibitions on tour. It lost $275,000 on the recent Revolutionary Decades exhibition. The AGDC has received funding for exhibitions from the Australia Council but in Pascoe's words 'has never had a capital base'. The directors have called a meeting on 18 November to discuss liquidation, despite an offer for some rescue money from the Visual Arts Board.

'I personally regard it as very sad because it did have an important role to play, not only in big exhibitions but small ones. And I am still not sanguine, as the galleries are, that they are effectively set up to move exhibitions around without the AGDC, or that its going to cost as little as they think it is. Or that there's going to be the logistic expertise.'

In the present climate, 'boards of arts organisations must really be very clear about what their responsibilities are. Not only morally but more particularly at law. The AGDC is a classic case. They know about the arts, but do they know good commercial practice? Conversely, the knights of industry may lack sensitivity to what makes management in the arts more difficult. Equally, there is the problem in administration. If people with an arts background want to be boss they must realise what being a boss means. It is not just an arty job, it involves budgeting, cost control, marketing, as well as artistic judgment. Frequently you hear it claimed that only an arts person can head a company. So it should be. Just so long as they recognise that the top job is management.'

'Management', I guess, like 'cutbacks' and 'parameters' is a word for the 1980s.

The Ballet strike occurred during a season of *The Hunchback of Notre Dame* in Melbourne. It lasted 26 days, until the board agreed to relieve Peter Bahen of his position. On 19 November 1981, a week after this article appeared, Stage Crisis Day was mounted as a public protest against the cutbacks to the Australia Council by the Fraser Coalition Government; and the introduction by the Council of a 'challenge grant' intended as an incentive to arts companies to embrace private sponsorship. Medibank was the original publicly-funded universal health service introduced by the Whitlam Government. Under Fraser it was privatised; but a new structure called Medicare was introduced by the Hawke Labor Government in 1983. Tony Eggleton was the current federal director of the Liberal Party and a feared power-broker.

During 1979 Richard Wherrett was appointed director of the new Sydney Theatre Company. At the time he was one of three directors of the Nimrod Theatre and the other two, John Bell and Ken Horler, had been regarded as more likely contenders. But Wherrett was well prepared and wasted no time in imposing a style upon the company, one which expanded and affirmed the *panache* that had by then come to be recognised as the Nimrod style.

Theatre of Panache

National Times, 29 November–2 December 1981

The final plays of the 1981 Sydney Theatre Company season at the Opera House is an occasion to give one pause: in the Drama Theatre is a work which leaves us looking at the corpse of contemporary theatre; and in the Opera Theatre the inspiration to make one start again. The first is *Chinchilla*, by—or rather based on a play by—Robert David MacDonald; a study in art deco of Diaghilev and his Russian Ballet. The second might be described as the apotheosis of John Bell in a return season of Edmond Rostand's *Cyrano de Bergerac*. Both productions are exquisite, and lift the company to a level of achievement well ahead of any company in Australia. By the same means they elevate the actor to the prime position—something that has never happened before in the subsidised theatre (except by default).

For a long time we have had a directors' theatre; for a while a playwrights' theatre. Now the STC is sweeping the theatre in a new season, towards—not exactly an actors' theatre, though that is part of it—but a theatre, in Cyrano's words, of panache. Style has always been STC director Richard Wherrett's style. He is at his best presenting actors as art objects—like the brilliant productions of Peter Handke's anti-realist plays which he directed for the Nimrod Theatre. He has a distinctive resource of imagination which makes his work compelling; and it would appear that it is the possibilities a play offers to the theatre, as much as any view of life which others might present, which leads him towards his choice of repertoire.

Sydney theatregoers, the State Government, rival theatres—not the least of them Nimrod—have been watching with close interest the performance of the Sydney Theatre Company, now ending its second year. We are not being offered 'the world's best plays'; or copies of Broadway productions, or ensemble theatre; or a classical repertoire; or an all-Australian theatre. The theatre now emerging is quite unlike anything since the old days of actor managers.

Wherrett now has, in his pre-eminent position as a resident of Australia's great architectural wonder and tourist attraction, the chance to give breadth to the best talent in Australia, and to exploit their abilities to the commercial limit. He also has the unique opportunity to make a fresh start, putting the varied experience of the other state company behind him. Already he has changed the fortunes of the director Rodney Fisher and the playwrights

Dorothy Hewett, Louis Nowra and Bob Herbert; he has given expression to the talents of the designer Brian Thomson, and actors Robyn Nevin, Nancye Hayes, Geraldine Turner, Noni Hazlehurst, George Spartels, Mel Gibson and others—also presently Peter Carroll as Chinchilla and John Bell as Cyrano.

Putting style before content has not always been a success. The opening production of the company, a conventional music hall spoof of the nineteenth century Australian melodrama, *The Sunny South,* missed the opportunity seized upon by NIDA in *On Our Selection*, of revitalising a piece of popular theatrical history. And Colin Friels' Hamlet was miscalculated at all levels, originating with the English director William Gaskill (who would have done better service on Edward Bond's work, for which he has a special affinity). The more recent *Cat on a Hot Tin Roof* was separated from the claustrophobic context of 1950s moral convention and left the actors looking simply dated. Others have been triumphant, like *Chicago*, in which the theatrical vitality defies one to pay attention to the script; *The Man from Mukinupin,* which created from the text a kind of visual symphonic poem; or *No Names…No Pack Drill,* which made out of a craftsman-like work a joyful journey into nostalgia for those who remember what Sydney was like during the Second World War.

The extremes of the two current shows demonstrate what is most liberating and limiting about this approach to the stage. *Chinchilla* is a play devised for the Glasgow Citizens' Theatre, which saw in the life of Sergey Diaghilev, the Russian Ballet patron, something of its own dilemma in presenting art for art's sake to a wholly industrial city like Glasgow. Rodney Fisher was apparently dissatisfied enough with the script to spend three weeks with the cast reshaping it and restoring historical fact. The name of the original author does not appear on the program. The resultant production is the portrait of a close, largely homosexual society, protected by privilege from reality: feckless, temperamental, self-indulgent. We see nothing of the art that it created, nor of the audience that received it. If there is a theme, it is that of *The Dresser*, Fisher's earlier success this year, that great artistry and great selfishness are not incompatible.

But where *The Dresser* was grounded in recognisable reality, *Chinchilla's* characters, in this production, move with measured grace in and out of silhouette-like pictures in an exhibition by Bakst or Erte. Like them, the characters are bereft of background—time, life, even death have no meaning except as a musical rhythm. The element that supervenes is style, expressed in the movement of the dancers, the extraordinary grace of the women in their Roger Kirk costumes, the ethereal lighting by John Rayment and Brian Thomson's stark white set; and above all the delivery by Peter Carroll of a stream of Wildean wit.

Apart from the mounting and the great lift it has given the cast to be privileged accessories to a kind of artistic conspiracy, the special achievement is the work of Peter Carroll. Carroll's style is mannered, and least comfortable in realist theatre. In the right hands he can give a blazing performance. He is more of a personality than a character actor, and this is by far the best thing he has done since his Benedick in *Much Ado About Nothing*, for Nimrod, which toured the capitals with such success. Huddled inside the stuffing of a black chinchilla overcoat he moves at a stately pace across the stage, dispensing a flow of repartee which conceals more than it reveals. Only the occasional outburst of peevish rage gives a glimpse of the mechanism with which this Diaghilev strives to control his own and others' allegiance. The performance is an admirable co-operative effort by producer, director, actor and designer to create something unique.

The question then is: is all this creative work worth the effort? If this play is an indication of where the contemporary European theatre is going, then we are looking at the death of the present movement. An art which turns inward upon itself in this way and retreats into the esoteric, becomes self-indulgent and effete. This production is no exception. Certainly the audience at *Chinchilla* on opening night were admiring but confused; and I wondered to what audience the work was really directed. This became clear, however, when I saw the new production of *Cyrano* designed for the big Opera House stage. There were complaints early on that the actors could not be heard in the circle. By the time I went to see it they were facing front and projecting for all they were worth. As an opera-goer remarked at interval, only the orchestra was missing.

And as much as *Chinchilla* describes an existentialist world of ever-retreating boundaries which demands that life imitate art, so *Cyrano*, in this late nineteenth-century romantic portrait of a seventeenth century musketeer, devotes his life to the splendid gesture. *Cyrano* is an affirmation of life as much as *Chinchilla* is a rejection of it—and as perverse, being equally grounded in the desire for life to be different, better ordered, more generous and more beautiful than it is. In short, *Cyrano de Bergerac* is an operatic production: splendid, extravagant, beautifully dressed by Luciana Arrighi, with superb virtuoso performances. It makes a grand tribute to the triumph of the human spirit over adversity and the flesh. This production expands admirably to the dimensions of the operatic stage, but it does more than that; it raises the skills of the actors to a new level of demand. The result is a work which would grace any stage in the world.

Of particular interest is the casting of Robyn Nevin, replacing Helen Morse as Roxane, the précieuse heroine who discovers too late that the face is not the window to the soul. Gothic girlishness is not naturally Nevin's style, but it needs a strong actress to carry vulnerability to the back row of the circle and miraculously she does it, conveying pampered femininity with as much force as the virility of John Bell's Cyrano.

Bell's performance has grown too, astoundingly, giving not only grace and crusty, self-effacing wit to the character, but a new heart-breaking warmth. His anonymous aria to Roxane in the darkness becomes a flood released from the containment of a lifetime; and the incomparable death scene duet with Nevin has the same liberating quality of a musical score. Equally there are new dimensions to the work of Robin Ramsay, as the wicked De Guiche, and Andrew McFarlane gives a fresh stubborn honesty to his handsome Christian. Altogether the production is a milestone: for a new truth which the actors have found within Rostand's florid sentimentality; and for the fact that it sets a new level for the aspirations of the performing arts in Australia. This is style, in Michel St Denis' sense of making a path to the truth through performance, and a long way from those many productions to which we have been too long and too often subjected, that seek to disguise incomprehension of a text by decorating the stage. While the STC remains solely in the Opera House—and the promised Wharf Theatre planned for experiment is fast evaporating—it looks as though the company will develop to be not unlike the Australian Opera, except that the work (with the exception of the selected texts) will be wholly indigenous.

The new season's works (including the Kaufman and Hart comedy *You Can't Take It With You*, Peter Shaffer's *Amadeus*, *Macbeth* and Pirandello's *As You Desire Me*) are as interesting for the challenge of their form as for their content. *Macbeth* presents one of the greatest problems for the modern director, and it defeated the Old Tote on its only venture into the Opera Theatre. The two Australian works are to be David Williamson's *The Perfectionist*, as yet an unknown quantity, and John O'Donoghue's *A Happy and Holy Occasion,* at least as challenging for its mixture of realism and expressionism as for its story of a Newcastle family. The STC's experimental season of one-act plays, *Shorts*, at the Stables Theatre recently, was an interesting insight into its approach to new work. The season was a training ground for inventiveness in which the playwright was mostly inconsequential, and the choice of personality actors ensured that the experiment paid its way.

Given all this evidence, it looks as though the STC will remain Sydney's most showy theatre company, billing star performers and star designers. It will not be a centre for new thought; its productions may be challenging, but not so their content—a politic decision and inevitable while the opera and ballet are held in special grace and favour by Canberra. This leaves the Australian playwright to Nimrod and the Ensemble, the serious interpretation of the dramatic text, the avant-garde and the stirring of the status quo to anyone prepared to take them on.

On Stage Crisis Day there was a call from John Bell and others for the arts to unite. And Bell himself is in a key position as director of Nimrod and principal actor for the STC. There is no question that the theatre needs a flagship to wave the banner for the whole profession and to be a cause for pride to the nation; equally that it needs a long-term investment at all levels if we are to keep the flag flying. Looking back it is hard to credit how far the performing arts have progressed in the last twelve years. Their leaders have a status now in the public mind unimagined in the days of the J. C. Williamson monopoly. And with status have come responsibility, influence and conservatism.

On Our Selection was adapted by George Whaley from the 1912 version by Bert Bailey and others, based on the stories of Steele Rudd. *The Dresser* by Ronald Harwood, with Warren Mitchell, Gordon Chater and Ruth Cracknell, was directed by Rodney Fisher for Helen Montagu at the Theatre Royal, Sydney.

The STC's repertoire in this early period was heavily influenced by the high rent of the Drama Theatre, then its only venue, and the status of the Opera House as an international tourist destination. The Wharf Theatre, seating 319, opened in 1984. With its scene shop, its administrative offices, rehearsal rooms and restaurant, it provided a genuine home and the opportunity to expand into more adventurous territory. In 2004 the 850-seat Sydney Theatre, with a scene dock, rehearsal rooms and restaurant, was opened opposite the Wharf.

A lot of what audiences enjoyed about the Nimrod style had gravitated to the Opera House with Richard Wherrett. Nimrod was feeling the pressure. In September 1979, I reported the appointment of designer Kim Carpenter (29) and tyro director

Neil Armfield (24) as directors ('New Turning for Nimrod') with the aim of setting a new direction. Carpenter resigned quickly. Armfield moved to Jim Sharman's Lighthouse Company in Adelaide in 1983. Chris Westwood had been appointed project director at Nimrod 1980–82, during which time she devised two workshops for women directors and writers, to address the lack of opportunity for women in the theatre, including the lack of good roles. It caused disruption at the time but its consciousness-raising gradually opened opportunities for directors and set male playwrights to redressing the balance.

Nimrod Faces Renewal Task

National Times, 10–16 January 1982

The year 1981 saw Sydney's Nimrod Theatre in the press more than it's ever been. The theatre whose name has been synonymous with larrikin style and the Australian playwright has been full of change and controversy. Audiences have been dropping. Subscribers have made their views felt. There has been a disturbing turnover of executives. Measures have been taken to democratise management and there's been gossip of a feminist takeover. All this reflects the confusion at the top and a period of unrest superseding one of stability. Nimrod's problems reflect a wider upheaval in the profession itself and the country at large.

The women's lobby at Nimrod, whose views have been heard during 1981, is again a reflection of industrial unrest; and their drive to gain the serious attention of the theatre industry for female employment has already had a significant impact. But these have been side issues diverting attention away from the almost unremarked advance Nimrod has made in embracing all these issues with the appointment of Aubrey Mellor as co-artistic director.

Nimrod is still the best barometer to gauge the weather for the Australian theatre, though Nimrod itself may not yet know which way the wind is blowing. Mellor's appointment coincides with, and has given force and stability to, a sudden reversal of Nimrod's direction. From being a happy-go-lucky inward-looking theatre company, it has taken upon itself the burdens of the world.

Before joining Nimrod last February, Mellor was a popular tutor at NIDA who in recent times had come to public attention with his lovingly studied productions at the Jane Street Theatre of *As You Like It*, *Mother Courage* and Louis Esson's *The Bride of Gospel Place*. The direction showed a care for the text and for actors' detail that singled him out from the crowd. However, his one production for Nimrod in 1976, Albee's gloomy *All*

Over, had been a failure, in good part due to the play itself. As a result some sages had concluded that Mellor, whose gentle, drily humorous manner hides a quiet determination and a taste for the bizarre and tough, had his place within the protected environment of the studio.

His impact upon Nimrod's stage was sudden and dynamic. He first burst upon us with George Whaley's devastating performance as the mad investigator in Dario Fo's *Accidental Death of an Anarchist*. Hard upon this was another political allegory, Václav Havel's *Protest*, in which Barry Otto gave three astonishing performances in different stories of betrayal. After that came Chekhov's *Three Sisters* which, though as a whole it was less complete than some of Mellor's work, still drew new strengths from actors and new insights into a familiar text. Cathy Downes and Anna Volska as Masha and Olga have never given better performances in that theatre. If Mellor has shown a technical weakness it has been that attention to detail has sometimes supervened over a central statement on the text.

But more interesting than the way he has sharpened his actors' skills has been the adoption of a central European bias to the repertoire. While Mellor is not alone responsible for this—it had been evolving earlier—he has been the instrument through which it has been defined. The move broadened Nimrod's horizons and coincided with a growing impatience with realist drama now long become conventional.

Until recently Nimrod's character has been domestic. It has been the home of the Australian playwright and has translated Shakespeare and the classics into an easy-to-take style for its audiences. It has not always been the subtlest of interpreters or the greatest respecter of a text; but what may have been lost in sensibility was made up in vitality. Now suddenly the direction is outwards. The unexpected has been the constant and the content assaulting. Nor has the view of the outside world been a happy one. Moral decay has been the theme of almost all the plays in last year's program. With President Reagan doing his best to plunge us into World War III, civilisation as we know it has a tenuous grip on the earth and Nimrod is seeking to add these troubles to our own. No wonder some patrons have retreated to the fun house run by the Sydney Theatre Company.

In itself some adverse reaction is not a matter for concern yet, except financially. Many of the Old Tote subscribers acquired by Nimrod have now moved on to the Sydney Theatre Company. There must be a period of adjustment.

In recent years Nimrod, founded to assault the establishment, has by default been the mainstream theatre in Sydney and its initial response to the reversal of that situation has been to see the world as a slough of despond. And we are in decay in this country. If there is one theme crying to be shouted about in the 1980s it is the swaggering self-centredness and acquisitiveness that consumes our thinking—in government, in business, in daily life. Mateship has given way to monetarism, the fair deal to the massive tax evasion industry; in the struggle the old, the crippled and the unemployed are pushed from the mainstream of society; we prey on those unable to defend themselves. We have entered the survival-of-the-fittest decade—and the fittest are wholly occupied with their own survival.

What has been the theatre's response to this? The established playwrights for the moment appear punch-drunk, the newer ones are taking up the cause of sectional interests or escaping into abstract forms or distant themes. For the moment our novelists are better documenters of the state of the nation than our playwrights; such periods of change are continuing and natural. Theatre directors have been restlessly looking for material with which to give expression to this uneasiness and one way is to show how much more decadent other people are than ourselves—*Lulu* and *Chinchilla*, for example. Or launching into raunchy escapism like *The Rocky Horror Show, Chicago* or even *Once Upon a Mattress*. Nimrod has gone further than the others in bewailing our condition and unconsciously pointing to the diagnosis. But as yet there is little passion or definition in the investigation, only a general feeling of malaise.

The lack of firm statement has reflected itself in the gap between play and performance. Neil Armfield's production of David Hare's *Teeth 'n' Smiles* early in 1981 was the first of the 'new policy' plays to cause controversy and certainly the assault was new. But the author's passion was dated and from far away, and the decay of British society had been told too many times since *Look Back in Anger*. Amplifying its rock music to the threshold of pain could not change that.

Caryl Churchill's ingenious device in *Cloud Nine* of exchanging gender roles to demonstrate the tenuous grounds on which conventional morality is based gave the actors a splendid romp under Mellor's hand but again its criticism was directed to a society different from ours. Ödön von Horváth's *Tales from Vienna Woods* is a compelling work, a bitter epic from Austria in the 1930s which examines, through the degradation of an ordinary young woman, the direction in which selfishness can drag a society. It is a fairy tale of decay crammed with the discarded corpses of old responsibilities. And yet the performance shared none of the rage against the time that drove the author but instead inhabited its own theatrical—and therefore finally harmless—world, just as did the recent South Australian production of *Lulu*, a play of related background. Looking at the Nimrod audience that night it seemed to me that they and Horváth's characters were not dissimilar. But the connection was not made.

The thinking conveyed from the stage reminded me of the well-intentioned social-realist playwrights of the 1930s and 40s. They chose their themes of drought and flood, racial discrimination, female exploitation from good motives but ones outside their experience and to which the theatre itself was not fundamental. With the exception of *Three Sisters*, *Accidental Death* and *Protest*, there was almost nothing in the year's program at Nimrod which I felt proved the theatre necessary, that could have expressed itself in no other form. And that includes the local works *Celluloid Heroes, Pinball* and *Eyes of the Whites*.

The play that came nearest to saying what Nimrod seems to be trying to define was a failure: Ron Blair's *Last Day in Woolloomooloo*. Despite the advances the company has made towards non-naturalistic theatre, it was unable to argue clearly Blair's symbolic plea for renewal within the Australian way of life and a more profound perception of its nature. The play is, admittedly, broken-backed, but so are some of Nimrod's most successful works. It made me wonder whether, in the present cacophony, it had lost the capacity to listen to the still, small voice.

The confusion between social concern and dramatic necessity has been central to the controversy over the women's lobby at Nimrod. Basically the motivation has been industrial rather than artistic; but artistic tension had been created by the introduction of a group with an overriding commitment to domestic issues at a time when others were being moved to look outward.

Briefly, the women's lobby at Nimrod began in 1980 with a workshop for women directors conducted by the English director Susan Todd. This was followed by a series of play readings for women writers and the Downstairs production of one of those plays, *Pinball* by Alison Lyssa. Most recent was a ten-week workshop by a group of actresses on music and comedy techniques, of which the current production *Desert Flambé* is an outcome. These activities led to employment for a number of women and to a general ferment of thought at a time when Nimrod was going through a transition period and seeking new directions. Some new talent was turned up, like the young director of *Pinball*, Chris Johnson. There were inevitably some clashes and some resignations.

Personalities aside, what was important about the women's lobby is a battle already won. It grew out of a crying need to draw attention to the lack of opportunity for women in the profession, to the dearth of experienced female directors, playwrights and technicians, and to the male orientation in most Australian playwriting. All this was manifestly necessary and proved politically timely, coinciding with a period of general upheaval in the performing arts. These women have engineered a change that must of necessity be continuing. Women directors and designers are beginning to get more work; male directors and male playwrights perforce are looking more carefully at women's roles. Management has discovered there is a market in the women's point of view.

But what we are talking about here is the effect of industrial action. Confusion has come when it has been disguised as artistic merit. Equal opportunity, anti-discrimination laws, rectitude and unequivocal language—these are the terms of the arbitration court; the stage has no place for them.

As yet it is too early to say what artistic gains have been made for women writers and artists. In this bid for attention the group have been quite as strident as Jack Hibberd, Graeme Blundell, John Romeril and others were in Melbourne in the 1960s, demanding with plays like *Customs and Excise* and *Bastardy* that the theatre be freed to debate Australia's sexual and political repression. That period raised the issues and gained attention for the rapid growth that followed; but it was not the period that produced the good drama. In five years' time we may look back on 1981—as we have looked on 1967—as some kind of turning point; as a period of healthy ferment out of which the good times grew.

Nimrod's artistic directors now make a good team; John Bell with his broad theatrical nous and Mellor with his imaginative attention to detail. The year of change ends with a good prognosis. What they need now is the playwright of renewal.

My prognosis was wrong. In 1984 Nimrod sold its theatre to pay off debt and moved to the Seymour Centre. The decision proved terminal. Aubrey Mellor and John Bell resigned in 1985. Richard Cottrell took over and produced a fine season of classics; but the spirit of Nimrod could not be recaptured in the cavernous new building. No playwright of renewal emerged in that time. The company closed its doors in 1987.

Lulu, an adaptation by Louis Nowra from Frank Wedekind's plays, starring Judy Davis and directed by Jim Sharman was presented in Adelaide and Sydney by the State Theatre Company of South Australia in 1981. John Osborne's play, *Look Back in Anger*, first performed in 1956, marked a turning point in the move towards working-class and socially critical theatre in Britain. *Celluloid Heroes* was a satire of the film industry by David Williamson; *Pinball* a polemical work about the custody of children by Alison Lyssa; and *Eyes of the Whites*, a political drama about race relations in Papua New Guinea by Tony Strachan.

Rise of the New Actor

National Times, 16–22 May 1982

It must be about twelve years ago that I recall sitting on the edge of the stage in the old NIDA theatre, the former totalisator shed at Sydney's Kensington in which the Old Tote Theatre was founded, talking to students about the critic's job and asking them if they realised they were talking a foreign language on stage—English, Irish, American—anything but their own. It was the time when renewed nationalism was stirring. In Melbourne the playwrights Hibberd, Romeril and Williamson were assaulting sexual repression with a barrage of Australian aphorisms. In Brisbane and Melbourne actors had already been arrested for performing Buzo's *Norm and Ahmed*. In Sydney *The Legend of King O'Malley* had defined the new larrikin theatre. The working actor who knew how to wear a costume, owned a repertoire of accents and prided himself on delivering on the instant whatever attitude the director asked for, suddenly found himself faced with an athletic singlet and lines like: 'Don't come the raw prawn with me, you bludger.'

About that time Richard Wherrett, now director of the Sydney Theatre Company, returned to Australia from Britain, where he had been working at the E.15 Acting School in London. 'E.15's approach to production was radical and collaborative', said Wherrett. 'It had a basis in the work of Joan Littlewood at Stratford East. I knew nothing else. Then I did a production of *Man of Mode* at the Tote [see p. 158]. I was very shocked to discover how passive the actors were.'

But all that is water under the bridge. Today, according to those who employ them, our actors are confident and the most popular earn fees appropriate to the executive class. 'Five years ago hardly an actor in Australia could earn $20,000 for a feature film', said Liz Mullinar of M&L Casting Consultants.

> Now top people can command $150,000—and no doubt it will be more soon. It will be even more exciting when they are getting half a million. Because then they will be recognised as international stars. I tell the producers that instead of moaning about costs they should be jumping for joy at the rising demand. It means the actors are actually drawing people into the theatre and the cinema.
>
> We are the only country in the world where there is more than enough work for good actors. That is one reason for the increase in fees. The industry is growing much faster than the supply of actors. There need to be many more NIDAs than there are—two more in Sydney and at least one in every other State. No wonder the handful that graduate each year are good, when 1,800 promising talents are turned down. The industry has so changed in the past five years in terms of professionalism that a great many people have been left behind.

So how have things changed and what has been the cause?

The film industry has brought money and the beginnings of internationalism, far outstripping television; but the groundwork goes back to those stirrings in the 60s and the determination to make an indigenous theatre.

'Part of the struggle to build up the theatre in the 70s has made actors more self-reliant and more versatile', said Nimrod director Aubrey Mellor, a teacher at NIDA during that period,

> and having acquired versatility to use it. The older actor took pride in being the same every night, in being unquestioningly what was required. The rise of the larrikin theatre required a new objective kind of performance. That leap from the old school of well-rounded, clear, polished work, to a personal performance, to the realisation that one can be true to oneself, is very great.
>
> Some actors cannot adapt—they prefer to hide behind technique. I'm not an actor. I like the job of building up character but could never drop my trousers or bare my soul. It's a matter of bravery. The acting style today is not presentation through technique but making a truthful response to every situation and allowing it to affect you. That way the response is always fresh and it seems to be true to what the theatre is.

There had been a steady move towards the selection of the more intelligent actor and rehearsals were now a group activity, said Mellor. NIDA had helped to make this change. 'There has been a deliberate policy to encourage the thinking actor at NIDA.'

Jim Sharman, who took over this year as director of the Lighthouse Company, has made a clean sweep with a new company of actors. South Australia has always felt the need for an ensemble and the young actors developed by the previous incumbent, Colin George, have made an impact on the national scene with their resourcefulness and intelligence—among them Colin Friels, Michael Siberry, Robert Grubb, Susan Lyons and Heather Mitchell. Sharman's style has a different kind of distinction.

> I think the idea of individuality has become more apparent in the past few years. You can feel the difference in the theatre. You don't go to the theatre to see the work of a director but to see performances. Actors are now accepting responsibility in a production. We have gone though a period of having a directors' theatre, a writers' theatre—these things are a matter of fashion. Now I think we are in a transition period and the actor is very important.
>
> The actors that interest me have an independence. The kind of actor who sits smiling at rehearsal saying silently, 'What would you like me to do?' is not an actor that appeals to me. Rehearsals should have a lot of ideas flying about.
>
> The most important part of the company is the repertoire. And that is what attracted my present company—they are interested in taking risks. After working with them on *Signal Driver, A Midsummer Night's Dream* and *Spellbound*, I think I can say that the most striking aspect of Lighthouse is the actors. They have a strongly individual approach.

Sharman's company includes two of the best new stage actors—serious, intelligent and distinctively versatile: Geoffrey Rush and Robert Menzies; and a group of established actors with a need to get out on the cutting edge.

Richard Wherrett's response to his new company is similar.

> Young actors—like Robert Hughes, for example, who is playing small roles for the STC this year. He is full of really interesting ideas—he never stops. On every aspect of the production. These young actors have never known the restrictions of not expressing their views to the director. Today's *Macbeth* rehearsal—everyone was putting in their bit. I love it.

Bill Shanahan, a former administrator of the Old Tote, has in five years as an actors' agent drawn to himself the lion's share of the successful new (and old) actors. He started out in business at the moment when the films

Caddie and *My Brilliant Career* were breaking the export barrier. His clients offer a wide variety and include Nancye Hayes, Geraldine Turner, Carol Raye, Noni Hazlehurst, Wendy Hughes, Judy Davis, Robyn Nevin, Robert Grubb, Barry Otto, John Orczik, John Hargreaves, Mel Gibson, Colin Friels, Sam Neill and Garry McDonald. In Mellor's view Shanahan is one of the few agents who fulfils his duty as a manager in the development of an actor's career. 'Some agents encourage young actors to go straight into TV—quick results by easy means. This is extremely dangerous to the development of young actors. It can ruin them for life.'

Shanahan works tirelessly in his overcrowded office in Woollahra, Sydney. At present the film business was quiet, he said, because of the tax laws. Filming would start in September and casting began in earnest in May. He refused to be drawn on individual clients—particularly about money—but he described the new actors as lacking in pretension and serious about their craft. 'The people I represent don't want to be personalities. They are about the business of acting', he said.

> Actors are now allowed to have an opinion and they do have a great influence upon the films they make and the plays they perform. Nowadays an actor can take an offer from overseas and not feel he must be grateful. The top film actors today are extremely choosy and more often than not turn down the Hollywood offers.

There were probably no more than eight or ten in that class: unless an actor had had exposure in the United States there was no interest. But those who were known had something to offer the American market. 'It gives them a confidence they didn't have before.' It was not the glamour that attracted a good film actor to a contract but the script, the director and the role.

Present-day fees were not lavish but realistic, he said. 'A few years ago even in the film industry actors were subsidising the product with their salaries. Today they can at last command a respectable salary in film and TV. But star actors will always subsidise the theatre. If they did not they would not have the chance to play the variety of roles they need to keep renewing themselves.' The theatre still remained of central importance to the life of an actor, he said, and his successful film actors would keep returning to the stage.

'Who would have thought five years ago', said Mellor, 'that young actors like Judy Davis and Mel Gibson would actually draw the public back into the theatre. On the other hand', he added, 'what Judy Davis finds so exciting about film is that they ask her opinion. She can influence the result.' This is something very new for the Australian actor.

There are those who prefer the life of the stage actor and some of these are moving also into directing. But in comparison the stage is still a cottage industry, as Wherrett has discovered. He has been the first of the state theatre directors to make a policy of promoting the actor's name above the title. But while the film stars do have an important influence on the box office, the stage stars' names—like John Gaden, Robyn Nevin and John Bell—still do not reach very far outside Sydney. Salaries for TV remain lower than film. A top actor could earn $1,500 to $2,000 per week for a TV series, said Shanahan. 'That is for a top series or an actor in demand. Not the soapies. They don't pay much. But TV fees have risen with the film competition.'

So who is the new actor? According to those who employ him or her, a confident, hard-working, versatile performer who wants to live in Australia and be true to our own way of life. 'One of the changes has come through Australian writing', said Sharman. 'The ambitions of the previous generation lay with London and the Royal Shakespeare Company. It's different now. We should remember that Hollywood has always used foreign actors as a matter of course when they are fashionable. Max Von Sydow and Liv Ullman were invited there but their finest work remains the work they did in Sweden.'

And what of the future? Limitless, according to Liz Mullinar. In the theatre Mellor believes that the new confidence and original thinking will enable artists to move out of the restrictions of the conventional company and gain their own following. 'I see no reason why we shouldn't develop our own Pina Bausch theatre in the 80s. Anything could happen.'

In film it comes down to the fact that the industry is growing up and the actors with it. Mullinar had the last word, about *For Love Alone*, from Christina Stead's subtle novel about a young teacher's obsession with a self-centred academic. She has been looking for the star. 'We came up with Judy Davis last time (*My Brilliant Career*) and the producers expect us to do it again. But look at the film itself. Five years ago we couldn't have made an intelligent film like this. The woman's role is so complex, so difficult. We could not have imagined it. It's a role for a great actress.'

From the perspective of 2005, the claims in this article read like fairyland. I can only justify it by saying that the growing success of the young film industry and empowerment of actors being proclaimed by the major theatre companies was, for a short period, engendering this optimism despite the financial constraints of the time. It contrasts cruelly with the report by David Throsby and Virginia Hollister, (*Don't Give Up Your Day Job: An Economic Study of Professional Artists in Australia*, Australia Council, 2003), on artists' earnings, which gives unemployment of actors at 90% and the average earnings from art practice of between $3,000 and $30,000 per year. The published article was illustrated with portraits of Judy Davis, Colin Friels and Geoffrey Rush.

Sharman renamed the State Theatre Company of South Australia the Lighthouse Company during his incumbency there in 1982–83. Others in the company of 12 actors were: Robynne Bourne, Peter Cummins, Melissa Jaffer, Gillian Jones, Melita Jurisic, Russell Kiefel, Stuart McCreery, Jacqy Phillips, Kerry Walker and John Wood.

Shanahan's comments about the film industry reflect the fact that tax deductibility then required the film to be completed within the financial year. So shooting began in spring with first screenings planned for the autumn.

Pina Bausch is director of her own mixed media dance company in Wuppertal, Germany. The company performed at the Adelaide Festival in 1982. One of her company who stayed was the Australian choreographer Meryl Tankard. Innovative dance and physical theatre became a strong element in Australia in the 1990s.

For Love Alone was released in 1986, directed by Stephen Wallace, with Helen Buday, Sam Neill and Hugo Weaving.

Death of the Pram Factory

National Times, 6–22 September 1982

Melbourne has tolled the bell on a social experiment that in the 70s made that city the leader in the most significant revival of indigenous theatre in this country. On Wednesday the Pram Factory in Carlton opened its last show, *The Bed Bug Celebration,* by John Blay. Today the wind whips up the discarded newspapers around the adjacent block, and the new sky-blue awning over the entrance contrasts with the peeling posters that have festooned the external walls for a decade. Inside, hired hands, no longer the dedicated labour of the old live-in collective, finish the makeshift proscenium arch stage they have erected for the performance.

Drummond Street is no longer the rundown place it used to be: the hunting ground of traders, students, intellectuals and knockabouts. The houses you could have bought for $10,000 back in 1970 are worth ten times that now, and the old crowd has moved further out. On 31 May 1980 the Pram Factory was sold at auction for $500,000 by its owners,

Paramount Prams Agency. It will be demolished to make way for an eight-storey office block and arcade of boutiques.

At the time there was an outcry. A campaign was launched in the press for a community arts centre. But it all happened too quickly—and in retrospect no one now involved regrets the passing—though some mourn the end of the hopes behind it. Bill Garner, one of the founding members of the Australian Performing Group back in 1969, and who has returned to act in the closing play, summed up the feeling: 'We kept the 60s alive through the 70s, in a kind of extended adolescence. Then we formed the ensemble to look to the 80s.'

In 1979 in a unique recognition of change the collective that had run the Pram Factory since it opened on 11 December 1970, voted itself out of existence. In its place was selected an ensemble of ten performers to carry on in a new spirit. But the gesture proved an empty one. 'The moral', said actor Denis Moore, 'is never inherit a theatrical history'. They found themselves on their own, with no common philosophy or direction and became in the words of the chairperson, Peter King, 'a professional playhouse, like any other'. Clearly they felt they had been dumped by those with whom the public and press constantly compared them.

What, in retrospect, was that group, remembered today as the nursery of a vigorous new 'alternative' Australian theatre? Writers like Jack Hibberd, David Williamson, Barry Oakley, John Romeril and Tim Robertson were part of it; and actors like Peter Cummins, Graeme Blundell, Bruce Spence, Max Gillies, Evelyn Krape, Claire Dobbin and Jude Kuring. *The Hills Family Show* and Circus Oz developed from the gymnastic emphasis of their performance.

Its special virtue was that all its life it remained a workshop, valuing the process above the product. The collective never became a 'professional theatre'; that was part of its capacity for lateral thinking and problem solving which has taken the individual members into many areas since.

A good part of their story is to be found in a decade of minutes and reports in the APG Archives, now up for sale to the highest bidder. They reflect vividly the way it was—passionate, faction-ridden, idealistic, at first naïve and later noticeably sophisticated in its politics and its purges: and throughout overlaid with socialist method and puritan ideology—the stuff of drama indeed.

The Australian Performing Group grew out of work at La Mama in the later 1960s, and was at first a group of dedicated people working in an

amateur capacity in experiments and exercises directed at creating a new
kind of knock-down drag-out all-Australian theatre. At the start there
was no constitution; but after taking a lease on the Pram Factory it was
soon proved that dedication was not enough. An executive was appointed,
a constitution drafted and a building appeal launched.

In February 1972 a proposal for a collective structure was put forward
with an eye on a grant application to the Australia Council; and provision
was made for six salaries. The proposal is a passionate document. 'Why
are we here?' it reads. 'Political reasons. The state of the nation is about as
rotten as proverbial Denmark's ...Theatrical reasons ... Australian theatre
in this century has been morally bankrupt, formally obsolete, politically
irrelevant and not Australian in any recognisable way...'. The style is
recognisably Jack Hibberd's.

The salaries approved were hardly princely—an average of $70 a week.
By 1974 they had risen to $90. Inevitably salaries proved a bone of
contention. By degrees an 'economic union' was devised based on sharing.
No one who had an external full-time job was paid by the collective, part-
timers earned for the work they did, and as they required it. At one point
actors who through the Pram began to earn large sums in film were pooling
their money.

The needs sometimes had their lighter side. An item appears in a 1974
report from John Timlin, headed 'Costuming the Administrator':

> My suit has lately come under severe criticism from artistic sources (I
> was accused of looking like an academic in Brisbane) and it is wearing
> thin at political levels ... Sartorially I am not keeping pace with the
> APG rhetoric and I therefore ask for a grant or loan of about $150 to re-
> equip.

The economic union at a further stage extended to communal living, a
pool of family resources, bulk-buying and the joint purchase of property
at Castlemaine.

'People don't realise', said Bill Garner, 'that for years we lived in the
building itself, on the principle of living with our work. The APG had a
systematic, domestic, economic basis. It became a community centre for
Carlton... it touched the *demi-monde*'.

The encounter with the *demi-monde* had its own problems. The APG
members might have been living on the breadline and squatting on their
own premises, but they were mostly middle-class in background—and
the morals of those who nicked the cheques and vandalised the plumbing

resulted in confrontations of ideology and with the police. In the end, said Timlin, the police agreed not to interfere unless they were called.

May 1974: 'With growth in activity and membership, responsibility has not grown equally. The situation is very demoralising. Robbery, theft, vandalism and irresponsibility is augmenting to an alarming and bewildering degree. Security is appalling.'

It was around this time that the Australia Council was heavying the group about the Company's Act requirements and the collective was restructured as a co-operative society, with the help of Timlin's new suit. He was becoming skilled at fund-raising over a wide range of sources. By the end of 1974 a basic grant by the Theatre Board of $100,000 was being favourably considered, 'dependent on the auditor being satisfied that our internal monetary controls satisfy the stringent requirements of public accountability. This in itself may mean uncomfortable changes within the group', Timlin told the collective.

But the disputes that had brought the group this far took their toll. Blundell and Williamson had been discouraged from membership by 1973, Hibberd came and went. By 1975 the APG had transferred its interest from writers to performance: there were more group creations, imported scripts, a new direction. And of course the group's needs were changing, as Garner pointed out. At the start they had bicycles and 'one clapped-out Holden owned by Romeril'. By the end of the 70s the Pram Factory had a car park.

The records are riddled with self-examination.

June 1975: 'What is socialist theatre? Chaos brigade or cultural axis of the socialist State? Popular or populist theatre: are we just trying to fill seats or making ideas of change accessible to large groups?'

November 1976: 'The critique, Loss of vigour, energy, enthusiasm and Australianness. Losing much with the reality of "out there"', and so on.

On 16 April 1979, after a series of such self-examinations and new experiment, the group decided the Pram should make a new start—and voted itself out of existence. In a paper tabled by Jon Hawkes it was said:

> the recommendation… is motivated by our belief that the APG is no longer a functioning *artistic* collective… The bulk of our current membership works here more and more sporadically so that increasingly the identity of the collective is seen as the *building* we work in and the full-time staff who operate it and carry out the APG's business. We offer *no* performers regular minimum wages even over short periods. There is no longer an economic commitment to the group.

Now the building is going too. The last show is a curious shadow of the APG's past. *The Bed Bug Celebration* is a play first submitted three years ago by the NSW poet John Blay and a personal project of Richard Murphet who directs it. It is a rewriting of the Mayakovsky play, taking Melbourne into the year 2029, and showing again the rotten state of Denmark Jack Hibberd pointed to in 1972. It is a play of technology that contrasts with the makeshift nature of the Pram and speaks warning to the bourgeoisie about a bleak future, which sits uneasily among the growing elegance of the new Carlton.

But the APG's legacy is one of which to be proud. Not only has it nurtured our major playwrights and Circus Oz, it has produced a breed of human being that has shown remarkable self-reliance in entering the outside world. Bill Garner explained why:

> The social experiment of the APG called on the initiative of the practitioner in a way that the professional theatre did not. We did not regard ourselves as employees. We were a co-operative of primary producers and as such put our hands to everything. We all faced the problem-solving. Problem-solving is no good to professional actors—they wouldn't last very long at the Pram.

Now a successful ABC TV writer, Garner says: 'For me the excitement has always been to be in on the beginnings of things. I never wanted to do the classics—we have done only one Shakespeare in the history of the Pram Factory... What I most lament in the passing of the Pram is the work process by which the shows developed. Out in the world... you are expected to succeed. But looking for new directions is a process that very well might not succeed. It is the looking that is important.'

The Almost Managing Company, the agency established by the APG, will continue in business and it handles many of the old collective. And some of them, like Garner, still yearn for the old work process. They are older and wiser (and richer) now, and the idea is hanging around that a new beginning with a new ideology could be made. Not in Carlton—but certainly in Melbourne. An experiment like the Australian Performing Group could happen only in Melbourne.

Others who have since made their name in other fields include Greig Pickhaver, Lindy Davies, Helen Garner, Sue Ingleton, Jane Clifton and Carmen Lawrence. The Almost Managing Company, later AMC Aust Pty Ltd, is today known as Bryson Agency Australia. Circus Oz thrives today as a lasting legacy of the APG.

The end of the Pram Factory was quickly followed by that of the Nimrod Theatre but much more acrimoniously. Between 13 and 18 December 1985 the *Sydney Morning Herald* published a series of debates and an editorial on the subject, accompanied by a flurry of letters to the editor. Under the heading 'The Great Nimrod Debate rages on' Ron Blair and I put the case for and against the company's survival. At this time the director Richard Cottrell had put a proposal to establish a repertory company presenting the classics for six months of the year. Ron Blair defended the need for this and the fact that several companies were now doing the work for which Nimrod was once unique. Cottrell, he wrote, was 'a man of great intelligence, energy and experience, who has clearly shown that he can make the Seymour work'. But the Nimrod board had rejected the proposal because it was 'a prisoner of the past'. In the event, Cottrell presented two seasons of the classics but the Nimrod finally came to a halt in 1987.

Final Curtain for Nimrod?

Sydney Morning Herald, 13 December 1985

On 21 November some four hundred people, myself among them, assembled at the Seymour Centre in Sydney for yet another 'save our theatre' demonstration of solidarity. They cheered spontaneously Nimrod's new director Richard Cottrell's call to arms as he denounced the Theatre Board's alleged demand for 'relevance' as 'ignorant, provincial and prejudiced'. The meeting claimed support for his new actors' company.

The Nimrod Theatre Company has been in financial straits for some years and its removal to the Seymour Centre has done nothing to improve matters. Following the resignation in September of artistic directors John Bell and Aubrey Mellor the staff was disbanded; Cottrell and his administrator Paul Iles were appointed in their stead. In the recent funding crisis the State Government backed the company but the federal Theatre Board voted thumbs down.

To those who attended the Seymour Centre meeting—many the same faces that had last year fought to save the Belvoir Street Theatre—the threat yet again was to employment opportunity. For those who refused support, this new all-British management was a betrayal of everything Mo on the Nimrod banner stands for. And yet, curiously, the abstention was no more than that. No champion has arisen to demand a return to Aussie aggression. The choice is Cottrell or nothing.

Nimrod has not in recent years shown itself to have the 'vision' and 'relevance' of 'pluralist theatre' and 'appropriate social forms'. A drum-banger for the Australian playwright through the 1970s, Nimrod lost its way when the death of the Old Tote transformed Nimrod overnight from a larrikin alternative theatre into Sydney's major company. After a short burst of hype (engineered by the then manager Paul Iles) the three-part directorship broke up leaving John Bell, with his heart in the classics, the sole remaining founder. Ominously the board of directors began to assert itself. There were assays into youth and feminism. Attempts at Australian work since that time have been whimsical and unhappy, not always the fault of the artists but of the company's internal divisions. Last year the Australian content was the first to be discarded.

What is left of Nimrod today? Not a building, even, nor a policy. Only a name. And a name that burdens the Seymour's future intentions. Until now the York Theatre, built in the Guthrie-inspired three-quarters round, has been no more than an unsatisfactory transfer house for proscenium-arch productions. Richard Cottrell has already demonstrated with *Arms and the Man* that he can use that stage better than any director. With his track record at the Prospect and Royal Shakespeare companies, the chances are that he will make us better Shakespeare than others have done. Sydney's directors have not been good on Shakespeare: the Old Tote's rare attempts were unhappy; after a couple of tries the STC have left well alone.

In a pluralist theatre there should be a place for a company recreating for Australians the drama of the past—in fact a pluralist theatre that fails to do so might fairly be charged with barbarism. It was, after all, John Bell who taught us to see *Hamlet* straight and on ice with Australian eyes during the fun-time of the 70s. Cottrell too, with his understanding of classic genre, could earn a place in the Australian psyche by examining the sources of our own drama which lie, whether we like it or not, in the 'appropriate social forms' of the English, Irish and European greats.

Basically, the problem of the Nimrod is a bureaucratic one of state/federal rivalry and one of the funding bodies' own making. There is no machinery by which a new venture can take over the funding options of an old one. If there were, the Nimrod ghost could have departed the scene long ago.

The issues are these: Sydney University needs a theatre company to occupy the Seymour Centre and public funding to maintain its building. The State Government needs such a company for the same reason and so is backing Nimrod with new money after old. The Theatre Board, on the other hand, is strapped for funds and looking for what it can throw back

Jenny Coopes' cartoon as published alongside Bob Ellis' contribution to the debate in the *Sydney Morning Herald*, 18 December 1985.

at the states. It has passed the buck to Council and is now offering practical funding on the original application of $345,000. Without Australia Council support the company will fold.

It has been an emotional issue for the Theatre Board, attempting to pension off Nimrod, the once-mighty hunter of the ocker theatre. But the old man had little fight left when he lost the roof over his head last year. Dragging him into an alien institution has proved fatal. He had already died once after the move from Nimrod to Belvoir Street in 1974. This time let him rest in peace. Then let's look at the proposal for something entirely different—a second major theatre company for the city of Sydney in 1986.

[As we go to press the Nimrod Theatre Company has yet to make a decision on the Australia Council's offer of $100,000 for 1986.]

Following publication of this article I received a letter from Paul Iles accusing me of xenophobia in calling the two men 'all-British', and stating he had been in Australia for seven years, was a naturalised Australian citizen and had promoted more

Australian plays than any other theatre administrator. Richard Cottrell was, and is, an Australian resident. Iles returned to the British theatre soon after. 'Mo' is a reference to the Nimrod logo by Martin Sharp, based on the stage face of the comedian Roy Rene (Mo). In Genesis Nimrod is 'a mighty hunter before the Lord' (10: v.9).

In the event, the Theatre Board did provide the needed money but it only delayed the inevitable. Nimrod closed in 1987. The arguments in this article are valid but in retrospect I did not take sufficient account of Sydney's changing climate, which saw the youthquake age and materialism replace quality-of-life. The Seymour Centre did not gain another theatre company but gradually Belvoir Street filled Sydney's gap.

PART VII
RETROSPECTION

During the 1980s I was occupied with managing the publishing business and continued to write occasional addresses advancing the cause of Australian theatre. Philip retired from the University of NSW in 1986 and began a series of experiments into Elizabethan stage practices. His partners in this were Wayne Harrison, at the time dramaturg of the Sydney Theatre Company, later director (1990–99) and the director and designer John Senczuk. In the glow of the forthcoming Bicentenary in 1988 Currency Press took on the monumental project of publishing a series of reference books on the performing arts. Philip, reluctantly, undertook the general editorship of our *Companion to Theatre in Australia*. While he did not live to see it published in 1995, it remains his legacy to the Australian theatre. He died in June 1993 after living with cancer for four years.

My journalism, thus far, had been directed to the future, in the hope of guiding by observation the work of actors, directors and playwrights, and by debating the decisions of the managers and funding bodies. From the mid-1980s, however, I had many opportunities to reflect on journalism and publishing, the practices of which had already radically changed; and my growing restlessness at the way the arts and literature were being tamed and manipulated by conservative interests. Dr Timothy Pascoe's observation about the arts in 1981, that work exhibited one year by an avant-garde gallery would be adopted by advertising the next, had come to pass. And yet, in the theatre, the creative and subversive forces that underpinned the New Wave revolution were no longer remembered. By the turn of the 1990s I was beginning see these labours as history and it offered me an opportunity to discuss the uses and misuses of art in a wider social and political context.

These reflections were first committed to paper on the occasion of Currency Press's twentieth anniversary. A party was held at the Wharf Theatre on 15 September 1991 at which a group of fine actors performed excerpts from our published plays, and we launched *Entertaining Australia*, the first by-product of the *Companions* research project. Philip and I were deeply moved by the occasion, particularly by the quality of the plays represented; but we were also troubled by the surprise behind their reception. Currency titles had, within a few years, reached into every secondary school and university in Australia; and yet the theatre itself had continued to discard this bookshelf evidence and pursue the new. The same thoughts came to me after a further ten years when, on my retirement, the Australian National Playwrights Conference held an evening of readings in Canberra. Barely a dozen titles—and fewer authors—were known to the actors and audience present.

We are a conservative country and yet we are not good at conservation. Hope of security seems, paradoxically, to lie in the next big thing. In the theatre when faced with the classics our response is a shallow one. Our lack of historical understanding prevents our trusting our masterpieces. We try to rearrange the work to make something superficially more accessible, for no better reason than that we lack the temperament to go deeper. Revivals of any kind are still rare and a response to crisis rather than opportunity. This particularly applies to the idea of an Australian repertoire. Titles become familiar to the general public because we study them at school, not because we see them in the theatre. How many times has Peter Kenna's *A Hard God* been revived? Or Jack Davis' *No Sugar*? Every theatre must have its war horses and in the classical theatre, as in opera and ballet companies, reviving the out-of-date is their mission.

This failure to conserve is endemic to all aspects of our performing arts—talent, creative teams, developmental programs—and equally we have failed to recognise social change and the arts' role in observing and reflecting it. But in 1991 it was morality that was concerning me. We had been through the 1980s. The theatre had suffered the cutbacks of the Fraser Government, the ceiling funding to the big companies which—permanently, as it turned out—diminished the independence of the Australia Council. Having sought to bring the business world onto the boards of these companies, the Council now found them blazing a path directly to Canberra. Eventually the Council brought them back into the tent by settling for a Major Organisations Board; but the members remain well protected by their connections.

In 1986 a genuine attempt was made to increase accessibility, downsize the Council; and reduce the drain on the public purse by encouraging better administration. This was a parliamentary inquiry into Commonwealth assistance to the arts chaired by Leo McLeay. It had virtues, the chief of which was that for the first time it took into account the whole of government's involvement. We sneered at it at the time, particularly its suggestion of devolving and decentralising the powers of the Australia Council; but in retrospect its overview is worth reconsidering.

A further major revolution of the 1980s was the decision of John Dawkins, the

Minister for Education in the Hawke Labor Government, to amalgamate universities and colleges of advanced education. It was a fatal error brought about firstly by the conflation of Education and Training into the one portfolio. This muddied the distinction between the two terms, understood by everyone employed in the business of education and training but disregarded by our law makers. The two, of course, are not incompatible but the environments in which they are taught are. Today our universities are reaping the whirlwind; generations of students whose interest has narrowed from seeking an understanding of the world and their place in it, to qualifying for a job.

Business, in 1991, was also in tumult. The rush of speculation that followed the floating of dollar in 1983 had led to the crash of 1987. A lot of corporations had lost their heads, CEOs trained to an industry—the public service too—were being replaced by Harvard MBAs with American salaries and no practical experience of their sector. The Berlin Wall had fallen and the New Europe was being hailed as a new economic zone; while in Beijing the students of Tiananmen Square had been gunned down for mistakenly believing in the promise of a new deal.

This was the moment when I thought a serious statement about the arts was in order. The speech later found its audience on radio and in the press but a party at the Wharf was not the moment for reflection. The address was somewhat mystical, enlisting Matthew Arnold's holistic view of culture, as a force for harmony and collaboration, to an argument of why we need the arts:

The reasons are simplicity itself. We need them because, in this time of economic rationalism and information overload, we need our mysteries—our myths—we need imagination and we need people who understand human nature. And we need these things very badly…

Within this total humane vision the creative artists in our community play a vital role. Along with our pure scientists, they are able to pursue truth in a disinterested way, regardless of the practical consequences. But it is a larger truth they pursue. They are those rare people who make connections in the life around us and translate them for us simply and powerfully, who direct our attention to the real priorities of life, who have the wisdom to see life steadily and see it whole. These are our writers, our philosophers, our painters, our composers, our stage interpreters. They are the guardians of civilisation's values, and in this so-called value-free society we need such people very badly.

Now if we look at the arts today from Arnold's perspective we begin to get a very different view from the current one. They no longer remain an optional extra, a hobby or entertainment to relieve the tedium of the serious business of living, but a resource with the power to transform our whole outlook upon life and make it richer, deeper and more harmonious. The more one thinks about this, the more one realises that the arts have in the 20th century been excluded from the mainstream of human discourse by the scientific approach itself: they have been deconstructed and rendered harmless; they have been categorised and assembled inside cultural centres, galleries and museums. And the artists themselves, along with the philosophers, historians and teachers, have been similarly marginalised from the 'practical' aspects of our life. Today our educational institutions are being forced to become information factories that teach functional skills but not how to think broadly or communicate clearly. But how can human beings function if they do not understand their own capacities? ('The Good Country and the Arts', 15 September 1991)

The sentiments were beyond imagining then and more so today. In composing them I was much influenced by the American educator Harold Taylor, whose understanding of the moral force and cultural possibilities of the arts is profound. But even as I was writing it the fight for respect for artistic endeavour was being lost. Worse, there was not even a fight. Until 1968 art and commerce had coexisted contentedly on separate territory. But a barrier between them had been arbitrarily erected by government, who went about setting them up in competition by supplying art with capital. This sent the commercial theatre into depression and forced the arts to become financially accountable. An enlightened government and a more thoughtful arts sector might have drawn up a long-term strategy directed to a common purpose; but our governments have never done better than tolerate the arts and within the arts themselves the wall between practice and theory, workers and thinkers, has been virtually insurmountable.

The Origins of Subsidy

That historical division was the subject of my inaugural Philip Parsons Memorial Lecture at the Wharf Theatre in December 1993. Philip had died in June and an annual address had been instituted by the NSW Ministry of the Arts. He had been determined to restore respect for the amateur theatre's contribution to our history with a substantial *Companion* entry; so I chose this as the subject of the lecture.

The one entry he wanted to write himself was the entry on amateur theatre. In the end it fell to me to take up his notes and complete the task. In the process I came to realise why he had been so insistent that amateur theatre be given a respected place in this volume. It is, in fact, the key to the personality of the Australian theatre today. I would go so far as to say that the health of our performing arts today is the legacy, not of the profession but of the amateur movement; and that throughout our history every original idea and progressive development has been advanced, directly or indirectly, not through the professional but through the amateur theatre. I believe we need to look at this history if we are to understand the structure and outlook of our subsidy systems; the changes in our commercial theatre, the dilemmas of our state theatres and the reasons why so many regional companies have failed. And further, I believe that after 25 years of government support we are narrowing, rather than broadening our perspective of the content, style and purpose of theatre: that subsidy and the media have created a procrustean bed into which we must fit our expectations of art and cultural expression. ('Yesterday the World, Tomorrow Australia', 1 December 1993)

This viewpoint is better understood today than it was then. It was greeted largely with bemusement, if not hostility. The amateur origins of most of our leading actors was, like our convict past, still something to suppress. I supported my argument with background on the improvisations of the colonial period, the aspirations of high art that came with the socially-responsible realist theatre, and from the 1920s the rise of amateur art-theatre, music and ballet companies, provided with professional teaching staff. Yet, in the 1960s and 1970s, the taint of 'amateurism' underwrote the thinking of those (largely British-trained) practitioners leading the campaigns on government subsidy. Legislation was brought against these groups that had supported legitimate theatre for fifty years, declaring only non-profit organisations with a board of righteous citizens would be eligible for government largesse.

Today at last we have realised the dream of those gurus of earlier generations: subsidy has enabled us to create a theatre artistic in purpose and professional in execution. The mission proclaimed by our major theatre companies is not to 'give the audience what it wants', as J. C. Williamson believed: or even, in Harry M. Miller's terms, to give them more than they expect. Their manifestos derive from the tradition of the amateur theatre: they contain sentiments about self-expression, education, and fulfilling the needs of the community.

And yet, at the outset, in our determination to create a profession comparable with anywhere in the world—the pursuit of excellence, as we have called it—we drove wedges between the community theatre and the profession, the universities and the profession; and even the profession and the commercial theatre. The very sources of the original inspiration and the very barriers they aspired to overcome...

The cost of this fragmentation has been high for the profession. At the outset of subsidy in 1968 commercial theatres were being demolished because there was no authoritative voice to prevent it. Today state companies are trapped in cultural centres of government devising, forcing them to become big business, but without the old JCW circuit to join for profit. Instead they have large corporate investors who demand dividends not in cash but in public exposure, cultural kudos and extra-mural fun for the executives. This seems to me to be more demeaning and less honourable than turning a quid... Government, in its insistence upon 'professionalism' on the one hand and a non-profit structure on the other, and pressured by the increasing demands upon its budget; has become more and more autocratic and bureaucratic, forcing artists to conform to accepted structures and strictures in the name of accountability.

That was 1993. The established amateur groups, waving the banner of 'the world's best plays', died in the 1970s. Since then we have seen cultural centres rise and temporary venues made permanent. But we have also seen the next generation, nationalistic companies of professionally-trained performers living hand-to-mouth on occasional project funding and the whims of public policy, die of exhaustion. Today there is little activity left in the middle ground. Most companies who survived succeeded in clambering onto the raft of triennial funding offered by the Major Organisations Unit. Those who failed died away or remained in the fringe world of independents.

The Rise of Aboriginal Theatre

In 1995 at an Australian literature conference at Vasser College, Poughkeepsie, Conneticut I reflected on the rise of one nationalist genre that gained a foothold in the 1970s: the Aboriginal performing arts. Of all the sectors within the arts this was one that truly represented our aspirations for a 'necessary' theatre. It sprang spontaneously from several sources: in Melbourne from the late 1960s with actor Jack Charles and the Nindethana group associated with the New Theatre and the APG. In Sydney it can be dated from the return of the director Brian Syron from the

Zac Martin as Sweet William and Justine Saunders as Ruby in the Black Theatre production of *The Cake Man*, 1975. (Photo: Robert Walker)

USA in 1968, his work on Kevin Gilbert's then fragmented play *The Cherry Pickers* (1971) and Robert Merritt's *The Cake Man* (1975). In Perth the poet Jack Davis' theatre-in-education play *Kullark* in 1979 led to a career in the mainstream as a leading playwright. Spontaneous events like Nimrod's revue *Basically Black* (1972) began to appear. Drama was seized as a platform for the civil rights movement and has grown as a powerful means of conveying to white—and black—audiences the emotional impact of public policy upon the recent history of Aboriginal society.

The essential quality that emerged from this early writing was a liberating humour in which the companionship of domestic life is celebrated. It was a revelation, something in which few white Australians had been privileged to participate. The white theatre collaborated in providing structural support and an introduction to the practices of theatre. Committed writers like John Romeril in Melbourne had introduced Aboriginal characters into their work. In Perth the director Andrew Ross had a close association with the work of Jack Davis and in 1982 founded the Swan River Stage Company (later the Black Swan Theatre Company) to support black performers and writers. In Sydney *The Cake Man* drew attention to the infant Black Theatre of Redfern before joining the mainstream. In 1983 it represented Australia in a World Theatre Festival season in Denver, Colorado.

Aboriginal theatre's crowning achievement, to date, however, remains Jimmy Chi's musical *Bran Nue Dae* (1989), conceived in Broome, assembled in Perth.

Bran Nue Dae in 1989 was a turning point in the short history of Aboriginal writing for the theatre. Twenty years of evolution: in writers, political activists, actors, dancers, singers and song-writers, preceded it. It was, surprisingly, only in the 1960s that Aboriginal writers began to be published in numbers which could be recognised as a body of work. This occurred as part of a gathering force of activism by a politically aware post-war generation of Aborigines and of white young people, particularly university students. In 1961 Aborigines had finally been given the vote. In 1965 Northern Territory Aboriginal pastoral workers were awarded equal pay with whites; in 1966 the first major land-rights strike took place; and in 1967 a national referendum overwhelmingly voted in favour of transferring judicial responsibility for Aboriginal welfare from the states to the Commonwealth Government. Isolated protests over local issues, mainly of living conditions on reserves, became by degrees an organised civil rights movement which gained confidence from the parallel movement in the United States. Coordinated protest had so far been impeded by traditional tribal rivalries and the diversity of languages. Skirmishes, massacres and protests had been rural and isolated; and many of them shamefully buried in a conspiracy of silence. What we had from the 1960s, by contrast, was a modern, open campaign led by urban leaders and using the weapons of politics and the mass media. ('The Future in Black and White', IDEA '95—2nd world congress of drama/theatre and education.)

Bran Nue Dae is the story of a boy called Tadpole who runs away from Broome to Perth and back again, and the people he meets on the way. The simplicity of the story belies the intellectual toughness of the mind that composed it. It is a story of interrelatedness, and had a benevolent effect not only upon its mixed audiences but upon the black communities. Many had been struggling with internecine debates about the appropriation of their stories and songs into these new art forms; and performers themselves appearing in roles that crossed tribal boundaries. *Bran Nue Dae*'s theme song, became a national anthem through the 1990s:

> There's nothing I would rather be
> Than to be an Aborigine

Chi's call for racial unity and celebration has since not been widely heard by the black theatre, any more than by the white. The black theatre's stories have remained largely personal, relating the pain of the stolen generation's displacement and other issues of identity and abuse. Recently the experience of urban Aborigines seeking their lost family and country has begun to surface. But much of the energy that went into that storytelling has now more effectively moved into film.

One quality to which Jack Davis' work drew my attention is what is called 'Aboriginal reality', the coexistence of both present material reality and a spiritual, telepathic reality, represented in various ways, often by ancestral figures. This has not developed in the theatre the way I had expected but has found its place instead in modern dance forms, particularly in the work of the Bangarra Dance Company, founded in 1989 and now a leading performance group with an international reputation. The other manifestation of two realities is to be found in the adoption of story-telling as a theatre form. With the rise of trained performers an increasing number have developed a confessional form of solo performance, beginning with Eva Johnson's *What Do They Call Me?* (1990), a three-part monologue, and Deborah Mailman's performance of *Seven Stages of Grieving* (1995). Ningali Lawford, Leah Purcell, David Gulpilil, Noel Tovey, Tammy Anderson and David Page are only some of the fine artists who have taken to the road, inviting audiences into their lives, re-thinking praise and blame, searching for lost origins, asserting their modern identity. We have the performers now and we have seen glimpses of what could be but we still await the emergence of an art form in the theatre that has its origins in an Aboriginal way of life.

That's a big ask. I suppose I am recalling the experience of finding *The Legend of King O'Malley*, back in 1970. The excitement lay not so much in the quality of the performance or the script, but in the communal energy, the sense of discovery, which said to me: 'Now we know what we are looking for'. I regained that triumphant feeling at the opening of *Bran Nue Dae* but it has not been repeated. Was it the lack of money that closed that path? (Chi's *Corrugation Road* was less successful.) Or was the show's gritty, satirical optimism not contagious? There hasn't been a lot for any of us to celebrate lately.

Creative Nation

The arts had a brief moment of hope and disillusion when in 1994 the Labor Government's *Creative Nation* statement was published: 'There has probably never been a better time than the present', it read, 'to reassess our national cultural policy':

> Australia, like the rest of the world, is at a critical moment in its history. Here, as elsewhere, traditional values and ideologies are in flux and the speed of global economic and technological change has created doubt and cynicism about the ability of national governments to confront the future. What is distinctively Australian about our culture is under assault from homogenised international mass culture.
>
> Ironically, our culture has never been more vital than it is now. At every level of society, Australians are engaged in cultural activities that are helping to re-invent the national identity, and most Australians would agree on the need to enhance and enrich our culture. To achieve this, cultural policy must enter the mainstream of federal policy-making. (*Creative Nation, Commonwealth Cultural Policy*, Canberra: Commonwealth of Australia 1994, p.1)

Brave words. And it is an impressive document drawn up by an eminent and caring advisory panel. In it they set out a Charter of Cultural Rights:

1.   The right to an education that develops individual creativity and appreciation of the creativity of others;
2.   The right of access to our intellectual and cultural heritage;
3.   The right to new intellectual and artistic works; and
4.   The right to community participation in cultural and intellectual life.

'Appreciation' and 'access' are the key words here. Sadly, *Creative Nation* made the same mistake as Nugget Coombs in the 1960s: of viewing the arts as product. The document opens new options for training and audience development, asserts the financial value of an artist's continuing moral rights to own the work and the financial benefit of public library lending rights, but betrays no more recognition than the IAC Inquiry or the McLeay Report, that until we have an industrial structure that allows more than 10 per cent of practitioners a way of exercising their skills lucratively at their art, no amount of education and appreciation will increase its vitality. And in recent years there has been less and less logic in the relationship, if such there is, between educational institutions and the professions they profess to supply. Most theatre, music and creative arts graduates have little hope of ever using these skills in paid performance. Before the Dawkins Plan such courses within universities were not practice-oriented and did not make such promises. Instead they offered a humane education as a basis for acquiring practical skills elsewhere. Today universities have brought this skills training onto the campus. NIDA, for example, offers an accredited BA degree. All this has added to students' expectations of a living on demand. But since 1999 feature film making has taken a nosedive. NIDA, once criticised for abandoning principles to feed the television industry, since the decline of ABC and SBS arts programming, has found even that outlet barred.

News and Entertainment

The change of government in 1996 brought with it, with a bang, the era of practical politics and practical reconciliation. A collection of essays called *Critical Perspectives,* which I edited for the Geraldine Pascall Foundation, gave me an opportunity to rail at the changes taking place in the press and the media: the presentation of news as entertainment; the manipulation of language and the illusion of intimacy created by television. I raised these issues in a speech at the Sydney Institute.

I believe that we are losing the power to imagine. I see an attack upon imagination at all levels in public life:

1. on television, meaning is collapsed into a kind of visual muzak;
2. in the education system, universities are stripped of any sense of the contestability of knowledge, geared instead to notions of quantifiable outcomes;
3. in the prevailing political ideology, the limitations imposed by economic reality are not only accepted but have become an end in themselves in the form of economic rationalism;
4. in the de-legitimising of intellectual discussion which has made the assault upon the ABC possible;
5. and lately I see it in the arts.

A curious paradox obtains today in our public life. The arts have been subsidised, industrialised and mainstreamed into amusement and advertising until they now reflect the needs of government and corporations. At the same time so arid has our capacity for empathy become, and so adversarial our attitudes to public issues, that in order to raise these issues in the public mind they must be shaped and dramatised. No news item on television can be related without an enactment or a graphic. The only way we can imagine ourselves into someone else's real-life dilemma is to make a comparison with fiction. 'It's like a Tarantino movie', we say. 'It's like something out of Dickens.' The more our parliamentarians and public figures talk of practical politics, the more they seek dramatic impact for their statements; the more these statements are edited, dramatised and subjected to photo opportunities. Where once our leaders ruminated in oratory, expecting and receiving our time and consideration, today they master the ten-second grab. The world has changed irrevocably since Vance Packard wrote *The Hidden Persuaders* and Richard Nixon's five o'clock shadow became the focus of a presidential election. Demand for instant gratification imposes other people's imagination upon our own, leaving us with an illusion of communication, of involvement in the exchange of ideas, of involvement in the democratic process; but which remains nothing more than that—an illusion.

Television, which more than any medium gives rise to that illusion, is a further paradox. It brings into our lives public figures and events with a degree of intimacy which no previous century could have imagined; and which even film cannot reproduce. And yet it discourages understanding. Put a debate on TV and the bulk of viewers change the channel. TV is antipathetic to argument; words are a minor adjunct to the power of colour, movement and music. TV has trained us to react within the narrowest of spectrums but not to engage. ('Amusing Ourselves to Death', Sydney Institute, 9 September 1997)

The speech went on to examine the funeral of Princess Diana, which had just gripped the western world, and the mass illusion of personal loss which it created. I reminded the audience that the forces at work were those of propaganda, the tool of mass disempowerment; and that it was a responsibility of the arts, which practise the skills employed in mass adoration and wedge politics, to be a social critic.

The originality, the lustful energy, the apparent lack of inhibition and in the case of indigenous art the arcane mystery; all these things are matters of astonishment to other countries, that so much talent comes from so small a population. And yet it is not being used as a social force for the public good. The artist's voice, which has always been a clarion call for change, is today hardly heard in the community. The arts patrons are heard, the government servants are heard, celebrities litter the newspapers. But when it comes to the big issues, the issues of God and Death, as Phillip Adams would call them, the arts is silent...

So, of what practical use are our arts and our artists? Can they help employment? Solve the Wik debate? Diminish greenhouse gases? Achieve industrial harmony? The answer is yes. Because they listen and observe. Because they make connections. Because they create fictions which reveal a truth. Because they challenge the accepted. Because they integrate the disparate. And lastly because they exercise the imagination. It takes imagination to foresee the consequences of our actions; it takes imagination to hear patiently the unwelcome facts, to see the other person's point of view; it takes imagination to embrace the abstract; to conceive of alternative ways of thinking, ways of living, ways of believing; to mend the fragmentation of modern life; to reduce the complex to the simple; to know when to hold one's peace. It takes imagination to engage in a disinterested debate. We are crying out for government to use their imagination.

At the top now we Australians are deeply divided: the country is in open revolt against the city; miners from conservationists; whites from Aborigines; Caucasians from Asians; the employed from the unemployed. Racism is a predictable response to our sense of powerlessness, our need to have someone outside ourselves to blame. People at the grass roots, however, know that reconciliation is essential to survival. Individual pastoral leases have made their own treaties; communities are forming action groups to address their own relationships; Aboriginal communities, in the past alienated from each other by tribal allegiances, are more and more united; and producing spokespeople of such magnanimity that our white leaders are simply outclassed. By the time the government succeeds in passing its ten-point Wik legislation—if it ever does—the many disparate communities of this great country will have already made their own reconciliations.

This was well before September 11, before the Bali bombing, the Tampa and SIEV–X incidents. Former Prime Minister Paul Keating recently commented about his successor: 'He's made an art form out of sadness and sorrow, rather than painting the picture of optimism and enlargement ... one would hope the cultural legacy is not one which is about some shared mourning or some foreboding about catastrophes.' (*SMH Weekend Edition* 28–29 May 2005, p.32) Which led me to the thought: would we have been a more thoughtful country if the photo opportunity had not become such a powerful tool? Would we have viewed Robert Menzies, for example, differently, had he appeared in living colour every night on television?

The Misuses of Language

In 1997, I found the issue of language manipulation related to these feelings of growing helplessness and manipulation. Any person whose business is words, is alert to the way that meaning changes but characteristic of this time was the way that meaning moved in the direction of profit and vested interest. Along with the privatisation of public services like electricity and transport, the word 'service' itself was disappearing from their titles. Intransitive verbs like 'grow' and 'progress' were being turned into transitive verbs to empower the subject. 'My business is growing' has become 'I am growing my business.' 'My work is progressing' is now 'I am progressing my work.' We have lost the proper meaning of that usefully un-emotive word 'disinterest', meaning divested of interest or impartial, today subsumed to mean apathy. And with the loss of the defining word comes the loss of the thing itself. So noticeable have such changes become that collections of manipulating and obfuscating language have made it into the best-seller lists.

As scholarship became competitive within the universities and research funding dwindled, obfuscation, or 'encraption' as one wit called it, became a disease among academics. Having as an editor been a victim of the epidemic I gave vent to my feelings at a 'The Scholar and the Stage Symposium' in Sydney in 1998. In this I recalled the rise of relativism and the gradual replacement during the 1960s of immutable texts with those of popular culture. The Dawkins reforms, I pointed out, came just as universities were attempting to come to terms with these confusions of increasing diversity—perhaps even because they were engrossed in doing so:

The philosophical upheaval within the universities meant that they were by this time no longer purveying the eternal truths in which my generation believed: government had to seek a practical model elsewhere. They chose the wrong model: the economic model. Staff gradually lost their tenure, funding diminished, the language moved from 'receiving an education' to 'purchasing a degree'. And now in the 1990s departments are being closed down as budgets are cut and the functional approach to education dictates which are the 'necessary' disciplines.

This apparent defencelessness, in my observation, has had a further debilitating effect on the expression of intellectual opinion; and encouraged territoriality. The pressures of increasing workloads, increasing competitiveness and job insecurity are making university staff self-protective and fearful. Now a new threat to the quality of education is causing further division: the level of literacy and diversity of culture among secondary students today.

There is no question that Australia's immigration has enriched our life enormously since assisted passages were introduced in 1947. And we can be proud that the great majority of our immigrants have been accommodated without the civil strife other countries have seen. We are proud of what we now call our pluralist society. What we have not yet learnt how to assimilate, much less appreciate, is that very cultural baggage—cultural capital it has come to be called—which all of us bring to language and to every other part of our lives.

Our institutions, on their part, have been accommodating. They have introduced affirmative action for students from non-English-speaking families, in relation to their grasp of written English and historical background. Our support of the disadvantaged has on the whole been exemplary. I would even go so far as to suggest that the new criticism, led by debates on post-colonialism and hybridisation, has been an enlightened response to this new mongrel society which we have become. The down side of this affirmative action, however, is that students, encouraged by the amalgamation of further education systems into university culture, are daily facing failure in their grasp of vocabulary, of comprehension and of cultural reference. I was only last month in Tokyo at a meeting at which these issues were raised about South-east Asia and Canada. Australia is not alone in this. Again the cause is the economic model imposed on an intellectual pursuit.

It's a question of values—what we value and how we measure it. In order for something to be valued it has to be defined; and in order for it to be protected or funded it must be measurable. And because the whole framework of our value system has been undermined by relativism; by the diversity of imported cultures; by White Australia's too recent recognition of the meaning of Aboriginality; and by the supervention of the global village; we have had to discard a great many imponderables in order to find ourselves a stable measure. The one we found was the currency of the marketplace.

But the things we value most are generally not a part of this particular metaphor. Our children, for example, are a pretty poor investment in material terms. And more intangible assets like clean air, a rich culture, ethics, religious belief, language, the arts, health and education. The things, in fact, which we would define as necessary to a civilised society. So in order to prove their worth, to keep their presence from being marginalised in the public debate, we change the terms we use to discuss them and force them into the economic mould.

As soon as we realise how inadequate, how ill-equipped economics is to measure value, the problem becomes clear. Government and business will never defend the university, only society will. And instead of cutting themselves off from society academics have a responsibility to embrace it. This doesn't mean popularisation, it means engagement. The arts particularly are in the best possible position to exploit and accommodate cultural diversity. Universities have largely lost the ability to engage with society. But the more they alienate themselves from the public, the more they lose faith with their greatest ally.

This changing language is a symptom of the changing values of our society and we could say the universities led the way when they took up the challenge of determining what was relevant; what objectivity meant, what was the meaning of significance. For it is university-educated people who walk the corridors of power. It is our peers who have grasped hold of the wrong metaphor and we have all conspired in this because we have left ourselves without a defence.

Among the most important responsibilities a university has is to teach a real understanding of language and its purposes. So much of the confusion in public debate today lies in the misunderstanding, misuse and manipulation of language. So much within universities is about correctness. It is becoming more and more difficult to conduct a disinterested debate, to define terms or to examine an unpopular opinion. A civilised country should not have to present performance indicators to defend the need for music and literature; or to examine the arguments in favour of limiting or expanding immigration. All social, and social justice, issues deserve free and fair debate. Regrettably, today, to express a view is to state an allegiance—and there's an end of it. ('Literacy, language and the Public Intellectual', 1998)

The Legacy of Subsidy

The performing arts were following much the same pattern. Within the Australia Council the Freedom of Information Act 1982 had stemmed the free flow of opinion within its walls. Mission statements, performance indicators, 1 per cent efficiency savings, not to mention sponsorship challenges and awards—and the apparatus that comes with these demands—were overtaking the subsidised organisations. In 1999 I gave a couple of addresses at the University of Western Australia directed at my concern at the entrenchment of various forces.

Firstly, the encasement of art in concrete. I used to be fond of saying that until the twentieth century theatres burnt down every ten years. And that was indeed true of Australia. This ensured flexibility for those working in the most ephemeral of arts. The great joy of the theatre revolution in the late 1960s, as my early chapters show, is the improvisation that directed the work and the found spaces in which they were performed. 'Don't make your audience too comfortable', Tyrone Guthrie said when his Minneapolis Tyrone Guthrie Theatre was being planned. And it is demonstrably true that the more comfortable an audience is, the less it is encouraged to use the imagination. Festivals are pressed to become bigger and bigger; special effects more and more dazzling. And the more that is provided the less attention is given to meaning and the more quickly the spectacle is forgotten. At the very moment when Sydney was pulling down its Victorian theatres and the new generation were creating their own venues, our masters were building, or planning to build, grand cultural centres in which to house the kind of work of which they believed we might one day be capable.

In the late 60s Philip and I went to visit Jørn Utzon at his home in Denmark. And at that meeting he described his plans for the interior of the Opera House, which by then he had been prevented from completing. He talked about the movement through the building in terms of a symphony: how in the slow opening movement the audience would walk up his grand Mayan staircase, and enter the foyer, how the colour, grey at first, would gradually increase in volume and variation as one entered the hall and conclude triumphantly as one took one's seat facing John Coburn's great curtain of the sun. All I could think of, as he was talking, was: what on earth do we have to put behind that curtain which could possibly fulfil these expectations? For nothing in the theatre ensures failure more certainly than too high an expectation in the audience. At that time the Australian Opera was still in its infancy and federal subsidy for the arts was only 12 months old.

The Opera House has fulfilled Utzon's dream of reflecting the quality of the city and becoming a building for the people. Day and night there are crowds around it. Every public celebration is centred on Bennelong Point. But only the select negotiate the complexities of ticketing to attend the performances. The staff work hard and imaginatively to increase use, with free concerts, philharmonic choirs; conventions, children's events. But the message of grandeur, of self-importance, is embedded in the overarching beams. It's the message every such public building has put out since the Comédie Française was built for the perpetuation of French tradition. It is not a message Shakespeare ever received.

The act of building the Opera House, and the centres in other states that followed, committed our major companies to a style of performance quite alien to the egalitarian nature of our society. Informality, community and active participation are the essential components of our mass activity: at sports matches, pub gigs, dance parties, street parades and so on. We are not short of audiences. Kids today know how to sniff out places without the aid of marketing. But our major arts organisations, trapped inside their edifices, have no chance of testing the mood of an audience: they are committed to timetables half a decade ahead. Seasons are cast, sets and costumes are budgeted and designed long before the director and conductor have begun to think about the work. It's an assembly line. Can anything be more meaningless? ('Cultural Policy and the National Debt' address to the X Club, University of WA, 5 October 1999)

And, of course, can anything be less economic? And yet the higher the cost the greater the need to preserve the asset. I commented that the Nugent Report spells this out in detail and argues persuasively ways of preserving the status quo: 'But no part of the report raises the question of whether their work is appropriate to Australia in 1999, whether we have invested our money in the wisest way. What to do about these mausoleums we built for our artists. Most particularly it failed to comment on whether all this globalised "art" has any meaning for Australians and whether our artists have the theatre they deserve.'

One of the big opportunities still awaiting the major organisations depends on a recognition of the distinction between globalisation and internationalism. *Phantom of the Opera* is globalisation; *Cloudstreet* is internationalism. It is not the work that needs to be standardised but the industrial structure; the network by which the success of a work can be maximised. We have seen how our Aboriginal artists have found their way to the major art galleries of the world; we've seen how movies like *Strictly Ballroom* and *Shine* have defied their lack of genre. But none of these works have yet made a proper financial return to their creators. That is where we need to corporatise and globalise.

All the innovation in this country has come, not from government, or big business or the legislature or the Church. Such authorities respond only when they have to: to electoral pressure and to practical results. Innovation comes from the individual and the small community interests. And it comes out of crisis. When we can't go further in one direction we are forced to seek another. The arts have reached that crisis. It's time to look around at what other interests are doing; to take lessons from the methods of the country communities in crisis; or the reconciliation movement. To forget the divisions between artistic genres and build again from the bottom. Divisions only remain as long as does the status quo.

At this point I went on to talk about football and how within a few years local loyalties and cohesion have crumbled before the commercial bulldozers. Since then we have seen the breakdown of ethical standards within these clubs, who buy and sell teenage players with too much testosterone and too little common sense. And by contrast South Sydney Rugby League, the struggling custodian of the league's working-class history, fought the Murdoch machine to the High Court to prove that community commitment has more stamina than financial investment. Why was anyone surprised? There are lessons in this for the arts community.

Employment

But what is that community? Like university students that once gathered to ruminate and plot in clubs and pubs, the bulk of artists today are too busy working at minimum-pay casual jobs, the only work that gives them the flexibility to accommodate their real work. A pattern they share with single mothers, carers and the disabled. Others are better off, applying their skills variously in advertising, corporate presentation and mentoring, counselling, IT and website design. Too little is known of how widely spread is the network of trained professional performers and musicians throughout our society or how valued is their contribution.

In this the arts are just one sector of society. But a sector now too divided by the hierarchy created to be a force for change. Only the practitioners themselves can create such a force, earn the respect of the community by demonstrating their value to society. There is a film industry lobby, a script writers' lobby; but little is heard from actors and musicians. In 1967 there was a successful TV: Make-it-Australian campaign; in 1982 a national Stage Crisis Day which led to a short-lived Arts Alliance. Something more comprehensive is needed today; a proper university-based study of the arts practitioner's way of life. David Throsby's reports for the Australia Council have set the agenda by demonstrating that over 25 years the rate of employment has not kept pace with expansion. That in 2004 the average earning of an arts practitioner from their art was $30,000. And for visual artists $7,000.

The McLeay Report of 1986 has been the only attempt to deal with the growing hierarchy and seek a way of making the arts more egalitarian and self-sustainable. And the first to look at both government and trade responsibilities. Aspects of the Labor Party had had an involvement in this since 1968, particularly in Victoria. The trade union movement had supported such initiatives as factory performances by the APG; and the federal ALP had a published Arts Policy aimed at a broader view of our culture than the pursuit of excellence. The Arts Action paper mentioned below was 'An Arts Action Policy for the ALP' to the Victorian ALP Arts and Culture Committee, which argues that the elite are not the custodians of excellence.

'The Council', McLeay wrote, 'is by no means the only form of government involvement in the arts. Council funding represents about 6 per cent of government cultural funding in Australia; perhaps 20 per cent of government arts spending'.

The report, quaintly titled 'Patronage, Power and the Muse'—perhaps a kindly attempt by Parliament to adopt the other side's language—made many resolutions, some of which (like triennial funding for major organisations) were implemented; but the argument fell apart on interpretation. While its motives were very much in line with the Arts Action paper of 1974, its resolutions were industry-based, urging means for developing potentially profitable sectors, like the recording industry. The Committee argued 'that the Council's proper field of responsibility is the subsidised arts. With limited exceptions, other, much larger, areas of cultural development are the province of other agencies.' The implication was that, in the scheme of things, the 'subsidised arts' weren't doing much for the economy. Without recognition of due process we can arrive at no other conclusion.

Nevertheless, I wish I had paid more attention to that figure of 6 per cent. There is worth in the idea that the Council stop viewing its constituency as the 'subsidised arts' and take account, as the McLeay Report did, of all levels of creativity. To see the artist's development as the most important component in building a pyramid, of which participation is the base and excellence is the peak. For a start we need to recognise and respect the contribution made to the quality of audiences by encouraging wide participation at the grass roots. In school drama, music and dance; in the amateur festivals; and in the many pro-am cooperatives that survive as long as their energies last; in the daily practice for pleasure. In creation and conversation on the web; in the purchase of CDs, in the enjoyment of radio, TV, concerts and film. All this is not about excellence but about a hundred other things, of which participation is the common element. Then for the improvement of skills we need training and we do have fine schools in every state.

At the next level we need a good look at the sources of employment at the end of the 1990s. We need small ensembles of every kind: avant-garde, popular and classical to give our performers steady practice. We need major production houses for legitimate theatre, classical and popular music; and a circuit of commercial entertainment; and we need distribution mechanisms both nationally and globally. And finally we need national and international stars. Ancillary to these we need a healthy film, recording and television industry; and academic practitioners to undertake research and development and provide the background for history and criticism.

But more than that, at this level we need a proper industrial structure. We need to take a hard look at the cultural real estate that gobbles up so much money. Is it right for our purposes in the new century? We need to see how one art form might advantage another, how the new digital technologies might overcome our isolation; how training in the arts might assist industry in changing its thinking in the conduct of industrial relations—to see the consequences of short-term planning, the advantages of a better environment. And most of all we need proper recognition of how the huge cultural changes, nationally and globally, have changed the way people think about the arts. And about 'excellence'. ('The Arts and the Pre-emptive Buckle', The Sir Frank Callaway Lecture, University of WA 10 October 1999)

The McLeay Report is worth revisiting. On 15 October 1986, following the release of the report, the Australian Theatre Studies Centre at the University of NSW held an all-day conference to debate it. The conference was particularly remarkable for the representation that attended: Leo McLeay, the Shadow Minister for the Arts Senator Stan Collard, the Chair (Donald Horne) and Chief Executive of the Australia Council (Di Yerbury), Professor David Throsby and representatives of the Victorian and Western Australian arts ministries, Actors' Equity, as well as playwrights and arts practitioners. The word spread rapidly that the Government was mounting a wholesale attack on the Australia Council and with a great sense of urgency

Currency put together from the conference a book of papers and opinion, called *Shooting the Pianist: the Role of Government in the Arts*, compiled and edited by Philip Parsons.

It makes interesting reading today, for the unity of the artists' defence of, and respect for, the Australia Council; and the clarity with which they expressed it. That view is captured sardonically in the title, which recalls Oscar Wilde's report of a notice he saw in a Colorado bar: 'Please don't shoot the pianist. He is doing his best.'

That best changed as a result of the report's recommendations and began an erosion of the autonomy enshrined in the 1975 Australia Council Act. The Australia Opera, the Australian Ballet and the Australian Elizabethan Theatre Trust orchestras, who had rebelled at the threat of ceiling funding, were separated into a Major Organisations Board (now Unit) and provided with triennial funding. Soon the State theatre companies followed. A Cultural Development Board was established as a mechanism for widening genre eligibilities, and has had a noble history (though in 2005 is being disbanded). Tax deductibility for donations was legislated under ministerial approval. However, its principal thrust to devolve the smaller companies and applications to the states was defeated by state intervention. And the recommendation that the 'contemporary' music scene and the recording industry be included in policy was dismissed out of hand.

On the darker side, the report recommended higher ministerial intervention in Australia Council affairs, including the submission of budgets and the issuing of ministerial directions. From being a council of peers it became 'the Commonwealth Government's funding and arts advisory body' with a logo to be stamped on all its merchandise.

The endemic problem of perspective, however, condemned the report in the eyes of artists. Philip wrote in his introduction to *Shooting the Pianist*:

> As members of the arts community, representatives of state arts ministries, the Australia Council and Mr McLeay himself rose in turn to speak, it became clear that they were not addressing the same issues, perhaps not even speaking the same language. To artists, support for the arts meant helping artists to create art, and that was exactly what the Australia Council was doing and doing very well. To Mr McLeay, support for the arts meant helping the taxpayer to get the art he or she wanted, and here the artists who call the tune at the Australia Council were clearly out for number one. Artists reacted first with bewilderment, then with alarm to proposals for change based on a failure to understand what art was about. Mr McLeay responded with sardonic patience to all this self-absorbed fiddling while Rome burned; change was in the air, proposals were

before the Minister, decisions were imminent, and if artists were not prepared for constructive debate they must put up with decisions made without them...

The history of the Australia Council, like the history of art, has been fraught with controversy, and of the artists' own making. But the Australia Council has succeeded, developing structures and programs that have met the changing needs of the art. And yet the McLeay Committee has managed to produce a report which not only ignores the contribution of the artist (without whom, as Dorothy Hewett reminded the conference, there would be no art) but represents them in passing as power-hungry, self-seeking and unrealistic.

Why has the artist, the furious centre of the funding debate in the 60s and early 70s, vanished from the thinking of the present inquiry? Because the public perception of the artist today has been replaced by 'the industry'. The arts industry is the invention of the arts lobbyists—themselves an invention of the 70s. To maintain and increase government funding of the arts, these spokesmen turned away from the quality-of-life arguments of the 1960s, which had identified, accurately, the intangible value of the arts to the human spirit, and instead addressed the political managers in their own language. They pointed to benefits created by past funding—spectacular increases in turnover and job creation, spin-off benefits to the tourism industry—and the rationale of arts funding became pre-empted by its incidental benefits. (*Shooting the Pianist: the Role of Government in the Arts.* Sydney: Currency Press 1987, pp.10, 13)

Process and Product

For the practitioner, the decision to tangle with government has proved a mixed blessing. When I recall the lasting influence of the tiny La Mama theatre; how rapidly David Williamson's *The Removalists* leapt from his typewriter to performance in Melbourne, Sydney and London, and how many participated in its success; or how the Sydney Theatre Company's entry into the Opera House Drama Theatre inspired a burst of epic theatre—and how today in the mainstream playwrights are constrained by the stage, the number of actors, by the taste of the sponsors, by the administration of the subscription season—is it any wonder we are, like John Howard, making 'an art form out of sadness and sorrow, rather than painting the picture of optimism and enlargement'?

This year David Williamson, our most successful playwright ever, has announced his retirement. And I was his publisher for 30 years. I look back on that history with pride and admiration but also with the feeling of a work unfinished. Williamson was not only in great part responsible for the building of the great theatres we have today, and their repertoire, he was the captive of it. At the outset in 1968 there was no doubt in Nugget Coombs' mind, or our own, that the cottage industry we were starting would become a viable artistic sector, respected by the world and contributing substantially to the economy. That seeding funding would lead, as in the film industry, to innovation, artistic development and commercial product. My reviews in the early years make it clear that was the intention. But that wedge between commercial and 'high' art intervened, creating instead a culture that disdained popular art and has become increasingly wasteful of its resources.

At the top there is only occasional collaboration between groups outside the exchange of performance spaces. There is limited opportunity to transfer successes directly to another venue. There is no interchange with the commercial theatre. The stage dimensions of the many arts centres are incompatible, adding greatly to touring costs. The domination of the subscription season and the complexities of touring put any idea of spontaneous celebration or festival collaboration out of the question. How can we keep going the process of art if product makes such demands on our resources?

Too many of the middle-sized theatres have closed or play only part of the year. The successful ones are being squeezed by rising costs and fixed seating capacity. The rise of real-estate prices, and noise and fire regulations, have closed many improvised venues for theatre, jazz and pop music. The outpouring of graduates from the training institutions has produced a growing network of cooperatives whose members choose to work independently. Among them one can find physical theatre, mixed media performance, political, documentary work and new writing of all kinds. This well of talent is our future; but without external support each lasts only as long as the energy.

The artist is the loser in all these cases. The preservation of funded venues has made the performer the disposable factor. Within the system people work hard at development and we still do have waves of new writers and performers entering the big houses. But their work is sporadically seen and often short-lived. And rarely have we seen the kind of long-standing creative partnerships of writer, actor and director that make for lasting work.

David Williamson stands out in all this. He made a break for the outside world in 1981 when a consortium of producers underwrote a production of his *Top Silk*. Something went wrong which led him back into the subsidised theatre system and held him to those familiar stages for another twenty years. In lieu of an Australian repertoire he became the war horse, answering the call of his audience, and we responded with devotion. Would he have written differently in a wider, more diverse world? Were there others who followed, or failed to follow, his path only because he was there? And if we had followed that early path towards sustainability that we set ourselves, would we by now have had our own version of Shaftesbury Avenue, with a new generation of entrepreneurs presenting our own favourite writers, composers and actors? We shall never know.

Is there a solution to all this? Not presently so, nor will there be until the practitioners themselves sit down and re-examine their position. We need to reduce unproductive employment by 50 per cent. We need individual artists to be more financially savvy than they presently are. We need to examine the history of the Australia Council and the achievements and consequences of its decision-making. We need to reconsider whether the structure of our boards of management and other external requirements set up in the Council's infancy are still the best governance today. And we need artists to stand up for themselves and earn our respect.

Then we need to draw up a ten-year national strategy aimed not at making bigger and better art but at freeing the artistic process.

Robyn Archer in her essay *The Myth of the Mainstream* is interesting on the subject of process. Product, she says, is the detritus of art.

> What we might buy to put on our wall is the detritus of the real act of painting, which happens in the studio. It's a helpful way of viewing art. You understand that a work is probably never finished, it is just a part of an ongoing process… While as audiences we may enjoy artistic detritus in all its forms, if we focus entirely on the product, we neglect to see just how vitally important the process is. (*Platform Papers 4*, Sydney: Currency House, April 2005, p.32)

It's the same argument Philip put back in 1986:

> The industrial view of the arts will never be able to make sense of a calling where intelligent people are prepared (as the McLeay Committee accepts) to put up with financial deprivation. These people will never have money, or power over others. The only power they will fight for is power on behalf of their art (and then the fighting can be vicious indeed). In the artist at work the industrial view recognises only labour producing a service, a product for a market. But the painter hoping his exhibition will sell out wants not only the money to live on but the assurance that he has discovered a truth and other human beings have seen it and want it on their wall. If the physical end of art is a product or a service, that product or service is itself only the means to a further end in which the final value of the art lies.
>
> Art is closer to religion than industry. As Dorothy Hewett told the conference, both required an act of faith. Consumer product is no more the end of art than the menu was the point of the Last Supper. When the Japanese declare a great artist to be a living treasure they do not mean he is a goldmine. Nor is it the

individual product they are acclaiming. It is the creative artist himself, the truth teller, prophet and celebrant of their world. And the truth-telling enterprise on which he is embarked is a journey of discovery; it is process, not product.

And so it goes on. Australia will need to be a much older, wiser country than it is now before we come anywhere near to resolution.

I've called this book *Not Wrong—Just Different*, because much of its pre-occupations have been consumed with finding expression for who we are, what we could be, what we might have been. Looking back over this career of forty years, at the excitement we all shared in determining public policy and applauding the extraordinary growth of individual talent and national cultural expression, I recognise that both despite and because of government support a huge amount has been achieved. My memory was that in the early days the arts were valued in a way they are not today. That they received huge space in our media and our consciousness in a way that has been lost. The Whitlam period is remembered as a golden period when government expanded funding and conveyed the illusion that it cared. Practitioners were once outspoken and debates have been robust, in the 1960s over the film and TV industry, censorship and the fight for arts funding, in the 1970s and 1980s over a policy and structure for the Australia Council for the Arts; over ceiling funding, triennial funding, the design of new arts centres, financial crises, bankruptcies. Most recently we asserted ourselves over the Free Trade Agreement. I no longer believe that it is the arts that are intrinsically less valued than they were in 1968; but that living is more complicated. And we justify doing nothing by believing we can no longer influence change. Donald Horne has written of those early days as *Time of Hope* when it was still possible for the individual to feel effective in the national conversation. Now the polls and the social surveys tell us that we are dumbed down and afraid to assert our views. That only the popular vote counts. But all over the country community groups are solving their problems by mutual help and without the government support on which we have for so long taught ourselves to depend. It is time the arts, too, began to examine their vested interests and their government-funded advantages and to think about restoring community. For, as Benjamin Franklin said as he signed the Declaration of Independence: 'We must indeed all hang together or, most assuredly, we shall all hang separately'.

Today, I believe that we take for granted the changing nature of our character and way of life. But we must never lose sight of the ever-present need to challenge the way we perceive ourselves, whether it is the need to find security in egalitarianism, or because our cultural palaces tell us we are a sophisticated and cosmopolitan country. The arts must engage in that challenge, reject the perception that they are entertainment for the good times. We must continue to question our actions, to enlarge our imagination, to collaborate with our rivals in seeking the way forward and to celebrate our little victories. To live up to, and speak out about, what we believe being Australian means. As this history shows, there was a time in living memory when the arts flowered because this process was uppermost. And Philip and I were there. Our culture is different now, much more divided, more hybrid, more demanding. If we don't want to continue making 'an art form out of sadness and sorrow' a new way to celebrate must be found.

INDEX

KATHARINE BRISBANE was a theatre critic for 21 years including a period as national critic of the *Australian*, at a time of radical change that saw the rise of contemporary drama, film and music in Australia. Educated at the University of Western Australia where she directed plays for the University Dramatic Society, she began her career as a reporter on the *West Australian* and by 1959 was its theatre critic. She joined the *Australian* in 1967, remaining until 1974, and later wrote for *Theatre Australia* and the *National Times*. She has been influential in setting the agenda for critical debate in Australian theatre and has published widely on the history and nature of Australian theatre in books and journals both nationally and internationally.

In 1971 she co-founded Currency Press, with her late husband Dr Philip Parsons (1924–1993) and remained managing editor and publisher until her retirement in 2001. In 2000 she established Currency House, Inc., a non-profit charitable association with the brief to assert the value of the performing arts in public life and to raise the level of debate. She was also a founder in 1972 of the Australian National Playwrights' Conference and its Chair from 1985–1990.

Her awards include the Dorothy Crawford Award by the Australian Writers' Guild for outstanding service to the Australian playwright (1985); the Sydney Theatre Critics' Circle Award for outstanding service to Sydney theatre (jointly with Philip Parsons, 1991); the Gold Medal of the National Book Council for services to Australian publishing (1994); and the A.A. Phillips Award by the Association for the Study of Australian Literature, in recognition of her work in Australian literary scholarship (1996). Both Philip and Katharine were awarded an AM in the Queen's Birthday Honours in 1993 for their services to Currency Press. In 1994 the University of New South Wales conferred on Katharine an Hon. D.Litt for services to theatre scholarship.